Ulf Hannerz

Cultural Complexity

Studies in the Social Organization of Meaning

Columbia University Press
New York

Columbia University Press
New York Chichester, West Sussex

Library of Congress Cataloging-in-Publication Data

Hannerz, Ulf.
Cultural complexity : studies in the social organization of meaning / Ulf Hannerz.
p. cm.
Includes bibliographical references and index.
ISBN 0-231-07622-3
ISBN 0-231-07623-1 (pbk.)
1. Culture. 2. Social structure. 3. Subculture. 4. Ethnology.
I. Title.
HM101.27H27 1992
306—dc20 91-23479
CIP

Casebound editions of Columbia University Press books are printed on permanent and durable acid-free paper.

Printed in the United States of America

c 10 9 8 7 6 5 4 3 2 1
p 10 9 8 7 6 5 4 3 2 1

Contents

Preface

There is a measure of continuity between this book and a previous book of mine, *Exploring the City* (1980), where a section in the concluding chapter is titled "The Social Organization of Meaning." What follows may indeed be seen as a more elaborate statement on the issues discussed in some fifteen pages there. In the present book, however, I have gone outside the framework of urban study within which I remained quite faithfully in the earlier work. Thus, while one chapter is again specifically concerned with the peculiarities of cultural process in cities, in general, I try here to develop a view of cultural complexity as such, to be considered within varied contemporary social matrices. I should add also that there are intermediate, but also brief, statements on some of the questions involved in a small book of mine in Swedish *Över gränser,* which appeared in 1983.

The good fortune of being able to spend periods at two think tanks was of great help to me in my work on this book. In 1984–85, I was at the Center for Advanced Study in the Behavioral Sciences, Stanford, for a year that allowed me to think more broadly than before about the questions involved and to get the project under way; this stay was aided by the Tercentenary Fund of the Bank of Sweden and by the National Science Foundation, United States (grant BNS 8011494). During the spring of 1988, I more or less completed a version of the manuscript (which has since gone through further revisions) while at the Swedish Collegium for Advanced Study in the Social Sciences, Uppsala. I am grateful to both these institutions, their helpful staff, and the stimulating colleagues whom I encountered in them, for supporting my undertaking in varied ways. I also wish to acknowledge the support of the Swedish Research Council for the Humanities and Social Sciences for the project "The World System of Culture," based in the Department of Social Anthropology, University of Stockholm, which has provided a framework for a considerable part of my work for some time.

I have benefited from the thoughtful responses to my presentations of parts and working versions in seminars or lectures at a number of universities and conferences: for a term as a visiting professor at the Ph.D. program in Anthropology at the City University of New York, in 1989; for a month as a visiting professor in the Department of Anthropology at University of Adelaide, Australia, in 1987; for a week the same year in the Departamento de Antropologia at Universidade Nova in Lisbon; on other occasions at the University of California, at Berkeley and at Santa Cruz; at the University of Frankfurt am Main; at University College London; at Stanford University; at the University of Trondheim; at the University of Tübingen; and at the University of Virginia. Parts of chapters 4 and 5 draw on a paper on the power of expertise presented at a conference on "Domination," arranged at Bad Homburg, October 1983, by the Max-Planck-Institut für Geschichte, Göttingen. Parts of chapter 6 were presented in a first version at the American Academy of Arts and Sciences workshop on "Meanings of the City" in Racine, Wisconsin, October 1984, and other parts at international conferences on urban anthropology; *"Cittá Nuova, Nuova Cittá,"* in Florence, November 1986, and *"La ciutat com a projecte cultural"* in Barcelona, February 1990. Chapter 7 has some of its origins in a lecture in the Centennial Lecture Series of the Department of Anthropology, University of Pennsylvania, in March 1986, later published as "The World in Creolisation," in *Africa* (1987), 57(4). Some fragments of the chapter have also appeared as "Notes on the Global Ecumene" in *Public Culture* (1989), 1(2), and in "Culture between Center and Periphery: Toward a Macroanthropology" in *Ethnos* (1989), 54:3–4. Another part of it is based on a lecture at the First International Conference on the Olympics and East/West and South/North Cultural Exchanges in the World System, Seoul, August 1987, later published as "Cosmopolitans and Locals in World Culture" in *Theory, Culture and Society* (1990), 7(2–3). A few paragraphs are derived from my keynote lecture to the Biennial Conference of the Nordic Association of American Studies in Uppsala, May 1987, "American Culture: Creolized, Creolizing," published the following year in a volume of conference proceedings under the same title. The chapter also draws on presentations at the Twelfth Meeting of Nordic Anthropologists, Stockholm, June 1986, in a session on macroanthropology; at the Annual Meeting of the American Anthropological Association, Chicago, November 1987, in a session on "Transnational Practices and Representations of Modernity"; and at a symposium on "Culture, Globalization, and the World-System" at the State University of New York, Binghamton, in March 1989. More continuously, I have benefited from the intellectual feedback in seminars at my home base, in the Department of Social Anthropology, University of Stockholm.

Of course, there is also that handful of good friends who have carefully and most usefully commented on the manuscript, in part or as a whole, in one version or other, at different points in time: Arjun Appadurai, Tomas Gerholm, Keith Hart, Stefan Molund, Roger Sanjek, and Aram Yengoyan. They may not necessarily have agreed with my point of view, and I have not always followed their advice or heeded their criticisms (although, often, I certainly have), but I have found their responses constantly stimulating; I am most grateful to them. One of the anonymous readers for Columbia University Press also offered especially constructive suggestions.

In particular, I am indebted to my wife and colleague, Helena Wulff Hannerz: not only because her own research on youth culture in London has given me some extra ethnography to think with (although it is only implicit in the pages which follow), but especially for her constant thoughtfulness, support, and willingness to listen, read, respond, and ask for more.

Ulf Hannerz

PART I

Forms

1 The Nature of Culture Today

> After all, the subject of anthropology is limited only by man. It is not restricted by time—it goes back into geology as far as man can be traced. It is not restricted by region but is world-wide in scope. It has specialized on the primitives because no other science would deal seriously with them, but it has never renounced its intent to understand the high civilizations also. Anthropology is interested in what is most exotic in mankind but equally in ourselves, here, now, at home.
>
> (A. L. Kroeber 1953:xiii)

Homo sapiens is the creature who "makes sense." She literally produces sense through her experience, interpretation, contemplation, and imagination, and she cannot live in the world without it. The importance of this sense-making in human life is reflected in a crowded conceptual field: ideas, meaning, information, wisdom, understanding, intelligence, sensibility, learning, fantasy, opinion, knowledge, belief, myth, tradition. . . .

With these words, another also belongs, dear to anthropologists: culture. There have been times when they have used it to stand for even more, but in the recent period, culture has been taken to be above all a matter of meaning.[1] To study culture is to study ideas, experiences, feelings, as well as the external forms that such internalities take as they are made public, available to the senses and thus truly social. For culture, in the anthropological view, is the meanings which people create, and which create people, as members of societies. Culture is in some way collective.

As I see it here, culture has two kinds of loci, and the cultural process takes place in their ongoing interrelations.[2] On the one hand, culture resides in a set of public meaningful forms, which can most often be seen or heard, or are somewhat less frequently known through touch, smell, or taste, if not through some combination of senses. On the other hand, these overt forms are only rendered meaningful because human minds contain the instruments for their interpretation. The cultural flow thus consists of the externalizations of meaning which individuals produce through arrangements of overt forms, and the interpretations which individuals make of such displays—those of others as well as their own. Perhaps the imagery of flow is a little treacherous, to the extent that is suggests unimpeded transportation, rather than the infinite and problematic occurrence of transformation between internal and external loci.[3] Yet I find the flow metaphor useful—for one thing, because it captures one of the paradoxes of culture. When you see a river from afar, it may look like a blue (or green, or brown) line across a landscape; something of awesome permanence. But at the same time, "you cannot step into the same river twice," for it is always moving, and only in this way does it achieve its durability. The same way with culture—even as you perceive structure, it is entirely dependent on ongoing process.

More precisely, the flow occurs in time and has directions. As a whole, it is endless; externalizations depend on previous interpretations, depending on previous externalizations. And the externalizations occurring now will bring about interpretations which in their turn lead to further externalizations in the future. Yet in details there are differences, as some of the externalizations are constantly present, some occur again and again, although in each instance they are short-lived phenomena; and some seldom or only once. In one way or other, also, the flow is everywhere, for as soon as people make themselves accessible to the senses of others, through physical co-presence or artefactual extensions, they render themselves interpretable. Whether it is what you intended or not, some meaning can always be attributed to you. But at the same time, some particular externalizations are available to everybody through the cultural flow, while others reach only a few.

Analyzing Contemporary Cultures: Meanings, Public Forms, and Distributions

Increasingly, in the twentieth century, the flow of meaning has come to make its passage through one general kind of scenery. It is a society with a far-reaching division of labor, which is at the same time a division of knowledge; in this way, categories of specialists are formed, and always at the same time a matching category of laymen.[4] It is a society where the state constitutes one framework for social life and the flow of meaning, and where culture is also in part commoditized, thus organized by the market. Formal education through schooling is widespread if not universal in this society, and literacy and electronic media play a part in shaping and channeling culture. The people here are a mixture of the sedentary and the somewhat footloose.

In this book, I am concerned generally with developing a certain view of culture and its study, but more especially with using that view as a guide to some of the peculiarities of the cultural flow in this kind of society, in which a large part of humankind now lives. Some anthropologists have seen their vocation as a study of "the Other"—with a preference for the most Other, as different as possible from that anthropologist's self which is most often rooted in an urban, industrial or even post-industrial, capitalist large-scale social order. I do not; I prefer to think of anthropology as a general and comparative study of society and culture, including, as Kroeber had it in the quotation above, "ourselves, here, now, at home." But my interest in the type of society just sketched is not merely a matter of turning the concerns of anthropology toward the West, and away from the rest. Those of us who live in Europe or North America no doubt find the outline of this society familiar enough. Yet it is not now only our society. It is rather a kind of society which has expanded, fully or partially, into just about every earthling habitat. The societies with which anthropologists have always had a special concern, in what for some decades we have called the Third World, have also—in large part due to their inclusion in a world system—become more or less close approximations to the type.

The fact that this kind of society has become so widespread does not necessarily mean that there is a global homogenization of culture. Certainly, it has often been assumed that sooner or later other cultures will become more like those of the West, and American culture especially has been taken to be a bellwether culture for others. There is also a predilection in the human sciences for speaking about past, present, and future society and culture in the abstract, while in fact one has only Europe and North America at the back of one's mind (and perhaps really only segments of them). Occidentalists, the people who study these regions and think about them, often have no very sharp sense of their own limits; not even of the internal variations within their field. The particular mixture of those attributes of society enumerated above may vary between instances, however; and while there are states, markets, schooling, media, and a division of labor in most places, this does not mean that the precise ideas and overt symbolic forms, the "cultural content," with which they engage must be the same. Even staying within the North Atlantic culture area of Occidentalism, for example, I know well enough that the societies and cultures of the United States and Sweden, my country of origin, are in some ways very different, against a background of commonality. More generally, and more importantly for the present and future practice of anthropology, it is now often within the matrix of the institutional forms just delineated that in any part of the world we will encounter the Other.[5]

How shall we refer to the culture of this kind of society? I am a little uncertain. "Modern" is a word with more associations and evaluative overtones than I am prepared to take on. "Contemporary" is preferable in being less loaded, although it is true that there are still other kinds of societies and cultures in the present which it is neither morally justifiable nor historically correct to see merely as remnants of the human past. "Complex cultures" in some ways serves my purposes better yet, although it is true that there have been societies of great cultural complexity in the past which have not shared all the attributes mentioned above. The ideal solution as far as clarity is concerned may be to use the label "contemporary complex cultures," but since that becomes a little unwieldy, I will in fact switch back and forth between the adjectives. ("Contemporary civilization" would be yet another alternative, suggesting complexity and large scale, and indicating openings to a research tradition to which anthropologists at present pay little attention; but perhaps it gives too little weight to variations within a highly inclusive whole.)

The term "complex" may in itself be about as intellectually attractive as the word "messy," but one of its virtues in this context is precisely its sober insistence that we should think twice before accepting any simple characterization of the cultures in question in terms of some single essence. I use it here not only as an overall descriptive term or as a call to caution, however, but also because it can be tied to the analytical point of view toward culture I want to put forth. The conception of cultural flow suggested above leads me to believe that the study of culture, generally, is best conducted through continued attention to three dimensions. As noted, culture has two kinds of loci: in human minds, and in public forms. But it is not in The Mind, or in just any minds. Rather, it is in particular ways in particular minds; and when it is public, it is made available through social life by particular people, to particular people.

The three dimensions of culture, to be understood in their interrelations, are thus:

1. *ideas and modes of thought* as entities and processes of the mind—the entire array of concepts, propositions, values and the like which people within some social unit carry together, as well as their various ways of handling their ideas in characteristic modes of mental operation;

2. *forms of externalization*, the different ways in which meaning is made accessible to the senses, made public; and

3. *social distribution*, the ways in which the collective cultural inventory of meanings and meaningful external forms—that is, (1) and (2) together—is spread over a population and its social relationships.

Now each of these conceptual dimensions can be seen in terms of degrees of complexity. I will not become entangled here with questions of precise measurement, but as a sensitizing notion, I think this can take us from a merely descriptive toward a more analytical view of complex culture. Some comments on each of the dimensions, seen in this light, may be in order.[6]

With regard to the first dimension, that of ideas and modes of thought, it is true that anthropologists have been wont to emphasize the intricacy of even what one would expect to be the simplest cultures. Indeed, complexity is shown here to be a multifaceted notion. Particular concepts can be seen as more complex when they have a greater number of denotations and connotations; a cultural whole which can be derived from a smaller number of fundamental principles is less complex than one which can only be described in terms of a larger number of such principles. Such understandings can also go to show, however, how difficult it would be to measure with any precision the relative complexity of cultures along this dimension. The basic units of meaning—"memes," "wits," or whatever else it has been suggested that they be called—are not easily delimited; and then, of course, cultural analysis cannot occupy itself with mere collections of meaning units, somehow seen as atomized and all distinctive at the same level. What matters more are the higher-level notions and ordering devices—"themes," "focal concerns," "galaxies," "key symbols,"—which turn the collections into structures, with some degree of coherence.

Nevertheless, it can hardly be disputed (and this is where we will leave the problem for the moment) that some cultures have larger inventories of differentiated meanings than others, which probably also involves a more complicated ordering, and that they also involve more modes of handling meaning: routinely, critically, expansively, or whatever. There would be such a difference, for example, between contemporary Sudanese culture, as it exists within the world system, and ethnographic-present Nuer culture. But the contrast obviously begs a number of questions to which I hope answers will be found in my continued discussion.

Complexity along the dimension of externalized forms seems like a more manageable notion. Simpler cultures use several such forms—speech, gesture, song, dance, adornment, and so forth, operating largely in contexts where human beings are in one another's physical presence. We have also come to realize that meanings can be "out there" in the environment, by way of indications about it which people make to one another. Thus, nature can carry culture—desert, forest, sea, wild plants and animals are invested with meanings. Yet, not all of nature is necessarily made cultural in this way. Some of it remains largely meaningless, outside the concerns of orderly human thought.

When a larger proportion of the physical environment is human-made, complexity in the forms of externalization of meaning automatically becomes greater. People hardly make things for themselves and one another without attaching meaning to them, whether what is created (and thereafter used) is the cityscape of Vienna, the American interstate highway system, a Moroccan plate of couscous, or a copy of the *South China Morning Post*. This means that the growth of human technology generally tends to increase cultural complexity along the dimension of externalization. More especially, however, there are those media technologies, ranging from writing to television, which make the cultural flow less dependent on face-to-face interactions, and which—having communication as their primary function—allow flexible, elaborate, intentional statements of meaning.

With respect to the third dimension, that of distribution, it is easy to say what the least complex instance would be—a total uniformity, where each individual involved with a culture has the same ideas and expresses them by the same means. The more complex instances are those where individuals differ in this regard, and where moreover they have some understanding that this is so.

Along all three dimensions, the type of contemporary society we consider here evinces a fairly high degree of cultural complexity. But again, the dimensions are interrelated. And the view I will take is that complexity along the first dimension, in contemporary culture, is in large part (although not entirely) a consequence of complexity along the latter two. The evidence suggests an interplay, for example, between forms of display on the one hand and ideas and modes of thought on the other. Not all ideas can be stated equally well in every mode of externalization; new external modes allow new modes of experiencing and new modes of thinking. When modes of externalization permit a more durable storage of meanings, this can also allow a growth of the cultural inventory over time.

Where the distribution of culture within a population is more complex, there can also be a larger combined cultural inventory. The individual may or may not have a direct hold on more ideas than has an individual involved with a simpler culture. What is more important is that he holds a smaller fraction of the whole. A greater complexity along the third dimension, in other words, leads to a greater complexity along the first dimension, as long as culture is seen as a collective rather than an individually based structure of meaning.[7] At the same time, to what extent and in what ways the culture as a whole actually coheres becomes a matter of social organization—how do meanings differentially distributed among people relate to one another?

Of the three dimensions of culture, anthropologists have been especially concerned with the first. Understanding structures of knowledge, belief, experience, and feeling in all their subtlety, and in their entire range of variations at home and abroad, is reasonably enough the core of cultural analysis. Secondarily, perhaps, anthropologists have occupied themselves with the relationship between the first and the second dimensions, with the way meanings find expression in a somewhat limited range of manifest forms—speech, music, graphic arts, or certain other communicative modes. On the whole, the least attention has been devoted to the third dimension, that of distribution.

Here, I will turn things around. I will take a particular interest in the distributive dimension, and some interest in matters of externalization, while I will attend least, and in large part indirectly, to questions of meaning in itself. Although this is a study of contemporary cultures, it is *not* a study of the ideas which have recently moved lives. My focus, one might say, is rather on the existential circumstances of meaning in society. As I have suggested, in cultural complexity, it is likely that complexity in distribution and in externalization has a large part in breeding complexity in the order of meaning. And the special concern with distributive problematics is based on a sense that anthropologists have been inclined to neglect them, at some cost. Whenever a culture is understood to be a collective phenomenon, it needs a sociology. When this sociology is left implicit, the danger is greater that it is a weak sociology.

The Organization of Diversity: Other People's Meanings

Studying culture in its distributive dimension is a matter of engaging with that classic issue, "the relationship between culture and social structure." There are ways of dealing with one or the other, but not with the relationship between them—some studies of the structure of social life are conducted or at least phrased as if culture does not matter, and a complaint against prominent recent tendencies in cultural analysis in anthropology has been that they evince a weak sense of social structure. But then there are also several ways of dealing with the linkage.

A possibility which various cultural theorists have entertained is that meanings and symbolic forms are predominantly generated in, or shaped by, particular types of social relationships; in Marshall Sahlins' version (1976:211), that there is a "dominant site of cultural production," a "privileged institutional locus of the symbolic process." Along roughly comparable lines, Mary Douglas (1970, 1978), the most Durkheimian of major recent anthropologists, proposes that the symbolic order represents the social order in its characteristic forms of "group" and "grid." More widely influential, and more Marxian, but still in a similar vein is the assumption that culture can in large part be studied as ideology, hegemony, domination, and at least occasionally, resistance. Maurice Bloch (e.g., 1977, 1985) thus argues that ritual is typically an underpinning of hierarchy; and Eric Wolf (1984:398) suggests that modes of mobilizing social labor—kinship, tributary, or capitalist—"impart a characteristic directionality, a vectorial force to the formation and propagation of ideas."[8]

Such views are not necessarily in conflict with the view taken here, but they should not be confused with it, for there is no more than a partial overlap. Rather than trying to find, somewhere in the structure of social relationships, a common denominator for the widest possible range of cultural phenomena—an enterprise which even in its more successful versions tends to be quite incomplete in its coverage—I am interested here in the sources of diversity, and in its consequences. This is a matter of confronting a customary commitment, in anthropology and elsewhere, to one particular understanding of culture as collective, socially organized meaning—the idea of culture as something shared, in the sense of homogeneously distributed in society.

The premise of cultural sharing, continuously reproduced in textbook definitions as well as in advanced theoretical treatises, is obviously deeply entrenched in anthropological thought, an intellectual default position to which one falls back whenever there is no insistent reason for thinking otherwise. Empirically, the stronger grounds for it are undoubtedly to be found in the cultural process of small-scale societies (more about this in the next chapter), but since these are the classic fields of anthropology, the special experience in them has had its more general effects. Yet the assumption of sharing also draws support from certain other theoretical or prototheoretical notions in anthropology, as well as from the practical constraints of field research, and from what has been an established convention in anthropological writing.

In the interwar golden age of American anthropology, as Aberle (1960) has noted, a strong although not necessarily explicit tendency was established to think of the nature of culture as analogous to that of language; and language, to do its work, had to be shared. (We may be more critical of so simple a view of language now.) In the British social anthropological tradition, meanwhile, the influential jural model of social structure concerned itself more with differentiation, but not in a way which really necessitated dealing with the issue of sharing versus nonsharing of meaning systems. In the analysis of social systems in terms of rights and duties pertaining to positions, it hardly mattered whether the people who acted differently also thought differently, or knew different things. On the whole, inquiries into belief systems were, in fact, largely based on a premise of uniformity within society. One could be concerned with the divisions of society, but find their representations in shared culture.

As field workers, too, anthropologists have often been predisposed to relying on assumptions of cultural sharing. A one-year stay in a distant community, with a great many unfamiliar people doing unfamiliar things, does not lend itself to much subtlety in pinning down variations in their interests, or values, or beliefs, or knowledge. Time and cultural competence may only suffice to find out what ideas people have in common, and to take such sharing for granted about rather too much. A good informant or two may have to stand in for the entire community as the ethnographer delves into the various domains of the cultural inventory. And then, as James Clifford has pointed out (1983:131–132), when whatever plurality of voices that were heard in the field are replaced by the single authorial voice of the conventional ethnographic text, uniformity is finally established: "the Nuer believe. . . ."

But the consequence of all this is to make cultural analysis asocial; to describe the collective phenomenon as if it were homologous to a personal meaning system.[9] And so when anthropologists claim to "take the native's point of view," we have not been in the habit of asking, "Which native?" For what the anthropologist saw must depend on the view of the person over whose shoulder he was glancing.

If one has doubts about the premise of cultural sharing, the unpardonable mistake would be to imply that it has itself been uniformly accepted by all anthropologists.[10] The patron saint of studies in intracultural variation is Edward Sapir, with his remarks on the nineteenth-century ethnographer Dorsey's brief note on a disagreement between his Indian informants—"Two Crows denies this." Dorsey, noted Sapir (1938:7), knew that he was dealing with "a finite, though indefinite, number of human beings, who gave themselves the privilege of differing from each other." In later years, a number of anthropologists—particularly Anthony Wallace, John Roberts, Ward Goodenough, and Theodore Schwartz—have taken an interest in developing more elaborate "distributive models of culture" (in the latter's term); these have certainly influenced my undertaking here, even when direct resemblances may be limited. The useful contrast between "the replication of uniformity" and "the organization of diversity" is Wallace's (1961). Not least on the basis of his unusually long field work association with the Kwaio of the Solomon Islands, Roger Keesing (1987a:161) has also argued that the study of culture must incorporate a sociology of knowledge, showing meanings as distributed and controlled; "cultures as texts . . . are differently read, differently construed, by men and women, young and old, experts and nonexperts, even in the least complex societies." And in his study of cosmology in the New Guinea highlands, Fredrik Barth (1987:77) states succinctly that distributionist view which, in a very different context, I will elaborate on here—"the distribution of the items of knowledge and ideas on the interacting parties in a population is a major feature of the organization of that body of knowledge and ideas; it is not only a matter of social structure but simultaneously a matter of cultural structure."

It may or may not be immediately evident how complicated a notion this is, and there are perhaps different ways of figuring it out. In a related formulation, Schwartz (1978a:423) states that distributive models of culture indicate "the mapping of a cultural system upon a social system." Leaving aside the matter of in what sense or to what degree either "the social" or "the cultural" show systemic properties, such mapping would be a simpler matter if the two could be seen as reasonably separate concepts. Yet, in fact, it is in part a consequence of the cultural flow through a population that a social system is created and recreated. As people make their contributions to that flow, they are themselves becoming constructed as individuals and social beings. Messages from others, in varied combinations and sequences, play their part in conducting them, with firmness and precision or by way of much uncertainty and drifting, to the series of stations they will occupy in life. In a process both cumulative and interactive, people make indications to one another about who they are and what other kinds of people are in their habitat, what is suitable conduct and what are desirable goals in life, and how to relate to other human beings and to the material world.

In the continuous interdependence of "the social" and "the cultural," it would seem, the social structure of persons and relationships channels the cultural flow at the same time as it is being, in part, culturally produced. I will take it to mean that, in Barth's words, a distribution of cultural items within a population is a matter of cultural structure is that people have understandings (also distributed in some way) of that distribution which may or may not be valid, but which in either case make a difference; these are meanings in their own right, and they affect the ways in which people deal with ideas and produce meaningful external forms. The major implication of a distributive understanding of culture, of culture as an organization of diversity, is not just the somewhat nit-picking reminder that individuals are not all alike, but that people must deal with other people's meanings; that is, there are meanings, and meaningful forms, on which other individuals, categories, or groups in one's environment somehow have a prior claim, but to which one is somehow yet called to make a response. At times, perhaps, one can just ignore them. Often enough, however, one may comment on them, object to them, feel stimulated by them, take them over for oneself, defer to them, or take them into account in any of a number of other ways. They may be understood or misunderstood. And as these responses occur, or even in anticipation of them, whoever has that prior claim may also respond to them. In such ways, the organization of diversity is part of the fabric of complex culture.

For its part, the social structure to which understandings of the distribution of culture refer I see as existing in the borderlands between culture and nonculture. I have twice already said that it is "in part" culturally produced, having in mind the fact that it is not entirely a cultural construct where people arbitrarily make distinctions by attaching meanings to themselves, to one another, and to relationships. Social structure, I take it, also involves demographic distributions of people with varying physical capacities; not least does it involve distributions of power and material resources. And even though these can also be grasped only by way of the meanings people attach to them, the possibilities of imposing just any meaning successfully are, after all, limited.

In brief, the idea of the relationship between culture and social structure which results here is quite far from that old and simplistic one where the somehow noncultural creates differentiation, and often threatens with conflict and disintegration, while shared culture, whether through consensus or hegemony, unites. Culture is distributed, and includes understandings of distributions. Social structure is based in part on cultural distinctions, in part on distributions of other characteristics; these characteristics are drawn into culture by being meaningful, but stand outside it insofar as the meaning is not wholly arbitrary. And the distinctions and the attributions of meaning on which social structure draws, of course, also entail distributions.

Culture, Culturalism, Culturology

Again, there are different ways of studying, or just thinking about, culture; for certain such ways, "culturalism" and "culturology" are sometimes used, perhaps with slightly different shades of meaning, but generally as labels of disapproval.[11] I am not a culturalist (but then I cannot remember anyone else, either, using it as a term of self-identification); a few more comments on my theoretical inclinations should suffice to show why.

My approach to a distributive understanding of culture comes out of a general theoretical stance perhaps best described as interactionist. People shape social structures and meanings in their contacts with one another, it proposes; and societies and cultures emerge and cohere as results of the accumulation and aggregation of these activities. Apart from the sources for such a view which I find in the cumulative research tradition of mainstream social anthropology (not least in its occasional recent turn toward processualism[12]), I draw to a degree on adjoining forms of interpretive anthropology, and not least on the kind of qualitatively inclined sociology which has its now rather remote beginnings in the early Chicago school.[13] If an amalgamation of these serves as the core of my perspective, it is also the vantage point from which I occasionally see openings toward a range of other research orientations, in and out of anthropology. (More about this later in the chapter.)

Where does this put me, then, in relation to "culturalism" and "culturology"? The former term usually suggests that the approach in question is strictly mentalist, or—at most—concerned with the relationship between things of the mind and their overt representations. It is held to be reductionist in that, from the assumption that human beings respond to everything in their surroundings by way of their culture, it proceeds to the conclusion that the study of culture is in itself sufficient for a complete understanding of human social life. For one thing, according to the critics, culturalism in this way often attempts to define—define away, rather—basic, perhaps irreconcilable conflicts over power and material interest as questions of cultural difference and misunderstanding. It is another aspect of culturalism that it construes human beings as products rather than as producers of culture.

As I understand it, to the extent that "culturology" differs in meaning from the other term, it is in the particular, mystifying emphasis it gives to this latter view. Knowledge, beliefs, norms, and values seem just to be there, timelessly present, or doing things on their own, or "through" people.I would argue that there is a connection between culturology and the "replication of uniformity" point of view toward the social organization of meaning. When it is claimed that everybody shares the same culture, then the individual can be anonymous, a nobody. The distributionist point of view necessarily brings people back in. And once you have to identify particular meanings and cultural manifestations with particular individuals and categories in social life, it would seem to be only a short step to seeing them as something other than mere cultural repositories.

In some of the anthropological work on distributive models of culture, it is true, there has been a tendency to see culture as frozen, rather than liquid, emergent, open-ended.[14] Even so, I see some affinity between distributionist thinking about culture and a viewpoint which takes actor and process seriously. As people are back in the picture, you sense that culture cannot just be there; whether it stays put or is made to move, people must do something about it. As actors and as networks of actors, they are constantly inventing culture or maintaining it, reflecting on it, experimenting with it, remembering it or forgetting it, arguing about it, and passing it on. There are not only static distributions of factual knowledge but also different ways of doing things with meanings, likewise unevenly spread out among people and situations. We speak of common sense and consciousness raising, of experts and dilettantes, of ritual, play, and critique, of fads and fashions. The covering terms I shift between, in suggesting this processual view of culture as activity, are "the management of meaning," or "the management of culture," or just "cultural management."[15]

Neither phrasing, as I see it, entails any premise that the activity need involve any measure of deliberateness or self-consciousness with regard to their implications for cultural process, on the part of either individuals or social systems as wholes; they may or may not. (Where such purposive manipulation of the social organization of meaning is involved, the more restrictive notion of "cultural engineering" is perhaps useful.[16]) In a cultural studies version of the classical actor-structure dilemma in social thought, I find myself, ambiguously but not alone, moving about somewhere in the middle.[17] A human being both possesses culture, meanings and meaningful forms which can be manipulated with some degree of deliberateness, and is possessed by culture, shaped by it and—to this degree—made somewhat robotlike by it.

With regard to the assumptions described as culturalist, the way I differ from them should be evident from what I have said about the relationship between "the social" and "the cultural." There are, as I see it, realities outside culture with which people must also interact, whether their grasp of them through their culture is perfect or imperfect. To elaborate: persons may be culturally constructed, but (usually) not out of thin air; there are also flesh-and-blood human beings to which the constructions are attached, and the number of such human beings, taken all together or divided into categories, can make a difference for cultural process. Power, similarly, may indeed be culturally defined, and much of the time symbolic references to it are made to stand in for the real thing, but in the end the ability to use force counts, and can be used effectively to back up one of competing definitions. Nature, of the non-humanmade kind, is really out there, and some of the ideas people may have about it serve them better in dealing with it than others. The control over material items, whether these latter are more "natural" or more modified through human intervention, may be distributed among human beings in a variety of ways.[18] The distribution is likely to be affected by culture, but once it is there it has consequences of its own, and I am not helped by pretending that it does not exist.

These realities are hardly altogether extracultural, then, but the kind of analytical closure held to be characteristically culturalist would not allow us to attend to them sufficiently for a proper understanding of how humankind lives. And there are situations in which the dynamics are so much over on the side of the interrelations between political, economic, ecological, and demographic factors that close attention to cultural definitions yields comparatively limited returns; something can be said in such cases for treating them more or less as given. My concern with a point of view toward culture here, then, involves no total program for the study of human life, or for anthropology. It is rather a matter of trying to detail a part of the program, with some rather scant attention to what is in the boundary zones of that undertaking. I will touch a couple of times on the demography of culture, and rather more often on the political economy of culture, to suggest the necessary openness of cultural analysis; but mostly, I stick to the problem field of the interrelations of culture in its internal and external loci, and their social distribution, as sufficiently complicated and important to warrant interest in itself. It is with reference to that problem field I attempt to identify relevant phenomena, scrutinize concepts, and consider suitable units of analysis, on the way toward answers to such familiar overarching questions as "What characterizes these cultures as wholes?" or "How does one live with a world of meaning like this?"

The Question of Scale

Because the view of culture as organized diversity links culture to social structure, it also inevitably leads us to confront problems of scale. Micro and macro may be terms out of place when culture is held to be merely replicated uniformity. Where there are differences in what is carried within minds, on the other hand, and differences likewise between relationships in what kind of cultural flow passes through them, then one must ask how the understanding of culture is affected by the circumscription of units.

A conception of culture without sensitivity to scale has consequences for the study of the smaller slices of human life as well as for the understanding of wider wholes. In investigations of small social units, involving some quite limited number of individuals in relationships to one another, it may lead to a neglect of the concreteness of the meaning systems involved; a lack of curiosity about the way ideas are linked to the particularities of interlocking personal experiences. I have something more to say about such microcultures in chapter 3. Here, I will devote more attention to the question of what a macroanthropology of culture entails. A couple of commentators from neighboring disciplines, arguing for reorientations in these, point us in what I believe is a useful direction.

Writing in the *Journal of American History*, Thomas Bender (1986) takes a critical view of the fragmentation of scholarship in the last couple of decades. Much of the most innovative work by American social and intellectual historians, he points out, has been devoted to recovering the pasts of particular groups in their society. But the result has been portrayals almost exclusively of "the private or *gemeinschaftlich* worlds of trades, occupations, and professions; locality; sisterhood; race and ethnicity; and family." There has been a strong dose of anthropological influence in this trend, Bender notes—regarding it as a mixed blessing. Although many of the parts are better understood than ever before, there is no image of the whole, no real concern with the public sphere. A notion of "public culture" is needed, to encompass the continuing, ever changing contest among social groups and ideas for the power to define the nation itself.[19] Bender is obviously interested here in returning political history to a central place in the discipline; but it is widened to include a strong concern with the politics of meaning in its entire range of forms, and in place of discredited understandings of the public sphere—with a consensualist bias and a suppression of discordant voices—there is a call for bringing these voices resolutely, along with those always heard, to the center. This is not to devalue the many particular histories of the recent past. Rather, it is to incorporate them into a new and wider synthesis.

Mary Louise Pratt (1987) contrasts a linguistics of community with a linguistics of contact, and argues for more attention to the latter. The linguistics of community assumes a unified, homogeneous social world where language exists as a shared patrimony—a kind of imagery which has been at the basis of most theoretical thought about language. The linguistics of contact examines the operation of language across boundaries, and would focus on modes and zones of interaction over difference and inequality. It is concerned with the workings of language as affected by differences of class, race, gender, and age; with the appropriation, penetration, or cooptation of the language of one group by that of another; with bilingualism, multilingualism, and translation; with the social conditions of the transition to literacy. As community is thus decentered, what has been on the margins of linguistic thought is moved to the core.

One would not do justice to Bender's and Pratt's arguments by describing them as in every way parallel. Bender's preference for the nation as still the most advantageous framework for synthesis clashes, for example, with some of Pratt's interests in transnational phenomena. The two have something in common, however, and this something also addresses anthropology, a discipline which Bender indeed identifies as a source for the tendency toward fragmentation which he opposes. They speak for a turn outward, from the small universes of community and homogeneity as things set apart, toward the ways in which such entities engage one another in diversity, within some kind of wider whole.

Anthropology has long been committed to both the close-up view and the overview, but as its practitioners have come to concern themselves more often with complex societies and cultures, ethnography and holism have drifted apart, with the former becoming increasingly devoted to miniatures—and often only to particular kinds of miniatures. No doubt there is here an implicit or explicit notion of an intellectual division of labor. The study of complex culture looks like a field already crowded, by everybody from art historians to sociologists. It may seem uncertain that there is anything that anthropology could add to its illumination, except possibly bits and pieces of ethnography of the slightly exotic or the mundane; unusual, hidden-away ways of life, or the everyday unofficial working of institutions. If in the historical discipline much of the study of parts alluded to before has been devoted to what the anthropologist-historian Bernard Cohn has referred to as "proctological history" (1987:39), history from the bottom up, much anthropology in the context of complexity has also been proctological anthropology. This, clearly, is often at the same time advocacy anthropology, moved by a sense of fairness, a conviction that there are people too seldom heard from, or listened to. ("On the mountains of Nova Sembla, or in the burnt valleys of Ceylon, wherever a wretch is found, he is my friend, my brother," wrote the eighteenth-century Swedish poet Bengt Lidner; gender considerations apart, a suitable motto for bottom-up anthropology.) Nevertheless, it may be reasonable to ask whether the fragments from the cultural whole are not increasingly often chosen on the basis of an evolving routinization of ethnographic genres, so that if we try to map the distribution of anthropological inquiries onto the distribution of cultural phenomena, we may find it uneven and fairly arbitrary.

In these and other instances, it is not likely that anthropologists would nowadays insist that the small units they work with can be seen as autonomous. It is rather that the larger frameworks within which they exist are not described, not investigated, but more often invoked, as generalized images. Commenting on this, and especially on the frequent choice of some kind of Marxian system image, George Marcus (1986:173) has rightly pointed out that one thing counting in favor of the latter is that it is *there.* Readers can be counted upon to be familiar with it; it is an intersubjective labor-saving device.

A recurrent problem here is that ethnography and system image may show less than a perfect fit. Too often there is, as Sally Falk Moore has put it (1987:731), a "zone of ignorance" between micro and macro, and consequently a need to expand ethnography at least into that space (if not further, to reach toward a more grounded system image). In the area of cultural study especially, however, it is also a fact that we are dealing with phenomena about which available system images tend to have little to say.[20]

What would be a productive stance for cultural analysis toward what we think of as macro: social structures extended in space, involving large numbers of people, and exhibiting large inventories of meanings and meaningful overt forms, differentially distributed? Of course, in units such as cities, regions, states, or the world, one could not aim at doing the ethnography of everything. Nor is the macroanthropology of culture probably so concerned with the quantitative aggregation of actions, or with the unintended consequences of such aggregation; favorite topics of types of macroanalysis which I would consider more socially than culturally inclined. Bender's and Pratt's proposals point in another direction, toward an overview of the cultural flow, and toward a focus on the points where its varied currents come together and mingle. True, Bender's conception of a "center" as the privileged locus of public cultural contestation may be more valid in some contexts than others; at times, the center is perhaps even nowhere to be found.[21] In any case, I will try here to pay less attention to the parts in themselves than to the interfaces, the affinities, the confrontations, the interpenetrations and the flow-through, between clusters of meaning and ways of managing meaning. For these are the places and the events where, in some way and to some degree, diversity gets organized.

Downscale, then, culture is likely to be characterized by the concreteness, the situational rootedness of its meanings. Upscale, it takes in increasing diversity. If a sense of a whole grows out of this, it is probably that of a moving interconnectedness, nothing less, not necessarily anything more. To get to the realities of contemporary wholes, we may often have to shatter the mystique of traditional anthropological holism (cf. Appadurai 1986b:758–759). Orderliness, harmony, durable equilibria, and smooth adaptiveness: all those characterizations are debatable.

A Western Under the Mango Tree

Come along now to Kafanchan, a middle-sized, multiethnic, polyglot railroad junction town in Nigeria; a site where it is possible to find all those aspects of the organization of contemporary complex cultures enumerated earlier in this chapter. What follows, however, is an ethnographic sketch of media use.

Nobody quite knows how many people live in Kafanchan, although local officials estimate that the population may be about 25,000. There is a busy, crowded marketplace; a number of schools, and a teachers' college; a post office; a great many drinking spots, for bottled beer, local brews, or palm wine; the palace of a Hausa emir, modest by the standards for such edifices in northern Nigeria; a couple of large mosques, and a number of smaller ones; and the homes of some twenty Christian denominations, not all of which are immediately recognizable as church buildings.[22] And over the rusty zinc roofs of the mostly one-story dwellings, since the late 1970s, there have been an increasing number of television antennae.

When I came to Kafanchan in the mid-1970s, there were three or four small bookshops and about as many record stores, and one could buy the major Nigerian newspapers from hawkers. But the town had no electricity yet, so that radios and record players operated on batteries, and the only two television sets were in places with private power supplies—the senior railroad employees' club, and the home of the chief medical officer. Yet as these were the years of the Nigerian oil boom, the Nigerian Electric Power Authority quickly extended its somewhat erratic operations (some customers claimed that the acronym stood for Never Expect Power Always), and TV sets were soon in considerable demand in Kafanchan. Moreover, a new open-air movie theater began to show mostly Indian and Hong Kong films. In earlier years, it happened once in a while that a mobile cinema outfit made a stop in Kafanchan to show a free movie and propagandize some line of commercial products. I remember one night hearing a speech on the virtues of canned margarine and watching an old black-and-white western under the large mango tree in front of the Emir's palace. The audience stood in a circle around the screen, as the picture could be seen on both sides; there was a sound track in English with live simultaneous translation into Hausa.

Literacy in Kafanchan is predominantly literacy in English. One learns to read and write in the primary schools in Hausa, the Northern Nigerian lingua franca, but fairly soon the transition is made to English as the language of instruction. The

Muslims in town send their young children to Koranic schools, usually for a couple of years or so, where they learn to read and recite verses from the Koran and thus acquire some familiarity with Arabic script. For most of them this remains a restricted literacy, however, and since to begin with most of the other schools had Christian missionary connections, the Muslims were for some time reluctant to send their children to these.

English is also the major language of print in Nigeria. There is some printing in each of the major Nigerian languages, especially Yoruba, Ibo, and Hausa, but if one browses in one of the small bookshops in Kafanchan, probably 80 to 90 percent of the titles one finds are in English. Much of the stock is made up of school supplies, self-help books, religious literature, and European classics. One shelf may contain the works of Nigerian and other African writers. The oldest of the bookshops was started by a North American mission and then taken over, in the period of decolonization, by the Nigerian Protestant church which was that mission's progeny. At least one of the other bookshops is likewise owned by someone who learned the trade in the mission bookshop chain. The world of literacy, one soon senses, still has a strong tinge of Christian missionary influence in much of Nigeria.

I mentioned that there are some record stores; easy to find, since they have loudspeakers in the street. What struck me about them was that you could inspect the stock, and then predict to what ethnic group the store owner belonged. Nigerian popular music has tended to be ethnically marked, again mostly Yoruba, Ibo, or Hausa. But most likely you will find some imported records as well. West Indian reggae has been very popular in Nigeria, and there may be some recordings by American religious vocalists, of the televangelist type. Recorded tapes have also become popular in Kafanchan in recent times. You could pick them up from a hawker who sells pirated copies out of a tall stack mounted on the back of his bicycle.

Switch on a television set in Kafanchan at night, and you may see newscasts in English and Hausa, an old episode of *Charlie's Angels,* a concert by Hausa drummers, commercials for detergents and bicycles, and a paid announcement of a funeral to take place in the nearest big city, where the TV station is located. The notion of funeral commercials struck me as innovative at first, but obviously it is an extension of the concept of the full-page advertisements wealthy Nigerians take out in their daily newspapers to announce the burials of their loved ones. Death and conspicuous consumption often go together in Nigeria.

A hole-in-the-wall school in the center of town provides a last scene. This is a small private enterprise, a commercial school started by one young Ibo immigrant who also employs another young man from the same hometown in the south of the country. For both, this is at least better than having no job at all. The two of them make up the entire staff, and the latter youth, the employee, teaches the handful of teenage pupils this morning. These are the children of traders in the town, or of peasants in nearby villagers, who have finished primary school but want some practical education (or their parents want it for them) of a type which their government does not do much to provide. So here they are, if they can afford the fees, acquainting themselves with a rather haphazard assemblage of ideas and skills.

With intensc attention in the case of some of them and obviously absentmindedly in the case of others, they follow the instruction which their teacher gives them in the elements of bookkeeping and business correspondencc. In a corner of the room one student pecks away slowly, slowly at a rickety old typewriter. One side of the room is open to the street, where every passer-by causes a small cloud of dust (it is the dry season), and where traffic from the nearby motor park starts the journey to surrounding villages or more distant towns. During the next period the teacher, who has noticeable dramatic talent, entertains his audience with jokes and riddles. The hour before the midday break is devoted to improving the students' knowledge of English vocabulary and idiomatic phrases, and to a reading of Macbeth; three or four students share each copy of the text.

It is Friday, so the afternoon is free; other schools and offices also close early for the Muslim holiday. Prayers are held at the central mosque, but since there are no Muslims in this school, many of the pupils are probably kept busy with chores at home or in the market place. Their teacher walks back to his rented room in an alley behind the school, where a group of young men (employed, underemployed, or unemployed) soon come together to talk and listen to records. There is a shelf containing detective stories, by Agatha Christie, James Hadley Chase, and others; Nigerian periodicals such as *Drum* and *Lagos Weekend* (a trashy scandal sheet); one old issue of *Newsweek*; and a few booklets from a correspondence course in creative writing which my teacher friend had embarked upon but apparently given up.

Machineries of Meaning

By now it ought to be impossible for anthropologists to pretend that media do not exist. As a sizable portion of the flow of meaning in societies passes through media, it must take a very willful disregard, or the most unthinking commitment to the ethnographic routines of the past, to leave them out of what is claimed to be a general study of culture.

Yet the growth and spread of media have had curiously little impact on the mainstream of anthropological as well as sociological thought. The strong tendency in both remains either to deal explicitly with face-to-face interactions or to pay little direct attention to the technical forms of social relationships and their implications. Meanwhile, quite outrageous statements are made in other quarters about the transformative social and cultural consequences of media, and serious media studies form an intellectual ghetto within the human sciences, its inhabitants talking mostly to one another. The great majority of them are Occidentalists, as media research has concentrated on the societies of North America and western Europe. But media are now reaching just about everywhere in the world to one degree or other, entering into varied combinations with one another and with that cultural flow which occurs through face-to-face contacts.[23]

It is another part of my purpose in this volume to try to assimilate a sense of the significance of media use into the overall view of contemporary cultural complexity. The idea is indeed to assimilate it, rather than to give it concentrated special treatment; consequently, media will be a recurrent topic in varied contexts in the following chapters.

The defining feature of the media is the use of technology to achieve an externalization of meaning in such a way that people can communicate with one another without being in one another's immediate presence; media are machineries of meaning. Of such technology there is little in the small-scale societies of the world: drum languages, smoke signals. Otherwise, the cultures of small-scale societies are cultures of face-to-face, oral flows of meaning. The cultures of complex societies, on the other hand, now make use of writing, print, radio, telephones, telegraph, photography, film, disk and tape recording, television, video, and computers. Yet only the implications of literacy have really, and only rather lately, claimed a more noticeable share of the awareness of anthropologists.

The media relate to all three dimensions of culture identified here before.[24] Obviously, they carry meanings; much media research is occupied in one way or other with content analysis. They entail a range of different modes of externalization, as technologies variously constrain and make possible particular symbol systems. Clearly, too, they have an impact on the distribution of meanings and meaningful forms over people and relationships.

Again, it is in the latter two dimensions I am most immediately interested, here as well. There is an echo here of Marshall McLuhan, who a quarter century or so ago fashioned himself as the superanthropologist of the electronic age, with slogans like "the medium is the message," "the retribalization of the world" and "the global village."[25] In McLuhan's pronouncements, of course, there was often a rather shrill technological determinism, and his claims concerning the communicative qualities of media could turn out to be confusing and implausible. Seeming at times as much a charlatan as a genius, he became the trickster figure of cultural studies, inspiring to some but making his entire field of interest intellectually disreputable in the eyes of not so few others.[26]

Yet the issues he raised—and at least dramatized—have become only more difficult to ignore. In the adage that "the medium is the message," taken in a reasonably strict sense, there is the general notion that what media communication is about is not just its more or less explicit, situationally varied content. Each medium, instead, through its symbol system, creates its own potentialities and enforces its own constraints on the management of meaning, in its way of reaching into people's minds, and possibly their hearts as well. Quite apart from particular referents, symbol systems relate differently to the senses, and to the inner capacities of human beings for processing information.

Surely McLuhan went too far in downplaying the significance of the explicit content of media messages, but a cultivated sensitivity to the particular media and nonmedia symbol systems, and to their distinctive tendencies of development as well as their interplay over time and in time, is essential to a grasp of contemporary culture.

Insofar as it refers to the organization of social relationships, McLuhan's macroanthropology is one that we can largely reject. The retribalization of the world creates no tribe. The global village is no village, and the television screen no village square. We are better off understanding the present world of media (or world *with* media, not to take too much for granted about their importance) on its own terms, rather than by way of these metaphors.

With regard to the distributive implications of media, the main fact is that the production of meaningful overt forms can occur in one place, their consumption in another; and since media often involve recording, meanings can be stored for later use.[27] Cultural flows can thus be extensively managed in space as well as in time.

Let us save the matter of time for later (chapter 5). As far as the spatial aspect is concerned, media have extended human experience and social life in many ways beyond the strictly local. Way back in early literacy, when reading and writing constituted a specialized craft, they were used in large part for administrative purposes. They helped hold empires together. Later, as literacy became more widespread, it could become a force of nationalism. In Europe, Protestantism and capitalism together initiated a flow of writing in vernaculars into print, and those who read and wrote the same language formed what Benedict Anderson (1983) has called "imagined communities." They felt that they had something in common despite the fact that they had never met. In the nineteenth century, lexicographers, philologists, and litterateurs became entrepreneurs of national culture. In yet more recent times, the intensification and multiplicity of media use have had a major part in setting up a new structure of relationships spanning the entire world. McLuhan's term was "implosion"; in the electric age, he wrote, there is involvement rather than containment. Yet "the global village" has too many overtones of the relative symmetries of cultural process in small-scale societies.

The overarching communication structures of the world today are, after all, center/periphery structures, heavily asymmetrical. By way of its superior power over the entertainment industry, news bureaus, the advertising industry, and the media through which they operate, the West strongly influences cultures in other parts of the world. This is commonly described and criticized as media imperialism; *Charlie's Angels* would be among its agents in Kafanchan. And this is just about where the concern with media power over geographical space stands now.

The ways media can bind time and space can create trouble for conventional assumptions about social relationships, society and culture. Following Weber, we think of social relationships as constructions of people "taking each other into account"; we also think of societies as made up of people in such relationships, and at the same time coinciding with particular territories. And we think of cultures as collective systems of meaning held by such societies. So, again, we expect that we can "map the cultural system upon the social system." But how, at present, do people "take each other into account"? Surely, not only in face-to-face contacts—not in a world of personal letters, telephones, demographics, and computerized campaign mail. We can take people into account, and in that way enter into some kind of relationship with them, even when we can never reach out and touch them. The Kafanchan school teacher and his friends in a manner stand in a relationship to the journalists on the staff of the *Lagos Weekend,* as they lap up the legends of a dream-and-scandal world created in the pages of that paper. It may be that neither party is aware of the particular identity of the other, but then anonymity can occur in face-to-face relationships as well. It may be also that the flow of meaning and influence is rather one-sided, but one could hardly make symmetry in this respect a defining feature of a social relationship.

The idea of a long-distance relationship between Lagos writers and Kafanchan readers may yet worry us less, as we can see them as members of the same Nigerian society. This, however, is not the extreme case. What about the relationship of the same young men in Kafanchan with the journalists on *Newsweek,* or the Jamaican reggae artist, or the Indian movie stars? Or for that matter, as those children in the one-room school struggle with *Macbeth,* do they not enter into some kind of social relationship with Shakespeare, and does not his play become a part of their culture?

Whatever we choose to think of as a relationship (and we are certainly testing the limits of the concept), it is obvious that media contribute greatly to making the boundaries of societies and cultures fuzzy. Perhaps the situation is to some degree clarified for us by Alfred Schutz' distinction between consociates, contemporaries, predecessors and successors (1967:15–16). People of all these categories can influence our thought and action in some way. Consociates are the people we can interact with directly in face-to-face relationships, the people with whom we share time and space; they predominate in small-scale societies but are surely everywhere else as well. Contemporaries are people whom we are aware of as living at the same time, about whom we make assumptions and whom we may influence in some ways, although we never meet in person. Our predecessors we cannot influence, but we may be aware of and be influenced by their actions. We can have no experience of our successors but can yet orient our actions toward them, anticipatorily.

The media give us more contemporaries. And perhaps some of them, due to the qualities of their symbol systems, do not only give us more contemporaries; they also make them seem more like consociates. Media may also increase our awareness of predecessors, like Shakespeare, and if he pondered the temporal consequences of writing, perhaps Shakespeare thought about his influence on his successors as well (although he hardly had those commercial school pupils in Kafanchan in mind).

Information Society, Postmodern Culture

Some of my preoccupations in this volume may appear connected to two concepts recently in vogue: information society and postmodern culture. It should help clarify the characteristics of my project, then, if I make a nod in the direction of these concepts and the discussion surrounding them, even as I then mostly leave them behind. (I do not claim to do justice to either of them in its own right.)

"Information society" belongs in a cluster with several more or less competing concepts: "the information age," "the learning society," "the knowledge society." The thrust of all of them is that in the late twentieth century, information has become more important than ever before. There is more of it, handling it keeps an increasing proportion of us busy, and it keeps growing faster and faster. In an essay a couple of decades ago about knowledge and time, Walter Ong (1968:3) suggested that at the beginning of history, it may have taken ten or a hundred thousand years for human knowledge to double, while at the time of his writing it took about fifteen years. If this is true, knowledge has more than doubled again since then, and probably the speed of growth has accelerated further yet.

Certainly, there is something to all of this. Occasionally, on the other hand, the imagery gets rather dubious. It is made to seem as if in the information age, humankind could enter some kind of ethereality, freed of dependence on material circumstances and material production, never again destroying or polluting its environment. But you cannot eat information, and it does not keep you warm. And if in the information society, more than ever before or anywhere else, knowledge is power, it is also true that power can control knowledge.

It is evident that we are getting a fair amount of self-serving rhetoric here, from groups of information or knowledge handlers who thus celebrate their own importance, or simply from the information technology industry. The real issues raised, however, are often directly relevant to the three-dimensional view of culture I have suggested above.

True, we have to cope with the ambiguities of some key concepts and their interconnections. Anthropologists have never established any real consensus on the relationships between "information," "knowledge," "meaning" and "culture." We would be puzzled by the notion that culture doubles every decade or two, as it is claimed that knowledge does. And what are we to do with the suggestion that not all information has meaning; that, in fact, meaninglessness increases in the information age?

It is not my intention either to become overly concerned with the regimentation of terminology here. At this point, I note simply that the increase in information, or knowledge, is in part a consequence of changes in modes of managing ideas, with a greater emphasis on more expansionist modes, thus involving the first of the dimensions of culture identified above; and in part this increase also results from a changing relationship between the first and the second dimensions, between "things of the mind" and externalizations. New technology allows more knowledge to be externally stored and in other ways managed.

But the third dimension, that of distribution, is also profoundly affected by the characteristics of the information society, and has a major part in the debates surrounding it. If there is "information overload" and "information anxiety," it is to a great extent because people cannot confidently enough manage the relationship between the entire cultural inventory and their reasonable personal share in it. When at times information appears "meaningless," it may again be that this information is somebody else's meaning. We often think of meaning, in a more restricted sense, as qualitatively superior information—well contextualized, relating to personal experience, perhaps thus to a wider range of senses and symbol systems. What is such meaning to you, however, may be a mere informational irritant in the eyes or ears of many contemporaries.

If knowledge is said to increase at a certain rate, but we are not used to speaking of culture in such terms, it is in part simply because knowledge in a narrower sense—what we regard as factual—is indeed what grows most rapidly (although it is true that mcasurements of the growth of knowledge are usually very oblique). There is no comparable proliferation over time of values, for example, or of aesthetic forms and sensibilities. Our reluctance to speak of this as a growth of culture, however, probably also has something to do with the assumption that what is cultural should be shared, in the sense of uniform distribution. The growth of knowledge, in contrast, is mostly very unevenly distributed.

This unevenness is another major problem of the information society. Not only do people's individual repertoires of information differ in content. They can also vary greatly in scope. And this is a matter not only of what at any one time is inside one's head, but also of what social and intellectual resources are at one's command for gaining access to information stored elsewhere. Under current conditions of information distribution, inequality is glaring, and as there are increases in the total inventory, there are no less obvious increases in relative deprivation, relative ignorance.

The arguments over the information society support the

view I take here that the distribution in society of meaning and meaningful form, and of ways of dealing with them, comprises problematics of its own, and that at least to a degree there is a dynamism internal to it. They suggest the value of giving some special attention in studies of contemporary culture and its overall management to those groups who are most actively and systematically engaged in cultural growth (if, after all, we can allow ourselves to use that notion), and who are also often on the privileged side when inequalities occur in, and result from, cultural distribution—experts, professionals, intelligentsia, intellectuals, or whatever in particular contexts they are called.

Even so, I would emphasize that the information society as usually depicted hardly coincides with the more general social framework for contemporary culture which I have already sketched; it is only an extreme variety of it. In an inquiry even into the particular consequences of the culture processing activities of certain groups of specialists for the culture as a whole, one cannot focus solely on them, because any mode of cultural management may also have its implications a step or more away from it within the interconnectedness. Therefore we cannot just ignore the marginals of the information society, the late stragglers into the information age (who are no doubt in the majority). On the whole, moreover, the information society is another Occidentalist idea, probably fully shared only with Japan (where, on the other hand, it has become an ingredient of the current national myth).[28] Indeed, since the beginning of Western colonization, the cultural inventories of Third World societies have also taken great expansive leaps, as complexes of alien meanings have been inserted into their life. But the organized large-scale production of knowledge new to the combined cultural inventory of humankind, as in Walter Ong's calculus and the characteristic division of labor of the information society, remain as much more the features of the center than of the periphery, and we are not narrowly concerned with them.

Postmodernism has also been tied to the growth of information and communication technology in this century, while at the same time, there has been an explicit emphasis on seeing the technology as embraced by advanced capitalism. Commentaries on the postmodern, very diverse among themselves, have in fairly large part been concerned with aesthetic aspects of culture—

literature, architecture, visual art. This is not least a matter of a sensibility, a "structure of feeling" (to borrow the phrasing which must recently have helped greatly in advancing Raymond Williams' position in citation indices). But it has been a key point that, in contrast with the modernism it is succeeding, in postmodernism the distinction between art and life is blurred; and so is that between high culture and popular culture. This is because life in general in latter-day capitalist society has become so saturated with images, in the media and through advertising, that art is no longer something set apart; rather, it is becoming more and more dependent on that other imagery.

The media have figured very prominently in postmodernist discussions, often in a rather McLuhanesque way. They are seen to be taking over from whatever may have been a reality outside them; messages bounce back and forth between them, taking on the leading part in constituting the environment of consciousness, a "hyperreality." But the media are also understood to be in the marketplace. Their messages are commercial, and the very fact that technology has come to allow the externalization of knowledge and culture to such a high degree facilitates commoditization. No longer are these latter so stably committed to the mind of the individual, who would thereby get some of his special aura, and no longer, either, is the individual so committed to them. The state also declines as an organization for the production and distribution of learning. This is the era of the transnational corporation.

Because there is such a proliferation of messages from everywhere in the media, postmodern culture is characterized by a multiplicity of perspectives and voices. It is a thing of shreds and patches. Juxtaposition becomes the prevalent experience as you zap your way around the television dial, or wander aimlessly through the shopping mall. When you have heard and seen everything and registered the contradictions, irony and skepticism make up a more likely stance than commitment and piety.

Postmodern times are times, as Jean-Francois Lyotard (1984:xxiv) has it, of "incredulity toward metanarratives." And the grand themes of history in which people believed under modernism (the march of progress, the emancipation of the proletariat) seem dubious not only because people are generally more inclined to doubt, but because of the specific place of postmodernism in time. Certainly, there is no real agreement on when postmodernism began, but it has largely been a 1970s and 1980s sensibility, growing in the wake of 1968—a period when first older metanarratives were discredited, and then the revolutionary, countercultural idea of 1968 itself gradually crumbled.

In part because of the loss of the master narratives, its interpreters have also said, postmodernism has little coherent sense of history. The past is raided instead for commoditizable nostalgias. The sense of place is likewise uncertain. In the media everywhere is here, and transnational capitalism thrives on uprootedness, importing workers, exporting work, being simultaneously present in the time zones of New York, London, Frankfurt, Hong Kong and Tokyo.

Is this the way we should see contemporary culture? My acceptance of the portrayal is only partial. Postmodernism comes close enough to the view of culture as an organization of diversity which I take here, and I find some of the comments on media and on the implications of commoditizing culture insightful or at least provocative. At times, on the other hand, the depictions of the postmodern age deserve some of its own incredulity. When it is claimed, for example, that identities become nothing but assemblages from whatever imagery is for the moment marketed through the media, then I wonder what kind of people the commentators on postmodernism know; I myself know hardly anybody of whom this would seem true.

It is a problem of postmodernist thought that as it has emphasized diversity and been assertively doubtful toward master narratives, it has itself frequently been on the verge of becoming another all-encompassing formula for a macroanthropology of the replication of uniformity, like any other conception of a *Zeitgeist*, or of national character. And of course postmodern culture cannot be coterminous with contemporary complex culture as the latter exists spread out over the world; postmodernist thought is again Occidentalist (once more, with Japan added). This is another instance of the transformation of a fairly small-scale European intellectual craft into a North American intellectual industry, and this time not only because of the large-scale American academic capacity in general, but also because nowhere else (Japan, then, possibly excepted) are the economic and technological foundations for postmodern culture so well developed as in North America (which also means that nowhere else are there so many people tuned into the consumption of commoditized images, and then ready to engage in theorizing about it). 1968, too, is largely an Occidental image. In many other places, it was just another forgettable year.

It is true that what is said to be characteristic of postmodernism is also what many people elsewhere may find attractive about America, and if we are to be attentive to transnational aspects of contemporary culture, this is not insignificant. But if they are aware of this kind of culture, it is likely to be an outsider's rather than a participant's awareness; a quite different thing. In the places where they live, media are present, but not everywhere. The role of the state in culture and learning may be under no real threat. They may themselves believe in one or another of the major metanarratives. Let us not ignore their varieties of cultural complexity.

In one more way do I take issue with theorizing about postmodernism. As a phenomenon of the last couple of decades, it has been a part of the ferment of ideas in the humanities, which has been immensely productive. At times, the engagement with the new sources of inspiration seems to entail a degree of intellectual amnesia, however, and as they are drawn upon for a reinvention of social theory, the results sometimes seem richer in hyperbole than in credibility. Where there has been a turn away from the established social sciences, in their own diversity, it has not been entirely without cost.

My point of departure here, as I stated summarily before, is in large part in a fairly durable tradition of social anthropology which, as it faces the organization of contemporary culture, may require some updating. Some of that must certainly come from the sources just referred to. But taking the point of view toward culture that I do, it seems to me arguable that we can benefit from a wider range of interlocutors in conversations across discipline boundaries: in media studies, in sociologies of knowledge and of culture, in the economics of knowledge production and distribution, in studies of professions and organizations, in information science. Such openings will also become apparent in what follows.

A Preview of Chapters

The chapters of this book fall into two sections. Part I, "Forms," including this and the four following chapters, is concerned in general terms with questions of conceptualization and with giving an overview of major variations of form within the social organization of meaning. Chapter 2, "Patterns of Process," thus takes its point of departure in a sketch of cultural process in small-scale societies, and goes on to ask in what ways a matching view of complex societies has to be different. It discusses two complementary sociologies of cultural process: a less abstract institutional view in which culture is seen to flow largely within and between the four organizational frames of form of life, state, market, and movement, and a more abstract formal view where culture in social relationships is seen in terms of six dimensions of symmetry or asymmetry. Some special attention is also given here to the cultural implications of the division of labor as a division of knowledge.

Chapter 3, "A Network of Perspectives," first elaborates on a notion of perspective as the individual building block in a distributive view of culture. From there, it goes on to scrutinizing the concept of subculture. The sizable body of writings relating to this concept is obviously relevant to a view of culture as an organization of diversity, at least in suggesting that the larger culture of which the subculture is a part is not homogeneous. Yet, often the term turns out to be merely a convenient label in descriptions of the more or less exotic ways of life to be discovered in the nooks and crannies of a large society. Perhaps if the ethnographic pleasures are great enough, nobody asks for conceptual niceties; anyway, here I try to specify the analytical implications of the concept. I also suggest that while subcultures are defined in relative terms as smaller units of collectively carried meaning within wider cultures, there is also a need for a concept of microculture to take into account differences of scale in absolute terms, and their implications for cultural form. The chapter furthermore includes a discussion of "the cultural apparatus," that complex of asymmetrically organized cultural production and distribution by which the meanings and cultural forms of the few reach the many. The social organization of meaning in complex cultures, it is suggested here, can be seen as an intricate interrelatedness between the cultural apparatus, in its various parts, on the one hand, and the subcultures on the other.

Chapter 4, "Unfree Flow," maps some of the economics and politics of culture, by surveying a range of different ways in which the flow of meaning through society is either deliberately constrained, or managed so as to involve some cost, in terms of material assets or power, to some, and of course a commensurate gain for others.

Contemporary complex cultures are, in the Lévi-Straussian vocabulary, "hot." These are cultures in the making, there is culture-building going on; the processual point of view keeps time in the picture. As the three dimensions of cultural complexity described earlier entail a synchronic view, one might even want to think of time, and diachronic differences, as a fourth dimension. It is not only a matter of culture history, of macrotime and irreversible, cumulative change. There is also microtime and its relations to macrotime, changes which occur and go away, changes which occur in some segments of a society but not in others, or changes which happen quickly here and then only slowly there. Chapter 5, "Growth, Flux, Coherence," is in part a discussion of this; concretely, not least a discussion of the roles that markets and media, intelligentsia and intellectuals play in it all. It also raises questions about the ways complex cultures hang together despite diversity and change. What are the characteristic forms of coherence work, and to what degree is coherence really a good thing?

If the first five chapters are fairly relentlessly conceptualizing, the last two, in Part II, "Sites," are attempts to apply the point of view thus developed to more concrete problems in the macroanthropology of culture. Anthropologists, it has been said, go to villages, but do not necessarily study villages; the villages may just be the places in which, or from which, other things are seen. But many things are *not* best seen in or from some single small rustic community. In chapter 6, "The Urban Swirl," I deal with cities as loci of complex cultural processes, and explore implications of their external and internal openness and of critical mass as a heuristic notion of cultural demography. I draw here for exemplification on the published materials concerning periods of intensive cultural productivity in three cities: Vienna, Calcutta, and San Francisco.

As collective systems of meaning, cultures belong primarily to social relationships, and to networks of such relationships. Only indirectly, and without logical necessity, do they belong to places. The less people stay put in one place, and also the less dependent their communications are on face-to-face contacts, the more attenuated does the link between culture and territory become. This is a fact we now encounter every day. In the final chapter, "The Global Ecumene," the stance toward cultural complexity developed in the preceding chapters is upscaled, as it were, to see what it suggests about the globalization of culture in the twentieth century. I stress the importance of center/periphery relationships in ordering cultural process, but I also point out that they involve diffusion as well as differentiation, and that contemporary views from the center have tended to give too little recognition to the generation of new culture at the periphery through the creative use of imported as well as local resources. Drawing in large part on Nigerian examples, I conclude by suggesting that creolization may be as useful a root metaphor as any in capturing the quality of those processes in which meanings and meaningful forms are shaped and socially organized between center and periphery.

This should set the stage for what follows. An earlier generation of macroanthropologists, concerned with civilizations as much as with savage minds, provides some inspiration. The concept of culture, Kroeber asserted, "gives anthropology a viewpoint of enormous range, a center for co-ordination of most phenomena that relate to man" (1953:xiv). With some rethinking of culture—instead of merely applying the concept loosely, or discarding it, or retreating with it into the hinterland—can we find that viewpoint again?

2 Patterns of Process

> In the ideal folk society, what one man knows and believes is the same as what all men know and believe. Habits are the same as customs. In real fact, of course, the differences among individuals in a primitive group and the different chances of experience prevent this ideal state of things from coming about. Nevertheless, it is near enough to the truth for the student of a real folk society to report it fairly well by learning what goes on in the minds of a few members. . . . The similarity among the members is found also as one generation is compared with its successor. Old people find young people doing, as they grow up, what the old people did at the same age, and what they have come to think right and proper. (Robert Redfield 1947:297)

> The metropolis is the genuine area of this culture which outgrows all personal life. Here in buildings and educational institutions, in the wonders and comforts of space-conquering technology, in the formations of community life, and in the visible institutions of the state, is offered such an overwhelming fullness of crystallized and impersonalized spirit that the personality, so to speak, cannot maintain itself under its impact. On the one hand, life is made infinitely easy for the personality in that stimulations, interests, uses of time and consciousness are offered to it from all sides. They carry the person as if in a stream, and one needs hardly to swim for oneself. On the other hand, however, life is composed more and more of these impersonal contents and offerings which tend to displace the genuine personal colorations and incomparabilities.
> (Georg Simmel [1903] 1964:422)

Small-scale ("folk," "primitive") societies have held a special place in anthropological thought. The village square, one may claim, has been the prototype locale for the ethnographer's encounter with the Other. It is predominantly with the help of observations made here, in adjoining alleyways and huts, and in the surrounding bush country, that anthropologists have thought and theorized about culture.

Elaborating on Robert Redfield's view, let us see how life goes on in and around the village square; the center of those activities and interactions through which a relatively simple culture is developed and maintained. It is the general qualities of the flow of meaning we are interested in; the ecological adaptation of the villagers, or the precise form of their social structure, matter less here. In some ways, we must also be aware, the view we will take of this process may be a caricature (or call it, as Redfield did, an ideal type), exaggerating characteristic features, rather than a wholly realistic depiction, of the circumstances of a simple culture.

Cultural Flow in a Small-Scale Society

What revolves around the village square is a face-to-face society. Its members stay within the same limited geographical territory and on the whole interact only with one another, but do a great deal of that. In the terminology from Alfred Schutz referred to in Chapter 1, they are fulltime "consociates," sharing a community of space as well as time. The division of labor is minimal—that is, not many distinctions are made between kinds of people, and there are not many tasks to allot differentially among them. Facing the same physical environment and having to use the same technical skills in dealing with it, people tend to replicate the same experiences. One might be tempted to say "raw experiences," but then experiences are really never raw. For, through communication, the society also makes available set ways of seeing and handling the environment. Its members have one opportunity after another to be on hand to see each other perform tasks and solve problems. In addition, as social distances are on the whole minimal and there are few natural barriers to the communication flow, they can also take in each other's comments on all this, in whatever modes of expression may be used for the purpose. The stream of events is quite repetitious; while there are situational improvisations, they tend to be variations on set themes.

People in this kind of society also know one another not

only segmentally, from particular kinds of activities, but as wholes, familiar more or less from the entire round of life. Not just for a few days or weeks or years, either, but to use a very culture-bound figure of speech, from the cradle to the grave—which, as generations follow each other, would most often mean from one person's cradle to the other person's grave. As there is no particular pressure to change, the life course of one individual prefigures the next in what appears like a chain of practically infinite length. ("Passed down from generation to generation for no apparent reason," as some humorist has said about Scandinavian-American cooking.)

This sketch of small-scale society certainly does not explain why this society has the particular culture that it has. On the other hand, it may have helped us see why it might rather effortlessly maintain considerable cultural uniformity, instead of traveling on the road of diversification. At every point, the tendency seems to be toward convergent or congruent understandings among the members of the society. As one of them considers the action of another member, he can view it and interpret it against a background of knowledge of the other's whole life. He can also then perceive that not only does this action probably match his own action in the same kind of context; it also fits into the other's life in the same way that his actions are integral parts of his own life. Personal experiences of different individuals tend to parallel each other, and are assumed to do so. They are readily transformed into collective representations in the Durkheimian sense. The formula for the social organization of meaning here, from the point of view of the representative individual, is that "I know, and I know that everybody else knows, and I know that everybody else knows that everybody else knows . . ." and so on, in a construction of massive intersubjectivity. (I will use this general type of formula again and again, as much of the complexity of the social organization of culture can be expressed in its variation.) There is no built-in strain between the point of view derived from an individual's first-hand experience and the items of interpretation and commentary kept in circulation, and reaching him as well, through social relationships.

Redundancy may be the key concept in summing up the character of cultural process in this small-scale society.[1] Action and context, part and whole, are mutually predictable; personal experiences match public messages; basically the same information, or complementary rather than unrelated or contradictory information, flows through many channels; there is similarity among people and repetition over time.

Again, not even real small-scale societies are likely to be precisely like this. No social structure can quite so successfully ensure uniformity of experience. There are everywhere some people who are physically strong and others who are weak, some who are hotheaded and others who are calm, some who become invalids through accidents; among sets of siblings, some people who grow up as older and others whose experience is that of being younger. What such matters of chance imply surely varies between societies, but their effects can hardly be obliterated altogether. In a more organized fashion, every society makes distinctions of some sort between men and women, young and adult, and among kinship groupings. And this means that experiences are not quite the same, intimacy is not total and universal, the flow of communication not unimpaired. Even with a minimal organized division of knowledge, some individuals may be recognized for their wisdom, and called upon in critical situations; there is a certain readiness among them to expand existing ideas a little way into unknown territory. Yet this wisdom is mostly based on a greater accumulated personal experience. Wise people in the small-scale society tend to be old people. As far as differences between the sexes are concerned, the women of the village talk over their experiences as they go out to look for edible plants and small animals; meanwhile, the men are out hunting. The long conversations follow different paths.

It is also a fact that, even if it would be in the nature of things that talk and observation together would make most knowledge shared, there can be quite consciously, and conscientiously, maintained arrangements of secrecy. Indeed, some of the smallest, otherwise most simply constituted societies (for example, in Melanesia) seem to be among those most intensely concerned with the organized withholding of knowledge.

"Culturality" and Contemporary Worlds of Meaning

Here and there in the world today, something at least reminiscent (all qualifications taken care of) of the culture centered on the village square may still persist as a bounded entity; and, in any case, we write about it in the "ethnographic present" to keep it alive as a part of our conceptual panorama of cultures. Obviously, however, one cannot export the view of culture which may grow out of its circumstances, and specifically assumptions about cultural sharing, to all kinds of other contexts, including that of contemporary complexity which we are dealing with here.

Certainly one should not underestimate either the amount or the significance of that shared culture which is present in complex, large-scale societies as well. Yet we must recognize the real intricacy of the flow of meaning in social life. As each individual engages in his own continuous interpreting of the forms surrounding him, how can we take for granted that he comes to the same result as the next fellow? There is nothing automatic about cultural sharing. Its accomplishment must rather be seen as problematic. With regard to complex cultures, it can be a matter of heated debate how much needs to be held in common, and what, and why.[2]

For one thing, contemporary complex societies systematically build nonsharing into their cultures, insofar as their divisions of labor are divisions of knowledge. But apart from this, there are the recurrent uncertainties. Communication in the complex society is uneven and fragmented. Many relationships (surely not all) are narrowly defined, and fleeting. One interacts with some people whom one hardly knows, and sees some people without actually interacting with them, while others are known only through hearsay. And it is not the same as in the small-scale society, where people are sufficiently alike so that what one individual does not actually know about another he may still have well-founded assumptions about. If there is redundancy in the cultural processes here as well, in many contexts at least it does not seem to come about in the same way. The actions and utterances of others are shaped by factors which are often imperfectly known. There is action without commentary, as well as commentary without observable action.

Thus, circumstances can promote ambiguity. Differences between people's points of view, working in combination with the segmentality and the greater distance of many relationships, render the full context of cultural externalizations opaque, rather than fairly transparent as it would be in the small-scale society.

People who make active use of certain cultural forms may intend them differently than they are understood by observers; different observers may not understand them in the same way either.

The telltale signs of such a cultural process in everyday life may be arguments, misunderstandings, and accusations of ignorance, and also those instances when we defer to expertise. And as proportionately less of the total cultural inventory is directly and fully shared by the individual, he may be more concerned than in a small-scale culture with certain kinds of metacultural knowledge: knowing one's own ignorance, knowing that others know something else, knowing whom to believe, developing a notion of the potentially knowable.[3] There may be a nagging suspicion that things are not what they seem to be, that a lack of intellectual tools prevents one from seeing concealed patterns, that large regions of reality can only be successfully dealt with by specialists, although they intrude into everyman's life.

In an essay by John Fischer (1975), one finds a quite conventional definition of culture as "persistent, socially transmitted and shared information," and the more unconventional notion of culturality as a two-dimensional variable; degrees of culturality, it is proposed, can be measured in terms of persistence and social distribution. Obviously, this would make some items in any one society more cultural than others. It would also seem to make some societies as wholes, such as that around the village square, more cultural than other societies, such as those of contemporary complexity. But for an overall, and comparative, view of the social organization of meaning, one cannot limit one's interest to either items or societies which are high in culturality thus defined. One has to deal, rather, with the entire field of variability in culturality, and with the realities underlying the variation. As we turn here to complex cultures, we must aim for a view which matches the scenario of cultural process in the small-scale society, but which does not hide their quite different circumstances. The second quotation above, from Georg Simmel, is explicitly concerned with the metropolis, and it again has overtones of classic folk-urban contrasts of which we may be skeptical, but it suggests some of those circumstances which pertain to contemporary complex cultures more broadly—the variety of sources and currents of culture, the differences in scale which make some meanings appear more personal than others, a complicated relationship between culture, technology, and space.

In the comparative study of culture, or of culturality, we must be prepared to deal with the implications of such a scenario as well. And we should attend both to the ways people make their own meanings, through the generative power of personal and situational experience, and to the way they take over meanings from others, in the communicative transmissions of interactions; we should note the ways in which cultural sharing ("conventional understandings," in the phrasing Redfield often used) may be established, but also the ways in which kinds and degrees of nonsharing are built into cultures. Rather than concentrating on what is persistent, we must ask, furthermore, how variations in temporality are built into cultural process.

Frameworks of Flow: State, Market, Movement, Form of Life

In thinking about patterns of process in contemporary cultures, I find it useful to shift between two analytical levels. One is a rather concrete institutional sociology of cultural process, using a familiar language of major organizational types and principles. The other level involves a more formal sociology, identifying the characteristics of cultural management in social relationships in rather abstract terms of symmetries and asymmetries along several dimensions. It is at this level that a coherent view of the social organization of meaning can be stated most rigorously, using a limited set of concepts. Variations at the institutional level can, in large part, be described by way of the formal level concepts.

In this chapter, I will argue first that four organizational frameworks encompass most of the cultural process in the world today, and I will also go on to identify six major dimensions of symmetry or asymmetry in that process. In between, I will devote some special attention to the central significance of the division of labor in the social organization of meaning.

In what kinds of relationships does culture typically flow in contemporary societies? Much as in the folk society, some of it passes between people simply in their mingling as fellow human beings. It passes also between governments and their subjects, or citizens; and culture likewise moves between sellers and buyers. Moreover, at times at least, there are the particular pressures of converts on nonconverts, organized and deliberate attempts to change cultures or parts of cultures.

For the four major frameworks which should take us at least a long way toward a comprehensive accounting of present-day cultural flow, then, I use the terms *form of life, market, state,* and *movement.* These do not work in isolation from one another, but it is rather in their interplay, with varying respective strengths, that they shape both what we rather arbitrarily demarcate as particular cultures, and that complicated overall entity which we may think of as the global ecumene. Within each framework, there can be great variation, between instances as well as in any one instance. Nevertheless, it seems possible to point to certain recurrent if not altogether universal tendencies in their organization of culture.

The first framework I will identify, for lack of a more precise term, as that of *form of life.* In contemporary cultures, to repeat, this is the framework which has most in common with what is the whole of cultural process in the small-scale society as described before, but here it is only a part of the whole. Certainly, it is still a framework of great importance; it involves the everyday practicalities of production and reproduction, activities going on in work places, domestic settings, neighborhoods, and some variety of other places. One characteristic of cultural process here is that from doing the same things over and over again, and seeing and hearing others doing the same things and saying the same things over and over again, a measure of redundancy results which is at least reminiscent of the small-scale society. Experiences and interests coalesce into habitual, enduring points of view. As the everyday activities are practically adapted to material circumstances, there is not much reason to bring about alterations in culture, as long as the circumstances do not change. In the form of life framework, consequently, there is a tendency toward stability in cultural process. If anything, unless there is some variety in the round of endlessly recurrent tasks, there is a vulnerability to boredom.

While every form of life includes some people and excludes a great many others, there are not necessarily well-defined boundaries between them, and people may develop some conception of each other's forms of life through much the same kind of everyday looking and listening, although here probably with less precision, less redundancy.

Within this framework, too, people's mere going about things entails a free and reciprocal cultural flow. There are no specialists in the production and dissemination of meaning as such, who are to be materially compensated for cultural work. As a whole, encompassing the variety of particular forms of life, this framework involves cultural processes which are diffuse, uncentered. The "commanding heights" of culture, as it were, are not here.

In the *market* framework, cultural commodities are moved. All commodities presumably carry some meaning, and are to that degree cultural commodities; but in some cases informational, intellectual, aaesthetic, or emotional appeal is all there is to a commodity, or a very large part of it, and commodities are intentionally shaped to carry such appeal. We will be especially interested in these, and could remind ourselves here that it has been one of the preoccupations of postmodernist thinking that the market economy as a whole, particularly in Occidental society, is increasingly one of signs. Even goods that eventually relate to people's physical and material adaptations, that is, are made to carry other, mostly pleasing, messages as well.

As meanings and meaningful forms are produced and disseminated by specialists in exchange for material compensation, more or less centering relationships are set up between producers and consumers—the cultural currents involved come from particular points. The market also attempts expansively to bring more and more of culture as a whole into its framework, its agents are in competition with one another, and they also keep innovating to foster new demand. There is, in other words, a built-in tendency toward instability in this framework.

The third framework of cultural process is that of the *state;* not the bounded physical area itself, but rather that organizational form which involves a degree of control over activities within a territory on the basis of concentrated, publicly acknowledged power. (It might have been preferable to use some such term as "regime," since basically similar arrangements of power can occur either above or below what is literally a state level, but since "state" is the more common term, and entirely appropriate in so many of the instances concerned, I will stay with it.)

As we now know it, the state, while still in the last analysis defined in terms of physical force, engages in the management of meaning in various ways. To gain legitimate authority, state apparatuses tend to reach out with different degrees of credibility and success toward their subjects to foster the idea that the state is a nation, and to construct them culturally as citizens. This usually involves a degree of homogenization as a goal of cultural engineering (although very occasionally, a state at least pays lip service to the idea of diversity, and somewhat paradoxically claims this as a value that unites it). On the other hand, the state also takes an interest in shaping such differences among people as are desirable for the purpose of fitting categories of individuals into different slots in the structure of production and reproduction. Beyond such involvements in cultural process, some states more than others engage in what one may describe as cultural welfare, trying to provide their citizenry with "good culture": that is, meanings and meaningful forms held to meet certifiable intellectual and aesthetic standards. Not least would this cultural welfare provide the instruments people may use in developing emancipated reflexive stances toward themselves and their world.

The state framework for cultural process concentrates material resources at the center for long-term cultural work, and the flow of meaning is mostly from the center outward. In at least one current of the cultural flow which the state sets in motion, the tendency is mostly toward a stability of meaning—the idea of the nation is usually tied to conceptions of history and tradition. But then again, we should know by now that such conceptions may in fact be spurious and quite contestable; when needed, traditions can be manufactured at short notice.[4]

The fourth and final framework of cultural process in contemporary life is that of *movements*. Clearly these are capable of exercising great influence—western Europe and North America would have been quite different during the last quarter-century or so without the women's movement, the environmental movement, the peace movement, or a variety of ethnic movements. We often describe these entities as "social movements," yet even when their ultimate concern is with the distribution and use of power or material resources, they are often very much movements in culture, organizations for "consciousness raising," attempts to transform meanings.[5] Movements tend to be less centralized in their management of the cultural flow than we usually find in the state and market frameworks ("each one teach one" is one formulation of a movement ideal), and there is also less concentration of material resources, as movements rely heavily on voluntary efforts. In this they are more like forms of life, out of which they of course tend to emerge, as people within the latter become dissatisfied with existing conditions or are threatened by changes.

Compared to what goes on within the form of life framework itself, on the other hand, movements foster a more deliberate and explicit flow of meaning, and are more outward-oriented, missionizing. Insofar as they are oriented toward specific changes or toward averting such changes, they are also more inherently unstable—they tend to succeed or fail. If they become entirely routinized, they are no longer movements in a strict sense.

Form of life, market, state, and movement can be rather commonsensically distinguished. What is important for our understanding of the cultures in which they have their parts, however, is that we see how they differ in their centering and decentering tendencies, in the relationships between power and culture which they entail, and in their cultural economies. They also have their own characteristics with respect to the temporal dimension of culture. The overall contemporary social organization of meaning results from the combination of these tendencies, and its variations result to a great extent from varying combinations.

Movements are thus more intermittently part of the cultural totality than the other three frameworks; the form of life framework is the only one which can never be altogether absent, although cultural critics at times envisage that dystopic human condition under which little meaning flows within it. If nowadays the entire inhabited earth is divided into states as political units, the degree to which these manage an effective cultural process covering their entire territories varies greatly. The organizing power of cultural markets, too, is variable. There is obviously some tendency for state and market frameworks to be in competition. Under the twentieth century forms of state socialism, there has been little room for market and movement frameworks in the organization of culture, and the state framework has coexisted, in one way or other, only with that of forms of life.[6] In the United States during the same period, on the other hand, with an unusual degree of cultural commoditization, the state framework has also played a major part in organizing at least some currents of meaning. There is no simple relationship of mutual exclusion here.

Yet combinations of frameworks, of course, entail interrelations; much of what goes on in culture has to do with these. States, markets and movements are ultimately only successful if they can get forms of life to open up to them. States sometimes compete in markets; nationalist movements have been known to transform themselves into states; some movements create internal markets for particular commodities relevant to their followings, and they can be newsworthy and thus commoditizable themselves in a wider market. (And what is called "movements" in art may be more like fashions in a market than they are like other movements.) Forms of life can be selectively commoditized as such, as life style news, and some of their particular items can also be restyled and marketed (ethnic home cooking turning into new varieties of fast food, and folk music becoming ethnopop, or world music); and so on, indefinitely. These entanglements, involving often mutually contradictory tendencies, also keep the totality alive, shifting, continuously unstable.

The frameworks are recurrent; their contents, and their interrelations, differ in time and space. While I claim that in combination they organize a very large part of the cultural flow, I would not insist analytically on forcing everything into them as a matter of sheer principle. Old-style personal patronage in the arts, for example, seems to hybridize characteristics from the state and market frameworks; the activities of foundations today, in support of cultural production, are of a similar nature. Some churches, when they are not simply arms of states, may be fairly state-like in their internal organization, although less tied to territory, and substituting moral force or supernatural sanction for physical force; but some are very market-oriented, some are certainly movements, and in some cases they provide inclusive frameworks for forms of life. Rather than using dubious means to crowd everything into the four major frameworks, we may just accept the occasional organizational forms that do not fit as we encounter them, and still look at them in terms of the same general variables. What is unambiguously covered by these four frameworks, however, certainly seems enough.

Identifying them should also make us wary of one very widespread tendency in social and cultural studies. Concepts of state, nation, society, and culture are conflated, so that when we speak of "societies," the units in question are usually the politically and territorially defined units of states, and when we refer to cultures, they are often units like "Swedish culture," "Romanian culture." Whether such conflation allows an adequate description of actual cultural flows and concomitant cultural boundaries is not an issue necessarily examined. What we should realize, instead, is that the flows of meaning organized within the four frameworks are sometimes contained within the state as a territory, or even within its smaller constituent units, and sometimes not; and that space is itself a factor of quite variable impact in the organization of contemporary cultural process. We will come back to this problem especially in chapter 7.

The Division of Labor as Distribution of Culture

At this point, it becomes necessary to discuss at somewhat greater length the part of the division of labor in contemporary cultural process, especially its importance in organizing complex cultural inventories. The division of labor introduces a basic duality into the cultural process, and this has a bearing on the conceptualization of the four frameworks above.

To repeat a point from chapter 1, a notable feature of the division of labor, compared to many other kinds of differentially distributed meaning, is that by giving shape to relationships predicated on a limitation of cultural sharing, it fosters its own form of cultural coherence, a complementarity of haves and have-nots. While factors such as allocations of time and physical labor are involved as well, the division of labor is to a great extent a matter of specialized knowledge, or occasionally some other kind of control over particular meanings, unevenly distributed in an organized fashion. (That this aspect of it is growing ever more important is, of course, one of the claims behind the notion of the information society.) Writing about a "division of linguistic labor," the philosopher Hilary Putnam (1975:227 ff.) has noted that we can all use certain words with a measure of confidence because there are some people who are expert users, who know exactly what they stand for.

There are words which are like a hammer or a screwdriver, tools that can be used by one person; and there are words which are like a steamship, requiring the cooperative activity of a number of persons. Too often, Putnam concludes, have words been thought of like tools of the first kind. The analogy between language and culture in this instance seems close enough. Where there is a division of knowledge, everybody does not have to know everything, as long as there is some access to the skills of particular other people. This is another way of collectivizing a meaning system. The sleight of hand in that paradox of man as a spider, living in a web of meanings he has himself created, consists of the fact that the web in this case is the work of many different spiders.

Through this interdependency, as we have said, a larger cultural inventory than any individual can competently control himself is somehow within his reach or on his horizon. In the United States, a *Dictionary of Occupational Titles* nowadays lists more than 20,000 different occupations (Bell 1976:93). But this, it would seem, at the same time means that there are also 20,000 different ways of being a layman. As the division of knowledge integrates cultural management into the material economy, much of our culture is only available to us at a price. Moreover, as large domains of contemporary cultures are managed by experts, the layman becomes vulnerable to the dispositions of others. Acquiring common sense turns out to be—in part—a matter of learning to be selectively incompetent. Whether princes or paupers, laypeople become clients.

Some years ago, in a leaflet available at downtown street corners in Washington, D.C., I came across this course outline:

> *Becoming an instant expert.* This course will give you the techniques and information on how to become knowledgeable enough in a matter of weeks to talk or write like an expert on any topic—computers, canoeing, the cotton exchange—you name it! This skill can be invaluable for freelancers, businesspersons or students. Topics to be covered include: finding the best written sources of information quickly, getting top experts to talk to you at no charge, what to ask these experts, discerning the good information from the bad, organizing your information into a coherent whole, and insuring that your collected information is accurate.
>
> (Open University, Washington, D.C., 1986)

You may not care to become an instant expert, and the course can hardly turn you into one. But the course description pinpoints some of the characteristics and problems of a culture organized to no small extent by expertise. There is the cash nexus, and perhaps some way of getting around it. There are the alternative sources of knowledge, and the difficulty of establishing, from the outside, what is real knowledge and what is dubious. Not least, the pieces must be be made to fit together.

Here are indeed some of the major issues in the social organization of meaning in contemporary complex societies. Can specialists be trusted? Can a coherent understanding of the world be reached, and a way of dealing with it be found, through a summation of the varieties of expertise? How are boundaries to be drawn between the realms where a division of knowledge is regnant and those where culture is collectively held in other ways, such as through more general sharing? How are complex cultures affected by the interrelations of coexisting modes of cultural management, differing not least in their stance toward the production and integration of meaning? To such questions we will have to return later on, particularly in chapters 4 and 5.

But the more or less complementary relationships between specialists and laypeople only make up one side of the impact of the division of labor on cultural process. On the one hand, that is, there are the relatively specific prestations for which the individual is materially rewarded, which are manifestations of his ideas and which constitute an outward flow of meaning of varying nature and scope; it aims at the public, the front stage. On the other hand, this individual's involvement in the division of labor is an important factor in his existential situation. His practice on the basis of the particular meanings allotted to him, his experience of the social relationships in which his practice involves him, and the access to material resources which results from these relationships, do much to give shape to his perspective in wider terms. The carpenter, the journalist, and the politician each has a world view colored by his line of work.[7] Perhaps such world views are to some degree transmitted, as a part of occupational training. But they can mostly not be exchanged, in their full range of expressions, for material rewards in the division of labor. Unlike specific know-how, they have no customers, at least probably not. Nonetheless these wider occupational perspectives may have sympathizers, in a community of the like-minded. Thus, in a way, it can turn socially inwards, toward a backstage.

This duality of the division of labor is reflected in the delineation of the frameworks of cultural flow above. It is important to understand that they refer precisely to cultural flow, not to social organization generally. I am concerned here, that is to say, with state and market as matrices for the production and dissemination of meaning and meaningful form, the front stage part. In other ways, obviously important in their own right although I do not deal with them directly here, both state and market are active in placing people within the division of labor, thus allotting them to their circumstances of material life and everyday practice.

To the extent that people located within the division of labor generate their own meanings and meaningful forms and circulate these through messages among themselves, backstage as it were, in a reciprocal free flow, I see this as cultural process occurring within the form of life framework, treating their ultimate connection to state and market for these purposes as given.[8] It may be protested that this conceals the overall importance of state and market; but it is not intended to do so. The point is simply that state and market affect contemporary cultures in two ways, directly and indirectly, through their own communicative channels as well as through the conditions underlying forms of life. At the same time as the influence of state and market on forms of life are recognized, however, one must accept the possibility that the latter can also have a degree of autonomy in their internal cultural process.

Culture in Relationships: Symmetries and Asymmetries

The four frameworks of cultural flow tend to combine a number of organizational features in characteristic clusters. Turning to what I referred to above as the formal sociology of cultural process, I now want to identify a number of dimensions of symmetry and asymmetry in the flow of meaning in social relationships, which allow us to see more precisely the convergences and divergences of these frameworks, and also how contemporary complex cultures differ from the culture of the ideal small-scale society. These dimensions are:

1. *baseline;*
2. *input mode;*
3. *input quantity;*
4. *scale;*
5. *material resource linkage;* and
6. *power linkage.*

Baseline refers to culture already in place. As people come into contact with one another, that is, or start on a new interaction, they may have available to them either more or less the same contextually relevant meanings or different meanings; they start out from similar or different points. The former case involves a relative baseline symmetry, the latter a relative asymmetry. The most complete form of baseline symmetry, again, is the "I know, and I know that everybody else knows, and I know that everybody else knows that everybody else knows. . . ." type of arrangement. It may be, however, that relevant baselines in a relationship first have to be explored and negotiated, rather than simply taken for granted.

Of course, one can hardly imagine a social organization of meaning which is in this way symmetrical in every detail. If there were one, the people involved would appear to have no need whatsoever to communicate with one another. But as far as communication is concerned, the point is that the greater the symmetry and the more limited the areas of asymmetry among the baselines, the more surely and effortlessly can meaning flow between the participants who have a sense of that distribution of meanings. What is explicitly communicated may be only the tip of an iceberg; since so much is already shared, contextualizations can be largely tacit. Ethnomethodologists have shown how much is thus taken for granted in conversations between people who assume that they know each other's personal meaning systems well—the "indexicality," as they would put it, of everyday speech where a baseline of far-reaching sharing is expected.[9] Where there is a greater measure of asymmetry between baselines, on the other hand, more effort to "take the perspective of the other" is generally needed to create an orderly flow of meaning; and there is also a greater risk of misunderstanding. But it is, of course, quite possible that the *outcome* of the cultural process will be a greater symmetry between the understandings of the participants.

The division of knowledge as discussed earlier provides examples of how baseline asymmetries are built into complex cultures. Again, when the division of knowledge creates specialists, it also creates laymen. (Most people are, of course, both; specialists usually in one field, laymen in all others.) The cultural constitution of these categories implies that the boundaries between their areas of cultural competence, and thus the forms of complementarity between them, are defined, more or less clearly, by convention or negotiation. Often enough, the social organization of meaning in these contacts is itself worked into routines. There are simple assumptions about the distribution of competencies and about the way to bridge the gap between asymmetrical understandings, when such gaps indeed have to be bridged. The communicative flow between specialist and client may be mostly in the direction of the specialist, or mostly from him. Seeking out a surgeon, an auto mechanic, or a barber, people act on the expectation that "he knows more than I about this." But they may still tell him more than he tells them, as the specialist's task in these instances is technical rather than communicative. There only has to be a prefatory communication first—about symptoms, or about desired outcome. Here, one party's comparatively limited understandings have to be expressed in a form which matches the other's more elaborate system of meaning—"if I say this, you can interpret it and act on it better than I can myself."

In other instances again, there is interaction with primarily communicative intent, but with the opposite asymmetrical loading; a specialist communicating some part of his more elaborate understandings to someone else, for the latter to act upon or simply to know. The specialist here may be a consultant, a journalist, or a teacher, or an artist of some sort. His assumption would seem to be: "you do not know this, but on the basis of what you do know, you should be able to grasp it."

Yet it must not be assumed that such bridgings of baseline asymmetry are never problematic. It is one of the small embarrassments of everyday life not to be able to tell an auto mechanic or even a barber exactly what you want from him; he somehow appears to have another understanding of what are shared concepts than you have. From his viewpoint, certain things are not in need of being said, or have only one self-evident way of being said. And the potential for controversy increases when those who are assumed to be specialists in communication cannot reach those whom they should reach. When teachers teach and nobody learns, or at least some students do not learn; or when art seems absolutely incomprehensible. There is some slippage in the social organization of meaning here.

One might add, as far as outcome is concerned, that laymen usually want access to specialist knowledge only in small portions. A certain viscosity in the flow of culture is involved here. Even if we could personally acquire more knowledge and thus rely less on specialists, the time and effort needed to do so, and to develop our skills in using it to an acceptable level, are not commensurate with our needs. Consequently laymen are content to remain occasional clients and leave most of the specialized knowledge where it is, calling for no more than that application of some part of it which matches their needs in particular instances. The baseline asymmetry largely remains in place, then, from one interaction to the next.

Let me present the other dimensions more briefly at this stage. What I refer to as the dimension of *input mode* relates to the fact that the actions of the participants in a relationship can make available similar or different kinds of meaning, and use similar or different ways of externalizing meaning. People may talk about much the same kinds of things, or they may have their subject specialties; or one party uses particular forms of cultural expression, such as music or painting, which others do not manage as actively, or at all. In a concert, someone sings; the members of the audience clap their hands (or whistle or boo, perhaps). In a political campaign, the office seeker makes speeches, plays ball, kisses babies, and marches in parades; the voter just votes.

By *input quantity,* I refer simply to the fact that participants may be equally or inequally active in supplying content to the flow of meaning. Friends, spouses, or colleagues are likely to be fairly symmetrically involved in this respect. The most extreme form of asymmetry here is a one-way flow of communication. Relationships between writer and reader, actor and audience, teacher and pupil are examples of varying degrees of asymmetry of input quantity.

Along the dimension of *scale,* relationships may be one-to-one, or one-to-many, or few-to-many, etc. Face-to-face relationships are often relatively symmetrical in scale, although there is asymmetry for example between a teacher and his pupils in a classroom. Literacy and electronic media are among factors which have greatly increased the possibilities of asymmetry of scale. In asymmetrical relationships along this dimension, the one can relate to the many either simultaneously or serially, over time. A great asymmetry of scale would seem to be the simplest way of making the leap from micro to macro levels in cultural process.

The remaining two dimensions bridge the divide between the cultural and what is at least in some sense extracultural, in line with what was said in chapter 1. The *material resource linkage* of cultural flow in relationships can be of a great many kinds, and identifying this as one dimension is hardly more than a way of acknowledging again the entanglement of cultural process with material life. It is true that some meanings simply have little connection with people's access to material resources. There are also, for example, many forms of practical knowledge which have such connections but are equally available to everybody; they may be easy to come by, for instance, in the form of life framework. This would be an instance of symmetry. As far as asymmetry of material resource linkage is concerned, we should be aware that it can both affect the flow of meaning and be affected by it (and these two possibilities are certainly often directly tied to one another). Where communication technology is available to some but not to others, this favors the former in their relative ability to influence the flow of meaning. In the market framework, those with greater material assets can better afford to buy commoditized knowledge; at the same time, of course, this exchange involves a redistribution of these assets in favor of the seller. And (as a major concern of studies in ideology) the cultural flow can also work to the advantage of some participants over others by disseminating, for wider acceptance, cultural definitions and evaluations which influence the general principles of material distribution in society.

It may seem odd, if one thinks of power only in terms of inequality, to consider the possibility of symmetry in the *power linkage* of cultural flow. If one regards power as a ubiquitous aspect of all human interaction, however, the difficulty disappears. In any case, the asymmetrical linkages may be more likely to draw our attention. Again, the linkage can work in two ways. Some participants in relationships may be more able to back up their messages with a threat of punishment if they are not accepted, or at least attended to, by the others. Conversely, some people may stand to gain more power than others if certain meanings become accepted. Again, ideology is a major example.

Identifying these six dimensions of symmetry or asymmetry gives us a few items of a vocabulary for talking about variations in cultural organization; perhaps in the form they have just been stated little more than a checklist, a sensitizing instrument, as along each of these six dimensions there is room for much variation. They allow us, however, to restate some of the differences between the several frameworks for the flow of meaning in contemporary cultures. A symmetry of baselines is fairly common in relationships within the form of life framework, although there are asymmetries here as well; asymmetries along this dimension often entail uncertainties in the cultural flow within all the other three frameworks. Asymmetries of material resource linkage are built into the market and state frameworks, and asymmetries of power linkage at least into the latter. The state and market frameworks typically involve asymmetries of input quantity and scale (which would usually go together); there is frequently more symmetry in these respects in the form of life framework, while the movement framework may often be in an intermediate position in this regard. Probably asymmetries of input mode are most common in the state and market frameworks, while they occur scattered in the other frameworks as well.

No doubt both symmetries and asymmetries tend to cluster for various logical or functional reasons, but the connections between them deserve to be investigated in each particular case. In gross terms, anyway, the dimensions may allow us to identify some of the differences in cultural process between societies. It is certainly not that relationships in a small-scale society are all necessarily symmetrical along each of these dimensions, or that relationships in complex societies, with complex cultures, are all asymmetrical. In the latter, however, the mix of relationships contains a greater proportion which are asymmetrical in one way or other, and this contributes remarkably to the overall construction of these cultures. This is one of the topics of chapter 3.

3 A Network of Perspectives

> Whenever some group of people have a bit of common life with a modicum of isolation from other people, a common corner in society, common problems and perhaps a couple of common enemies, there culture grows. (Everett C. Hughes 1961:28)

> For most of what he calls solid fact, sound interpretation, suitable presentations, every man is increasingly dependent upon the observation posts, the interpretation centers, the presentation depots, which in contemporary society are established by means of what I am going to call the cultural apparatus.
> (C. Wright Mills 1963:406)

The Boat people of southeastern China—derogatorily known as the Tanka—engage in fishing and shipping for their livelihood, and live their everyday life on their boats. What the landliving Chinese see of this strikes them as very un-Chinese, and they tend to assume that the distinctiveness of the Boat people is rooted in a separate origin, but in fact it seems to be a matter only of the fairly extreme ecological adaptation to an aquatic life. There are practicalities in the way of going about things, and a specialized knowledge, which the Boat people do not at all share with their compatriots.

Yet Barbara Ward (1965, 1966, 1977), who studied the Boat people in the small island village of Kau Sai, on the outskirts of Hong Kong, found that they were far from isolated from the rest of Chinese and Hong Kong society. They had variously well-developed and accurate conceptions of the characteristics of other Chinese groups, derived from their contacts with these and used in interactions with them, but also commented upon among the Boat people themselves—Ward's own discussion of all this has been in terms of "conscious models." Such interactions with other Chinese occurred continuously at the fringes of daily living—for example, in trade. But it also happened that individuals of the Boat people would leave the waterbound life and assimilate to the surrounding population. To have had some preliminary understandings of what pertains to land living could then be a useful resource in getting started.

The Boat people usually referred to the habits and preferences of the various groups of landliving Chinese with which they were familiar in a rather matter-of-fact way, without any particular measure of respect. They took a rather different view of another set of meanings, those which in traditional China were propagated especially by the literati.

"Because we are Chinese" is the answer Chinese informants most often give to their anthropologists when asked why they follow such and such a custom, Ward noted; and even in as marginal a group as this one, the conception of Chineseness has its historical basis in the fact that in traditional China, the literati and the administration which they staffed provided a notably effective organizational framework for the maintenance of nationwide cultural coherence. One could spend decades in the examination system, gaining forever more understanding of Confucian social thought. Only some groups—but including the Boat people—were excluded from sitting for examinations. And this system penetrated the land. Although there were considerable local cultural variations, there were resident scholar-officials practically everywhere, serving as models for a life according to the nationally acknowledged standards, and using their power to enforce these in at least some domains of life. To people in Kau Sai, the literati model was something to aspire to, even as they knew they must fall short of it, for it was the real Chinese way.

The twist to the story here is that since there are in fact no traditional Chinese literati any longer, they are now an agency of cultural coherence maintained only in memory, by the Boat people and presumably among many other Chinese. More than ever, these highly respected all-Chinese standards are now the Boat people's views of literati views, with whatever imprecision, misunderstandings, and blank spots this may entail, rather than the actual standards once known to and propagated by the literati themselves.

Yet the literati were never quite alone in spreading a sort of national Chineseness in the village communities of China.

"When we next do plays," Ward found, was the time when the Boat people of Kau Sai village really felt that visitors should come and see them. Then the single drab street filled up with people; colorful processions with lots of firecrackers, hawkers and peddlers, lion dances, public gambling of many kinds, as well as a visiting troupe of professional actors from the city, who performed with intensive participation by the local audience. Cultural performances, and theater especially, continue as one broad current of cultural flow through which common motifs and themes reach all Chinese.

In this chapter, I concentrate mostly on two major tendencies in the organization of cultural flow, represented in the quotations from Hughes and Mills above, and the interrelations between them. Both tendencies are illustrated in the case of the Boat people. These Chinese certainly have that "common corner," with "common problems," from which grows a set of meanings uniquely theirs. The traditional Chinese cultural apparatus, on the other hand, was made up to a great extent of the literati.

In the more abstract terms introduced in the preceding chapter, what above all defines these tendencies are symmetries and asymmetries respectively along the dimensions of input quantity and scale. Among the Boat people themselves, presumably, there is on the whole a mutual give and take in the flow of meaning within a form of life framework. In contrast, the cultural apparatus of the literati (organized in this instance within a state framework) consists of a flow of meaning from a relatively few officeholders to the great Chinese majority.

Before turning to these matters, however, I want to outline a view of the individual's share, or version, of a culture as a collectively held structure of meanings; a view which is consonant with what was said in chapter 1 about "bringing people back in" through the distributive conception of culture. This view will then serve as a stepping stone for the continued conceptual elaboration.

Perspectives and Horizons

Several of the anthropologists concerned with distributive models as mentioned before have had their own neologisms to denote the individual's portion of culture—"mazeway" (Wallace), "propriospect" (Goodenough), "idioverse" (Schwartz); Bourdieu's "habitus" is again in some ways a similar notion.[1] My own preference is "perspective," both because I see some value in using a more everyday term, and because it makes especially well the point (around which most sociology of knowledge, where it is also often used, revolves) that things look different depending on where you see them from.[2]

People, that is, manage meanings *from where they are* in the social structure. At any one time, the individual is surrounded by a flow of externally available, culturally shaped meaning which influences his ordering of experiences and intentions. Yet he is not merely a passive recipient of all sorts of available meaning, and he does not just contemplate it in the stillness of his mind. As soon as he has begun to form a conception of himself and the world, and of what is desirable and not desirable, he is actively involved in dealing practically, intellectually, and emotionally with his particular situation. Thus, he will concern himself with meanings especially as they appear to relate to his own experiences and plans; to his involvements with other people, for one thing, and to his material needs and interests, for another. If need be, he may extend or modify the meanings available to him, acting improvisationally and innovatively "on the basis of" them rather than fully "in line with" them. His practical reason, that is, has a cultural foundation, but as he draws on extant meanings their forms may be made to vary and change. Meanings are used as equipment; in their management there is a strong factor of relevance and intentionality.

The perspective is the device which organizes the attention and interpretation which an individual gives to externally carried meaning, as well as his production of such meaning, whether deliberate or spontaneous. As I understand it, the perspective exists in a tension zone between culture and social structure, insofar as there is no assured congruency between situational experiences and demands on the one hand and available, ready-made meanings on the other. But the tension can be resolved when there is such a close fit. The small-scale society, insofar as it has an undifferentiated social structure and a continuous, nearly all-inclusive cultural flow, is more likely to minimize this tension than complex societies are.

How are perspectives generated?[3] A brief excursion into

what I think of as a variant of role theory (although it centers on activities and experiences, rather than norms) helps us get an overall view. If we see social life as consisting of a set of situations, we can view roles as characteristic involvements in such situations. Societies have different, and variously large, sets of typical situations, and consequently variously extensive role inventories. In small-scale societies, the role inventory is modest; in the complex society, it is large.

Roles are of many kinds, however we somewhat arbitrarily decide to classify them. In the complex society, as we have seen, a great many of them (but perhaps only one per individual) relate to the society-wide division of labor, others are defined by household activities and kinship, others again by leisure preferences, neighboring, or even the fleeting chance co-presences created in our traffic through physical space. Each individual has roles of many or all of these kinds; they come together in his role repertoire. Roles may be linked to one another in some way, so that if you have a particular one, you are also likely to have the other. Gender, age, or ethnicity is often the basis of such recurrent role clusters. But if clustering is not so tight, there can be much variation between role repertoires, rather than some handful of predictable constellations.

In principle each role, each situational involvement, can contribute to an individual's perspective, both by way of the cultural flow through that situation and in terms of the nature of the individual's particular practical involvement in it. People's perspectives as wholes, that is to say, may be taken to reflect their entire role repertoires. Moreover, they may do so not only at a single point in time. As perspectives are built up more or less cumulatively, they reflect previous involvements and experiences as well. The perspective is a biographical structure.

To the extent that people in complex societies have more varying role repertoires, the perspectivation of meaning implies less replication of uniformity, less extensive cultural sharing. Here, we should remind ourselves of the various views of "where the action is" with regard to cultural generativity referred to in chapter 1. The sound and fury of cultural production may well be particularly great on some sites within the social structure. Yet it is not obvious, as role repertoires differ, that everybody in a complex society is involved with these sites in the same way, or at all.

This basic understanding of diversity, however, has to be qualified in certain ways. For one thing, it is important to realize that there are many kinds of situational involvements which everybody, or nearly all, or at least a great many, share. These naturally tend to homogenize perspectives. Furthermore, not all situations are equally important in the construction of a perspective. We spend less time in some than in others, and attach different weight to them. If certain kinds of situations are thus perspectivally peripheral, so to speak, they would have less impact on the variability of perspectives. Being a mother or a factory worker should influence one's personal meaning system more than being a sometime bus passenger; these are the kind of experiences where one would find one's most resonant metaphors.

Accumulating and organizing experience, the perspective goes on to generalize it in responding to new experiences and new demands for action; it becomes a personal paradigm, fosters certain habits of mind. Consciously—or, at least as often, unconsciously—preferred styles of maneuvering with meaning develop. In Veblenesque terms, there is a trained capacity for handling the world in a particular way, and a trained incapacity for handling it in any other way. A differentiated buildup of sensibilities occurs as a consequence of an uneven exposure to, and acquisition of competence in, varied symbol systems in the cultural flow. And interests are established which guide the active management of meaning in social relationships.

Moreover, with perspectives go horizons. The correlate metaphor draws attention to the "reach" of a perspective, and to the fact that especially nowadays, people can see quite variously far. There are those who engage habitually only with a limited range of ideas, drawn from some handful of nearby sources in the cultural flow through society. From a large world of meaning, they carve out something smaller.[4] Yet there are also those others whose ideas involve them, to some degree or other, with much more of the world: those whose ideas may be of more kinds, coming directly or indirectly from more sources.

Last but not least (and this is certainly related to differences in horizons), perspectives are perspectives toward perspectives. Knowingly or unknowingly in contacts with other people, one takes their perspectives into account, as one construes these. Not only anthropologists have distributive models of culture, that is; there are also folk models of this kind. I have pointed to the "I know, and I know that everybody else knows, and I know that everybody else knows that everybody else knows" formula already. This is probably as close as one can get to demystifying the Durkheimian notion of "collective consciousness," an arrangement which takes meaning out of the domain of the individual whim to make it over into something more solid and real.[5] It is hardly more than a special case, however, in a very large family of highly variable, and variously extensive, formulae of this general type: "I know that you believe this, but I do not," "I believe you know more about this than I do, and I believe you know that you do," "I know, and I believe you know, but I also believe they do not know that we know," to suggest only a few of the possible arrangements. Sometimes they are evanescent; guiding the flow of meaning and thus changing the latter's distribution from the baseline arrangement, they may bring about their own transformations. In other instances, they remain stable over time, setting segments of society apart. There are also such formulae as "I know that, unlike certain others, I believe this." As one forms an understanding of the perspectives of others, one may put one's own perspective into perspective as well.

As a social organization of meaning, culture can be seen as made up of an extremely complex interlinkage of such formulae; a network of perspectives, with a continuous production of overt cultural forms between them. In this manner, the perspectivation of meaning is a powerful engine in creating a diversity of culture within the complex society. Call the network a polyphony, as the perspectives are at the same time voices; term it a conversation, if it appears fairly low-key and consensual; refer to it all as a debate, if you wish to emphasize contestation; or describe it as a cacophony, if you find mostly disorder.

Clusters of Symmetry: Subcultures and Microcultures

Through the interaction of perspectives, culture is produced. How many people have to be involved in order for us to see culture as a collective phenomenon? As few as two, or as many as millions.

If we want to think of the meanings managed in a dyad as "a culture," it makes sufficient conceptual sense.[6] There is hardly any logical reason why the term should be reserved for complexes of meaning carried by larger units of social relationships. Certainly, one would hardly expect to find anywhere two people who together keep "a culture" going in perfect social isolation, without being influenced by anybody else. On the other hand, at least as things are now, neither do cultures carried by a thousand people, or ten million people, or a billion people, exist so splendidly alone. There is something fairly arbitrary about bounding any culture-carrying unit of social relationships today.

More often, it is true, cultural studies are concerned with the meanings handled in somewhat wider sets of social relationships than the single dyad. We may still want to begin by thinking small, however, at least in a relative sense, about the social organization of meaning; and this is where we make our approach to the notion of subculture.

The term "subculture" is widely used in anthropology as well as in sociology, and has even inched its way into everyday speech.[7] It may be fair to say that it has been a greater success socially than intellectually.[8] There are even the ambiguities built into the very word—does "sub" make this type of culture simply a segment of a larger culture, or is it something subordinate to a dominant culture, or is it something subterranean and rebellious, or is it substandard, qualitatively inferior? While the first of these alternatives is undoubtedly that most solidly established in academic discourse (and the only sense in which I use the term here), all the others have a way of sneaking into at least more popular usage, and at least as overtones, with a great potential for confusing issues.

Strikingly enough, one of the main weaknesses of writings on subcultures is that they often give scant attention to what happens at the interfaces within the larger culture. Subcultural ethnographies have thus tended to be internalist. The "sub" prefix, which should signal that this particular cultural unit is in some part characterized by its embeddedness in a wider whole of differing cultural characteristics, is virtually ignored.

The celebrated work of the "Birmingham School" (emanating, mostly in the 1970s, from the Centre for Contemporary Cultural Studies at the University of Birmingham) cannot be accused of such neglect; it has concentrated heavily on the oppositional character of post-World War II British youth cultures, and on their position within the British class structure.[9] Yet here as well, one may be less than entirely satisfied with the precision with which concepts and ethnography are handled. Such dissatisfaction is in fact voiced in an autocritique by one of the directors of the center, Richard Johnson, who notes that

> there is a pressure to present lived cultures with which one sympathizes deeply as peculiarly homogeneous and distinct. Indeed, sometimes the "cultures" replace the people and the social relationships. Cultures as whole ways of life are humped about by the same sort of people and bump up against other great slabs of meaning humped about by others. There is a definite tendency to what I call the "continental plates" theory of culture. (1986:302–303)

These are difficulties which, drawing on a small body of useful critical writings on subcultural theory, some older and some newer but mostly of interactionist persuasions, I will try both to cast light on and get away from here.

Everett Hughes' terse statement, quoted at the beginning of this chapter ("Wherever some group of people have a bit of common life . . . there culture grows"), is one admirable—if not exhaustive—formulation of the initial conditions for the development of subcultures. A similar and equally well-known view has once been stated by Albert Cohen: new cultural forms can emerge, he proposed (in theoretical work provoked by a study of juvenile delinquents), where a number of individuals with similar problems of adjustment are in effective interaction with one another. Initially, it may be a problem for them that no model exists for the resolution of their difficulties. But they can create one themselves, and test it and develop it gradually. A major factor is that of social validation. "Exploratory gestures" play a part here: if you stick your neck out just a little, I will stick mine out just a little, too, and perhaps even a little further. And as this continues, the participants become equally committed to the emergent product (1955:53–61).

Restated in the terms used here, the subcultural process delineated by both Cohen and Hughes involves a baseline symmetry of perspectives among participants, cumulatively stabilized and amplified by the back-and-forth flow of meaning among them. An early feeling that "I suspect that you have the same vague sense" changes into the familiar "I know, and I know that you know, and I know that you know that I know." In the place of a somewhat amorphous awareness of the lack of fit between available meanings on the one hand and one's problems of existence on the other, a rich structure of ideas comes into being (partly located "out there") directly relevant to one's situation. Much as in the small-scale society, the tension between social structure and cultural flow is largely resolved, although this time not on a society-wide scale. There is a relatively free reciprocal flow of meaning between the participants in the cultural process; people stick their necks out together. On the whole, in the terms suggested before, there is not only baseline symmetry but also a symmetry of input quantity and scale in the relationships involved, since in principle and in the long term, at least, individuals give about as much as they take from one another.

With time, naturally, such a subculture can become an ongoing concern, persisting largely within what I have described in chapter 2 as a form of life framework. New participants can be enculturated into it without making any particularly innovative contribution to its form. But by participating in keeping its particular traffic in meaning going, they contribute to maintaining it as a supportive environment for the perspectives of those involved.

For a conceptual clarification of the subculture concept, the essential thing about Hughes' and Cohen's formulations, and my adaptation of them, is the simultaneous emphasis on cultural distinctiveness and relational anchorage. As a collective phenomenon, a subculture belongs to a particular social relationship, or to a set of relationships. But it need not encompass every aspect of the flow of meaning within this relational segment of the social structure; only what is more or less distinctive about it, as contrasted to the flow of meaning elsewhere in the same society. The subcultural aspects of the cultural flow in a relationship may thus well be inextricably entangled with culture that is less peculiar to this segment of society.

The relational anchorage of the subculture concept, for its part, suggests that the unit of participation in the subcultural process need not be at the level of individuals, whole and indivisible. Instead, it is minimally defined at the level of particular social situations and relationships. In principle, it is certainly possible that the same subcultural distinctiveness is present in all the different social contexts in which a specific individual participates; that is to say, this individual is totally encapsulated in a single subculturally marked segment of the social structure. But this is not necessary. People can be involved with one subculture, rather, through one role, or a constellation of some of their roles, and with other subcultures through other roles in their repertoires.[10]

Beyond prompting this brief explication, Hughes' and Cohen's formulations are useful in pinpointing the ideal conditions under which subcultures are likely to develop and continue to exist as arrangements of cultural sharing. People should not only be in similar circumstances, in order to generate similar perspectives. They should also be in effective interaction, and in some measure isolated from others—in this way, their reciprocal flow of meanings becomes a comparatively large part of the total cultural flow reaching them.

To repeat, these are the ideal conditions, but real life is not always quite like this. The symmetry of perspectives is often only relative, for reasons both internal and external to the relationship engaged in subcultural construction and maintenance. Even people who are intensively engaged in mutual communication and collective problem solving may not take part in the situation immediately at hand in exactly the same way; some intrinsic asymmetry can already be involved here. (While spouses in middle-class Western society, for example, often share a great many activities and objectives, they need not evolve entirely the same perspectives toward these.) But what is at least as important is that people who are superficially in the same situation may see it in different ways because their total, more or less integrated, personal perspectives result not only from that one situation, but from their various situational involvements in their entirety; that is, from their role repertoires as wholes. And compared to the relative overall transparency of small-scale society, the windows through which people engaged with subcultures can look into one another's perspectives may be rather small.

It would appear, then, that the stronger, more inclusive subcultures are those which can draw on, and integrate, larger segments of the role repertoire, seen in terms of both the relative salience of particular roles and the sheer number of roles. And some subcultures remain weak because they draw on a shared involvement only in some limited field of activity, with continuous intrusions from a diversity of perspectives generated elsewhere in the round of life.[11]

This is one aspect of the general question of the embeddedness of subcultures in a larger whole. The isolation of subcultures can only be a matter of degree, and if it were perfect there would be no reason to describe these entities as subcultures, rather than simply as cultures. Yet as I pointed out before, much writing on subcultures looks mostly inward, toward their distinctive cores rather than toward their interfaces with whatever is outside, and its orienting vocabulary rather exaggerates isolation. The subculture may be seen as a "social world," a term with strong connotations of self-sufficiency.[12] Or if some wider order is acknowledged, it is described as a "mosaic of subcultures." The image is pleasantly vivid, but it becomes most revealing as it allows us to examine its imperfections.

The mosaic as a root metaphor—a notion with an internal complexity which would allow the analytical elaboration of our understanding of how subcultures connect with one another—suggests for one thing that the subcultures, as "pieces," are all of one kind, all largely homogeneous in their internal characteristics, and all hard-edged. All this is questionable, and the mosaic turns out to be in large part a negative root metaphor, a tool for understanding what subcultures are often not.

As I have already suggested, what goes on in the management of meaning in any one social relationship, or set of relationships, tends to be a mixture of what is subculturally distinctive and what is not. We have likewise seen that subcultures can overlap in individuals, who may not keep them entirely compartmentalized within their perspectives, with varied consequences for overall cultural organization. In neither of these instances does the idea of subcultural hard edges seem particularly helpful.

Furthermore, what is subcultural can itself be distinctive in several ways. The idea of sharply bounded subcultures would seem to imply that the meanings relevant to the definition of the boundary are so distributed as to be present on one side and absent on the other, with unambiguous overt forms. In fact, there may be gradations of different kinds, rather than clear dichotomies. Much the same meanings may be given different external form on different sides of the boundary; or the same overt form may be differently interpreted on the two sides, by being placed in different contexts. (Part of the polysemy of forms in complex cultures may thus originate, at least, in a differentiation of meanings between perspectives.) Rather than a contrast between presence and absence, there may also be a mere difference in the frequency of use, or the salience, of various meanings and their manifest forms. It seems likely that subcultural boundaries are by nature more often blurred than clear—except in those instances where cultural forms are understood as emblems of social distinction, markers of identity, in which case the alternatives in category or group memberships should not be too fuzzy.[13]

Yet another problem with the notion of the subcultural mosaic is that it may imply that all social relationships are equally involved in subcultural process, engaging in producing or reproducing distinctive clusters of meaning where the connections between perspectives have been rather well worked out and elaborated, relying to a fair extent on symmetries between them. To repeat, there are zones of complex social structures where relationships are carried on in a fleeting manner, with only limited communication. If we want to think of the shared understandings existing here as also subcultural in nature, we must still admit that the structures of meaning in question can be of extremely limited depth and richness. The kinds of intricate cultural orders which students of subcultures usually dwell on, then, exist rather as islands in a sea; or we may say that the distribution of subcultural phenomena over the structure of social relationships is variously thick and thin.

In a mosaic, again, most—if not all—pieces are usually of the same size, and they are laid out side by side. Subcultures, as socially distributed clusters of meaning, vary both with regard to the size of their inventories of distinctive meanings and the size of that set of social relationships which carries them; furthermore, they do not always exist side by side. The "I know that you know that I know" formula can work with varying scope and precision, depending on how intensely contextualized meanings and their expressions are.

All of which is to say that diversity within a complex culture, at least as much as it is a mosaic, comes out as clusters of meaning at varying levels of generality, sometimes nesting inside one another: subcultures, subsubcultures. An ethnic subculture may splinter on the basis of class, and then again on the basis of age and gender, as each entails a further differentiation of perspectives among the participants in the cultural process.[14] And so one can proceed all the way down to those complexes of meaning which belong to particular neighborhoods, gangs, workplaces, or households.

This ordering of collectively held meanings at different levels of generality needs to be well understood if certain kinds of unnecessary confusion are to be avoided. In a hierarchy of generalizations, it may thus be that at the apex, cultural sharing of the "I know that you know that I know" type can refer to quite highly decontextualized understandings, of an "in principle" variety. The trouble is, of course, that people most of the time have to work out their forms of life in specific contexts, and here shared understandings may pertain to the application, or nonapplication, of principles under these circumstances. These understandings, however, may be shared among the people in these contexts, but not shared with people outside them, even if there is agreement with the latter on matters of more or less decontextualized principle.

A couple of examples are in order. Fredrik Barth (1969:13) has related how southern Pathans could find the behavior of Swat Pathans so strange that the latter could indeed be held as "no longer Pathan"; there seemed to be too much basic cultural difference. Barth, however, could explain the conduct of the Swat Pathans to the southerners in terms of specific ecological constraints, and the southern Pathans could then bring themselves "grudgingly to admit that under those circumstances they might indeed themselves act in the same way." In other words, difference had been shifted from the most generalized to the contextualized level, but only with the help of the anthropologist as a cultural mediator.[15] Without such assistance, it seems, there would have been, at the level of high principle concerning essential Pathanness, cultural sharing without a recognition of sharing; the one knows and the other knows, but neither knows that both know. Which is the formula for the social organization of meaning designated "pluralistic ignorance."[16] One senses the same kind of misunderstanding in the view of the landlubber Chinese toward the Boat people.

And obviously much of the "culture of poverty" debate, peaking in the United States in the 1960s, revolved around similar confusions, and resulted in competing corruptions. The problem with the "culture of poverty" concept was that one reading of it showed the culture as somehow an independent poverty-producing force, invulnerable to ameliorist meddling; the poor would hold some set of absolute values which, irrespective of context, would keep them poor. The inevitable response to such a view was to point to the part of socioeconomic and political factors in generating and reproducing poverty. As the argument went on, unfortunately, the next step was sometimes to declare that there was no culture of poverty whatsoever. A much more realistic view, in light of the evidence, would have been to regard a culture of poverty as resting largely on the next lower level: that level where collective understandings are tied to a general type of context.[17] Shared poverty generates cultures of poverty, rather than vice versa. People in a poor neighborhood (such as that in Washington, D.C., where I did field work in the late 1960s) do have a web of contextualized understandings among themselves, of the "I know that you know that I know" type, with which outsiders would mostly be unfamiliar.

In sum, it is possible that shared culture at some level of general principle gives rise to different cultures at the level of specific contexts; and it is possible, perhaps even common, for the latter differences to be misinterpreted as differences of principle. A more subtle issue is whether, or under what conditions, principles of higher generality can go on persisting in their pure, decontextualized form, without being affected through some kind of feedback by being contextualized in particular ways, or by being declared nonapplicable under prevailing circumstances. This question is more seldom raised.[18]

At the lowest level of the contextualized specification of culture, to repeat, we find that which pertains to particular, concrete, limited sets of social relationships. As one reaches this point, however, a certain qualitative change in the nature of shared meanings may be involved. In the formation of perspectives, I have said, there is an interplay between concrete personal experiences and more generalized understandings and dispositions. The former are at the basis of the latter; the latter then frame the interpretation of the former. With regard to collectivized understandings, we would usually assume that it is the more generalized versions of meanings which count most; never mind what are their histories within individual perspectives. At this lowest level, however, we may find shared meanings directly tied to specific, likewise shared, experiences of people, settings, and events.

For such cultures, it may be useful to have a special term; I think of them as microcultures.[19] Usually, they would be the smallest parts of some wider social whole where any kind of distinctive meanings or meaningful forms are maintained. Yet the main point may not be that we have reached some final point in the cultural segmentation of social life. While the subculture concept, when we take "sub" seriously, problematizes embeddedness, the microculture concept is more absolute than relative. There may be some approximate maximum size beyond which it becomes much more difficult to construct a culture on the basis of such concrete shared experiences, a common biography. That maximum is itself no doubt dependent on social organization and other contextual factors. One might venture the opinion, nonetheless, that while subcultures can involve millions of people, who can rely on relatively generalized shared understandings, microcultures may seldom reach beyond a few dozen people, or a hundred.

As an aside, then, I would note the possibility that if the concreteness of shared experience is the defining feature of the microculture, it need not in principle be a subunit of a wider cultural universe. If some small social unit, let us say a community of hunters and gatherers, maintains a considerable degree of autonomy, we may think of its structure of meanings and meaningful forms as "a culture" rather than in subcultural terms, and yet in its workings it may have the characteristics of a microculture.[20]

Cultures of such concreteness and limited social extent have largely been ignored as matters of conceptual and theoretical concern by anthropologists and sociologists, although they often provide the raw materials for ethnographies. When microcultural facts get written up, that is, they tend to be transformed into subcultural or cultural facts, at higher levels in the hierarchy of generalization, decontextualized to a degree.[21] Yet this may be to miss something essential about the nature of the culture of complex societies. Much cultural process takes microcultural form; microcultures allow people to move back and forth between the concrete and the more abstractly general not only in the inner workings of their minds, but with the support of the collectively known. For, of course, microcultures do not *only* deal in the currency of particularities. They allow, rather, a socially recognized conversion between what may be gossip, on the one hand, and philosophy, on the other: the grounding of the general in the specifics of the face to face.[22]

Perhaps the one major recent exception to the disregard for microcultures has been in the surge of interest in organizational or corporate cultures. Here, analysts are sometimes concerned with the influence of particular individuals and events on shared meanings; but often the organizations are already too large to really fit into the microcultural frame, and as management experts take over cultural analysis, the concern with shared meanings tends to become prescriptive, a question of how to make company ideology pervasive. The "Japanese model" is ever present, and corporate culture becomes a matter of efficiency, eventually to be measured in dollars and yen.[23] This is hardly where an overall understanding of the role of microcultures in the organization of diversity can be expected to grow.

Our view of subcultures within the context of the larger whole suggests that they relate to one another in a variety of ways. They can crisscross in the same individuals, and they sometimes arrange themselves like Chinese boxes. They can also reflect one another. Just as perspectives in general are in large part perspectives toward other perspectives, subcultures tend to be collectivized perspectives toward perspectives. There are subcultures which mostly turn only inwards, toward their own corner; where the people involved largely engage in transacting meanings relating to internal group activities. But there are also some that turn in very large part outwards, constituting a running critical commentary on some Other. And most of them may be in between, sometimes minding their own business, sometimes preoccupied with the flow of meaning in their social environment, but not infrequently engaging in constructing bridges.

People may accept a difference between themselves and others with indifference, or exaggerate it, or play it down; all ways of creating some semblance of order among subcultures. The culture of poverty controversy, with its ethnic overtones, could be seen as yet another chapter in the history of such management of subcultural difference in America, usually moving in several directions at once. There can be a search for ways of reaching across cultural gaps, ways of making different strands of thought intelligible and acceptable in one another's terms, or in those of some stratum of cultural commonality previously not sufficiently explored ("if you had been in their shoes . . . "). Or there are flat assertions of irreconcilable differences.[24] The conspicuously other may be rejected and ridiculed, and if one has the requisite power at one's disposal, one may put pressure on that other to become more like oneself. Or one may defer to that other from a distance, conceding superiority or more general validity.[25] Or again, that other may be made a model for one's own aspirations—the kind of thing sociologists have for some time dealt with under the rubric of "reference group theory." The subcultures of young and liminal Americans during much of the twentieth century could hardly have taken the forms they did without a notion of Black culture, understood as involving a fundamentally different, existentially superior approach to life; the hardline culture of poverty concept turned upside down. As alternatives are encountered among the subcultures on their horizons, people may stick to their own understandings more emphatically than ever, or drift ambivalently or opportunistically between contraries, or undergo cultural conversions.

Working out stances toward other subcultures within one's horizon, drawing contrasts or at times parallels, can be a way of sharpening reflexively the contours of one's own. Thus ethnic groups, classes, and other social entities make assumptions of cultural difference vis-à-vis one another, which whether well-founded or not serve to sharpen social distinctions and constrain interaction, and at the same time to strengthen cohesion within the group. As others are seen to play a different game, by different rules, social boundaries are strengthened, and stereotypes grow. In sociology, "labeling theory" developed at one time to deal with similar phenomena: the selective classifications which nondeviant people make of deviants, and the social consequences of these classifications. When, for some reason or other, individuals or groups are labeled as deviant, they are set apart from the rest of society. In this state of separation, according to labeling theory, they might turn yet more exclusively to others similarly classified; and so the distinctiveness of their subcultural process is further accentuated.[26] The tendency in all these instances is toward making people more subculturally encapsulated, limiting overlapping allegiances.

Countercultures—not only the 1960s instance in Western societies, but others as well, in other times and places—also exemplify this general tendency in the management of meaning.[27] The defining feature of countercultures is their strong externalist orientation: their raison d'être is that of standing as an alternative, radically opposed to some other set of meanings (usually that of a "dominant culture"). The counterculture is inherently adversarial. It may not merely constitute a developed, embodied critique of what is there in the opposite culture, however; at the same time there may be a rhetorical strain (much as in labeling) toward constructing the image of the latter in a one-dimensional manner, disregarding the ambiguities and contradictions in it, out of which the counterculture once grew, but which also still remain.

A final general comment on subcultures: it is important to realize that they are everywhere. If subcultural studies have frequently exaggerated differences and distinctiveness, they have at other times been prone to disregard variations that actually are there. The result has been to imply that some people are involved with subcultures, and others not. Terms like "mainstream culture" or "the dominant culture" are much used as contrastive devices, at times when we are really focusing attention on what is not-dominant, out-of-the-mainstream. When we turn directly to the parts of complex cultures to which these designations are presumed to refer, however, it is a little intellectually embarrassing that their homogeneity may vanish like a mirage. If one takes the example of the United States, let us assume that "the dominant culture" can be described as middle class, and white Anglo-Saxon Protestant. (Let us also assume, as usual, that ego's perspective is conventionally male.) But then you have to make the reservation that the teenagers are into some youth culture or other; and that the women are into women's culture; and then some of the men are involved with gay culture. And possibly you should also qualify your assumptions about the very young and the very old. And can you generalize about rural people and people in towns and city dwellers, all together? And what about the apparent paradox that the dominant people, the political and economic elites, are perhaps not wholly to be counted among the carriers of the dominant (in the sense of most widely distributed) culture?

There may be rather more commonality of culture among some of these than there is between them and people who are involved with more dramatically distinctive subcultures. The differences between their perspectives may be more subtle, more limited in extent. In their own distributive models, too, people may more often disregard the differences, and be "lumpers" rather than "splitters." But everywhere, the flow of meaning has to relate to the nuances in perspectival conceptions of relevance, preference, and truth.[28]

Such a view has yet another implication for the way we look at subcultures. We often seem to think that subcultures need explanation, while "mainstream culture" does not. And not only do we contrast the former to the latter; we also tend to assume that subcultures are instances of specialized evolution departing from the general mainstream base. (Even an analysis like Albert Cohen's, as summarized above, lends itself to this reading.) Yet, obviously, no such common base can be posited; at least, not as having existed any time recently. In a society where the cultural flow is varied and uneven, it is an open question which meanings have reached where, and when. Historically, as circumstances change and as groups of varying cultural heritages are differentially drawn into them, present subcultures may simply be the children of earlier subcultures.[29]

The Cultural Apparatus

The view toward complex cultures from subcultural studies is mostly sideways, horizontal; decentered, we might also term it. There is not really so much a mosaic as a variously heavy layering over the social landscape of partially overlapping, imprecisely bounded sets of meanings and overt cultural forms. From any one point in that landscape, individuals or groups engage more actively with some of these, and have some knowledge of a greater or smaller proportion of the others, depending on their perspectives and horizons. But because of the tendency toward internal symmetry in the organization of subcultures, and their limited reach in society, no perspectives, and no voices, really appear privileged in cultural process.

There is also, however, a vertical view, from the top, looking down (or alternatively, from the bottom, looking up); focusing on what C. Wright Mills described as the cultural apparatus—composed "of all the organizations and *milieus* in which artistic, intellectual, and scientific work goes on, and of the means by which such work is made available to circles, publics, and masses" (1963:406). What defines the cultural apparatus, I would suggest, is that it connects one person or a relative few (creators, personified symbols, performers, players) with a greater many who are more passive (clients, spectators, audiences), in relationships the core of which is a provision of meaning. These relationships are thus asymmetrical in terms of scale, and also with regard to input quantity, as some parties are more active than others. It is the cultural apparatus that occupies those "commanding heights" of cultural dissemination (but also—we will come back to this—some lesser heights).

If the cultural apparatus is identified in terms of the two asymmetries of input quantity and scale, other asymmetries tend to follow. Its specialists are usually part of the division of labor, operating mostly either in the market or the state frameworks of cultural flow; more about this in chapter 4. They receive material compensation for their work. (Some are in movements; here, material compensation may be less certain.) An existing asymmetry of power linkage may be at the basis of the functioning of the cultural apparatus, and its workings may also strengthen this asymmetry. Quite often, there are asymmetries in input mode as well. This is not merely a simple consequence of the asymmetry of input quantity, the fact that when the flow of meaning becomes almost a one-way phenomenon, audiences can only respond in simple, compressed ways if they can respond actively at all—as in the case of applause in exchange for a skilled performance. Such communicative constraints apart, the asymmetry of input mode also comes about because as the production of meaning and meaningful forms is made a part of the division of labor, some means of cultural expression become much more highly developed within the cultural apparatus than outside it. The cultural apparatus does not altogether monopolize music making, writing, and painting, but it is still true that many people engage little or not at all with such cultural forms as producers in their own right, and may encounter them mostly through the cultural apparatus, as consumers.

In principle, the cultural apparatus includes all those specializations within the division of labor which somehow aim at affecting minds, temporarily or in an enduring fashion; the people and institutions whose main purpose it is to meddle with our consciousness. Some things are very clearly part of it. For one thing, there is ritual, or at least ritual-like performances (parades, coronations, inaugurations, festivals, commemorations or whatever), types of occasional events, with new versions forever coming into being.[30] It is tempting to see ritual in the small-scale society as the forerunner of the cultural apparatus; at times, an occurrence of intellectual, aesthetic, pedagogical, and morally authoritative import, all rolled into one. True, ritual in the small-scale society does not always have much in the way of a specialized personnel. But it is focused, fixing attention on particular objects or occurrences; and in this manner, like the cultural apparatus, it contrasts with that cultural management which is diffused and refracted in a rather unconscious manner among various everyday practical activities and interactions.

Much of the cultural apparatus, however, is of a more continuous nature than ritual, agencies at work day after day. There is hardly a more central complex within it than education, in the sense of institutionally specialized transmission of knowledge and development of cultural competence.[31] (About 75 percent of the world's children now receive some sort of primary education, and about 20 percent of the world's population arc students.[32]) Education plays a large part in shaping the kinds of living creatures required to keep the complex culture going. It differentiates among them in some way which will eventually influence their placement in the social structure, and it may attempt to create just the right number of each kind for the desired division of knowledge.

From one point of view, we may likewise see legal machineries, engaged in the formulation and interpretation of binding rules, as parts of the cultural apparatus. It includes much of organized religion, and it encompasses capital-C "Culture," the production of works of special intellectual or aesthetic merit, usually by identifiable individuals, as well as what goes by such names as popular culture or mass culture. Museums and exhibitions belong in the cultural apparatus, as well as spectator sports. Artists, teachers, priests, sports stars, and broadcasters, for example, are unambiguously in it. So are a range of mediators between producers and consumers: agents, publishers, critics, engaged in selecting, supporting, disseminating, interpreting.[33]

Yet it is not easy to delimit the cultural apparatus precisely, for there are a great many borderline cases. In its entirety, of course, the division of labor includes the work of blacksmiths and barbers as well as that of poets and professors. We would assume that the latter but not the former belong in the cultural apparatus. The haircut is an externalization of cultural skill just as the sonnet is, and one should not disregard the contributions to the cultural flow which result from the activities of the barber or the blacksmith, or for that matter the engineer or the veterinary, or the butcher or the construction worker. It is true that they all add something to the wealth of meanings carried by a culturally constructed environment. Yet the involvement of the blacksmith and the barber in the creation and dissemination of meanings is mostly a byproduct of work on our physical surroundings, or our bodies, and we do not usually seek out these kinds of specialists to have our consciousness worked over. Their work is not primarily communicative in character.

When the barber becomes a hair stylist, however, his place in the cultural apparatus may already seem assured. The case of the production of material goods for the consumer market is similar. Artifacts can come with some rather simple meaning attached to them, and they may end up carrying a greater symbolic load only because of the experience one has of using them. But often, particularly through packaging and advertising, such goods now come to the consumer shaped by a commodity aesthetic. Perhaps the best we can do is to think of the involvement of goods and services in the cultural apparatus not always in either/or terms, but often as matters of degree.

Asymmetries in the Media

What really makes great asymmetry of scale possible in the dissemination of more elaborate statements of meaning is cultural technology: the media. Although the part of face-to-face relationships in the contemporary cultural apparatus is not negligible, it is through print, radio, television, and sound recordings that the meaningful productions of one individual or a mere handful of people can reach millions.

The tendency toward asymmetry is not inherent in all media. Literacy can operate in a manner of perfect symmetry of scale, and as a two-way communication: I write a letter to you and only you, and you write a letter to me (or we leave notes on one another's office desks, or on the kitchen table). Telephones similarly serve as a decentralized media technology. The only qualification here—not an unimportant one—is that someone else, centrally placed, controls the mail and the telephone system and could intervene in the conduct of our relationship. Photography, likewise, is in large part deployed in symmetries. We can look at one another's snapshots, and—in more affluent societies—home movies or videos, of family, friends, and vacation scenes. These can all be the media of microcultures.

Real asymmetry, where it occurs, is not always experienced in the same way, either. People sometimes respond to those others who appear in the one-way media as if there were a two-way flow, and as if the relationship was one-to-one rather than one-to-many—in short, as if they had a "real relationship" with them.[34] And those who entertain no such illusions can still relate differently to persons if they see them in moving pictures than if they merely read of what they have said or done. This is that spurious McLuhanite global village of electronic communication, with its particular symbolic capacities. In fact, through the asymmetry of scale, some become more "village personalities" than others; celebrities, personal carriers of meaning, or even meanings personified, in a certain resemblance to the concreteness and intimacy of the face-to-face microculture concept. But the small scale is here only at one end of the relationship.

As further media varieties are introduced, their implications for more symmetry (of a real kind) or more asymmetry in cultural processes nowadays often come to the forefront of debate and speculation. Will more media bring us closer to Orwell's 1984, even as we leave the actual 1984 further behind us, if media power keeps cumulatively concentrating in the same hands? Or will a computer literate society make totalitarianism and its knowledge hoarding impossible, as more people can answer back, and as the hackers will always get the secrets in the end? Does cable television allow more of a two-way flow, or will it remain mostly a matter of narrowcasting rather than broadcasting, a lesser degree of asymmetry of scale?[35] Yet if these are the more typical questions, there is also reason to think of more qualitative issues, relating to asymmetries of input mode.

At times, new media simply take over the symbol systems occurring in the nonmedia cultural flow, in part or as wholes, or the symbol systems of media already in existence. There seems to be a measure of inertia here. As time passes, nonetheless, they tend to go through a maturation process, and to a considerable degree they evolve their own, or at least their own modifications, depending on the particular constraints and possibilities of their technologies. By now, media symbol systems taken together, far from being second-rate substitutes for nonmedia symbol systems, can do just about anything the latter can do, and more—consider how zooms, slow motion, flashbacks, and other technological tricks allow filmmakers to manipulate attention and manage meaning in ways intrinsic to the medium.

Some of these media symbol systems become widely accessible for active use by more or less the entire population; others do not. Take literacy as an obvious and at the same time sufficiently intricate example. Most people involved with contemporary complex cultures tend to be literate and, as we have noted, reading and writing are also available for symmetrical use. But literacy is not just an either/or matter. We can read more or less and write more or less, and do both either more or less well. Jack Goody, who has done more than anybody else to open up literacy as a field of anthropological study, has emphasized that literacy is a "technology of the intellect."[36] It can aid an individual in working out ideas for himself.

In a way, oral language does not actually "stand for" something—in its ephemeralness, one might say (perhaps at some risk of being misunderstood) that it rather "passes for" it. When, on the other hand, the written words are there on the page before you, you need not occupy your mind with the struggle to remember them. You can lean back and consider them from some intellectual distance. You can pause over a passage or go back and forth in the text, elaborating your critical sense of it.[37] Furthermore, the intricate maneuvering with ideas is aided not only by ordinary word-after-word-after-word prose. Particular literate inventions like tables and lists help us order our understandings of contrasts and relationships, and organize large quantities of information for quick access.[38] Setting his own work to begin with in the context of the debate among anthropologists and philosophers over a "Great Divide" between primitive and modern modes of thought, Goody suggests that literacy has had a major part in moving us from the former to the latter, with such differences between them as there may be. But there is no real "Great Divide," no sharp break between contemporary literate cultures and what one might facetiously call an idiocy of oral life. Rather, there has been a long series of small and large steps by which humankind has gradually realized the potential of writing.

True as that may be, it is equally clear that all people do not use literacy as a tool of criticism and more elaborate intellectual constructions nowadays either, although some do more of this than others. Shirley Brice Heath (1983) has portrayed very convincingly the practices of reading and writing in two working-class communities in the southeastern United States: a literacy of street signs and birthday cards, of cereal packages and newspaper obituaries, of shopping lists and car license plates. This is petty literacy, not the high-power critical literacy of the bookish. (Not that there are necessarily only these two varieties.) And we can safely assume that literacies such as these differ not merely in frequency and intensity of use but also in the cultivation of levels of skill, with regard to reading as well as writing.

One more point about literacy. We are prone to assume that literacy is an indivisible package, in the sense that people both read and write. Yet most of us do a great deal more of the former than of the latter, and here and there the asymmetry of literacy has been even more striking. When general literacy was to be introduced in Great Britain at the beginning of the industrial revolution, the ruling class, according to Raymond Williams (1975:131), felt it was enough to teach working people to read but not to write. The masses should be consumers of texts, not producers. (Even this was dangerous, as they could start reading the wrong things.)[39]

In recent times literacy has become the dominant root metaphor for thinking about the fact that skills in the use of symbol systems can be cultivated, to different levels; that is, symbol systems are not to be taken as unproblematically available as soon as they have found external form in one production or other. We now hear, in the affluent countries of the Occident, of computer literacy, film literacy, television literacy.[40] There is surely a rhetorical element here, used by the enthusiasts and entrepreneurs of particular media. Just as it is now taken for granted that a literacy of the written word is a fundamental human right, and that the illiterate is a cultural invalid, the causes of both computer education and film education can be advanced if the illiteracies in question can be identified both as individual stigmata and as social ills. They become cultural welfare problems.

A small problem in using the literacy metaphor across the board is that different kinds of symbol systems require quite different degrees of skill cultivation to allow people to handle them at all. It does not take much developed skill to make some elementary sense of film or television. This is obviously one of their great attractions—you get in at the basement level for free. You will get nothing at all out of the written word, or numbers, or the computer, on the other hand, until you have devoted some time and effort to picking up some basic new skills. (This is not to say that there is no such thing as film or television literacy.)

What is more important, however, is that in the cases of a number of contemporary media symbol systems, it is virtually impossible for most people to get involved in producing messages. They can only be consumers of messages—readers rather than writers. This is true, for example, of more complicated film productions, as well as of some kinds of music. Involvements with the cultural apparatus thus often result only in different levels of literacies of reception. It is sometimes argued that the highest level of skill in handling a symbol system must entail an ability to manage it with proficiency as a producer of symbolic forms—only then can one also be a fully competent consumer. In the case of the symbol systems employed mostly in the media, such active handling cannot be widespread. Nevertheless, the absence of such practice does not seem to be a real obstacle to the development of a high degree of analytical and appreciative skill; lots of cineasts do not make movies, and there are book people whose own writing skills hardly go beyond the requirements of petty literacy.

The problem of the asymmetry of input mode in the cultural apparatus, especially as constituted by media, then, is that it allows little active participation in the production of certain kinds of symbolic form. At the same time, the presence of the cultural apparatus may allow people to cultivate a sensibility to symbolic forms which, without it, would not have been available at the same level of development at all.

Subcultures and the Cultural Apparatus

The horizontal and the vertical views toward contemporary cultures must meet somewhere. Yet the interplay between subcultural processes and the working of the relatively centralized cultural apparatus is continuous, complicated—and often neglected, in theory and in ethnography.[41]

Subcultural studies, turning inward, dwell on the production of homemade structures of meaning, in sets of face-to-face relationships; if they turn outward at all, they speak of fragmentation and diversity. Studies of the cultural apparatus emphasize the dissemination of ready-made culture; the way in which, in Mills' phrasing, "men live in second-hand worlds," and the cultural apparatus becomes "the lens of mankind." As theorists of "mass culture," many writers in this vein have been preoccupied with the spread of sameness.

Undoubtedly, much of whatever general cultural sharing one finds in complex societies depends heavily on the effective dissemination of meanings from a center. The work of the literati made it possible even for the Boat people, with all their maritime idiosyncracies, to take their Chineseness for granted. Probably there is now more such sharing than there was in that period where the division of labor (often in the form of inherited occupations), ethnic diversity, and other factors of subcultural differentiation were already firmly in place within the social structure, while educational institutions and media technology were as yet weakly developed.[42]

Nonetheless, the rhetoric seems often to be carried too far in this direction. The very notion of the mass—compact, undifferentiated, anonymous population—must be a problematic one in social analysis anywhere, in the concept of mass culture as well as that of mass media. As Raymond Williams put it in *Cul-*

ture and Society (1959:319): "There are in fact no masses; there are only ways of seeing people as masses."[43]

Seeing people as individuals, we find the meeting point of the cultural apparatus and subcultures in their perspectives. This is where the asymmetries of one and the fundamental symmetries of the other come together, as a cultural management problem to be resolved, or just somehow muddled through, on an individual or again a collective basis.

The flow of meaning which people receive through the cultural apparatus is not always automatically channeled into their subcultures. Bookish people, surrounded by the face-to-face relationships of the unbookish, are often regarded as a bit odd, asocial. And it is true that media such as those of writing and print tend to undermine the capacity for thought control of the face-to-face community. With a reader in their midst, people cannot be confident that they know what he knows. Moreover, he who has read often knows that the others do not know.

The consequences of such unevenness of cultural apparatus impact presumably vary. In an extreme case, perhaps, a subculture (or at least a microculture) can break up because of it; too little sharing is left. At other times, individuals desert their subculture, although it remains the going concern of others; again in other instances, they may remain engaged with it, but with a qualified commitment, even in a state of inner exile.

Different media can have intrinsically different individualist or collectivist implications at the receiver end, implying more or less privacy in cultural apparatus involvements. A reader, in the act of reading, has to attend closely to the text, and the presence of others is a threat of distraction. The classic age of the book, George Steiner (1980:188–189) suggests, is already past; its typical figure was a man (yes, a man) sitting alone in his personal library, while the rest of the family, elsewhere in the house, was enjoined to avoid unnecessary noises. By now, in Western society, the home has hardly any taboo spaces or sacrosanct hours, and the radio, the television set, and the record player have crowded out the bookshelves. The new activities of looking and listening are in themselves less individuating; as people engage in them together, in a sort of shoulder-to-shoulder relationships, each one of them knows (or so he believes) what the others hear and see as well. The flow of media meaning can be instantly incorporated into a web of face-to-face relationships.[44]

If there are such intrinsic immediate differences not least between media in the cultural apparatus, it is also true that all the currents of meaning from the latter can be channeled into subcultural or microcultural traffic at least indirectly—often, by way of characteristic institutionalized forms. As far as the written word is concerned, parents thus read bedtime stories to children, conversations over the breakfast table deal with stories in the morning newspaper, and academic seminars discuss important monographs.

Assume, anyway, that whatever output of the cultural apparatus we have in mind reaches the population involved with a subculture rather evenly; and moreover, that the same output also reaches a number of different subcultures. How can we then view its part in subcultural process? The end result is hardly total homogenization, a death of subcultures as perhaps the "mass culture" thesis would have it, for that whole range of factors remains present which differentiates populations and supports the development and maintenance of subcultures. Rather, from the point of view of the population engaged in a subcultural process, the cultural apparatus and its messages become a part of that situation which has to be defined and for which an adaptation (perhaps moral and intellectual as well as practical) has to be created. And that part may be more or less problematic.

For some subcultures, clearly less. Their internal shared perspectives get additional support. They can feed voraciously on the offerings of the cultural apparatus, working exchanges over the popular music scene, art exhibits, the contents of books or newspapers, television programs, or what you learned in school today, into the internal cultural flow.[45]

For other subcultures, just as obviously more. Too many messages are affronts, or at least reminders that the bearers of the subculture are not members of that community on whose baseline assumptions these messages build.

One has to consider, then, the origin of these messages. The currents of meaning through the cultural apparatus, of course, also originate in perspectives somewhere in society. And as (in an era of nation-states) a language is sometimes defined as a dialect with an army, a "mainstream culture" can be seen as a subculture in command of a more widely reaching cultural apparatus. This, as far as overall cultural management is concerned, is what makes some subcultures privileged vis-à-vis others of their kind.

Attending to the influx of cultural apparatus messages into one's subculture (if, indeed, they come from outside it), then, is much like the management of subcultural difference in general, as discussed earlier. Perhaps the cultural dividing line here is one to which it is harder than usual to be indifferent, although it need not be entirely impossible, and is in any case a matter of degree.

I want to return here for a moment to what was said before about differences in levels of contextualization, and about the American "culture of poverty." I argued then that the latter existed as a collective adaptation to a set of circumstances. Just a little further on, I suggested that in the long run, such a specific contextualization of principles of a higher generality could lead to a reinterpretation of these principles themselves.

Is this likely to happen in the particular American case in question? The effectiveness of the American cultural apparatus, if it remains as it has been, would lead one to expect that the answer, on the whole, is no. For as people are continuously reached by statements of the more general principles, either in a more decontextualized form or in the contextualized mainstream versions, through media, schools, and in other ways, poverty subcultures such as they are have little autonomy. Linking back to the mainstream by way of the shared higher level principles is likely to be the kind of subcultural accounting that most satisfactorily eases the strain between subculture and cultural apparatus messages.

Yet this particular mainstream cultural apparatus is not always so effective, and others can be less so. It is quite possible for messages emanating from a cultural apparatus with pretensions to general reach to fit so poorly with understandings developed in a subculture that their impact on people's perspectives is limited. A large number of people may not even attend to them. (The Church of England, according to an old joke, is the Conservative Party in prayer.) When the message is not clear, it may be misunderstood. If it is obvious enough, it may meet with skepticism, ridicule, and rejection. Perhaps too much is sometimes made of the notion of cultural resistance, if that is taken to mean a kind of heroic, conscious, obdurate refusal of the flow of meaning from a dominant cultural apparatus. What goes under that name in some interpretations of contemporary cultures seems at times more likely to be a subcultural process going on in its own terms, taking rather distracted notice of what passes on its outskirts.

One should be aware here, too, that when the largely one-way flow of meaning in which the cultural apparatus engages cannot be guided by significant feedback concerning the responses to its messages, it carries its own burden of inefficiency. It does not know who listens, or what is heard. Polling is one tool in the social organization of meaning introduced into a variety of contexts to ensure some informative return flow back to the managers of the cultural apparatus, but with an asymmetry of input mode as well as of input quantity, its content is usually impoverished.

What has been said so far about cultural apparatus/subculture interrelatedness rests on a couple of oversimplifying assumptions. One is that the cultural apparatus treats everyone in the same way, rather than differentiating its messages; the other is that it is itself a unitary institutional phenomenon. Neither is entirely true.

If, according to Mills' usage, we employ the concept of cultural apparatus in the singular to denote a large number of agencies with certain similar characteristics, we must be aware that this singular form is somewhat treacherous. It is not always terribly well integrated, as its parts may not all be controlled from the same quarters, sometimes work at cross-purposes, and have very different reach. A range of factors influence the level at which they insert themselves into the flow of meaning. When agencies of the cultural apparatus operate in the market, it is one strategy to reach for the largest possible number of consumers, with some common denominator; but the opposite strategy of finding a niche in some particular segment of the market may also work. And again, if some media technologies likewise lead to great asymmetries of scale, others, and not least some of those more recently developed—desktop publishing, cable television—allow more specialized audience identifications.

Some agencies of the cultural apparatus, while controlled by people of one subculture, certainly intend their messages for general consumption, or even for people fairly well understood to be engaged in other subcultures. There may be some shadowboxing here, in that it is often argued by the people in question that it is their perspectives toward the others' perspectives that govern their productions: "We only give people what they want," "This is what they need most." But then there are also segments of the cultural apparatus deliberately producing a cultural flow for internal consumption within the subcultural population itself. That is, the cultural apparatus is variously internal or external to given subcultures.

Some scrutiny of the idea of class culture is instructive at this point: an instance of maximal importance, and also of a complexity which we should not underestimate; not only important in its own right, but also as an example of how larger-scale subcultures cohere. That there is some such thing as class culture in just about every contemporary large-scale culture seems undeniable. At the same time, the scope, intensity, and coherence of the entities in question seem rather variable, and the conceptualization of the phenomenon sometimes none too clear. How do class cultures come into being and stay there, as subcultures with their own internal processes, and affected at the same time by the cultural apparatus?

Following Everett Hughes' notion of "where culture grows," as discussed before, it would seem that a distinctive culture would be generated in a class as such, particularly because of "common problems and perhaps a couple of common enemies." If, that is to say, relations to the means of production (which is what I take class, strictly speaking, to be about) are in themselves a particularly fertile source for the generation of meanings and symbolic forms, this would follow from the problematic combination of conflict and cooperation in relationships between classes.

But then Hughes' formulation also implies some complications. As class cultures are presumably above all developed and maintained *in* classes (rather than largely *between* members of different classes), the members of the class have to be in interaction with one another, and the very situations which define them as class members do not always guarantee social relationships internal to the class, and extending throughout it. Instead, the membership may be spread over a variety of habitats (the classic Marxian "sack of potatoes" question), and segmented into categories which have little except class position in common, but which internally share a great deal more.[46] Each occupation within a class thus tends to have its problems and experiences, its own characteristic forms of personal relationships to members of other classes, its ingrained habits of thought evolved out of its work habits. From these circumstances, one could not expect a single unitary structure of meanings to grow; it would rather make for a loose collection of more restrictedly distributed subcultures.

Certainly members of a class tend to be thrown together for interaction in the form of life framework outside of the work situation, even if in the latter they are to some extent separated. By and large, for one thing, they may live under similar material circumstances, with whatever commonalities result from this. And this would still make for some wider unity, in entities like neighborhoods and kin networks.

But class cultures—as we usually recognize them—also depend, in one or more ways, on the asymmetrical workings of the cultural apparatus. What happens, for example, in education? The controlling perspective of a unitary educational apparatus may belong to one class or another, but hardly to all classes at the same time, so that for some class, at least, it must be an external source of meaning. An overarching system of education is certainly, and with some justification, held to be one of the agencies of cultural homogenization in a society. Even so, one must view the impact of its messages against the background of whatever subcultural variations have developed by other means. If these messages are indeed undifferentiated at the source, the same for everybody, they may return in a loop to the class culture where they originate, strengthening it most likely, and turning out to be rather readily assimilable. To people of any other class culture, in contrast, they may appear to some degree alien—to what degree, of course, depends on the extent to which a subcultural perspective is already formed on the basis of class existential conditions and internal interactions. The resulting strain, in line with what I have argued before, may become an additional source for perspectival, and in the case of a collective process, subcultural development: how to respond to the ongoing experience of inconsistency? The unitary message, that is, becomes subculturally refracted.

Then, on the other hand, it is also quite possible that the single educational apparatus contributes to the shaping of class cultures more directly, more fundamentally. Sooner or later, as its interns rise through it, it may differentiate its messages. The members (at least, members-to-be) of one class are subjected to one kind of educational processing, different from that of members of other classes. They become constructed, for the purposes of their placement in the division of labor, as people who know and think certain things, and who do not know and think certain other things.

Given the importance of formal education in contemporary cultures, one must take seriously the impact which this may have on the homogenization of perspectives within the population assigned to one class. The flow of meaning in its internal interactions is hardly independent of what the educational apparatus has made of its members, even if there is still that strain between its teachings and more autonomously generated understandings.

In such respects, a class culture may bear the stamp of an external cultural apparatus, one which is outside the direct control of the members of the class (and which usually includes more than the agencies of education). And let us now widen the scope of the argument: the same could be true of the culture of any other segment of society whose members are somehow set apart for particular cultural treatment, on the basis of gender, ethnicity, or whatever.

But then again, such a unit may also set up its own internal cultural apparatus; in the case of a class, perhaps in the form of publishing and continuing education. Some classes, in some places, do more of this, and some much less. The same would be true of other kinds of units. One constraint, obviously, is that for any growth of a cultural apparatus, there would have to be a material basis for its support within the population concerned.

In other words, while the core of the social organization of meaning in any subculture is the relatively symmetrical, free flow between people of reasonably similar perspectives (similar, that is, at least in relevant aspects, and with or without an input into that flow from an external cultural apparatus), we should allow conceptually for the possibility that it may—in addition to this—include an organization of internal asymmetries. Maintaining a cultural apparatus of its own is clearly especially important for those subcultural communities which are in themselves internally varied as well as spatially spread out, in order to prevent the drifting apart of their varied subsubcultures and microcultures.[47] Here, it could develop as a more or less conscious means of fostering cultural coherence from the inside. It is, on the other hand, possible that it results as insider entrepreneurs find a market niche in the particular desires of members of their subcultural community.

The distinctiveness and cohesion of a large-scale subcultural unit such as a class culture (or an ethnic culture, or a gender culture), to sum up, involves a complicated equation of whatever kind of replicated experience gives it its essential unity, whatever internal diversity may at the same time tend to pull it apart, whatever unity is imposed through a directed cultural flow from the outside, and whatever is done within the population involved to offer, and attend to, a relatively centered internal presentation of shared meanings.

As an afterthought, it may be added that perhaps one had better see the internality of any subcultural apparatus as a matter of degree. Perspectives have a tendency to shift as they are removed from the symmetrical flow and inserted instead into an asymmetrical structure. This is due to the changing material base, which sets them apart, and also to the attention that is being focused on them from consumers, and the greater deliberateness with which they tend to be stated, once they are part of a cultural apparatus.[48] Yet it would not seem difficult, in many situations, to recognize the difference between what is more directly derived from a subculture and that which is an outsider's rather uncertain, less experientially grounded, perspective toward the subcultural perspective.

We should note briefly one additional type of cultural apparatus/subculture interplay. The kinds of instances referred to so far involve subcultural units which are, presumably, distinctive primarily at the level of meanings—the first of the cultural dimensions identified in chapter 1—and which fairly certainly have an existence independent of cultural apparatus input. But then there are those contemporary subcultures which are in large part characterized by their different entanglements with the cultural apparatus and with specific media symbol systems, marked consequently by the forms they employ to bring involvements with media and the cultural apparatus generally into face-to-face relationships. Here, the distinctiveness of subcultures is to a greater extent a matter of that second dimension of culture, the forms of externalizations, in its interrelations with the first dimension. Academic subcultural communities—"invisible colleges," to use Diana Crane's (1972) term—show some of this; they are integrated by print, computer, and telephone as much as by seminars, conferences, and think tanks. Contemporary Western youth cultures of the more conspicuous varieties revolve around video and stereo; subcultures such as those of hackers or cineasts do not just open themselves to the media, but have indeed come together around them.

In such subcultures, one tends to find—perhaps beyond a familiarity with the classic works of the respective media, where such exist—a self-conscious intellectual or aesthetic capacity for appreciating subtleties, and sometimes a concern with investigating the limits of media potentialities or of the individual's own media-using skills. Favorite metaphors and modes of imagination can be drawn from the way meaning is managed in print, film, or computer programs. Because of the shifts in media involvements between the generations, the young can be literate with respect to their preferred symbol systems at levels which are quite alien to older generations. And the subcultures oriented toward the written word can perhaps collectivize the critical mode of their variety of literacy, and use it by ingrained habit as a resource in the management of meaning even at moments when there are no pages to stare at or flip back and forth.

Conclusion: Symmetries and Asymmetries Reassembled

I have devoted most of this chapter to questioning two routine ways of depicting contemporary cultures: one tending toward centrifugality, in emphasizing the fragmentation and isolation of subcultures, the other toward centripetality, in depicting homogenization and massification by the cultural apparatus. I would not want to overstate the case. There is some validity in both depictions. First of all, however, they need to be brought together, instead of being kept apart as poles between which our rhetoric swings altogether opportunistically. For when they are brought together, we understand that they cannot both be wholly true, in their strongest versions, at the same time.

Secondly, they must each be taken apart, and the elements reassembled into another whole. Here we see the institutions of the cultural apparatus (a term one may want to retain, as the collective label for those various agencies—in principle of uncertain connections to one another—which have in common their operating along certain dimensions of asymmetry) as tied in their productions to particular perspectives, and reaching variously far, toward people with either similar or other perspectives. And we see subcultures as clusterings of perspectives; variously clearly bounded, sometimes nesting in one another, sometimes crosscutting; in some places rich in content and form, in other places poor in the same respects; basically defined in terms of symmetries of cultural process, but at times including certain asymmetry as well. We may even see—to introduce one more possibility—how the cultural apparatus can present different subcultures with images of one another, thus perhaps giving them more sharply defined characterizations than they may get in their more direct but often muddled contacts. The cultural apparatus in this way actually mediates between subcultures; yet this can mean keeping them apart through stereotyping (when the cultural apparatus is in the market framework, its bias is to make its commodities spectacular), as well as bringing them closer through acts of benevolent interpretation.[49] The rhetorician of cultural politics may get lost in this maze. The careful ethnographer must find his way.

So much for focusing on symmetries and asymmetries of input quantity and scale. In the next chapter, we will be concerned mostly with linkages of cultural distribution to material resources and power.

4 Unfree Flow

> An economist is one who knows economics, and economics is primarily the science of commodities. A commodity is something which is exchanged and, therefore, has a price. It is usually something which can be produced and consumed—that is, created and destroyed. At times, knowledge possesses all these properties, and hence it can claim to be a commodity. It is, however, a very peculiar commodity and has very peculiar relations to other commodities.
>
> (Kenneth Boulding 1970:142–143)

> The manipulation of information—withholding, distorting, and concealing it—is crucially important in controlling human affairs. This has been known throughout human history; and this knowledge has been essential in many professions and trades, including those of spies, blackmailers, politicians, the military, merchants, and businessmen. All governments, to a larger or smaller extent, have lied—directly or by omission—to their subjects. However, it may fairly be said that it is our century which has witnessed for the first time a new civilization, in which the entire power system (i.e., control of the population by its rulers) is based on the control of information.
>
> (Leszek Kolakowski 1989:65)

The flow of meaning, we tend to think, should not be fettered. Freedom of expression, free speech, the free flow of information—opprobrium faces whoever tampers with them.

But then "free" is not an unambiguous word. It can mean "unconstrained," but it can also mean "without cost." And the two need not go together. The "free flow of information," for example, has been held to serve as an alibi for the domination of the center (with its news bureaus, its advertising agencies, and its communication satellites) over the periphery in the global information order; and thus the periphery, arguing that to it, such lack of restriction might in some ways be costly, has at least attempted to suggest policies for constraining that flow.[1]

Such restrictive rules and practices have not been rare, either, in human life. People have, in fact, been quite inventive in devising ways of controlling the flow of meaning.

In this chapter, I will take note of a range of costs and constraints relating to cultural flow; costs (to some, and gains to others) in the sense of asymmetries of power and material resource linkage, and constraints which channel the distribution of meaning and meaningful form in society. I will thus say something about the alignments of distributions of meaning with power and material interests through ideology, secrecy, and censorship; about the use of culture to make personal and collective distinctions; about various constraints on the management of meaning in the market place; and about the cost of expertise to the layman. This will be in the manner of a whistle-stop tour of some of the more interesting sites for the social organization of meaning. One could stay longer in each place, but the aim of this tour is breadth and variety rather than exhaustive inquiry into particularities. Before all this, however, some more general considerations of the relationship of culture to power and material life.

The Curious Economics of Culture

In the study of small-scale societies, anthropologists have been prompted to develop cultural points of view toward the economy, but hardly economic points of view toward cultural process. In these societies, at least as we have habitually viewed them, the entire design for living is displayed, delivered as a package, simply as people go about the daily round in one another's presence. Such exchanges of goods and services as occur are on the whole not related to any differential access to meaning. One hardly gets closer to a free flow of meaning than this.

If any economic principle of culture is at work here, it is one which is anomalous in the context of most economic thought. As one of the major figures of nineteenth-century American anthropology (although remembered perhaps mostly as a Boas adversary), Major John Wesley Powell, told a congressional committee in 1886: "Possession of property is exclusive; possession of knowledge is not exclusive, for the knowledge which one man has may also be the possession of another." (Quoted by Boulding, 1966:3) In the cultural flow, that is, people can give something away and keep it at the same time. Telling people what you know does not result in your knowing it any less. In fact, if your offerings are accepted, their value may even be enhanced for you as you simultaneously hold on to them. You may become more "cognitively secure," as it were, by realizing that others agree to the validity of your ideas. Moreover, you may benefit from the coordination of their actions with yours which may follow from such acceptance. Or you may at least be honored as a source.

In the quintessential small-scale society, such a free flow of culture appears to work out well for everybody. The meanings which are passed around have much the same use value for everybody. In our textbook view of the advantages of cultural sharing, we see no zero-sum games involved. Over time, at least, everybody contributes in the same or similar ways.

The same kind of cultural process is widespread, if hardly equally dominant, in contemporary complex societies, where it is characteristic of the form of life framework. As the eminent economist of knowledge, Fritz Machlup put it, "every person alive (and not in a coma) has at his disposal an almost continuous flow of free knowledge" (1980:179–180), but since no choices are involved and no alternative opportunities given up, it does not ordinarily count except as a free good in the economist's scheme of things.

But then there are also those meanings, and manifestations of meaning, to which particular people have some sort of special relationship; instances in which the "Powell principle," if we may call it that, does not quite hold.[2] It matters to these people, in some way or other, whether or not that special relationship is maintained or altered. The particular distribution of culture in question has consequences for them in terms of what material goods or what services it allows them to get from others. These are the cultural phenomena of unfree flow.

In Karl Polanyi's familiar terms (as used and partly elaborated by later anthropologists), one might say that the free flow of culture entails a generalized reciprocity.[3] And Polanyi's two other basic economic forms, redistribution and market exchange, then have their parts in organizing cultural management as it becomes entangled with power and the material economy.

If the form of life framework for the flow of meaning is linked to generalized reciprocity, the other frameworks relate variously to these other economic forms. In the market framework, typically, clearly delimited units of manifested meaning—know-how or its products; a session with a palmist, or a novel—are paid for directly by particular customers at particular times. Under a redistributive arrangement, the ideas held by particular individuals or categories are offered, translated into overt form, either to a collectivity as a whole or to its individual members in a somewhat indirect exchange for material resources, which are first collected at some organizational center point and then allocated to the holders and producers of specialized meaning. While such an organization is not unique to the state, it is obvious that it fits especially well into the state framework. In its central accumulation of resources, it makes possible large-scale, long-term effort. Combined with coercive extractive power, it can ensure that material resources are available for a provision of meaning both to those who can afford it but do not necessarily want it and to those who may want it but who probably would not have participated in clear-cut market arrangements; the latter is the foundation of policies of cultural welfare.[4] (Coercive power can furthermore be used, certainly, to impose a flow of meaning on unwilling recipients.) Yet people can obviously also come together voluntarily according to a redistributive principle for purposes of promoting the production or distribution of meaning. In the movement framework, cultural flow often depends on a combination of generalized reciprocity and redistribution, possibly with market exchange playing a subordinate part as well.

It would seem that different principles of the economics of culture to some extent have areas of application where each works either well or less so in organizing the cultural flow. But this is only true within limits, and it is equally remarkable how vaguely and shiftingly the boundaries may be drawn between the zones where market exchange, redistribution, and the free flow of generalized reciprocity respectively reign. It is also true that where one organizational principle is preferred and more fully institutionalized, the others may also be present; interstitially, supplementarily, unofficially. As complex cultures differ in such respects, it is clear that the economics of culture in itself has to be a cultural economics, giving adequate recognition to the role of arbitrariness and convention.[5]

Ideology: The Distributive Problem

If in some ways the political economy of culture does not seem so distinctive, there are ways in which the same qualities of culture as allow a free flow also impinge on the special relationships between some people and some culture. When you can give ideas away and retain them at the same time, you can afford to be generous. In contrast, it is less easy to maintain allegiance to any number of contradictory ideas, and especially to act in line with all of them. Thus, if somebody accepts your ideas and therefore has to discard or reject competing ideas, in belief or in action, he may really be more generous than you are as the donor.

There are about as many definitions of ideology as of culture, but this is one way of looking at what it is about.[6] An expansive cultural flow fundamentally originating in one perspective (usually the collective perspective of a group) states basic understandings or ground rules for action, interaction, and exchange which, when accepted by others, result in an asymmetrical distribution of power and/or material resources. In the simplest form here, you can profit from sharing, without sharing the profits. But if ideology is not a matter of outright sharing, a replication of uniformity, it can at least involve a coordinated network of perspectives, one dominant and others somehow receptive to it and thereby subordinated.

Ideology may be explicit and deliberately worked out as a philosophical system, or it may be—at most—intuitively understood even by its instigators as an aspect of their general perspective, and expressed through everyday practices. And not all contributions to the cultural flow which are in line with one ideology need originate in the group ultimately identified with it; hegemony is certainly most securely established when people help keep it going whether or not it is to their advantage. Hegemony as cultural power may be having one's way with people against their interests, but not against their will.

But if this is what ideologies strive toward, and what hegemony is, then the big question here is how it is accomplished; the ideologue faces a distributive problem. This does not decrease, either, as we recognize that although there is hardly anything in a conceptualization of ideology such as ours to intrinsically confine it to large-scale social structures—it is entirely feasible to locate an ideological analysis even at a microcultural level—ideology is usually thought of as a macrophenomenon. It seems doubtful that the dominance of a particular perspective can be effectively promoted within a wider structure only through the flow of meaning in a decentered web of interpersonal relationships, leaning toward symmetries of scale and input quantity.

The cultural apparatus, on the other hand, would seem to show greater promise as a tool in the move from sectional perspective to hegemony in complex cultures. And before we move on, with a mere nod toward the fact that studies in ideology have been a major intellectual growth industry for some time, we will dwell just for a moment on the implications for ideology of the view of cultural apparatus/subculture interconnections sketched in chapter 3. To this will be added some remarks on the characteristics of the market and state frameworks in the promotion of ideology.

Much of the concern with the power of the cultural apparatus in contemporary cultures has indeed been a concern with its penetrative ideological force, as organized either in the market or by the state. Hegemony is accomplished, it is suggested, through a sort of flooding of perspectives, either through a massive redundancy of messages in sheer quantitative terms, or through a use of cultural forms of peculiar qualitative potency.[7] As the ability to manipulate symbol systems through media technology improves, consumers are tempted into a dream world of commodities, and citizens become the audience in an electronic theater state.[8] And not only may each of the various agencies of the cultural apparatus—rituals or related performative genres, educational institutions, the legal machinery—disseminate ideologically marked messages on its own, they can also support each other, as when schools inculcate the propriety of complying with the law or rehearse proper ritual attitudes.

Persuasive as such views of ideological outreach may be, we can sense what are the counterarguments. Before getting to them, however, the question may be broached whether ideologically marked messages flow more readily in one or the other of those frameworks in which agencies of the cultural apparatus tend to be situated, the state or the market.

In some ways, it certainly seems that the state framework lends itself particularly well to the advancement of ideology (which may be an ideology in support of the state itself, or the ideology of whoever controls the state). The redistributive principle for funding should be very appropriate to work of cultural construction and dissemination which concerns basic, long-term principles for social life. It allows drawing material support for such work not only from those enthusiastically in favor of it, but also from those who might gain from it in the long term, yet could not be trusted to support it voluntarily in the short term; even from those who would not gain in the long term either. In contrast, on the face of it, it might seem intrinsically contradictory to place such meanings and their overt forms as commodities on the market, where free choice is supposedly exercised on a short-term, piecemeal basis; not least since the ideology should thus be bought by people whose interests might well be opposed to it. Moreover, while hegemony may entail a furthering of an asymmetry of power linkage, there is already, in the state framework, such an asymmetry present to be drawn upon in ideological promotion—the state can put unique means of compulsion to use to enforce attention to at least some of those parts of the cultural apparatus which it controls. In *The Invention of Tradition,* Eric Hobsbawm has an ironic passage about "official new public holidays, ceremonies, heroes and symbols which commanded the growing armies of the state's employees and the growing captive public of schoolchildren" (1983:264).

All the same, the promotion of ideology through the market place surely has its possibilities as well, which is why contemporary Western ideological analysis so often focuses on phenomena such as popular culture and advertising. It is one aspect of this that the large-scale production and dissemination of culture may tend toward monopoly or oligopoly, not least where it requires large investments, as in media technology. In this way the freedom of choice is obviously limited; cultural commodities representing all imaginable alternative ideologies may not be available. More fundamentally, along such lines of argument, there is the question of how the cultural market works in the short term and in the long term. In any particular instance, people may seem to pick what they want from available commodities, thus exercising the freedom to choose. Yet over time, being at the receiving end of the commoditized flow of meaning also means having one's perspective shaped by it, being culturally constructed by it; no longer just taking possession of that culture, that is, but perhaps becoming possessed by it. And when this happens, the freedom of the market becomes a fiction; the consumers are hooked, incapable of warding off whatever is the ideological import of cultural commodities. As a state may mold its citizens, the market may thus to some degree mold its customers.

There are good reasons to take seriously the impact of the cultural apparatus on ideological dissemination. Yet for another couple of reasons, it is also possible that this impact on the perspectives of people at the receiving end superficially appears greater than it is. For one thing, where there is a coercive element involved, there may be public compliance without private acceptance. For another, due to the very ubiquity and familiarity of cultural apparatus meanings, they may be what people fall back on in their exchanges until more personal perspectives have been identified—before a relationship has shifted from being shoulder to shoulder to being fully face to face, as it were.

And then we reach the point where the counterarguments against the effectiveness of the cultural apparatus in the service of hegemony are to be heard, the question marks surrounding it noted. Some of them relate to the variable characteristics of the cultural apparatus itself. How insistent on the purity of their ideological message are its agencies? Do they really stand in unity behind the same ideology? We have accepted the possibility before that thinking of the cultural apparatus in the singular may at times be misleading. It may not speak with only one voice.

Even more basically, there are the doubts one may have about the willingness of recipients to accept, across dividing lines of interests, the gift of ideology.[9] In the form of life framework, within which subcultures mostly grow, the tendency toward pragmatic routinization and stability entails a sort of protection of any ongoing order of things. Once an ideology has indeed reached in here, this can be a haven for hegemony, where its more or less one-way flow of meaning can be complemented by a multitude of crisscrossing minor currents carrying much the same message—often enough in an implicit form, in which it is less available for argument. But at the same time, that repetitiveness of the form of life internal experiential and communicative order can be a shield toward any intrusive ideology, a constant source of tacit or explicit critique of meanings which do not fit. Between it and the cultural apparatus, there may be only the incessant battle of conflicting patterns of redundancy. Now and then, the would-be donors of ideologically marked meanings thus turn out to be stuck with their offerings.

Ideas Withheld and Forbidden: Secrecy and Censorship

Ideology, to repeat, is expansive. It is a matter of pushing meanings forcefully through the obstacle course of the social terrain. But personal or group interests can also be served by withholding meanings.

Restrictive practices in the management of meaning are essentially of two kinds. There are those which prevent a cultural flow from occurring so as to affect directly what people can know (thus relating to the first dimension of culture, as identified in chapter 1), and there are those which aim more immediately at restraining the use of particular forms of externalization of meaning even among those knowledgeable enough (relating to the second dimension).

Secrecy in itself is of the first kind; an instrument through which an uneven distribution of knowledge may be carefully cultivated. In Simmel's words, "the secret offers, so to speak, the possibility of a second world alongside the manifest world; and the latter is decisively influenced by the former" (1964:330).

That hidden world is one of notable organizational variation. One might distinguish, to begin with, between microsecrets and macrosecrets. The former, involving bits and pieces of information about particular individuals and events in the immediate surroundings, are parts of the management of meaning in microcultures. Very concrete and specific, they are also often matters of passing concern. At the other end of the scale, secrecy can be institutionalized as a pervasive line of division within the society as a whole. In our vision of the totalitarian society (that to which the quotation from Leszek Kolakowski at the beginning of this chapter refers), there are those who know and those who do not. A form of cultural engineering, mostly within the state framework, secrecy here turns into a more general, enduring, and systematic management of entire domains of meaning, with censorship as a key tool of control. This is hegemony the other way around.

Then secrecy can also entail a number of different distributions of knowledge, and of ignorance, and of knowledge of ignorance. Often control is most securely maintained if the secrecy is itself secret—people should not know that they do not know, because if they know that they do not know they may try to find out.[10] Where knowledge becomes power mostly by way of prestige, however, the opposite may be true. The possession of secrets is flaunted. Others should be made to know that they do not know, and also made to know that to know is superior. This appears to be the major form of secrecy in those small-scale societies which are on the whole characterized by a free flow of meaning.[11] There is, so to speak, so little viscosity in the cultural flow here that just about everything will get around unless one takes special steps to promote the ignorance of others. Yet it is also very difficult to keep secret something that is tangibly vital, so that what is secret tends to be something esoteric, and as important as it can be established to be by convention—among those in the know, as well as those not in the know.

And then there are "leaks"—another member in the family of flow metaphors—which occur when someone among those who know deviates from a rule of secrecy. What should be contained within gets out. Sometimes the very fact of the leak becomes a secret among another set of people. Or it becomes widely known, while it remains a secret who was responsible. And if frequently the leaked knowledge in itself is significant enough, it can also come to stand more generally as a reminder of what is not leaked, of the fact that somewhere, secrets are being kept.

In most of these cases, the inequality of knowledge—the deliberate maintenance of an asymmetry of baselines, if one wants to put it that way—is to the advantage of someone, at someone else's expense. The idea of free flow is negated in both the ways initially referred to above. As an extreme and peculiar case, however, there is also what one may describe as "universal secrecy"; the attempt to prohibit offensive kinds of meaning, such as pornography, or representations of violence, or heretical beliefs, in order to cleanse a culture as a whole rather than to manipulate distributive inequalities. If ever achieved, this would be the secrecy of nobody vis-à-vis everybody, the sharing of the absence of something—at which point, of course, secrecy ceases to be involved, and there is only ignorance, or innocence. Perhaps this absence can also work out to the greater advantage of some people relative to others, although the advantage would appear more complicated than that based on uneven distributions. As a conscious goal, universal secrecy is sometimes pursued by states, and rather more often by movements. The former may use censorship; the latter may advocate it.

The active practice of censorship is a matter of stopping the cultural flow in the phase of externalization, to prevent it from reaching into people's perspectives. It may be the work of an obscure official inspecting newspaper copy, or rest on the decision of a local library committee, or come about as an agitated crowd burns the books by which they feel symbolically violated. Crises in cultural history have revolved around censorship; its many forms in contemporary cultures, and the heat it can generate as an issue in cultural management, was shown on a global scale, with any number of local permutations, in the 1989 Salman Rushdie affair.[12]

Decisions to prohibit ideas are not often completely effective, however; they rather force the ideas underground. Controlling the broad and visible channels of the cultural apparatus may not be entirely impossible, although even here both producers and recipients of messages may find ways of getting around censorship, and poking fun at it: allusions, historical metaphors, cultural cryptography. It is extremely difficult, on the other hand, to prevent meanings from circulating in the rather inaccessible symmetries of face-to-face relationships.[13] Here, they may survive over long periods, perhaps to reemerge into the open as old institutions of censorship crumble. Soviet culture under *glasnost* is an example. Another is the revitalization of intellectual life in Spain in the post-Franco period; a reconquest of the cultural apparatus by the ex-subterranean.

Making Distinctions

The kinds of restriction of cultural flow which works primarily at the level of externalized form, rather than knowledge as such, is exemplified not least by those instances where people take a proprietary interest in particular means of expression as matters of identity and social distinction, personal or collective. The people involved do not conceal these forms, and the latter are not in short supply as far as the proprietors are themselves concerned, as for their part they can act in the same way again and again, but they want to limit competition in the use of the forms in question (or simply assume limited competition, until somehow other users appear). As these people exhibit their cultural properties to others, they want to make themselves thereby appear intrinsically attractive, preferred choices as partners in relationships. They are not offering prestations of meaning in direct exchange for material assets, but are rather looking for social assets in the form of desirable contacts, influence, interpersonal power. There is a kind of exchange, that is, but the cultural externalizations are (in Malinowskian terms) valuables rather than commodities: gifts creating obligations. More indirectly, material benefits may be gained in the relationships thus formed, but it is likewise possible that only immaterial rewards will flow through them.

Insofar as there is competition for whatever assets are involved here, the treatment of meaning as property obviously cannot create only winners. "Property is theft," as Proudhon said, or at least has zero-sum qualities. Those with less attractive identities—who may not engage in much monopolization or promotion—are the losers (perhaps finding among each other such comfort as they get).

In some instances, such distributions of meaningful attributes are based on ascriptive principles, so that one is born to the cultural emblems of one's social unit. Ethnicity thus channels social organization by having group members signal a general kind of availability to one another and distance to outsiders, through their appearance and conduct.[14] Royal houses in Europe and elsewhere similarly attempt to engage the loyalty of their subjects through the use of a distinct and powerful symbolism. In other instances, the identification with particular meanings is acquired, but it can still involve group or categorical membership rather than individual identity. Through the exhibition of certain styles or tastes people can sort one another out as desirable partners in various types of relationships. Often this reflects a selective involvement with the cultural apparatus; showing a sophisticated consumer appreciation of its more intricate productions of symbolic form (mostly capital-C Culture) becomes, in the term popularized by Pierre Bourdieu, "cultural capital."[15]

Achieved categorical distinctions such as these are not least important in a mobile society where detailed knowledge of other individuals is not readily at hand, but where ascriptive principles are not effective. Yet people can also manage meanings in such a way as to promote a sense of more uniquely individual desirability, again both through appearance and modes of action. The differentiated cultural product here is the personality, in the popular sense of the word. ("Charisma" is an extreme case.) One need not assume that even the small-scale society is immune to such competitive nonsharing—it is to no small extent a microcultural phenomenon in complex societies as well—but once more, work on meanings as personal identity may have a special place in a society where many relationships have to be formed through one's own efforts. It has been widely recognized in Western societies in recent years that work on personal identities is often carried out with a conspicuous frenzy particularly in large cities; a phenomenon that sociologist Orrin Klapp has referred to as "ego-screaming" (1969:80).

What we have concentrated on so far are the ways in which the competition for advantage in relationships through identity and distinction can constrain the cultural flow, by hindering some from making active personal use of forms which they may be fully familiar with, but which belong to somebody else. Royal impersonators have tended to be frowned upon, ethnic "passing" likewise. We must certainly be aware, however, that the search for distinction also can be expansive, a factor underlying the insertion of new forms into the flow.

When the cultural forms claimed as property lose their attractiveness to oneself or to others, or are taken up by too many people, or simply by the wrong people, the right kind of distinctiveness can only be reinstated if one comes up with something new. To take one example, LeRoi Jones (later Amiri Baraka) has suggested in his book *Blues People* that this has been a motivating power behind continued Black American musical creativity (1963:220). While a distinctive music has been a highly esteemed ethnic marker for Black Americans, others have again and again appropriated its forms; to this Black musicians have responded by digging yet deeper down toward the roots of their music, and coming up with further variations. If the view is correct, it would seem that the sequence of distinction—assimilation—new distinction thus keeps a complex of cultural forms from ever stagnating.[16]

Here, of course, we may cross the border toward outright commoditization; the reethnicized music perhaps strengthens a sense of personal Blackness, but it also becomes a distinctive brand of cultural goods in the market. And so we encounter, briefly, the same type of diversification in yet another current of the flow of messages: obviously brands are attempts to construct "personalities" for commodities, to remove them—in most cases through qualities of packaging and advertising extrinsic to the product itself—from an essential sameness in a crowded field of products for mass consumption, and thereby build competitive distinctiveness and customer loyalties.[17] To repeat, there is more than simply a mechanism of cultural restriction here. We come back for a moment to the culturally expansive implications of the search for distinction in the next chapter. Now, on the other hand, we turn to some other ways in which knowledge can be, as Kenneth Boulding put it, "a very peculiar commodity."

Credentialism, Copyrights, and Other Constraints

In the camp at Wallaby Cross, on the outskirts of Darwin in the Northern Territories of Australia, reports Basil Sansom (1980:24 ff.), the more regular inhabitants are more or less urbanized Aborigines, fairly loosely organized into "mobs." These camp dwellers derive some of their income by acting as hosts, patrons, brokers, and protectors of visitors—other Aborigines who come to town from the hinterland for a drinking binge. In the negotiations which occur within and between mobs, with the visitors, and with the authorities in town, there is a strong sense of rights in rhetorical property. Social, economic, and political advantages depend on who has what rights to what words—"I caan give you that word, ask that olfella"; "That my word you usin! You leave my word! You got no *business* with my word!"

There is here, it seems, a category of "knowledge you may have but may not act upon." Such a notion occurs here and there in world ethnography, also in places where on the whole one expects the free flow of culture to be regnant.[18] The camp dwellers at Wallaby Cross actually seem to have inherited their sense of rights in cultural property, if not the properties themselves, from the Australian Aboriginal tradition. In a brief paper on the economics of orality, Michaels (1985) has discussed how that tradition has allowed rights of performance to be monopolized but also negotiated in an economy of sacred knowledge.

And there are other ways in which some users of some knowledge can claim precedence over others. In colonial British Africa, it used to be that one could come across tailors proudly exhibiting homemade signs announcing that they had been "trained in Her Majesty's Prison"; there are also the tales of hapless job applicants in India with calling cards or resumés describing them as "B.A. (failed)." These are claims from the nether reaches of credentialism; a principle for the social organization of knowledge widespread in Occidental societies, but also now what Dore (1976) has described as a malady of the Third World, a "diploma disease."[19]

According to credentialism, specialization should be uniformly packaged and clearly labeled. In the relative anarchy of actual cultural flow, there may be different ways of coming by a particular kind of knowledge; through trial and error, by reading books, through apprenticeship. The credentialist predilection, however, is to recognize and legitimize (or at least privilege) only one way, or some limited few, mostly in the shape of formal education, through specialized institutions in the cultural apparatus. Credentials take the forms of academic degrees, certificates, membership of exclusive groups of practitioners. Often they come as a part of that complex described as professionalism—well established in some locations within the division of labor and knowledge, and anxiously sought by specialists in various other locations.

If professionalism and credentialism are valued in the West, it is also clear, as Dore shows, that they have been expanding globally. And this does not only include a deference to diplomas from the West, or to diplomas proclaiming Western-derived varieties of knowledge, which is what Dore primarily refers to. The strain toward credentialist forms is also evident in non-Western lines of knowledge; for example, among indigenous healers in Africa, who (spontaneously or with state encouragement) are forming professional bodies and setting up new training colleges (cf. Last and Chivanduka, 1986).

Laymen, as consumers of specialist services, stand to gain something from credentialism, for through it they may have some guarantee of required skills. When it is a matter of qualities and degrees of knowledge which are not obvious to ordinary people, or when the results of application are not immediately known, it is helpful to have some way of predicting whether someone has the requisite knowledge to perform acceptably. This is why the public tends to go along with credentialism, and why, in attempting to keep the knowledge market under some control, states also more or less favor it.

On the whole, credentialism is a macrophenomenon. As Randall Collins (1979:62), one of its leading theorists and critics, has suggested, it is such easily announced, easily inspected claims to knowledge, rather than the knowledge itself, that can most readily channel relationships in a large-scale market with a large measure of anonymity. Writing about healers in an area of Tanzania, Steven Feierman (1986:216) notes that those who become most engaged in the National Union of Traditional Healers and its offshoot organizations are "healers who travel, who practice in towns, and who do not specialise in caring for relatives and immediate neighbours"; the latter type of practice, in contrast, is embedded in long-term local relationships of trust and reputation to which official credentials would add little.

If under some conditions credentialism seems in certain ways beneficial to the public, however, it often carries built-in advantages to credentialers and credentialized (often the same people), and other side effects on cultural distribution, which are not equally desirable to all. Insofar as the specialists themselves control the channels by which skills are acquired and do the credentialing of new practitioners themselves, they can act as gatekeepers and restrict the number of competitors and, thus, also the supply of knowledge. And while there is not necessarily a close relationship between actual knowledge, credentialed knowledge, and actually needed knowledge, credentialism tends to create standard packages of skills which are not to be subdivided. The credentialed can thus control the practice of some of their more accessible know-how as well as that which is more esoteric. None of it will be available in any bargain basement of the division of knowledge, there will be no barefoot this or that. Uncredentialed knowledge becomes another instance of "knowledge you may have but may not act upon."

It is also true that credentialed knowledge tends to be of a more general, decontextualized type (or, alternatively, one built up only in a single type of context). Consequently, recontextualizing it in a wider range of specific situations may involve its own problems, and sometimes the result turns out to compare poorly with local knowledge, subcultural or microcultural stuff which is uncredentialed.[20] In addition, when labor markets become increasingly organized in terms of knowledge credentials, and when there is a glut of more or less credentialed job seekers, there arises the possibility of credential inflation; more people pay in the universal currency of credentials for jobs which do not really demand their acquired level of skill.

The restrictions on use of knowledge among the Australian Aborigines, to get back to them, seem not so much to be a matter of credentialism, with its emphasis on institutionalized forms of knowledge acquisition, but rather remind us of another set of contemporary principles for obstructing the use of particular knowledge, when one cannot prevent that knowledge itself from spreading: patents, copyrights, and a range of related rights.

These are means of safeguarding the material rewards for specialized management of meaning, in these instances of an innovative nature; as Ploman puts it (with reference to copyright), it is "a method to link the world of ideas to the world of commerce" (1985:25). What is acknowledged here is that major peculiarity of knowledge as a commodity: as soon as certain constructions of meaning are given external form they are, by the nature of cultural flow, "given away," unless durable exclusive rights to the externalizing itself can be maintained through special means. Much skill and effort may have gone into developing them as originals, but once they are there they can be easily copied. Patents and copyrights establish the idea of cultural property, and thereby also the possibility of punishable cultural theft (in a less paradoxical sense, that is, than Proudhon's).[21]

There are those instances, certainly (in capital-C culture especially), when the link between creator and creation in cultural production is held to be so strong that copies are intrinsically devalued; they may be mass produced to perfection, but the main value, the cult-like "aura" in Walter Benjamin's term (1969:220 ff.), is really attached to the creative work embodied only in the original. A signature can link creator with creation as both process and product (while at the same time it places the latter within a corpus, thus identifying a context of interpretation).[22] In such instances, some copying becomes forgery; one sort of acceptance of the idea that only the original really counts.

If oral cultures such as those of the Aborigines have oral economies, with some sort of copyright notions, such ideas have been taken much further, although by way of slow and uncertain development, in relation to print and other media technologies operating in a developed market framework.[23] Through absences and presences, they channel cultural production; a facet of cultural history deserving continued exploration.

At present, the historian Neil Harris (1985) has noted, much of Western popular culture is affected by copyright laws; somebody *owns* Superman. And this means that nobody else can produce Superman for profit where this copyright is upheld, not in comic strip form, and not as a movie or on the stage or on a greeting card, either. Nor, for that matter, can one freely produce too-close Superman imitations, insofar as it may be held that it is the general concept of a Superman that is protected—from this point of view, old Captain Marvel was a questionable character. According to American copyright law, one can only use somebody else's copyrighted characters in order to criticize them and parody them. (True, in times when a large part of popular culture takes a parodical turn, this can be a significant exception.) Yet the purpose of copyrights and their affines, of course, is not only restrictive, for they are intended as an incentive to original productions, and to making the fullest possible use of these, in every niche to which the protection extends. When the same comic strip figures appear on greeting cards, on stationery, on sweat shirts, in theme parks and on the stage, and do so on a global scale, then rights in them also inspire a quite expansive mode of cultural management.

Copyrights, however, require a reasonably efficient interaction between state and market. Where for one reason or other this does not occur, cultural flow is affected; and as markets and states are often not coterminous, issues of this kind often in some way or other involve the diffusion of cultural commodities across state boundaries.

Until late in the nineteenth century, for example, in the United States, foreign novels were not protected by copyright, while local authors were. This was, in fact, not greatly to the latter's advantage. On the other hand, as Wendy Griswold (1981) has pointed out, it had interesting consequences for what they would write. The country was flooded with the imports, and one reason why the works of American authors during this period in particular seemed to reflect a peculiarly American character, deviating from the typical themes of their foreign colleagues—more small towns, more social mobility, more social reform, and more humor—was probably that only in this way could they secure a foothold in the market.

At present, a similar situation obtains with regard to cassette music piracy, although at least according to some observers, it does not seem that the results are the same. Dave Laing (1986:336), discussing the implications of international piracy for the music scene in the Third World, suggests that when "in many countries, pirate tapes of Madonna or Stevie Wonder cost less than half the price of locally made recordings," fledgling local recording industries are hurt, and the supply of recorded local music begins to dry up. There is a certain irony in this, for if Laing is right, while piracy is often viewed first and foremost in terms of its infringements on the rights of the artists and the corporations of the metropolis, the pirates may in fact be among the more active agents of cultural imperialism. But more about this kind of issues in chapter 7.

Culture as Power: Expertise

Finally our exploration of the varieties of unfree flow takes us to expertise, and the costs of depending on it. To reiterate, through the division of knowledge, a larger cultural inventory than any individual can competently control himself is somehow within his reach or on his horizon; but only at a price, and that price is not always just pecuniary. Sometimes, people may indeed see specialist abilities simply as extensions of their own, and at least in principle may enter into relationships with specialists voluntarily. At times, however, there is a sense that, in these relationships, we surrender our autonomy to some degree, and become vulnerable to the dispositions of others; laymen thus become clients.

While this may occur just about anywhere we confront specialized occupational knowledge, it is useful to distinguish from other occupations two main types which tend to become especially prominent in views of the relationship between power and expertise. One of them we may call technocrats; the other, professionals—in a narrower sense. (In a wider usage, both might be termed professionals.) It is characteristic of both that they have large quantities of organized knowledge in their minds, or at least at their fingertips; this knowledge has been acquired, to begin with, through some more exclusive wing of the formal educational apparatus, and is then expanded or maintained through experience and, probably, continued collegial contacts. But the knowledge of technocrats and professionals is not only noteworthy because of its quantity. Its application also shapes the lives of people generally to an unusual degree.

The expertise of technocrats and professionals fits into society in different ways. The power of technocrats is impersonal in relation to most members of the public, and mediated by those whose part in the division of labor it is to be generalists, professional laymen, specialists on specialists—the politicians and administrators who orchestrate expertise more or less adeptly as a part of being in charge of wider wholes. Through the generalists at the top, the technocrats exercise their powers on a large scale. In contrast, professionals in the narrower sense are experts who offer their services more directly and personally to individuals or groups of the general public.

Technocrats tend to be provided for through redistribution, while the professionals are fairly often in the marketplace. But neither arrangement is absolutely necessary, although either one no doubt leaves its own mark on the way expertise is put into practice. Because the knowledge of both technocrats and professionals is so difficult for anybody outside their own ranks to evaluate, their practice is likely to be characterized by great personal or—at least—collective autonomy. This is strengthened, however, in the case of professionals by the fact that they have a great many clients, rather than being wholly occupied, as technocrats usually are, with one or a few. In any case, credentialism will probably have a major part in bounding either type of group.

Whatever there is of a connection between expertise and power is based on the fact that as the interaction between expert and layman begins, there is a notable asymmetry of baseline knowledge; and more or less regardless of what happens in the interaction, much of that asymmetry will remain. As we noted in chapter 2, if there is a transfer of knowledge from the one to the other, it is only in small portions, relative to the overall scope of expertise. While experts may use some measure of secrecy and credentialism to maintain their niche in the knowledge economy, it is, on the whole, already safeguarded by the fact that it would be very costly for individual laymen to try to invade it.

In fact, there may be no transfer of knowledge at all and, in that sense, no cultural flow. The expert may just use his knowledge to affect the circumstances under which the client lives, and the client may have to make up his own interpretation of the changed circumstances. Such an operation can be performed quite directly in the relationship between a professional and his individual client, or by technocrats by way of a mediating structure. Because in the latter case the same expert action will probably be imposed uniformly on everybody without exception or modification, and because it is rather likely that any communication of expert knowledge that occurs here will filter only ineffectively through the mediating structure, it may be a fair guess that members of the public are more likely to experience technocratic applications of knowledge as unpredictable, inexplicable terror.

But let us concentrate on the contacts between professionals and ordinary laymen, those encounters which occur in everybody's lives. Professions tend to be seen as engaged in service to their clients, but insofar as the latter are not in complete control, those who give service also take power. The clergy, it has been said, are the archetypical form of this kind of expertise, although in recent times their power has declined. By now, doctors may be the most conspicuous example, but there are various others—lawyers, social workers, financial consultants, career counselors, teachers at least in some aspects of their work.

We can see why clients sometimes view themselves as

dominated. To the client, the contact with any particular kind of professional may well be a unique experience, an interaction the result of which may be life or death, illness or health, poverty or prosperity, the integrity of his family or its dismemberment; a moment of crisis. The expert can make authoritative interventions which fatefully affect wide areas of a client's life without his fully informed consent. Despite any code of service, the fear of the predatory professional may linger. And the client may be left alone with the burdensome task of reintegrating his entire existence around whatever is the outcome.

In an expertise-saturated society, moreover, the sense of dominatedness does not all have to focus on one particular expert or on one kind of expertise. If ideology is a wholesale form of culture as power, professional expertise is a retail form. For the client, however, many such experiences can come together in one more diffuse feeling of dependence, intensified perhaps by the uncoordinated and even contradictory demands they may involve.

We may also discern, on the other hand, that this sense of domination need not be fully reciprocated. Because of the difference in perspectives toward the relationship, the expert may not quite recognize his power. For him, the world may be divided into a multitude of delimited fields of knowledge. He, for his part, deals with only one particular kind of facts of life, in a long series of relationships. The expert-client relationship is for him mostly a routine. In some instances, at least, there may be dominatedness without intentional domination.

"Regard for professional expertise compelled people to believe the voices of authority unquestioningly, thereby undermining self-confidence and discouraging independent evaluation," writes Burton Bledstein (1976:xi) in his history of the ascendance of professionalism in the United States. With the passage of time, the critique of professionalism may even have reached a point where domination is taken for granted in expert-layman interactions. But then there are experts and experts, and laymen and laymen. It is hardly possible to abolish the enduring knowledge asymmetry in the relationship between them, but depending on the particular nature of the initial baseline asymmetry, and on the quality of the flow of meaning that actually occurs, there may be more or less of the sense of surrender.

At times, what the expert communicates about the situation of his client may even intensify the feeling of disqualification. In his comparative analysis of Western and Chinese health care systems, Arthur Kleinman (1980:107–108) points out that both popular and professional discourse in the medical field in the West is replete with the metaphors of war: "fighting" infections, "vanquishing" disease, "invaded" by pathogens, immunological "defenses." (Chinese practitioners of popular medicine, on the other hand, are more likely to say that illnesses might have been caused, advertently or inadvertently, by ghosts.) Martial metaphors are widespread in Western culture, and it may be a mistake to make too much of their recurrence in the medical field (cf. Lakoff and Johnson 1980:4ff.). Yet they could have some implications for the definition of illness and the medical encounter: a state of crisis; the existence of a scheming enemy whose aim is destruction; a need for hierarchical organization in the battle.

In the semantic interface between expert and client, there may be much that in this way moves the latter into uncertainty and anxiety. In the medical domain, words such as fever, cancer, heart, drugs; in the legal domain, suit, trial, defendant—these have a symbolic resonance of fatefulness to an individual for someone not accustomed to relating them to personal experience.[24] In combination with a chance and superficial exposure to an unknown, specialized technical vocabulary, such words may carry at least one unequivocal message: lay understandings stop here. If someone else is better equipped to handle the crisis, the layman is prudent to submit to his authority. Terms such as "need" and "care," less dramatic but absolutely central to many kinds of expert-client relationships, also suggest the vulnerability of the client and his passivity after surrendering to the expert; they seal the treaty.

Meanwhile much of this vocabulary can be Janus-like. It does not necessarily carry the same overtones to the experts involved, in part because the cases in question are less fateful to them, but also because their training and accumulated experience enable them to attach more precise analytical meanings to terms. Some of the vocabulary of greatest emotional power, including various metaphorical usages, may for that matter belong mostly in the traffic in meanings between laymen, or between client and expert, rather than within circles of expertise.

Expert-client communication, however, is not always like

this. Kleinman's analysis of the various forms of Chinese healing practice suggests that where explanatory models are to a greater extent shared, as they are between clients and shamans, the informative give and take is also greater than it is between patients and the Western-style doctors in China, where explanatory models tend not to be shared. Chinese-style doctors are, apparently, in some ways in an intermediary position. They do not share much of their explanatory models with their patients, and their communication with the latter is partly couched in a technical idiom which is inaccessible to the latter, partly an attempt to translate professional conceptions into popular terms.

To understand why there is more or less of the sense of submission—even more or less of actual submission—it seems that one must examine the traffic in meaning between expert and client. How does the client comprehend expert knowledge? How is it matched with his own understandings, and in which way are the latter sustained or altered by expert-client interaction? How are the issues described which bring client and expert together? Is the mode of thought and communication of the expert a reflection and refinement of that of the layman, a specification of his general will, or is there a distortion, in some way and to some degree, which results in an exercise of expert domination over clients?

While this structure of communication may to some degree be institutionalized on its own terms, however, the traffic in meaning is also likely to proceed from a specific asymmetry of perspective baselines. On the whole, all clients are not equally disadvantaged in their understanding of the nature of professional expertise and in their attempts to translate it into their own terms. A more knowledgeable client may need to be told less, but is often told more. And in some instances, the layman gets exactly what he asks for, and knows it.[25]

The client who would seem best equipped to approximate expert knowledge, and to engage in communication about expertise, is probably someone who is virtually a colleague, or an expert in an adjacent field. There need be little experience of surrender here. A client to whom the use of a certain kind of expertise becomes routinized would be in a reasonably similar position, building up his own connoisseurship of expert action and an independent ability to evaluate it. A further question here may be to what extent familiarity with *some* variety of similar expert reasoning is helpful to a client in finding a meta-analytical framework which allows him to take on the expert on more equal terms. There are, of course, several facets to this question—the part played by the client's awareness of such cognitive and communicative competence merely in building his self-confidence, the real ability to scrutinize the enactment of expertise which this competence entails, and the readiness of experts to recognize it in a layman.

In large part, the conditions which make surrender more or less avoidable would seem to be much the same for layman-professional and layman-technocrat relationships. It would appear that the laymen who directly confront the technocrats—the expert generalists, the specialists on specialists—would stand a better chance of preserving some independence, although we know that they sometimes fail as well; then the consequences may be unusually conspicuous, scandals in the public domain.

In any case, the unquestioning belief in expert authority of which Bledstein writes may wax and wane. In parts of the world, not least at the periphery of the present global order, where new and alien modes of expertise are introduced from the center, professionalism and technocracy are perhaps not immediately challenged. In the Occident, the situation in the late twentieth century is hardly what it was a hundred years earlier. At the same time as expertise may try to expand its operating zone, the critique of expertise is increasingly vocal and systematic. To the tensions generated here, we come back in chapter 5.

Culture flows, but in large part not unrestrainedly. As much of the cultural inventory of your complex society is made up of other people's meanings, your getting complete access to them, and full use, is not always in these people's interest—and sometimes, if they are willing to let these meanings and their externalized forms come your way, then some catch may be involved. At the same time, you, too, may be holding on to what you have. The distribution of culture which results is the aggregated outcome of the working of a variety of principles and strategies of individual and collective management of meaning.

As we have seen, however, what is restrictive in one way—identity distinctions, copyrights—may in some other way count among the factors which encourage creativity and cultural expansion. And, here again, there are also a number of other ways of handling culture to inspect.

5 Growth, Flux, Coherence

> The genuine culture is not of necessity either high or low; it is merely inherently harmonious, balanced, self-satisfactory. It is the expression of a richly varied and yet somehow unified and consistent attitude toward life, an attitude which sees the significance of any one element of civilization in its relation to all others. It is, ideally speaking, a culture in which no important part of the general functioning brings with it a sense of frustration, of misdirected or unsympathetic effort. It is not a spiritual hybrid of contradictory patches, of watertight compartments of contradictory consciousness that avoid participation in a harmonious synthesis. (Edward Sapir [1924] 1985:314–315)

> . . . the culture of any society at any moment is more like the debris, or "fall-out," of past ideological systems, than it is itself a system, a coherent whole. Coherent wholes may exist (but these tend to be lodged in individual heads, sometimes in those of obsessionals and paranoiacs), but human social groups tend to find their openness to the future in the variety of their metaphors for what may be the good life and in the contest of their paradigms. (Victor Turner 1974:14)

The notion of "culturality" referred to in chapter 2 included persistence as one of its dimensions; that is, the more durable some item of meaning or meaningful form, the more cultural would it be. And indeed, as anthropologists have increasingly come to confront situations where many things seem less than solid, they seem often to commit themselves to the task of identifying, even celebrating, some layer of stability underlying changes which, it is implied or argued, are relatively superficial. The *longue durée* is where culture is.

Yet there is in this a danger of a curiously one-sided picture of human life—providing, no doubt, a useful antidote to the tendency of change and its agents to claim all our attention, but hardly a credible view of the contemporary social organization of meaning as a whole. Again, whatever we may detect that is persistent below the surface, the complex cultures of our time are quite noticeably in a state of flux. It seems at least as natural to think of them "in process" as "in structure." They are involved in change in microtime and macrotime, in change reversible as well as irreversible, changes affecting them as wholes or only in parts. The management of meaning proceeds within them in different directions and at varying speed; in other words, there is a differentiated distribution not only of meanings and their overt forms, but also of kinds of cultural processes. And as such divergent tendencies might threaten to pull the cultures apart, other ongoing processes keep them from doing so—to bring about, after all, some measure of coherence. The vitality of these cultures has much to do with the ways in which gaps, overlaps, contradictions, and unequal intensities in cultural management are built into their patterns, and worked on there. This chapter is concerned with several ways in which complex cultures are on the move, as well as with the ways in which they more or less cohere. As before, I emphasize social-organizational aspects, with some attention to their interplay with the technology of culture.

Common Sense as Standard Operating Procedure

As change is indeed not everywhere, always, let us begin by identifying a mode in the management of meaning which we all engage in much of the time, and which in its ideal-type version provides us with a contrast to flux; I will describe it as common sense.[1]

Common sense is cultural "business as usual"; standard operating procedure, one's perspective at rest. Meanings develop and survive here through the redundancy of social life. In action as well as interaction, common sense involves an unreflective use of meanings which are close at hand and which have mostly already turned out to be convenient enough in dealing both with people and with the material world. Using them in a stable form or improvising within limits, one scarcely knows that one acts upon them, and one would be hard put to describe or explain how and why one acts upon them. Often, we just assimilate them for our own use as we see them displayed in the actions of people in our environment—learning is embedded in living. If actually at any one time we have received explicit instruction in them, this fact is gradually overshadowed by their being part of our everyday modes of being.

As a form of cultural management, common sense allows one to get along comfortably much of the time. It has to do with unchallenging and unchallenged routines. One speaks not *about* its meanings so much as *in terms of* them. In reasonably stable environments, common sense tends to a degree of cultural inertia. There is no need to keep on producing new and different meanings. Common sense tends to be especially at home in that framework for cultural process I have labeled "form of life." Yet they must not be entirely identified with one another, since within that framework nonroutine moments occur as well.

With regard to further social-organizational aspects, it is clear that common sense is founded on sharing, or at least the assumption of sharing. While not all culture that is shared is common sense, no meanings fully belong here unless it can be more or less taken for granted that other people, of sound minds and exposed to the same relevant realities, also accept them. "Cognitive security," I called this before; meaning is socially validated, made something solid and real rather than an individual whim. In this instance, as everywhere else, the social organization of meaning is a matter of perspectives toward perspectives. Knowingly or unknowingly in contacts with other people, one takes their perspectives into account, as one understands these. But this instance is one where there is an assumption of symmetry between perspectives. Perspectivation, consequently, is in effect disregarded.

Common sense is, in a way, everywhere; but not with the same content. In a complex culture, that is to say, some common sense is for everybody, but much is most definitely not that common. Intricate issues of distribution are involved here as well. At one level it may be true, as Robin Horton (1982:228 ff.) has proposed, that common sense does not vary much even between historically separate cultures. As a mode of ordering reality it may operate in large part with those basic categories of perception which have evolved with human adaptation over the ages, such as above/below, in front of/behind, before/at the same time/after, self/other. On the other hand, much of the stuff of living to which common sense is regularly applied may be very specific in cultural terms; in a complex society, subcultural or even microcultural.

Numerous varieties of common sense coexist, that is to say, working along more or less similar principles, but applying them to different materials.

Thus, there are kinds of common sense that a member of a complex society shares only with comparatively few others—people who are in much the same location in the social structure as he is, and exposed to the same currents of cultural flow. These meanings may be bounded in their contexts of relevance. Preeminently a management of routine meanings, common sense often even serves people best in those specific familiar milieus where the routines usually have their place. The meanings may be carried, in their most concrete versions, by the physical features of these milieus and by the characteristics and biographies of their personnel. Common sense can be what one has to know about prevailing winds, that piece of land or this street, or about particular individuals as types of personalities. It is alluded to in nicknames and anecdotes, among people who know one another and live under much the same circumstances. Consequently, it does not travel well.

In his " . . . as a Cultural System" series, Clifford Geertz (1975) has gone further toward identifying the characteristics of common sense. It involves seeing things as neither more nor less than what they seem to be, to stay adaptively in touch with the facts of life and to steer clear of such subtlety and imagination as could entail an overproduction of meaning. Common sense is ad hoc, concerned with the one "here and now" rather than with the logical integration of many. It is therefore rather tolerant toward inconsistency. Proverbs can all be wise, and—at the same time—in direct contradiction of one another. And there is an underlying assumption that common sense is for everybody. Anyone in possession of his faculties can have a share in it without special effort. The world is familiar and can be approached without esoteric knowledge, special technique, or peculiar giftedness.

Common Sense Upset: Changing Circumstances, Perspectival Clashes

Common sense, then, is intrinsically oriented toward a stability of meanings. Yet even where one variant of common sense has been dominant, it may not be immune to change. The circumstances of life may be altered, or they come to be seen in a different light. There is a failure or rejection of routines. Perspectives are intensified, at least temporarily; later on, common sense may be reestablished, in an old or a new form.

Take, as an example of such turbulence among routine meanings, what happens in a crowd—the sort of thing sociologists and social psychologists have usually placed under the rubric of "collective behavior." We might as well say that a kind of instant cultural process is going on here, a management of meaning involving the immediate spatial and temporal present. The attention of some number of people, available to one another's senses although hardly known to one another personally, becomes focused on some unusual occurrence, and impressions as well as overt reactions are formed interactively. Whatever preexisting perspectives the participants may hold are undoubtedly involved (the notion that crowd behavior would be an exhibition of some precultural "raw humanity" seems dubious), yet there is at the same time an intense traffic in new meanings. In chapter 3, the sociologist Albert Cohen was cited concerning the significance of "exploratory gestures" for cultural emergence. When one sticks out his neck a little, the next person could stick hers out a little further. The short-term microculture of a crowd would appear to depend a great deal on such cumulative interaction. On the other hand, the precise degree of congruence between perspectives is not readily established under crowd conditions. The actions of participants, whether intended as communications or not, are likely to be fragmentary and ambiguous, open to varied interpretations. And decisions about interpretations are made quickly, without much deliberation. Crowd cultures may thus be structures of misunderstandings, although this is not inevitable. At times, they may turn out to have some effect on enduring meaning systems, as common sense returns. Often, they merely become brief cultural parentheses.

Or take as another instance of the destruction of a particular version of common sense what can happen to a community in a disaster; the "collective trauma" of the people of Buffalo Creek, West Virginia, portrayed so well in Kai Erikson's *Everything in Its Path* (1976:189). First there is "a quiet set of understandings that become absorbed into the atmosphere and are thus a part of the natural order." Then a dam bursts, and people find their habitat and their way of life laid waste. For a long time afterwards, there is disorientation and a feeling of vulnerability.

Many changes in the external circumstances of life come more gradually. Thus, people have time to change their understandings; with more or less awareness of what is going on, but often with less, as common sense recontextualizes itself. Here, too, new culture emerges through social process. There are interactions over the meanings of shared conditions.

Apart from such circumstantial inducements of change, however, any variety of common sense which is part of a complex culture also has to cope continuously with the diversity which engulfs it. As perspectives are distributed over the social structure and as people stand with regard to the currents of the cultural flow, some people may even find no established form of common sense available to them with which they can be altogether comfortable. They are in their very own corners, not in a "common corner" (as in the formulation by Everett Hughes quoted in chapter 3) with someone else. If others are in a similar situation, they are not interactively in touch with them.[2] The fit between the received meanings of the cultural flow and the requirements of their situation continues to be poor, or highly relative.

People like these may participate in the cultural traffic as hostages, fellow travelers, reformers, or rebels. They carry on with established meanings because they must (and power may indeed be involved here), not because they embrace them; or because these meanings are just reasonably convenient in the absence of real alternatives. Or they do what they can openly to protest against them, or they subtly attempt to undermine them or introduce shifts in them—none of this necessarily at any very high level of consciousness. Mixed in with other people's symmetries between perspectives are their asymmetrical arrangements: "I do not believe this, you believe in it and think I do" or "both of us know this, but you think it is important and I do not." Within such perspectives, a potential seems to exist for changes in the social organization of meaning. But meanwhile, these perspectives may also be rather inchoate, lacking in established symbolic form.

Even those who are more or less committed to some existing version of common sense, however, will now and then find themselves in situations where it is undermined. As one watches the panorama of meanings put on display in the complex society, even within the form of life framework, provocations toward reflexivity occur again and again. One's own most salient understandings and those understood to be correspondingly significant to others mutually frame one another in one's mind. Again, since perspectives are in no small part perspectives toward other perspectives, fewer things can be fully taken for granted. As Bourdieu (1977:164 ff.), one of the commentators on the nature of common sense—in his terminology, *doxa*—points out, what "goes without saying" (at least in any explicit, self-conscious way) no longer does so when it is in fact said, when it becomes embroiled in argument and has to be seen as one variant among other meanings which are also available. As a critical stance toward *doxa* is made possible, a field of opinion is constituted where orthodoxy and heterodoxy clash. Instead of security in one's convictions, contacts with others here threaten with the social destruction of reality.

In the conditions of a complex society, any variety of common sense may become a little less stable, more fragile and embattled, more aware of its limits; perhaps a little less like the ideal-type version, although still not entirely different from it. The recurrent confrontations with alternatives which contradict it can result in uncertainty or ambivalence, or in an orthodox mode, in an emphatic reassertion of those truths one feels should be self-evident. They may also foster sensitivity and reflectiveness, and cultural creativity.

Some such perspectival inclinations may be spread out in a fairly diffuse manner in the populations of complex societies, insofar as just about everybody has some opportunities to find routine assumptions upset. What McLuhan called implosion—the turn from containment to involvement—and saw in large part as a media effect, is after all in many ways a more general tendency in the societies of today.

It is also true, however, that the perspectives in question show up in particular concentrations in certain locations in the social structure. Members of ethnic minorities have often attested to a "double consciousness," made up from clashes between perspectives from within their own group and those prevalent in the surrounding society. Humor, as a subversive play with conventions and established ideas, can draw on such a source of heightened sensitivity, and the best American comedians have often been minority members—Jewish or African-Americans.[3] And as has been pointed out often enough, Marx, Freud, and Lévi-Strauss, explorers of the human condition beyond what is official or obvious, likewise have a minority experience in common.[4]

Yet the heightened awareness of perspectival clashes need have nothing to do with ethnicity. Complex societies have other kinds of interfaces between varieties of common sense, other kinds of marginality. Some are created biographically with the passage of time, in the experiences of the socially mobile, the exiles, or the homecomers who, after having been away, cannot regain the taken-for-grantedness of old ideas.[5] In these instances, there may be a double encounter between perspectives; a current perspective toward one's own past perspective (and perhaps imaginatively, the opposite as well), and an acute awareness of what others in one's current milieu take to be common sense. If irony is one kind of thought and expression generated under such circumstances, nostalgia is another.

Making Meaning in the Market

Common sense, within the contexts where it is most fully operable, is culture for free, generously shared because nobody gains anything by withholding it from others: again, generalized reciprocity in the flow of meaning.

But as we have seen in the preceding chapter, people can also find competitive advantage in distinctive offerings, exchanging their efforts in the production and dissemination of meaning for material and social rewards; such opportunities may open up and then fade away. If perspectival encounters and clashes is one recurrent source of new meaning in complex cultures, the possibility of gains in cultural marketplaces is thus another.

There is a three-in-one example in an article by Mulkay and Turner (1971) on competition and innovation among North African Muslim saints, nineteenth-century French painters, and contemporary scientists. (In the first of these instances, Mulkay and Turner draw mostly on Gellner's work; in the second instance, especially on that by Caroline and Harrison White; and in the third, on a variety of sources.)

In North Africa, the transmission of *baraka,* the sacred power, has been hereditary. But the saints have been comparatively comfortable economically, and as men of peace they have tended to enjoy long lives, so that they have had more descendants than local markets for saintly services have been able to absorb. In other words, there has been an overproduction of saints; a shift, one may say, in the demography of culture. The responses to this situation on the part of those saints who could not find a place for themselves in their rural home areas have been various. Some have become latent saints, hoping for new opportunities to come up later. Some could establish themselves in another rural locale, practicing largely in the style of their fathers. But for those who have migrated to urban areas, the conditions for saintly work have been different. It has been necessary to compete with others for new adepts, recruited by way of conversion and enthusiasm. This competition has often been characterized by ritual innovation, with a special appeal to the poor, illiterate segments of the urban community. Ecstatic dance and music, acrobatics, fire eating, snake charming, and unusual techniques of breathing and fasting have become part of distinctive performances which, while earning the disapproval of puritan, orthodox urban Muslims, allow new saintly niches to be carved out.

In France in the first half of the nineteenth century, there was an overproduction of personnel in another area of cultural endeavor. In the century before, a new hierarchical structure of academics had professionalized painting. Facilities for training had been improved, and artists also gained a higher status. Thus painting gradually attracted increasing numbers of young men. Then the structure changed again. The Royal Academy came under the control of a small gerontocratic elite, emphasizing traditional styles and themes. Rewards in the form of prizes and official purchases went to large historical paintings, of a type a growing number of painters could ill afford to work on. In order to have a regular income, to buy paint and canvases as well as to cover living expenses, many of them, therefore, turned to genre paintings, landscapes, and still lifes—frowned upon by the Academicians and the large salons, but becoming popular with the ascendant bourgeoisie. Soon, the new art forms were also linked to a new structure of critics and galleries, building reputations and sales apart from the old institutions of the art world.

The expansion of the natural sciences in the twentieth century, Mulkay's and Turner's third instance, has been conspicuous. There has been a rapidly growing number of openings for scientists, but an even greater number of people are attracted to them, and there is not room at the top for everybody. As a result, there is competition for recognition within the research community, and for the grants and career opportunities into which recognition can be converted.

Training in the sciences tends to take the form of apprenticeship. Young trainees work with established scholars, who may well prefer to direct their adepts to problems close to their own areas of interest and competence. For such reasons, one might expect science to show a steady, cumulative growth. But competition encourages another pattern. Intense research activity leads anomalies in ongoing research orientations to be identified quickly, with the consequence that new problem fields are opened up. Competitively inclined researchers realize that there is a promise of great returns if one moves into these fields quickly, and diminishing returns if one remains in them later. Waves of invasion and exodus between research fields are the result, as scientists try to beat one another to the glittering rewards for significant new knowledge.

The search for distinction in these instances, one might say, is on the part of the cultural producers. They innovate in order to find a materially rewarding niche in the market for their commodities, and thus for themselves. Yet the cultural market can also serve to provide distinctions allowing consumers to sort themselves out; and fashions are the obvious example here of the way tendencies toward competition stimulate cultural flux, in many fields ranging from clothing to the latest in intellectual -isms. What is sought here, obviously, is often less a sense of absolute originality than that of belonging to the select, or at least not to a hopelessly outdated minority. And when one no longer shares a fashion only with the right people, it is time to move on. In these times, at least, there is little that is spontaneous about fashions in many fields. They are deliberately engineered in the cultural apparatus, making yesterday's meanings and their manifestations obsolescent (at least until some time in the future, when they can be recycled with new profits).

The competition for advantage through distinctive meaning-making surely does not result in entirely uncontrolled, undirected innovation. New meanings, and new forms for old meanings, have to face the test of markets which tend to be neither wholly predictable nor wholly unpredictable. What is entirely unattractive to everybody is less likely ever to see the light of day. What has a limited market may be too expensive to produce, except perhaps for those who are already doing too well to be bothered. Some innovations will be pushed for a while, then withdrawn, after having failed. Yet the temporary circulations of failures also contribute to cultural flux.

The Critical Spirit: Expanding, Connecting

Cultural innovation, or preparedness for innovation, as it develops out of perspectival clashes is in large part unplanned, accidental. Innovations resulting from a struggle for gain in one marketplace or other are to some extent spontaneous and hardly conscious, in other instances quite deliberate, institutionalized cultural engineering. Contemporary societies, however, also institutionalize original work on meaning in other ways within the division of labor. Insofar as the latter is a division of knowledge, it is not just a matter of an uneven distribution of access to facts. There are also different modes of handling meaning, some of which are more expansionist than others.

The contrast with the prototype small-scale society can again offer some insight. Here, as in other societies, common sense is a prominent mode of cultural management. Yet it does not stand alone. Even here, where the organized division of knowledge is minimal, when people are in a situation where their own common sense does not suffice, they may turn to some individual equipped with that higher form of common sense, wisdom. To repeat (from chapter 1), wisdom is in part a matter of accumulated experience.[6] But it also involves a certain readiness to expand beyond what is known and certain. What wisdom tends not to do, on the other hand, is to keep on pushing beyond what is practical for given ends. It is built up rather haphazardly, and it is applied largely opportunistically. Nor is it usually reproduced systematically.

The more institutionalized, conspicuous complement to common sense in the cultural management of small-scale societies, activated, according to one familiar line of argument, when common sense is somehow incomplete, uncertain, or threatened, has been ritual. It may focus attention on a problem to be dealt with, a critically important task to be accomplished. But again, ritual is normally not culturally expansive. Mostly, it has been seen in the anthropology of small-scale society as a sort of self-regulating mechanism of culture, working in a context of long-term stability. It may contain liminal phases, where social structures and structures of meaning are loosened and a more or less free play with alternatives is allowed. For a moment, there is not only what is but what might be. Even so, in the end established structure returns.

In the complex cultures of the contemporary world, however, there may be no such return; flux remains, even feeds on itself. Not least, a critical spirit which seems almost self-propelling continues to guide and motivate efforts to expand as well connect culture. The cultural management activities we cannot ignore here, that is to say, are those of the people described (by others, but not least by themselves) as "intellectuals" or "intelligentsia."

The premise that these people are by definition culturally expansive requires some scrutiny, since there are wider usages. Edward Shils (1972:3), one of the most prolific writers on the subject of intellectuals, suggests that in every society, "there are some persons with an unusual sensitivity to the sacred, an uncommon reflectiveness about the nature of their universe and the rules which govern their society." These, in his view, are the intellectuals; people who want to be "in frequent communion with symbols which are more general than the immediate concrete situation of everyday life and remote in their reference in both time and space"; people who need to "penetrate beyond the screen of immediate concrete experience."

The emphasis on a management of meaning which goes beyond the obvious, the immediate, and the entirely situational and ephemeral is clear here; this is something other than common sense. But do the people who are sensitive to the sacred and who reflect over the universe and society's rules necessarily think critically about them? Or could they just as well be the custodians of stably defined higher levels of meaning, hidden from other people, or simply of little concern to the latter in the everyday business of life?

The latter kind of specialized cultural managers are known from many societies—literati, priesthoods, elders of the tribe. They are there as soon as an organized division of knowledge begins to appear. They maintain an orderly picture of the cosmos, and much like most ritual, their handling of meaning may help give stability to social life. On the other hand, there is often little in the way of cultural expansionism here. Commenting on the work of French colleagues on the systems of thought of the West African Dogon, Robert Redfield (1962:362) noted that the Dogon learned men—including Ogotemmeli, the sage immortalized by Marcel Griaule (1965)—appeared to view knowledge as substantially fixed, to be progressively revealed to them and their successors as they passed through life. Clearly, they preserved and communicated a form of higher learning. But, Redfield asked, were they intellectuals? One would have liked to know something about their discussions with one another, but he missed "evidence of criticisms of tradition, of important original contributions by individuals, of notable reformulations."

In a stricter sense, Redfield thus seems to have felt, people of learning need not be intellectuals. Apparently, there is some sharing of assumptions here with Alvin Gouldner (1976, 1979), whose formulations concerning "cultures of critical discourse" I draw upon. The cultures of critical discourse are fundamental orientations to the management of meaning which are in some ways in distinct contrast to that of common sense, and which have become major forces of cultural growth and fluidity.[7]

In cultures of critical discourse, Gouldner suggests, everything can be discussed and problematized. The culture is self-monitoring and reflexive, oriented toward pattern and principle. Thus it is capable of moving from statement to autocritique in infinite regress. There is a striving toward expressly legislated, context-free meanings; the latter become cosmopolitan rather than local. (Gouldner cites Basil Bernstein's sociolinguistic contrast between elaborated and restricted codes as a source of inspiration here; the culture of critical discourse employs an elaborated code.[8]) The validity, the authority, of statements within such a culture is based on their conformity with explicit procedures and principles and should be independent of the originator's social position.

Cultures of critical discourse, Gouldner also argues, now come in two major varieties: that of the intelligentsia and that of the intellectuals. The two terms, one Russian and the other French in origin, both out of the nineteenth century, are of course often used interchangeably. They both refer to people somehow preoccupied with ideas—people whose perspectives tend not to rest but to keep working on meanings in themselves and in their less routinized relationships to action and material life. If the terms are to be applied at least as ideal-type labels for two somewhat distinct categories of people, however, this would be based on the fact that they engage with the culture of critical discourse in rather different ways, and perhaps not to the same degree.[9] The intelligentsia, according to Gouldner's usage, are in some way or other technicians. As they push ahead with their cultural work, a domain of knowledge is turned into a discipline, and on the whole they are content to remain within its boundaries. The notion of "normal science," as discussed by Thomas Kuhn in *The Structure of Scientific Revolutions* (1962), provides a key to the understanding of their activities. The intelligentsia concentrate on solving puzzles within a paradigm. They become experts, quite likely credentialed. Certainly they produce new knowledge in this manner but—in a term familiar to anthropologists—there is also a tendency toward involution.

Intellectuals, in contrast, are less bound by paradigms, because none exist in their fields of activity, or because several compete. They stand in opposition to the normalization of cognitive work, and often transgress the boundaries of conventionally defined fields of knowledge. Credentialing intellectuals is more difficult.

There can be learning and abstract, esoteric knowledge without cultures of critical discourse. The tendency toward a relentless continuation of inquiry on the part of intellectuals and intelligentsia in their present forms, however, has no doubt contributed much to the accelerated growth of cultural inventories. Probably the intelligentsia—committed to one line of inquiry and pressing on with it, thus rolling back the frontiers of the unknown—are responsible for a large part of the growth of factual knowledge, the rise of the "knowledge society." The cultural management concerns of the intellectuals, on the other hand, above all involve issues of coherence and incoherence; they often investigate, and fill in, the internal spaces of a culture rather than its frontiers.

It is the business of intellectuals to carry on traffic between different levels and fields of meaning within a culture; to translate between abstract and concrete, to make the implicit explicit and the certain questionable, to move ideas between levels of consciousness, to connect ideas which superficially have little in common, to juxtapose ideas which usually thrive on separateness, to seize on inconsistency, and to establish channels between different modes of giving meanings external shape. (If each single intellectual cannot do all these things, two or three might be enough). Not least are intellectuals concerned with the center-periphery relationships intrinsic to culture itself; that is to say, with the critique of developing and passing facts of life in terms of durable core values.[10] The thinking of the real intellectual (that is, the ideal intellectual) seems not fully domesticated. If the intelligentsia at times lean toward involution, the intellectuals with their disregard for conventional boundaries and constraining structures may indeed be forever liminoid—that relative of the liminal which Victor Turner described as not returning the world to where it was before, but rather going on and on, more likely undermining the prevailing order and sacredness itself.[11]

"Almost self-propelling" was the way I described the critical spirit, or in other words, the cultures of critical discourse, above. How autonomous is this power of cultural expansionism? We may well accept here that it can draw some of its strength from circumstances external to itself, including some of the kinds we mentioned before. Some people may just seem to be born intellectuals, others are spontaneously turned into intellectuals because of particular experiences which provoke them into going further than most others in questioning common sense. Marginality and encounters with contrasting perspectives can foster intellectual leanings just about anywhere, including small-scale societies; Victor Turner's (1960) Ndembu informant Muchona would seem to make a better example of an independent critical mind than Griaule's Ogotemmeli.[12] It is also demonstrably true that competition rears its head here as well. The scientists in Turner's (another Turner) and Mulkay's sketch, weaving opportunely in and out of research fields, convert the growth of knowledge into a profitable curriculum vitae; the critical spirit may thrive in the market. And certainly Gouldner's suggestion that the culture of critical discourse typically is self-monitoring, infinitely moving on to new stages of autocritique, is better understood in theoretically collectivist rather than individualist terms. The single scientist or intellectual may perhaps reach the point where his mind finds a comfortable resting place, but then his peers will descend upon him. The culture of critical discourse is to a degree confrontational. It has its areas of "I know, and I know that you know, and I know that you know that I know," but its cutting edge is rather represented by some other kind of formula, such as "what you think, I should try to disprove," or "what you are satisfied to know, I will go beyond." As Robin Horton notes, "rival theory rather than practically significant experience provides the ultimate challenge to any given body of theory and the ultimate source of anxiety for the theorist" (1982:247).[13]

The fact of overriding importance, however, is that the spirit of inquiry has been institutionalized as a part of the management of complex cultures. No longer do knowledge and theoretical formulations come about mostly as unanticipated outcomes of practical experiences. As Horton also points out, there has been a reversal of process in that configurations of experience are instead selected and devised in order to serve the growth of meaning (1982:246). The continuous development and scrutiny of meaning has become more or less a goal in itself. Intellectuals and intelligentsia are integrated into the division of labor and into the political economy of culture (and this is so, even if—on the one hand—the discipline orientation of the intelligentsia is rather readily accommodated within the division of labor, while—on the other hand—the job of the true intellectual would seem to be to ignore it). They are remunerated for thinking and for making known what they think, and they may have been intentionally trained for it. Through that dominant pattern of organization, these modes of cultural expansionism have become something quite different from the chance buildup of personal wisdom, or the idiosyncratic musings of a spontaneous intellectual surrounded by common sense thinkers. And if at times the goal of cultural growth is one in terms of which market competition can take place, there are some forms of life which revolve around it, where expansionist thought is part of the routine, and it is also deemed important enough for states to make sure that it is covered by their redistributive economies.

The Distribution of Intellectuals and Intelligentsia

The application of various modes of managing meaning varies both with situations and with people; this we must not forget. Intellectuals may not have to theorize about parking their bicycles; most of them can use their common sense to do it. Similarly, members of the intelligentsia do not always operate as powerful but one-track minds. Common sense as portrayed above may not seem particularly appealing, yet undoubtedly each one of us has common sense notions which we can satisfactorily rely on in most of our settings of everyday life. We can in fact hardly do without them. Conversely, to repeat, situations occur where people who are neither intellectuals nor intelligentsia, by trade or inclination, are forced out of their commonsense assumptions, and may feel the oncoming strain to shift gear and continue inquiry.

On the other hand, intellectuals and intelligentsia are recognizable as categories of people. To the extent that the respective manners of processing meaning involve native predilections or more or less chance responses to personal experience, these people may be rather randomly distributed over the social structure. As distinctive occupational varieties of cultural management, however, intellectuals as well as intelligentsia have their characteristic distributions, and some further comments on this topic may be useful. The habit is quite widespread, in thought and writing on this question, to link intellectuals with the humanities, and the intelligentsia with technology and natural science. In this manner, the culture of critical discourse seems to turn into what C. P. Snow at one time described as "the two cultures" (1964).

No doubt there is some tendency for intelligentsia and intellectuals to distribute themselves in this manner. The discipline orientation, the stricter and conventionalized criteria of relevance, the presence of accepted paradigms, make science and technology a likely ideational habitat for the intelligentsia. And the concern with values in the humanities, as well as their less paradigm-laden character, would more closely match the mode of meaning management of the intellectuals.

Yet things are hardly quite this simple. It is indeed possible for some to operate in the natural sciences rather more in the manner of an intellectual, and in the humanities, there is no dearth of people functioning more like an intelligentsia, moving on and on with the production of new knowledge, or other new meaning, within a limited field of specialization. This is equally true of the social sciences.

Of course, neither intelligentsia nor intellectuals necessarily make their home in academia. Within the cultural apparatus, there are diverse loci for the expansive modes of cultural management, in the arts, in the media, in education. It is from these bases they reach out most consistently, through the relationships of the few to the many, to meddle directly with the multitudinous forms of common sense and their leanings toward steady states. Among the scientists and technicians of the intelligentsia, many are engaged in developing new knowledge which tends not to be disseminated as such but which affects greater numbers of people more indirectly, by altering their material environment. In human affairs, one would probably expect to find the intelligentsia as managers and administrators, in fields where an expansive style is useful in handling ideas (and where there is constant movement between decontextualizing and recontextualizing), and in the professions. The British have had the reputation of preferring generalists, people with a broad education in the liberal arts, for higher decision-making and administrative positions, rather than people with a narrowly specialized training: a leaning, it would seem, toward intellectuals rather than intelligentsia.

It is true, obviously, that the involvement with critical discourse in some of these areas is a matter of degree. Likewise, it should be clear that everybody whose occupation it is to handle information of some sort is not necessarily for that reason either an intellectual or a member of the intelligentsia. Even when such activity involves handling large quantities of data, it can be quite routinized, nowadays aided by information technologies which greatly limit the need for individual mental effort. To handle knowledge correctly and effectively, one may only have to know which file to look in, what buttons to push. "Knowledge worker" is one designation which conveys the relatively uncomplicated nature (and modest prestige) of such participants in the contemporary division of labor.

Lastly, we should remember that intellectuals and intelligentsia are not only involved in cultural process as producers of meaning. They can also be at the receiving end. It is reasonable enough to expect that in each domain of meaning, laymen are more given to common sense than are the intelligentsia or intellectuals whose area of expertise it is. Those who are laymen in one field may function as intelligentsia or intellectuals in others, however, and they may well allow their general familiarity with a culture of critical discourse to filter, unpredictably and imprecisely perhaps, into their practice of laymanship as well.

Intelligentsia, Intellectuals, and Ideologies

Much of the sociology of knowledge has been preoccupied with intellectuals, intelligentsia, and their relationships to ideologies. I will be brief on the point, only to locate it within the present overall view of cultural complexity.

If the two main tendencies in the cultures of critical discourse are distinguished as they are here, it would seem that the intelligentsia as such is not necessarily too problematic in its ideological dimension. Its representatives in various occupations are mostly involved with some particular rather narrowly defined objective, just as people in most occupations are. While it differs in entailing a more expansionist handling of meaning within its niche, the intelligentsia need be neither more nor less ideologically inclined than anybody else, in the sense of desiring to permeate society as a whole with its favorite ideas, and thereby to reorganize it according to its interests. Also, as the members of the intelligentsia have reasonably clearly identifiable places in the social structure, the anchoring of their various perspectives, and with them such ideological leanings as they may have, is about as obvious as such matters get.

With intellectuals things get more complicated. The truly liminoid intellectual seems to have no privileged perspective of his own. He is, Ralf Dahrendorf has argued, like a court jester, outside as well as inside the social order, not committed to it and therefore able to speak uncomfortable truths without fear (1970: 54–55). And like that medieval predecessor, he would have "the duty to doubt everything that is obvious, to make relative all authority, to ask all those questions that no one else dares to ask."

Or is the perspective of the intellectual, in a slight variation of the same basic notion, composed of all perspectives in society, as they reflect one another—the encounter of common senses described above, only made systematic and all-embracing? This is largely Mannheim's well-known, and much debated, position in *Ideology and Utopia* (1936:156). "Free-floating intellectuals" (the term is actually Alfred Weber's, brother of Max) are created through an education that replicates "the conflicting purposes and tendencies which rage in society at large."[14]

Mannheim's view, of course, is often held unrealistic. The opposite view is that associated especially with Gramsci: intellectuals like other people are rooted in particular locations in the social structure, for there is no way not to be. And any such location can be used as the base for that work on meaning which consists of the refinement in more general, abstract terms of the typical everyday practices and durable interests associated with it (1971:5 ff.).[15] Some people are intellectuals in these terms without being employed as such; *Homo faber,* Gramsci affirmed, cannot be separated from *Homo sapiens.* Whether longshoremen, farmers, or business executives, they become the "organic intellectuals" of their group, their class, or for that matter, their gender. Others also are intellectuals by occupation, and manage meaning from the positions they thereby come to hold in society, whether reasonably autonomous or fairly directly beholden to somebody else. If intellectuals are concerned not least with the center-periphery relationships of structures of meaning, the core values in terms of which other ideas, experiences, and practices are scrutinized are in each of these instances those which are congruent with their positions. Consequently—and especially when it turns into an engagement with a society or a culture, more or less as a whole—their work on meaning tends to be ideological.

Of the two points of view, Mannheim's (and Dahrendorf's) is most in line with the notion of the intellectual as forever autocritical—whatever perspective he holds is that of which, in his infinite disloyalty, he takes an opposing view next. Yet here again we probably do better by not assuming that the individual intellectual is self-sufficient in his endeavors. If particular individuals, and circles of individuals, have some degree of commitment to particular perspectives, it is the community they all form together that keeps the critical inquiry from grinding to a premature halt. (Along the lines made familiar by Simmel, it is a community held together by conflict.) In any case, the two points of view may represent two sides of one reality. Konrad and Szelenyi (1979) have attempted to synthesize them, identifying a tension between the generic and the genetic being of intellectuals. (Actually a tension closely related to that between social structure and cultural flow, noted here in chapter 3.) Generically, intellectuals transcend particular conditions. Genetically, they cannot exist apart from them.

One aspect of this kind of understanding of intellectuals, accepting that they have at least their specific points of departure in the social structure, from which some may get further than others in their cultural work, is that it can contribute to an understanding of the relationship between intelligentsia and intellectuals. For if all groups in a society can have their own organic intellectuals, so can its various intelligentsias. To this fact we will soon return, but not until after we have taken note of some of the ways the media relate to cultural expansionism.

The Media in Time: Storage, Scrutiny, and Cultural Growth

To the extent that the media operate within the market framework for the flow of meaning, we tend to see them mostly as helping accelerate the passage of all sorts of cultural manifestations into history, by packaging them as news. Much news, of course, is basically more of the same, variations on a limited number of set themes. There has also been a continuous trend, however, to turn forever wider domains of meaning into news genres, and thereby to commoditize them. Food recipes become news. Some individuals are turned into celebrities, and their day-to-day comportment becomes news. And in recent times, everyday life in Western societies has been made into the "life style" news of careers, gender, household organization, child rearing, and the latest word in popular psychology. If media have a persuasive power, such news may well do more than only reflect changes. It may speed them up, it may again make people more acutely aware of what might otherwise be mere common sense. And it may delegitimize the old as it legitimizes the new.

The combination of new machineries of meaning with the market can affect the practices of intellectuals as well. In his "mediological" treatise *Teachers, Writers, Celebrities,* Régis Debray (1981:86), has lamented the decadence of French intellectual life which in his view has come with the dominance of television and the attraction of electronic stardom—"those who laboriously chiselled away at meaning, who worked with ciphers and secrets, are giving way to the lay-out artists, the curators of archives to the manufacturers of surprises."[16]

But then even as media, when set into one particular organizational framework, may be used to produce cultural obsolescence, they also, perhaps more fundamentally, give humankind greater opportunities for cultural storage, and cultural critique.

Memory is the time dimension of culture. Naturally, the general shape of life as it is lived not least in small-scale, nonmedia societies makes sure that much meaning is effortlessly kept alive at least in microtime, through redundancy. Knowledge and beliefs are inscribed into the environment, and personified by individuals. To a degree, there are mnemonic devices everywhere.[17] But as time passes, and there is a shift of personnel at least over generations, and as conditions may change, "living memory" becomes less sure of itself. When societies march toward the future, the rear end of detailed history also moves, unless records are made. That past of the nonmedia, or protomedia, society which is distinct from the present can in large part be remembered only through the spoken word. Here, therefore, particular feats have to be performed with the latter. Craft mnemonists—minstrels, genealogists—may be in charge of history, and a genre like oral poetry is, among other things, also a mnemonic technique.[18] Nevertheless, it is difficult to maintain precision history this way, without specific storage technology. Ray Bradbury's *Fahrenheit 451,* both a novel and a film, is a fantasy of what craft mnemonists would be like today or tomorrow, in the wake of a large-scale destruction of writing: mumbling intellectuals, repeating for themselves the texts of Swift, Plato, Darwin, and Schopenhauer which the authorities have outlawed.

In fact, media societies have little use for the deliberate mental practice of mnemonics, for media help give culture another kind of staying power. Even if it is true that each generation to some degree rethinks history through perspectivation, media (to the extent that they involve recording, which of course not all of them do) allow the process by which the past changes to become to a greater extent cumulative, rather than substitutive or assimilative.[19] In macrotime, an awareness can be fostered of many pasts, arranged into periods, and of cohorts of predecessors, rather than one past, within itself almost timeless.[20] And the members of media societies can normally entrust desirable knowledge, or any desirable cultural form, to encyclopedias, cookbooks, desk calendars, instruction manuals, computer software, tapes, or video cassettes, in a confident expectation that they can find it there, whether they want it tomorrow or in ten years. Thus, increases in the complexity of meaning systems—complexity in the first of the dimensions identified here, in chapter 1—become much less constrained. The accelerating growth of human knowledge would clearly be impossible without such storage.

In the end, there may be an embarrassment of riches. Once upon a time, the past was scarce. Not much of it survived. Now we can know not only the great events of history in great detail. Increasingly, it is at least technically possible for us to immerse ourselves in the trivia of earlier periods as well. The cultural heritage becomes a problem of disposal, of selecting a past, perhaps planning a past for the future, as a matter of cultural policy (perhaps especially in the state framework, but not only there). Should everything be stored? Or how should the past be systematically sampled? Should one select the typical, or the best?

And indeed, something can happen to the the criteria of quality in themselves. Media recordings do not only allow manifestations of meaning to be produced at one time, and then stored more or less forever—they also allow more sophisticated patterns of consumption. Consider again the point made in chapter 3 about literacy: a spoken word is an event, a written word a thing. The latter remains, while the utterance disappears immediately. It is through the ability to conserve the products of the elaborateness and flexibility of the linguistic mode that the greater possibilities for scrutiny, reflection, and new syntheses are realized. For such reasons literacy has long been central to the management of meaning among intellectuals and intelligentsia. In Gouldner's view, it is characteristic of the culture of critical discourse that its meanings are explicit, decontextualized, stated in an elaborated code. Language obviously has the potential of meeting these requirements better than most other symbolic modes; written language does so especially. It seems typical that

Charles Kadushin, in his study of American intellectual life, found the latter revolving more around journals than anything else. Out of a list of 42 major journals, the most influential intellectuals claimed to read 16.5 each on a regular basis (Kadushin 1974:40–42).[21]

Dominant as literacy may have been, and may still be, in our conception of a critical stance toward meaning, however, the possibilities of other symbol systems should not be disregarded in this connection; and the continued development of media makes this point even more significant. Shils, in the statement cited earlier, goes on to suggest that intellectuals can express their special quest for meaning in many ways—oral or written discourse, poetry, plastic form, or ritual, to mention a few. True, his and Gouldner's pictures of the typical intellectual differ in some ways; but even if we lean toward the latter's point of view, we can see that it should be possible to be both intellectual or intelligentsia in the terms of other kinds of symbol systems as well, insofar as these have some potential for the development of meaning systems through critical reflection. And this is also to say that in terms of contrasting cultural management modes, it is quite possible that some painters, say, may lean more toward the intelligentsia than toward the intellectuals. Rather than pursuing the wide-rangingly liminoid, they develop an area of expertise; genres are their disciplines, and they investigate the frontiers of their symbolic mode.[22]

"Painting is a kind of research," said one of the artists interviewed by Deborah Ericson in her ethnography of the Stockholm art world (1988:101); and the spirit of inquiry as a collective commitment seems to be captured in Bruce Lippincott's depiction of the jazz musicians' jam session:

> One of the greatest joys of jazz is this camaraderie, when everyone is attentive, economical, in good spirits; then the ensemble melody is played with no brazenness; the solos are related to the mood of the entire piece; each new soloist takes, without premeditation, the final phrase of the former soloist and tries to develop the ideas of it, then hands it on to the next man. When the piece is finished, each man feels glad he was part of the whole. (1958; quoted by Merriam and Mack, 1960:220)

Moreover, by allowing a greater variety of symbolic products a greater durability, more media can become technologies of the intellect. The possibility of preserving particular feats of human creativity can allow a masterful musical performance or a brilliant film director's work to set enduring standards of excellence for the management of meaning. Elite sports, from football to boxing, have similarly come to depend on the careful analysis of recorded past performances.

Critical Discourse/Common Sense Interrelations: Spin-Offs and Movements

Summarizing things so far, then, complex cultures include a multitude of more or less contrasting versions of common sense, which in themselves lean toward stability but which may be upset as conditions of life change or as these versions come upon one another; there is some strain toward innovation as situations of competition entail a demand for distinctive products and markers; through cultures of critical discourse, an expansionist management of meaning has been institutionalized; and the media tend to contribute to both flux and cumulative growth.

This is a very schematic way of looking at matters, but it already brings to notice how diverse are the methods by which complex cultures keep in motion. There are great variations in the quantity and durability of the contributions various modes of managing meaning make to the total cultural flow through society. In much of everyday life, meanings are embodied intentionally or unintentionally by a constant stream of acts which in their general types are repeated again and again, without any one of these acts carrying much greater weight in cultural process than any other. They are quickly absorbed into the collective mass as largely anonymous contributions, and become influential only aggregated in that mass, through such redundancy as they build up when people all do their part, in view of one another.

In the market, such as in the case of popular culture, the number of particular cultural productions (of hit tunes, say, or television comedies) is much smaller, but because these tend to have unrivaled access to the asymmetries of the cultural apparatus, each one of them reaches out a great deal more widely. Yet these productions are also rather ephemeral. Mostly here today and gone tomorrow, they may be remembered again largely in terms of the themes and categories they exemplify, rather than in their own specificities.

Then there are the works of greater individual distinctiveness in their handling of meaning and form, often the work of intelligentsia or intellectuals; often what we think of as capital-C culture. There may be a considerable quantity of works here, but most of them do not become widely known. Some are forgotten, dead ends; some are stepping stones for others. But there is a selection process going on among them, by which some get marked as more meritorious than others. And these few, understood as unique items, may become prominent in the cultural flow as as a whole, not least over time, as they more than any other individual productions are kept in circulation—permanently exhibited, reproduced, taught about.

But then again, all these ways of managing culture do not go on side by side, separately from one another. They intermesh, again in more ways than one. To take the view of cultural complexity as one sprawling interconnectedness, we must attend to this as well.

In their book *Knowledge Application,* Holzner and Marx (1979:23–25) note that other societies in history have had their communities of specialists in esoteric knowledge; alchemy, acupuncture, astrology, or whatever. But, usually, these domains of knowledge have been rather insulated, and ordinary people have gone about their lives without being much affected by them. What is peculiar, probably unique, about contemporary cultures is the way science casts its shadow over all other domains of meaning, and styles in the handling of meaning—not least common sense.

We have touched on this before: complex cultures, for all those involved with them, include areas of organized incompetence, maps (uncertain and fallacious perhaps) of other people's knowledge, notions of what in principle can be known. As one stands there with one's variety of common sense, one is aware that the many specialties in a more expansive handling of meaning are nearby, as potential guides, perhaps, but often as adversaries or judges.

One of the ways in which specialist knowledge can come to influence the commonsense understandings of laymen, and for that matter the structures of meaning of other specialists or of intellectuals covering wider fields, we may think of as spin-offs of cultures of critical discourse. Clusters of meaning and expression may diffuse from one to the other without being originally intended, presumably, for such a general distribution, and without much in the way of an all-embracing purposive organization to bring about that spread.

In two books, Sherry Turkle (1978, 1984) has described such spin-offs. The first study is of the impact of psychoanalytical ideas on general culture, especially in France during the 1960s and 1970s. French society long resisted Freud; in conspicuous contrast, it has seemed, to American society, which rushed to embrace him. Yet Freud himself was suspicious of that latter welcome. To reiterate, in the economics of culture, the recipient of new meanings may be more generous than the donor, if those new meanings crowd out old established ones, or ideas which might actually be of better use. And to Freud, the American reception seemed superficial in its generosity—"psychoanalysis was so deeply subversive of common-sense ways of thinking about the world that to understand it was to resist it" (Turkle 1978:5).

What happened in the United States, it seems, was that psychoanalysis by and large became merely another discipline within the developing division of labor; the circumscribed domain of knowledge of another medical intelligentsia. It can hardly be denied that psychoanalytical notions, and not least bits and pieces of a psychoanalytical jargon—the superego, the Freudian slip—have entered at least at the fringes of commonsense meanings in America. But this, Turkle suggests, is little compared to what happened in France when resistance there finally broke down. The wave of psychoanalytical ideas reached linguistics, poetry, economics, philosophy, and mathematics. It continued into child rearing as well as into politics. Perhaps there were soon as many tendencies in French psychoanalytical thought as there were varieties of cheese, but it was a field of ideas cultivated as much by intellectuals as by any specialized intelligentsia. And they both played their part in spreading these ideas yet more widely.

Psychoanalysis has had an impact on the way humanity (in the Occident, in any case) views itself, at least in large segments of it, and apparently in different ways in different places. The same has been no less conspicuously true in more recent years of the concepts of the computer intelligentsia. The computer seems "good to think with" even as we do our own thinking about our own thinking. Turkle's other book, *The Second Self* (1984), deals with various facets of this cultural development, ranging from debates within the computer intelligentsia—and, one should add, among its intellectuals—to its growing spin-off effects among American adults, youth, and children. "The computer stands betwixt and between," Turkle (1984:24) notes in a reference to Victor Turner's writings. As the clown and the madman are at the edge of the social order, so is the computer at the edge of mind, directly or indirectly, for growing numbers of people.

There are spin-off success stories, then; the products of the expansionist modes of cultural management can at times penetrate more widely shared structures of meaning. Yet it cannot be safely assumed that merely because laymen have some idea of what intelligentsia or intellectuals have been up to they necessarily have an accurate understanding of it—not even a thinned-out but essentially matching understanding, an "I know that you know" useful in organizing access to the cultural inventory. Psychoanalysts and members of the computer intelligentsia must sometimes conclude that lay people know less than they think they do about the fields in question. Here as elsewhere, when perspectives develop toward other perspectives, new misunderstandings are also generated: an in-between, shadowy cultural territory—the property claims to which everybody assigns to someone else.

As a form for cultural change, movements differ from spin-offs for one thing in their higher degree of organization and self-consciousness. They are a matter of people coming together to construct new shared understandings on the basis of shared circumstances. Old commonsense notions may have become unsatisfactory as material conditions change, and so one may need to blow the whistle on the changes, as in the case of the environmentalist movement. Or, as in the instance of at least the first phase of the contemporary women's movement, new sets of relationships have to be created where old, but not very elaborated and systematized understandings, opposed to established (and in this case male-oriented) common sense, have a chance to be interactively worked out in a more complete, coherent, intellectual and symbolic form. Instead of talking to people with other perspectives, one speaks at least for some time with one's own kind; "consciousness raising" liberates the hostages of what it suits other people to take for granted.[23]

In a way, cultural process in movements may resemble what we have seen as typical of subcultures; relying mostly on a symmetry of baselines as well as of input mode and quantity, to refer back again to the dimensions outlined in chapter 2. Movements are not just like any subcultures, however. While the latter quite commonly include an awareness of differences at their boundaries, movement thought is more than usually contrastive: we used to think/we now think, we think/they think. From the point of view of movements there are still people out there waiting to be persuaded or recruited, potential converts as well as adversaries. Thus, the movement management of meaning is two-sided, aimed at both insiders and outsiders, usually in somewhat different ways. All this has a part in the way movements contribute to cultural flux.

But movements often differ from many ordinary subcultures in yet another way. True, they may be made up to a great extent of "ordinary people," giving their own and each other's perspectives a collective working over, concerned with matters which have been in a common sense domain before and which will perhaps return there later. Often, however, movements are more accurately described as an organizational form by which a flow of meaning is established between a culture of critical discourse and a destabilized common sense. In this manner, they have at least something in common with the spin-offs. The changes in the structures of meaning of laymen are not altogether autonomous but are further energized, as it were, through close connections with some smaller number of people engaged more systematically in a culture of critical discourse. Movements, that is, have gurus.

These people who are in the forefront in the activity of scrutinizing established ideas and dismantling them may have found their place there by different routes. They may be "organic intellectuals" in Gramsci's sense, starting out from the same perspective as other laymen but just pushing further by their own inclination. Perhaps some are critical intellectuals at large. Or they may be in their particular positions due to the division of labor, as concerned intelligentsia with special expertise in a relevant discipline, perhaps transforming themselves into intellectuals by placing their knowledge in a wider framework of values.[24]

It is also conspicuously true, especially in societies with a generally high educational level, that a notable part of the most engaged audience of movement gurus, and a large proportion of the movement activists, are often laymen of that particular kind: people who have more than a passing acquaintance with cultures of critical discourse generally, people who are themselves intellectuals or of the intelligentsia, prepared metaculturally to take a critical view of common sense even when the area of knowledge in question is not one where they have an expertise of their own. If they are not themselves in this instance pioneers at the cultural frontier, then they are at least skilled consumers. As such, too, they can be a mediating category between specialists and laymen of a more genuinely commonsense persuasion.

Intelligentsia Takeover Bids, Populist Responses

In movements such as just described, laymen largely accept guru guidance. Contemporary cultures, however, also exemplify more confrontative relationships between laymen and expansive expertise.

Ivan Illich has noted that when he learned to speak, "*problems* existed only in mathematics or chess; *solutions* were saline or legal, and *need* was mainly used as a verb" (1977:22). Changes in the meaning, and frequency of use, of such terms have become "the fodder on which professions were fattened into dominance." That blend between power and service in the interactions between experts and clients in the division of knowledge which we noted in chapter 4 is no longer what it used to be; this is what Illich suggests.

Some kinds of intelligentsias, it appears, have had a way of expanding their domains, and attempting, at least, to make compliance with their expertise more often compulsory. Illich labels them "the disabling professions" (1977). In a similar vein, Christopher Lasch has critically described the family as nowadays besieged by helpers—social workers, doctors, and teachers (1977). This is also part of the knowledge society.

It may be in the nature of things in complex cultures that there are two contradictory tendencies: on the one hand, an intensification of the division of knowledge which creates new specializations, and thus new or larger niches in the material economy, and on the other hand a desire on the part of laymen to have sizable domains of general knowledge, to a great extent of a free-flow, commonsense type, where people can rely on their own cognitive resources instead of paying for the skills of others, and where they can maintain personal autonomy and enhance self-worth. The former of these two tendencies, in that case, may itself be strengthened by expansive modes of cultural management, especially by the paradigm commitments of intelligentsias.

Illich, as well as others commenting on this kind of development, and especially the push to make expertise binding, adopt Howard Becker's notion of the "moral entrepreneur" (1963:147 ff.). What Becker especially emphasizes is that "rules are the products of someone's initiative"—they do not materialize from thin air. But that basic insight into cultural management should in this case be complemented by another: the entrepreneurship is not only moral but also cognitive. A perspective toward knowledge cultivated in one area is made to expand innovatively into others as well, and unique powers are claimed for it and its mode of problematization. From their specialized experiences and concerns, experts may derive a root metaphor through which they can elaborate their conceptualization of other large areas of experience, and render them understandable and familiar. At least some members of a given intelligentsia, that is, have become its organic intellectuals, and they have turned their disciplinary perspective into an ideology for hegemony. Nonetheless, they remain committed to the division of knowledge, as the source of their authority.

The most conspicuous example of such expansiveness seems to have been "the medicalization of society," with illness as its root metaphor. Zola (1977:62) has noted that American newspapers can offer comments by physicians or psychiatrists on divorce, intermarriage, ethnic conflict, school failure, feminism, antimilitarism, nonvoters, disrespectful children, or any number of other issues that happen to be current. But other professional categories, from clergy to economists, can be similarly inclined to shape the world in the image of their concerns.

There is something paradoxical in the authority of specialists here, to the extent that they achieve their authority on the basis of their mastery of a form of critical discourse; for the culture of critical discourse is not supposed to recognize authority. But the point is that the culture of critical discourse is most fully displayed *within* the community whose members show a similar competence. In the expert-client interaction that competence tends to be encapsulated as an achieved fact, a halo, instead of coming under direct challenge.[25]

Intelligentsia takeover bids, anyhow, need not be quietly accepted; critiques such as those of Illich, Lasch, and Zola reflect the recent countertendency. The resistance may originate simply in intelligentsias with competing agendas (probably the most accurate summary description of the strongly anti-expertise 1960s cultural revolution in China). It may also unite, if only in opposition, intellectuals of more free-floating varieties—like Illich and Lasch—and the advocates of common sense views. Anti-expertise, anti-intelligentsia streaks are present in both modes of meaning management. In common sense, there is the will to see the world as familiar and accessible; and consequently the resistance to, or even contempt for, esoteric knowledge and decontextualized theory.[26] In its own groping way, common sense can be somewhat expansive; and, under the conditions of contemporary cultural complexity, there may be some readiness to accept the intelligentsia as its avant-garde. But when expertise encroaches on its domains, claiming special privileges in understanding matters which common sense has previously taken care of on its own, with satisfactory results, then the fighting form of common sense is populism; *doxa* turns into orthodoxy.[27] Experts can be denied power, because their knowledge is denied as well. If their institutional dominance is too well established, it may at least be resisted through the guerrilla warfare of ridicule and sabotage.

As far as conflict between intellectuals and intelligentsia is concerned, there is something here again of the old contrast between hedgehogs and foxes (cf. Berlin 1978). Intellectuals are foxes, they know lots of things. Generically at least, they transcend particular perspectives. Intelligentsias are more like hedgehogs. While they begin knowing some little thing in a corner very well, they proceed to assimilate so much to it that it ends up being a very big thing, almost everything. This is an alarming development to foxes, who may be worried that they will be left with very little to themselves, and who in any case may feel that the hedgehog does not know everything there is to know, and certainly not from every point of view, about the big thing it claims to master.

The critiques of expertise on the part of common sense and intellectuals may share a dislike for the conventional boundaries of knowledge domains drawn by the intelligentsia. Intellectuals may have their doubts about these boundaries as a matter of conscious principle, as they concern themselves with interconnections and wholes. Common sense, with its ad hoc approach to things, may not be too bothered by problems of integrating knowledge for their own sake, but in dealing with what is at hand it may find that the division of knowledge is a nuisance.

Apart from this rather uncertain unity of opposition, however, the adversary relationships of intellectuals and common sense to expansive expertise may be largely independent of one another, having different bases. It is true that intellectual critiques of expertise now and then make explicit reference to the worth of the common sense point of view, another instance of a recurrent attraction of some intellectualism to populism. But the reciprocation of this sentiment is uncertain. The common sense stance is of course in many ways, at least by implication, just as critical of the intellectual mode of managing meaning as it is of that of the intelligentsia. And while the preoccupation of the intelligentsia with solving problems may have its appeal to common sense, the imaginative leaps of intellectuals may leave it behind, devoid of sympathy.

The Division of Labor and Subculture Segmentation

The dividing line between a largely common-sense–based general knowledge and the variety of specializations in a complex culture is a frontier that shifts back and forth. Now, you have a new kind of expertise casting doubt on established popular practices and competences. Next, there is a new "do it yourself" wave, to save you money and make you feel good about yourself.

Yet, as the division of knowledge moves on, there is also another tendency in the social organization of cultural process.

The historian Robert Darnton (1975), reminiscing about his brief experiences as a *New York Times* reporter, suggests that the journalists in the newsroom really had one solution to the everlasting problem of whom to write for: they wrote for one another. There, in "the snake pit," they found readers who would devour their stories, and who would go on, if they had done poorly, to devour them as well. Conversely, it was their peers who would show the most acute appreciation for an assignment handled cleverly.

In his well-known study of the occupational life of American dance musicians around midcentury, Howard Becker has portrayed a related situation (1963:79 ff.).[28] The musicians played popular music for money, in bars and taverns, ballrooms and night clubs, country clubs and hotels, for what they considered audiences of squares. There was not much in the way of shared tastes between the audiences and the musicians. When the former requested polkas, the latter longed for opportunities to play jazz, the only music which gave them intrinsic pleasure. Among themselves, the musicians showed hostility and contempt for the squares on whom they depended for their livelihoods. Much of their life styles—dress, language and all—expressed their desire to set themselves apart. They saw themselves, in Becker's phrasing, as people possessing a "mysterious artistic gift," and for that reason they should be free from control by outsiders who lacked it. They might subject themselves to playing the polkas and the rumbas because they were constrained by the rules of the marketplace, but their own central institution was the jam session. After the dance was over, the squares had gone home, and the establishment was closed, they could stay behind to play according to their own aesthetic standards. (And, as suggested above, the resulting jam session could be seen as an inquiry into the possibilities of music.)

What the ethnographies of both journalists and jazzmen point to is a dialectic of division of labor and subculture segmentation which is widespread in complex cultures. This is based on the duality of cultural process resulting from the division of labor, as already mentioned in chapter 2. The individual may be materially rewarded for specific prestations based on his specialized skills, but at the same time he develops a more general perspective grounded in his overall experience in practicing these skills and in his reflections on them. And if he is communicatively in touch with others engaged in the same specialization, they can together develop and maintain a subculture.

With such subcultural evolution, there is a tendency for the practitioners of a specialization to turn inward toward one another in their attentions. The peculiar, perspectival experiences, beliefs, and values of the specialists find the most authentic appreciation only within their own circles. It is, therefore, tempting to give the public only as much as is necessary to safeguard the flow of material resources, and otherwise to turn inward toward subcultural process, where the symbolic rewards are richer. Thus we get the ivory tower of academics, the art which only artists (or highly trained critics) can quite make sense of, the values and concomitant esteem rankings of the pressroom, the joys of the jam session, and perhaps not unrelatedly, some of the undergrowth of political and administrative life. Whereas intelligentsia takeover bids crash into common sense, the evolving subcultures of cultural expansionism drift away from it.

The division of labor/subculture segmentation dialectic is at hand widely in contemporary cultures. Whenever the interest turns to matters of method or procedure, to socialization and career patterns in the specialization, to its history or its existential problems, the community of specialists is likely to be more engaged than members of the public, who ask only for the immediately useful products of a trained skill. But the dialectic has a particular inherent force, probably, where specializations involve the more expansionist modes of cultural management. Here, as specialists continue to press ahead with the exploration of fields of meaning and with the experimentation with the properties of symbol systems, they are likely to leave the general public further and further behind. What is practical is less important than what serves a given line of thought; and the work turns inward to the specialist community not least because it is often organized as a competition between rivals, whether individuals or schools.

While science may show this pattern most clearly, Susan Sontag's comments, in *Against Interpretation* (1967:295–296), on the accessibility of 1960s art are also to the point. Increasingly the terrain of specialists rather than open to the generally educated, the arts in recent times have demanded "an education of sensibility whose difficulties and length of apprenticeship are at least comparable to the difficulties of mastering physics or engineering." And, Sontag points out, the art she has in mind is cumulative, with works full of historical references to preceding works, sometimes as much acts of criticism as of creation.

The philosopher Alfred North Whitehead once remarked that "it is a profoundly erroneous truism . . . that we should cultivate the habit of thinking of what we are doing. The precise opposite is the case. Civilization advances by extending the number of operations which we can perform without thinking about them" (Quoted by Medawar 1984:195).[29] When more understandings can sink into common sense, active and deliberate cultural management can proceed toward new goals. The expansionist management of meaning depends on this. The various specializations can thus keep raising the levels of their own common sense, far beyond what constitutes common sense among nonspecialists. And of course, in the communities of expansionist specializations, remaining at their respective commonsense levels earns no accolades. This is often what underlies the ambivalent or hostile attitude toward those who carry their subcultural meanings to nonspecialists: a less praiseworthy cognitive entrepreneurship appears to be involved, picking up knowledge where—as mere common sense—it is cheap or even free, and peddling it where it is expensive, accepted as scarce and original insight.

The specialists in expansionist cultural management, finding that their objectives are best served by relationships encapsulated within their own subculture, have to face one problem—how to support themselves while mainly taking in one another's laundry. They must be a part of the material economy in some way. Making their products available to the general public through market exchange often seems less suitable or attractive, since it may be difficult to sell them piece by piece, to particular customers at particular times. The market solution may be somewhat more feasible in societies where intellectuals and intelligentsias of various sorts together make up a sizable population, with some cognitive preparedness for appreciating one another's output. In many contemporary societies, however, there is hardly an internal quality-conscious market of this kind, and even where it may be expected to exist, the producers of cultural goods may be in for some disappointment.[30]

A longer-term patronage, functioning through a centralized redistributive mechanism, may be the main alternative where markets do not suffice. But from the point of view of the specialists, the solution becomes very imperfect if the control over material resources thereby comes to rest in an institution dominated by more narrowly commonsense views, or even explicitly populist values, or other set doctrine. And their interests are best served, they may feel, if control is delegated at the earliest possible point to people of their own kind, to shape their own segment of the redistributive structure as they see fit, or to make their own internal market arrangements. The "peer review" is seen as the superior instrument of enlightened decisions, and the specialist community strives to incorporate itself in the structure of society in the form of a guild.[31]

In Western societies especially, communities of professional expertise have indeed often achieved considerable autonomy along such lines, partly because of the difficulty of assessing the competence of their members from the outside, partly on the expectation that cultures of critical discourse should provide built-in self-monitoring. But it is in this area of the organization of reward structures for intellectuals and intelligentsia that many of the more heated issues in the political economy of contemporary complex cultures arise—"the control of science," "government support for the arts," "the sponsorship of culture."[32] And as different groups find fault with different organizational forms and their cultural consequences, and as power alignments change in societies, the organization of cultural management becomes fluid here as well.

Connecting the Disconnected

Anthropologists who think of cultures as meaning systems have tended to view cultural integration as a matter of logic and style. Edward Sapir exemplified such thinking particularly clearly in his contrast between genuine and spurious cultures, from which one of the beginning quotations of this chapter is drawn. It is, Clifford Geertz proposed some decades ago, "the sort of integration one finds in a Bach fugue, in Catholic dogma, or in the general theory of relativity" (1957:34). One grasps it through contemplation, it would seem, and the elements which thus come together in unity exist apart from social life, apart from the messy complications of differences between people. Such coherence has been sought, and sometimes found, by anthropologists and other observers in complex cultures as well. Not only among the Zuñi, the Dobu, and the Kwakiutl but also among the Russians, the French, the Americans, the English, the Italians, the Japanese, the Mexicans, and the Swedes has that unity of character been detected, of one description or other. Yet, every time, voices are soon raised in protest. The portraits are not really plausible. Among these people there are too many differences, too many exceptions.

Perhaps it is possible to find that here and there in their overall structures of meaning, even such large populations can arrive through their interactions at some kind of unity, some points on which they think alike and where they conduct themselves according to a recurrent, recognizable, conspicuously distinctive pattern. Such unity, if it occurs, may be more noticeable to an outside observer than it is to the people involved.

This conception of coherence, however, largely disregards the fact that cultures of this kind are characterized rather more by their internal diversity than by any overarching uniformity. What can we mean by coherence, in the case of cultures where perspectives diverge and then clash, where people may seek advantage by being different, where groups of people are forever pushing further and further away from the taken for granted in their search for new understandings, where the gains of expertise are suspected to be at the expense of common sense, and where in a division of knowledge specialists prefer to speak to other specialists?

An understanding of coherence which does more justice to the particular character of complex cultures must be built around the fact that people can also to one degree or other make sense of other people's meanings; the ideas, and the externalized forms of ideas, which are primarily integral, actively managed parts of the perspectives of other members of their society. It is one thing, this is to say, to arrive at a logically—perhaps even aesthetically—satisfying integration of the core elements of one's own perspective, based probably on personal interests and central, recurrent experiences. Although even this may be difficult under the circumstances where a life is drawn in many directions, it would be rather more like that Bach fugue, or religious doctrine, or a scientific theory. These, after all, are also the products of individual minds, or of groups acutely concerned with creating works of unity together. But it is rather a different thing to have a perspective toward other perspectives which somehow can be deemed a satisfactory bridge to them; a perspective which maps as large a part as possible of the landscape of distributed meanings, and which does so with some degree of accuracy and appreciation.

Coherence in a complex culture must be measured in such terms. It is greater when more people's perspectives make sense of other people's perspectives. This can hardly be more than a vague orienting notion, but it suggests on the one hand that diversity is not necessarily synonymous with incoherence, and on the other hand that coherence under the conditions of diversity is problematical. There are built-in tendencies toward disconnectedness and incoherence. Thus, coherence is something that people have to work at, and something which is achieved to a higher degree in some areas of meaning and probably by some people, vis-à-vis particular others or generally. And because of growth and flux, the work on coherence is never done, never carried once and for all to completion.

Certainly some cultural coherence seems easy to come by, somehow natural and effortless. Within the network of perspectives of the complex culture, some perspectives link up with others and their meaningful products in ways which are hardly entirely predictable, through elective affinities in interests or ingrained habits of thought.[33] These interactions can allow existing orientations to be confirmed, and embodied in new ways, or they can point toward further developments. Through whatever is more or less held in common at some general level by cultures of critical discourse, intellectuals or intelligentsia may find affinities in one another's perspectives. This possibility we have identified before.

But we also have a vocabulary for different types of coherence work and coherence workers in complex cultures. The author Ralph Ellison (1964:xiii) has reminisced about the part the notion of "renaissance man" somehow came to play in the imaginative life of his circle of boyhood friends growing up, with a sense of frontier freedom and adventure, in the Black American community of Oklahoma City. They were youths who refused to "know their place," who appreciated jazzmen and scholars, movie stars and Black cowboys, writers and clever bootleggers, the eloquence of a preacher and the style of a headwaiter. In their fantasy, at least, they could play with the ways in which all these people contributed to their culture.

"Renaissance man" is indeed one of the labels we attach to people who to some degree succeed in bringing together in their own perspectives domains of meaning which cultural specialization has increasingly set apart. In the strictest sense of the term, a renaissance man is not only knowledgeable about these domains, but also creative in his handling of the materials of each of them; he contributes innovatively to the production of culture. This is a rare achievement and no doubt getting more so, but it can still inspire those whose curiosity and self-confidence knows few limits.

More modest than the renaissance man, another social type which we identify with cultural coherence work is that of the amateur, or dilettante, or dabbler. Reflexive commentaries on the management of meaning treat him with varying degrees of ridicule or respect. The critic Jacques Barzun calls him indispensable, in a world "where mankind is now divided into two cultural classes of haves and have nots" (1982:30 ff.). He may be incompetent and scatter his energies, and act generally as an anachronistic nuisance in an order of things where areas of knowledge split and then split again. But this primitive among specialized sophisticates is freer than they are, and, Barzun continues, as he moves among the various forms, styles, periods, and persons in his stumbling but uninhibited way, he can intuitively help promote a common language of discussion and criticism.

In some ways, the amateur in Barzun's portrait seems to be much like the true intellectual in his concern for unity and his disregard for boundaries. His relationship to the culture of critical discourse, however, seems appreciative rather than (at least, to any greater extent) personally creative; with regard to capital-C culture, he is a consumer rather than a producer, a member of the fan club of the intellectuals and the intelligentsia, rather than of their own club.[34] And in the cultural marketplace, he may be a fickle customer. As a dabbler in different fields of meaning, his loyalties are apt to change quickly. The trajectories of fads and fashions in culture are shaped to no small extent by the dilettantes.

The threat of cultural disconnectedness also provides the basis for different kinds of intermediaries who engage in a variety of coherence activities in the management of complex cultures, thereby developing their own niches in the cultural economy. They can build those bridges of understanding between laymen, on the one hand, and intelligentsia and intellectuals, on the other, which the members of the latter categories do not want to be bothered with constructing themselves. Intermediaries may be reviewers, popularizers, critics, translators, commentators, or again, course instructors who tell you how to become an instant expert. (True, not all of these are only intermediaries). They may reformulate an alien complex of meanings in the terms of a more familiar one, or they can explicate the standards by which esoteric cultural products should be evaluated. As in the case of art and music critics, they may deal with work in one symbolic mode through another which is radically different.[35] Whether under such varied conditions the cultural renditions of intermediaries are always accurate reflections of the original works is an inherently difficult issue here, as is indeed the notion of accuracy itself: the *traduttore, traditore* problematic, that is to say, becomes very real. Yet in some way or other, the coherence of culture is increased, as the network of linkages between meanings and meaningful forms becomes denser through the mediations.

Intellectuals, too, are particularly concerned with coherence, in their own way. In large part, the aim of their discourse is to identify and criticize old and new incoherence, within as well as between perspectives. Surely this is one way of making culture more connected, in that it brings together what might otherwise be left apart, lack of fit undetected or ignored. As it points the way toward more coherent alternatives, nevertheless, it spotlights the lack of coherence that is actually there. In large part due to such predilections, intellectuals in contemporary societies tend to develop, in a term coined by Lionel Trilling, "adversary cultures" (1965). Moreover, as intellectuals proceed with their critiques and with their new constructions of coherence, they frequently do so in terms which become increasingly remote, less immediately intelligible from the perspective of many others. As coherence increases in one way, it may thus decrease in others.

Movements, also concerned on variously wide fronts with a kind of cultural critique, are in a way like intellectuals writ large: advocates of coherence in some area, but conspicuously engaged in the denunciation of some incoherence, some contradiction. The sort of cultural spin-offs from the meaningful constructions of specialists into more general culture also contribute to cultural coherence, at least where they do not simply convert ignorance into misunderstanding. Intelligentsias, on the other hand, by pushing ahead in various directions with little apparent concern for the no-man's-lands of meaning which may line their paths, or for keeping the lines of communication open to the rear, would seem to bring about much unintended incoherence. Yet their academic branches have at least one specific kind of coherence work which is characteristic of them: interdisciplinary work.[36]

Conclusion: In Praise of Spurious Cultures

A complex culture, I have said before, has to be seen as a moving interconnectedness. We find it to be an interconnectedness between meanings and forms which carry them, but at the same time, through the social organization of meaning, it becomes an interconnectedness of people.

The images of a coherence reaching toward perfection are not particularly apt here: the Bach fugue and so forth. Cultures change in ways which some regret and which please others—sometimes, in ways which seem to be to nobody's liking. There are misunderstandings, both working and nonworking, and productive confusions. It is most unlikely that, in the end, there will be a stylistic unity of a kind that offers intellectual and aesthetic delight. But in his storehouse of metaphors for cultural integratedness, Clifford Geertz also has that of culture as an octopus, not the best coordinated of living things (1973:408). Our kind of culture bears a stronger resemblance to this inelegant animal. In the complex societies of today, among the masses of people involved, surely all—as individuals—have a brain superior to that of the octopus; but as each of them applies his own perspective, the aggregate outcome may give no more impressive evidence of coordinative ability—sometimes rather less.

The shift of image, however, is not just a matter of lowered expectations. The contemplative appreciation of formal unity is replaced by a judgment of adaptiveness in action. What the octopus does may not be pretty, but it manages to live on and get around (even if it is not very efficient, either).

This is worth keeping in mind with regard to complex cultures. So far at least they, too, have mostly kept muddling through. And it is arguable that there is some virtue here in being just incoherent enough.[37] Geertz prefaces his comments on the octopoid character of cultures with the point that systems can hardly afford to be both very complex and highly interconnected; the combination could immobilize them (1973:407). Better spurious and alive, then, than genuine and dead. Victor Turner pointed repeatedly to a similar line of thought, of which the quotation at the beginning of this chapter is one instance. In the long term, societies could best retain a broad domain of resilience if their cultures carry with them a store of variant models, some perhaps seemingly nonfunctional, one of which might turn out to be adaptive even under drastically changed conditions (Turner 1977a:70).[38] (This view, of course, provided as good a rationale as any for an interest in liminality.)

Being culturally incoherent enough, and at the same time coherent enough, does something, then, for adaptation as well as adaptiveness—in the short term and in the long term. The division of labor, and consequently the division of knowledge, is an instrument for dealing efficiently and well-informedly with the world as it is. Somewhere in this type of social organization, there is an expert for almost every occasion and every problem. If you know where he is and how to use him—and if you can make him serve you—his expertise may be almost as available as what is in your own mind. But over time, the diversity of perspectives and meaningful forms which are not immediately interdependent in any useful way, and even the conflicts among them, may contribute to "the wisdom of the system," to the extent that there is anything that deserves to be designated by the latter term. The various segments of a complex culture may more generally serve as laboratories and reservoirs for the culture in its entirety, to be retrieved and put into new uses if opportunity or need arises. One cannot be sure that one set of meanings, and one way of managing them, will not ever be able to saturate an entire culture and run away with it even to the point of the self-destruction of a society. But in its flux, the complex culture may have at least the semblance of checks and balances. Ideologics of domination provoke ideologies of resistance. When one intelligentsia carries its ideas rather too far, it is confronted by commonsense skepticism, becomes the favorite target of intellectuals, and perhaps brings a movement into being, to raise an oppositional consciousness among laymen. And reactions upon reactions upon reactions keep the whole from ever stagnating.

In some places and at some times, however, much of this seems to happen faster and with greater intensity than elsewhere. There is more flux, more diversity to be made sense of. There are metropoles and there are renaissances, sites and periods where the management of meaning reaches unusual heights.

PART II

Sites

6 The Urban Swirl

> Only the coming decades will show the crime that Hitler perpetrated against Vienna when he sought to nationalize and provincialize the city, whose meaning and culture were founded in the meeting of the most heterogeneous elements, and in her spiritual supernationality. For the genius of Vienna—a specifically musical one—was always that it harmonized all the national and lingual contrasts. Its culture was a synthesis of all Western cultures. Whoever lived there and worked there felt himself free of all confinement and prejudice. (Stefan Zweig 1943:16)

> I love Calcutta. . . . I have lived here all my life. The best of whatever is being done in the arts in India is being done here. There is great intellectual vitality here. A lot of very good Bengali writing is being done here. The Bengali theatre is very much alive here. The coffeehouses here are full of people with ideas. Only filmmaking has not attracted many intellectuals, yet from a filmmaker's point of view no city could be better, because all kinds of things happen here all the time.
> (Satyajit Ray, in interview with Ved Mehta, 1970:410)

More than other human habitats, a city is a place of discoveries and surprises, whether pleasant or unpleasant; a place where it is likely that you see things today that you did not see yesterday, and encounter people who are not like yourself. "The rapid crowding of changing images, the sharp discontinuity in the grasp of a single glance, and the unexpectedness of onrushing impressions. These are the psychological conditions which the metropolis creates," wrote Georg Simmel in his essay on mental life in the big city (1964:410). Simmel wanted to abstract a psychology, a state of mind. Yet these are also cultural conditions. In the city we find, in the most concentrated form within a limited space, the kind of cultural complexity that this book is about: the greatest variety of subcultures, the most elaborate cultural apparatus, a number of contrasting but interlinked modes of managing meaning.[1] Thus, cities should have some special appeal for cultural studies.

And especially some cities, at some points in time—quattrocento Florence, Berlin in the 1920s, perhaps the black South African township Sophiatown in the 1950s. . . . But not all such instances are equally well known and documented. In this chapter, to cast some light on the conditions as well as the nature of urban cultural process, I will look at available materials concerning three cities, Vienna, Calcutta, and San Francisco, during periods when they are generally recognized to have been places of unusually lively cultural production.[2] The materials in question include works written during these periods, by people who were themselves participants in local cultural process. I have also drawn on synthesizing historical overviews and on biographies. I have done no work on little-known primary sources, and I have no new facts, since my intention is not to contribute to research on the three cities, but merely to use them as sources for understandings of certain kinds of cultural flow. Rather than writing intellectual history, I am raiding it.

This incursion is not without risks. Many of the sources for my interpretation already see Vienna, Calcutta, and San Francisco culture not as summations of individual achievements but indeed as collective phenomena, particular instances of the social organization of meaning. Yet, histories naturally deal more with the people whose unique works are still with us, as capital-C culture, than with those who mostly reproduced whatever, under the circumstances, was common sense. They remember successes, not failures, heroes rather than hangers-on. And little people do not write their memoirs. We cannot from such accounts draw a conclusion that this was the way Vienna was as a whole, that this was what Calcuttans were like. But perhaps we can see how those individuals who have made themselves remembered, as they did what they did, could draw on their contacts with one another, as well as on conditions and experiences they may have shared with many. And in this way we can hope to discern such peculiarities of cultural process, and conditions of cultural process, as are more likely to be found in cities than elsewhere, although certainly not in every urban community to the same extent as in Vienna, Calcutta, and San Francisco.

Particular historical moments are involved in these three cases. I look at Vienna in that *fin-de-siècle* period which has fascinated many intellectual historians; at Calcutta in the nineteenth century, when it was the site of what has become known as the Bengal Renaissance; and at San Francisco mostly in the 1950s, the time of Beat culture—which was, in fact, also referred to as the San Francisco Renaissance. Let us first remind ourselves, concretely and without much analytical ambition, of the characteristics of the three cities respectively in these periods, and point to some of their most notable inhabitants. (Assuming that to most readers, Calcutta is the least familiar of the three, I allow it a little more space.) After that, we come back to the cultural peculiarities of urbanism.

Vienna: The Final Years of an Imperial Capital

At the turn of the century, Vienna was the capital of an old and declining empire. There was a rather comfortable cohabitation between the imperial court and the old aristocracy on the one hand, and an affluent liberal bourgeoisie on the other; feeding together, it seemed, on operetta and whipped cream. Those who lived secure lives had with time become addicted to what critics called *Schlamperei,* a loose inefficient sloppiness, widespread in administration as well as in business. The gerontocratic streak was epitomized by Emperor Franz Joseph, who would muddle through on the throne for two-thirds of a century. In the life of the Establishment there was a strong sense of propriety and decorum, even as the gap between assertions and realities grew wider. "It was very beautiful, I enjoyed it very much"—this was the emperor's set phrase for almost fifty years when an opinion was called for. The last time he had made a more personal (and unfavorable) remark, about the new opera building, the architect had killed himself.

Yet this was also the setting in which new ideas and modes of expression grew. Sigmund Freud lived here, of course; so did Theodor Herzl, a litterateur who became the father of Zionism; other writers like Arthur Schnitzler, Stefan Zweig (for some time, the most translated author in Europe), and Hugo von Hofmannsthal; Gustav Mahler and Arnold Schönberg in music;

the painters Klimt and Kokoschka; the architect Adolf Loos; the publicist Karl Kraus; the philosopher Ernst Mach. Ludwig Wittgenstein grew up in this milieu. Adolf Hitler began his adult life in Vienna in this period, trying to establish himself as a painter and absorbing the ascendant (although still hardly dominant) ideology of Germanic superiority in both its quasi-scientific and its rather more theatrical and mythological local versions.[3] And when one of the emperor's closest advisors was warned that a great war could lead to revolution in Russia, he is supposed to have retorted, "Who is to make that revolution? Herr Trotsky in the Café Central?"[4]

To the writer Hermann Broch, this was the period of Vienna's "gay apocalypse." He also called it a "style democracy," for what brought its classes together were its aesthetic values, a hedonistic pleasure in arts and festivities. At the same time, other forces were tearing the social fabric apart. Industrialization had brought masses of people into the cities (Vienna trebled in size in thirty years), to a harsh existence in multiplying workers' suburbs; and political radicalism, on the part of both the working class and a threatened stratum of artisans and shopkeepers, had begun to express the realities of the emergent industrial class structure. Germanic nationalism clashed with the ethnic pluralism of the Habsburg empire, and with an Austrian liberalism which had only reaped its share of power in the aftermath of military defeat. And both by way of modeling ethnic unity and through the anti-Semitism which were often part of them, this and other European nationalisms in turn stimulated interest in Zionism, at least in parts of the large Jewish population of Vienna and its empire.

About one-tenth of the Viennese were Jewish at the turn of the century. They, and those other Jews for whom Vienna was the natural center, ranged on a scale of assimilation from those clearly in the mainstream of liberal urban life, to eastern Jews for whom ethnicity and religion were central facts of daily existence; people arriving recently from centuries in the *shtetl* to confront a city where life was with strangers. The obvious success of many of the former, and the equally conspicuous cultural separateness of many of the latter, both fed anti-Semitic prejudices among the non-Jews. And these prejudices, in turn, made especially members of the intellectual Jewish bourgeoisie acutely sensitive to the problematic relationship between being oneself and being a Jew.

Much of the creativity in Vienna was the reaction of a younger generation to what they found untenable in the existing situation: as an escape from it or as a critique of it. They were mostly sons of the bourgeoisie, many of them largely assimilated Jews, but they had been reluctant to follow in the footsteps of their fathers as pillars of society. Stefan Zweig has described in his autobiography how even as schoolboys he and his friends fled in their imagination from the solid but dull education of the Viennese *Gymnasien* to a world of literature, art, and ideas about which their parents knew nothing. They read French, German, and English journals, and talked and talked and talked about what they read. They hung around theaters and art exhibits. Whenever they liked something, the senior critics in the major newspapers would probably describe it as "decadent" or "anarchist." But they on their part sensed, in the words of another among them, Hugo von Hofmannsthal, that the order which had thus far prevailed stood on *das Gleitende,* it was slipping away.

Hofmannsthal's anonymous teenage debut as a lyrical poet had amazed literary Vienna. Soon after, he became a member of that coterie of writers known as *Jung-Wien,* including also Stefan Zweig and Arthur Schnitzler, assembling regularly at the Kafé Griensteidl, and presided over by Hermann Bahr, an author and journalist who seemed forever tuned in to the latest fashions in the arts. Born in the provinces, and after having been "thrown out of every university in Austria" (according to Spiel 1987:85), he had spent time in Berlin and Paris in the 1880s, and had thus returned to Austria with the resources of a cosmopolitan cultural broker.

For Hofmannsthal, who defined some of the experiences of his generation, the poet was one "who binds up in himself the elements of the times"; one who establishes relationships, one who takes a fragmented reality and uses language to give it cohesion. Reared on aesthetic sensibility in his family, Hofmannsthal came to see human feelings and instincts as an untamed, dangerous force in society. This psychology must be acknowledged and domesticated, given an outlet in new symbolic forms. As he turned from poetry to drama, Hofmannsthal became preoccupied with a politics of ritual, one where nobody should feel left out; a version of the theater state. Habsburg does not seem far away here, although new conceptions of psychology and its connections to politics had altered old visions. Nevertheless, there was not just despair, but perhaps a belief that cultural engineering could avert the disaster.

As Hofmannsthal strove to create unity between the self and the world, he found underpinnings for his poetic experience in the theory of knowledge set forth by a Vienna contemporary, the philosopher-physicist Ernst Mach, whose university lectures he attended. The world, Mach proposed (as Hofmannsthal and his friends understood him), consists only of our sensations of it. In that case, Hofmannsthal, Bahr and other writers concluded, a poet, working in all forms of expression on the range of his experiences of the world, knew reality at least as well as the physicist. Mach's philosophy also influenced the Austrian socialists, as well as Robert Musil, who wrote a doctoral dissertation on it (as, in a more distant corner of the Habsburg empire, did young Bronislaw Malinowski)—one example of those remarkable Viennese cross-currents to which we will return.[5]

Arthur Schnitzler, Hofmannsthal's older friend and colleague, combined the medical career his father had demanded of him with his vocation of writing. In both fields, he was drawn to psychology. The combination of them, of bourgeois professionalism and the life of *Jung-Wien*, probably gave a particular intensity to his understanding of the conflict between social constraints and personal desires, and to his concern with variety and change. Freud, who avoided meeting Schnitzler (even beyond his usual unconcern for Viennese literary society) commented repeatedly on the similarities between their work, and even wrote to him that he feared meeting his double.[6]

In art, the impressionistic, personalizing perspectives of the *Jung-Wien* circle found their closest parallel in the work of Gustav Klimt which, exemplary of the *Jugendstil* (that is, art nouveau), also celebrated a generational discontinuity. Of modest origins, Klimt had begun as a decorator of the many large official buildings rising in the late nineteenth century in Vienna as well as in other cities. As his talent earned increasing recognition, he made his way into more affluent circles in the capital, where he became a leader of the Secessionists, a grouping of artists, craftsmen, and architects so known because they had broken away from the historically imitative manners favored by the leading art institute in Vienna. Writing in the first issue of their journal *Ver Sacrum* ("Sacred Spring"; the title was drawn from a Roman ritual in which youth were consecrated at times of national crisis), Hermann Bahr saw in the work of the Secessionists a war on "actionless routine and ossified Byzantinism."Klimt (who soon seceded from the Secessionists as well) experimented with a lusciously ornamentative, provocatively sensuous style. Occasionally his work caused controversy, especially a series of ceiling paintings for the University of Vienna, which offended the self-images of academic elders. Yet Klimt also became the favorite of enlightened society families, imaginatively portraying their women.

Both *Jung-Wien* and the Secessionists engaged in what one may describe (with a term popularized many decades later, and elsewhere) as a culture of narcissism. They elaborated on the deeply personal and the subjective, things confined by previous rulings to the nether regions of the mind. This was indeed one kind of protest, but one which in its aesthetics had not quite broken out of the framework of Habsburg culture.

But there was also a strand, mostly somewhat later in time, of more radical opposition to the pretenses of officially established culture, and to the institutionalization of doublethink and doubletalk. Here the search for simplicity of form contrasted sharply with the indulgent, decorative established culture.

Through its leading protagonist, Karl Kraus, an agemate and former schoolmate of Hofmannsthal, this cultural current had been present already at Kafé Griensteidl; but Kraus had not sat at the table of *Jung-Wien,* and when that establishment was torn down, Kraus, still in his early twenties, wrote an ironic piece portraying the members of the group less than gently. (One of them responded by beating him up.) Kraus' next major victim was Theodor Herzl. Already admired as a literary connoisseur and self-confident dandy by his fellow high school and university students, Herzl had become the Paris correspondent of the *Neue Freie Presse,* Vienna's leading newspaper, solidly Establishment and one of the most respected in Europe; returning from France, he became the literary editor. In Paris, however, he had followed the Dreyfus case, and this experience had made him more self-consciously a Jew, and the first major spokesman for Zionism. Few of the Jews in the mainstream of Viennese life were prepared to take his scheme of resettlement in some distant Jewish land seriously, however, and on their side Karl Kraus also came down, in a biting pamphlet.

Yet Kraus as a critic and satirist worked over a much wider range of topics, being usually strongly for or strongly against; and the latter more often. He, too, had been invited to join the *Neue Freie Presse.* Instead, he had chosen to start his own irregular but approximately biweekly *Die Fackel,* "the Torch"—mostly, and after some time wholly, written by himself. ("I no longer have any collaborators. I was jealous of them. They put off the readers I want to lose for myself.") *Die Fackel* turned into a one-man campaign against sham in public life, and a running commentary on the crisis of language. Kraus' politics changed over the years, as did his religion (Jewish, then Catholic, then Jewish again). But on language and public morality he was consistent, an advocate of purity, simplicity, integrity, and precision. From this position he could attack Bahr, Zweig, and Hofmannsthal, the popular operettas of Lehar, not least the style of writing and the surreptitious biases of the *Neue Freie Presse,* psychoanalysis (and especially its popularizers), police corruption, militarism, advertising, and Jewish name changes. And he could be just as strong in his praise of some things, and certain people: some durable favorites of the Burgtheater stage, as well as that strange, debauched, but at the same time somehow innocent *ur*-hippie Peter Altenberg, also for a while a Griensteidl regular (but at yet another table), knowing everybody, yet without real enemies, whose ephemeral writings on Vienna, life, and personal experience Kraus found just as genuine as he found those by Hermann Bahr artificial and manneristic.

While there were Viennese literati households where Kraus' name was pointedly unmentionable and where copies of *Die Fackel* would not be seen (and while the *Neue Freie Presse* kept systematically silent about him), his intellectual influence was enormous. It increased also through his public readings of his own works, as well as of whatever else he considered important literature. These recitals were electrifying performances, where he made full use of gesture, the entire register of his voice, and his great ability to mimic. Kraus would have liked to be an actor but was too small and ugly (with a slight back deformity) to have any real chance. His one appearance in a public production, at age nineteen, is said to have been "ruined by outsize wig and ill-fitting costume" (Stern 1975:37).

What Kraus labored to do for the written and spoken word, others also undertook in other realms of cultural form. The architect Adolf Loos had first been allied with the Secessionists, but found their decorative mannerisms unacceptable. Decoration, he wrote in his famous essay on "Ornament and Crime," was a sign of decadence, lack of civilization, evil; criminals tattoo themselves, and savages make the most intricate patterns. From the latter Loos insight followed the remark that one of the most prominent Secessionist architects was a "Papua in the pay of the state."But Loos was not merely a polemicist. Some of the most controversial new buildings in Vienna were examples of his striving for simplicity.

Kraus supported Loos; Loos became the patron and adviser of the young artist Oskar Kokoschka; and Kokoschka was enthusiastically reviewed in *Die Fackel*. It could seem that Kokoschka's violent, emotional expressionism was something very different from the measured exactness of Loos' architecture, but then Loos was determined that art and architecture were to be kept separate, and Kokoschka in his paintings showed another kind of depth and purity which contrasted with Secessionist prettiness (although it is true that Klimt had also given early support to young Kokoschka, and that the latter continued to admire Klimt).

In music, it was Arnold Schönberg who most directly drew sustenance from Kraus. Musical life in Vienna had been conflict-ridden at least since the dividing line had been drawn between Brahmsians and Wagnerians, and musical audiences were mostly conservative in their tastes—"as far as music went Vienna had to be dragged into the twentieth century," writes Spiel (1987:169). Gustav Mahler, chief conductor and later director of the Court Opera for a number of years around the turn of the century, had worked hard to revitalize its repertoire, but in the end found the support for his efforts so weak that he felt obliged to resign and leave for the United States. Schönberg, a painter and writer as well as a composer, was if anything even more acutely controversial, and opponents repeatedly disrupted performances of his works. For Schönberg did nothing to appease the conventional musical assumptions of audiences. The sound of music was less important than its logic. It was this concern for the purification of musical thought, and for that release of its potential which he would find more fully in twelve-tone music, that Schönberg saw paralleled in Karl Kraus' critique of language, and which may have led him to autograph a copy of his *Harmonielehre* to Kraus with the dedication "I have perhaps learned more from you than any man should learn if he desires to be independent."

Calcutta: The Bhadralok and the West

If the predominant image of Calcutta today is that of one of the world's urban infernos, there is a competing image of the city as a center of cultural ferment; "a city of furious creative energy," in the words of the eminent anthropologist Surajit Sinha (1972:7). And this has remained true after the Bengal Renaissance. If Rabindranath Tagore was a child of this renaissance, the filmmaker Satyajit Ray has been one of its internationally known grandchildren.

Like most port cities of Asia, Calcutta is a product of Western colonialism, and the Bengal Renaissance was in large part a matter of an encounter between Bengali and European cultures. The East India Company established a trading post here toward the end of the seventeenth century, and from then on, the settlement just grew and grew. A sizable European community developed, while the most prominent grouping on the Indian side was one of commercial and administrative middlemen: the banians, a cover-all term for the people who as brokers, interpreters, bookkeepers, advisors and investors became the foreign merchants' affluent partners in enterprise. Some of them had occupied similar positions in the service of Hindu Rajas or the crumbling Mughal Empire, and now transferred administrative and commercial skills as well as a cosmopolitan orientation to the new frontier.

By the beginning of the nineteenth century, Calcutta society already had some historical depth. A British visitor would describe the houses of the established Bengali families, with Corinthian pillars in front and English furniture inside. Wealthy Calcuttans would be satisfied only with the best horses and the most elegant carriages. There were also occasional signs of decadence. "Young men from affluent families were allowed to dissipate with opium, women and kite-flying contests," writes one commentator; "the degeneration of the youth was due to the indulgence given by the fathers who were too busy making money and enjoying the blessings of a care-free existence in an irresponsible society" (Nag 1972:143).

It was a society in many ways strongly oriented toward the West. While, in the early years of the settlement, just a little knowledge of the English language would be seen as a great asset, many people would soon have a thorough European education. Nonetheless, Anglophilia was only one part of the story. The dominant families were mostly high-caste Hindus, and the internal order of Indian Calcutta depended on considerations of caste and religion. Rituals could be occasions of major expenditures, and a major organizational feature was *daladali,* that factionalism which in no small part revolved around matters of caste. The *dal,* led by a *dalpati,* could be a multi-caste faction, although there were also single-caste factions. It served not least as a tribunal for the settlement of disputes over inheritance, marriage, caste rank, and intercaste relationships. But faction leaders could also involve their followers in other issues and campaigns. Some *dals* were large and others quite small; some were short-lived, while others existed for generations.

This was the Calcutta of the Bengali, or more precisely of the broad stratum of the *bhadralok,* "the respectable people," who self-consciously distinguished themselves from the urban and rural masses. The *bhadralok* (or, more or less synonymously, the *babus,* a term sometimes used with pejorative connotations) were the people who could either live from wealth already acquired, or who occupied the various new niches opening up for people with some Western education and some familiarity with European modes of operation. The Bengal Renaissance, when it got under way, was theirs.

Meanwhile, there was also the Calcutta of the Europeans. Most of them had come to India for quick profits, with little interest in the local population, or good will for it. The areas of contact between them and the Bengali were about as limited as they could make them, with profits and comforts intact. Yet there were also sectors of British society in Calcutta who had a greater impact on Indian life by way of their cultural involvements. From the eighteenth century onwards, the city had its British intelligentsia of administrators, doctors, lawyers, engineers, officers, and priests. These were people who both read the classics and stayed in touch with debate in the home country. To their social events—garden parties, dances, theatrical performances—select Bengali acquaintances would also be invited. This was one way in which the Calcutta British were cultural mediators.

There were also colonial institutions with a particular impact in stimulating local intellectual life. In the later decades of the eighteenth century, after a period of unusually rapacious exploitation of Bengal, the East India Company had shifted to a policy involving greater cultural sensitivity. In a new generation of administrators, many took a deep interest in Indian languages and Hindu civilization, actually pioneering Orientalist scholarship. To pursue such interests they formed the Asiatic Society of Bengal, and somewhat later the College of Fort William was founded, as an "Oxford of the East," to instruct officials in many fields of learning, but not least those pertaining to the languages and modes of thought of India. On the college staff were Indians as well as Europeans, for the British Orientalists gathered pandits to work with them on building a body of systematic knowledge.

In the Calcutta context, and in the training which the College of Fort William gave to civil servants, Orientalism came to stand for more than a branch of scholarship. It turned into a cultural policy of pouring, as the historian David Kopf (1975b: 218) has put it, "the new wine of nineteenth-century civilization into the old bottles of Indian institutions and practices with dynamic results."[7] Moreover, the British Orientalists and their activities did much to stimulate the interest of the Bengali themselves in a cultural heritage which had suffered from fragmentation and decay. The College of Fort William became the nucleus of a new cultural apparatus, not involving the Bengali only, but having its greatest impact among them. Printing presses were started, at first depending largely on college patronage, but gradually building up their own markets. This allowed the dissemination of Western knowledge and ideas; the educated people of Calcutta took great interest in philosophy, science, and literature. But because classical Indian texts were also translated into Bengali and other contemporary Indian tongues, printed, and commented upon from new points of view, a new distribution of knowledge about Indian history and about Hindu doctrine was likewise brought about, undermining Brahmin control of the sacred domain.

Through these activities Bengali was developed as a written language, but only by way of a lengthy two-front battle with Sanskrit on the one side and English on the other. Many pandits continued to dismiss Bengali as a barbaric tongue unfit for subtle expression; when they deigned to use it, it was in such a Sanskritized form that no layman could understand what they were saying. On the other hand, many of those Calcuttans who would take an interest in written materials preferred English, finding that what was available in Bengali—at least in the early decades—was too limited and too unsophisticated.

Yet Bengali grammars, dictionaries, and various other materials were published, and a Bengali press developed. The scholars at the college may mostly have been concerned with matters of high culture. They were closely allied, however, with the Baptist missionaries at nearby Serampore, who had the best printing establishment in the region. The missionaries engaged more in popular educational publishing, and spread the idea of the importance of the renaissance (the original one, in Italy) to cultural development in Europe. They also emphasized the contribution of printing to a cultural breakthrough.

Other linked institutions followed. A School Society and a School Book Society, voluntary associations run largely by prosperous Bengali with some British supporters, fostered the growth of education and made educational supplies widely available. Hindu College was set up mostly to ensure that the sons of the new elite could gain a largely Western education. Yet again the background assumptions were largely Orientalist: the goals were modernizing in a way which would fit into an Indian framework, rather than Westernizing and entirely secular. Slightly later there was also Sanskrit College, open initially only to Brahmin boys, and offering not only traditional Sanskritic studies of rhetoric, sacred literature, law and grammar, but also a successful science curriculum including mathematics, mechanics, chemistry, and medicine.

The result of this influx of new ideas, and of new ideas about old ideas, and of this growth of new institutions, was to create another diversity: new distinctions, new debates. And these then kept changing throughout the nineteenth century. In its early part, there would seem to have been two major camps, associated with the *dals* led by the Deb and Tagore families respectively.[8] The most famous member of the former family is Radhakanta Deb, whose grandfather had become enormously rich as a banian and established the dynasty through financial power as well as the politics of marriage. Radhakanta, inheriting both wealth and position, spoke good English, read British authors, took a strong interest in Western science, and attended lectures and scientific exhibitions. He was a benefactor of Hindu College, secretary of the School Society, and an active member of the School Book Society; moreover, he was a classical scholar who compiled a Sanskrit encyclopedia, appearing in seven volumes between 1822 and 1858. A visiting British bishop described him as anxious "to vindicate his creed in the estimation of foreigners"; which is to say that he was skilled at the kind of cultural accounting which entails arguing about one system of meanings in the terms of another. In many ways, Radhakanta seems to personify the Orientalist ideals of cultural syncretism. Yet he is generally remembered as a strong conservative, not to say Hindu reactionary, for there were things in the Indian heritage that he was not willing to abandon.

The Tagore family were Brahmins, but belonged to a grouping which at some point had been ritually defiled, and they therefore held an uncertain and rather modest position within the social order of caste. On the other hand, they had soon turned to cooperating with British interests, and gradually they had become very wealthy. Radhakanta Deb's contemporary, Dwarkanath Tagore, was the leading entrepreneur in Bengal, involved in banking, shipping, textile industries, tea plantations, publishing, and a range of other lines of business. After he had dinner with Queen Victoria on a visit to London, the queen noted in her diary that "the Brahmin speaks English remarkably well, and is a very intelligent, interesting man" (quoted in Kling 1976:169–170).

Dwarkanath's personal commitments on cultural and religious issues may not have been so pronounced, but he and his family were associated with the man on whom much controversy focused for several decades in the early nineteenth century: Rammohun Roy, a maverick often described as the father of the Bengal Renaissance. Rammohun was a fairly late immigrant to Calcutta.

His ancestors had long been in the service of Muslim rulers in Bengal, and at an early age he acquired a knowledge of Arabic and Persian (and the Koran), as well as Hindu learning. Apparently, this multiple exposure soon made him critical toward certain Hindu beliefs and practices. He also traveled extensively in India in his youth, reaching as far as Tibet. As a young adult, he took up work for the East India Company where he was closely involved with Europeans. At the same time, he engaged in business on his own, successfully enough to allow him to retire, in his early forties, in Calcutta, as a man of independent means, engaging in scholarship, philanthropy, and cultural politics.

Rammohun, it seems, had already spent some time in Calcutta earlier, and had been influenced by the Orientalists. With time, he had taken an interest in Christianity, and had become impressed with the uses of Occidental culture in the Indian context. He studied Unitarian texts closely and corresponded with leading Unitarians in Europe. But although some of his Christian associates might have expected that he would eventually become a convert, his real goal was to purify Hinduism and build an Indian monotheism. Authentic Hinduism, he argued, had been corrupted with time, just like Christianity. Acknowledging the affinity between all major religions, Rammohun and his associates formed the *Brahmo* movement, which would later (after Rammohun's death) split several times due to conflicts over doctrine and practice as well as because of personal discord, but which continued to be an influential force in Calcutta life.

Rammohun did translations and introductions, and wrote tracts and pamphlets in a Bengali prose which drew a great deal of admiration. He published a Bengali grammar, as well as weeklies in Bengali and Persian. He engaged in public debates with Hindus as well as expatriate Christians, and founded a school and a college. (He had been involved from the beginning with Hindu College as well, although his adversaries kept him off the governing body.) Rammohun also followed the affairs of the world, took great interest in the French and American revolutions, and donated funds to aid the famine-stricken Irish. He attacked polygamy, child marriage, and the maltreatment of women. The issue which excited most feeling, however, was that of *sati,* widow burning, a Hindu practice which had in fact become increasingly frequent in Bengal in the early nineteenth century. Rammohun campaigned against it, even to the point of going to the funeral pyres to argue with participants in the ritual. It was on this question especially that he found himself confronted by the circle around Radhakanta Deb.

The battle spread over many arenas. Not least was it fought between newspapers, with Rammohun's *Kaumudi* and the Serampore missionaries' *Darpan* on one side and the conservative *Chandrika* on the other; they were similarly aligned on several other issues as well. Rammohun and the missionaries saw *sati* as an epitome of cruelty and injustice. The Hindu conservatives described it as an act of great virtue and self-sacrifice on the part of the widows, and an integral part of Hindu religion. Rammohun found no support for it in those scriptures that he thought were the only acceptable sources of Hinduism. Meanwhile, British officialdom, committed to business and otherwise to making no unnecessary waves, was not too eager to become involved. Yet, in the end, at a time when the British at home and abroad were becoming increasingly confident in their own social and cultural superiority, a governor-general recently arrived in Calcutta banned *sati*.

By this time, around 1830, a more clear-cut Westernizing tendency was gaining strength. James Mill's *History of British India*, a book admitting little of value in Indian society and culture, had been published in England in 1818, and was very popular with many British civil servants in India. A cultural policy antithetical to that of Orientalism came into effect, associated especially with Thomas Babington Macaulay, who as president of the General Committee on Public Instruction wrote that famous minute on education where it was proposed that funding should be wholly concentrated on the propagation of Western knowledge and values—"a single shelf of a good European library is worth the whole native literature of India and Arabia."

Macaulayism led to further cultural polarization among the *bhadralok*. The Hindu conservatives around Radhakanta Deb formed a society, *Dharma Sabha*, to defend "the Hindu way of life"; however, it still took pride in conducting its meetings according to strict rules of parliamentary procedure. This was a powerful and affluent group of people, and according to Sarkar (1970:18), a historian of the Bengal Renaissance, at the meetings of the society, "the street would be jammed by [their] private carriages."The *Dharma Sabha* opposed Rammohun's *Brahmo* movement, but was perhaps even more scandalized by the new goings-on at the Hindu College, which was fast becoming a bastion of secular Westernization. The key figure here, if for a few years only, was the young Henry Vivian Derozio, a Eurasian who had been educated by a Scottish freethinker in one of Calcutta's private schools, and who at age seventeen became a teacher at the college. Derozio (also a poet) impressed his followers with his integrity and his searching intellect, and encouraged debate and the questioning of authority among his students. It has been argued that Derozio was an Indian patriot and nationalist; however, this was not a matter of cultural nationalism, for he saw the progress of India rather in terms of a modernity of a distinctly Occidental kind. And his young followers, the Derozians, engaged in acts which were shockingly countercultural with reference to orthodox Hinduism. They ate beef and drank liquor; when they were required to utter mantras at prayers, they would quote the *Iliad* instead; and when one of the students was asked to bow before the goddess Kali, he reputedly greeted the image with a "good morning, madam."

After various incidents, and a campaign against his corrupting influence, Derozio was forced to resign from Hindu College. He died from cholera in less than a year. His influence did not disappear, however, as his followers, known collectively as Young Bengal, continued to form a strong current in Calcutta intellectual life.

The Hindu conservatives also had to struggle against the influence of the Christian missionaries, who were more interested than even a Macaulayist government in transforming entire personalities and thus saving souls; they were, of course, vehemently opposed to Derozian secularism as well. The missionaries at the time were of a rather elitist inclination and concentrated much of their efforts on the Western-educated city people who had become alienated from the mass of their countrymen.

Times went on changing. By 1854, when the College of Fort William was officially dissolved, it had for a long time existed in name only. After Rammohun Roy had died, his *Brahmo* movement had declined; then it was revived by Debendranath Tagore, Dwarkanath's son, father of Rabindranath, and a former pupil in the school founded by Rammohun. But now the movement, and its offshoot organizations, increasingly emphasized traditional culture, opposed Christian missionaries and the Westernizing extremism of Young Bengal, and moved closer to Radhakanta Deb's conservatism. One prominent member of the Tagore camp, Rajnarayan Bose, founded a rather short-lived "Society for the Promotion of National Feeling" and lectured on the superiority of Hinduism to other world religions, a stance rather different from Rammohun's universalism. The Tagores themselves organized the Hindu Mela, an annual cultural fair displaying Indian arts and crafts and offering prizes to writers, artists, and athletes; Rabindranath Tagore made his debut at the Mela, reciting his own poetry, at age thirteen.

By then, however, the *Brahmo* movement had split, and later split again, as it wavered between cultural ideals. One radical wing broke away and demanded that Brahmins in the movement should discard the sacred thread, that intercaste marriages should be actively promoted, and that men and women should join in the same religious services. This group, turning itself into something more like a mass movement, published popular literature of uplift, promoted temperance, ran night schools for workers, and called on the latter to assert their rights. But it had a rather high-handed leader who provoked internal dissension, and when he married his minor-age daughter to a chief, conspicuously against *Brahmo* principles, another faction formed, devoted to democratic republicanism and the liberation of all people. By now, this offshoot of Brahmoism had come rather a long way from the Hindu mainstream.

The nationalist and revivalist tendencies which were gathering strength in Calcutta society in the second half of the century had something to do with the changing economic climate in British India. The first half had been characterized by economic cooperation between the British and Bengali entrepreneurs, and the belief in such collaboration had found cultural expression as well, through voices such as those of Rammohun Roy and the Young Bengal group. During the latter part of the century, the Bengali more often found themselves as dependents and subordinates rather than partners of the Europeans. Entrepreneurial groups from other parts of India were also squeezing the Bengali out of niches in trade. In culture and in politics, this turned the *bhadralok* increasingly toward critique, opposition, and protest.

In the work of Bankimchandra Chatterjee, the first major writer in Bengali, the changes are reflected visibly enough. Bankimchandra, a colonial civil servant, was a cautious man, and greatly influenced by European thought. But he was suspicious of Western interpretations of India, and of the long-term usefulness of foreign domination to Indian progress: in order to shape its own future, India must have a history, a culture and a language of its own, and pride in them. To such ends Bankimchandra devoted his efforts: by publishing a paper which convincingly showed that a great range of issues could be sophisticatedly discussed in Bengali, and through a number of novels on social and historical themes where the Bengali could even be shown, as in *Anandamath,* his best-known book, rising against an alien regime. Yet critique also had to be self-critique, and among the urban, Westernized *bhadralok,* Bankimchandra found too much opportunism and self-centeredness, too little cultural integrity.[9]

In the early 1870s, a swami from western India, Dayananda Saraswati, later gaining fame as the founder of the *Arya Samaj* reform movement within Hinduism, made a prolonged visit to Calcutta. His experiences in the city, as described by his biographer Jordens (1978:75 ff.), offers one view of the special qualities of the city. The variety of beliefs and attitudes with respect to religion and political and social issues, and the variety of individual combinations of such beliefs and attitudes, was striking. The swami found heated debate and deep distrust even between the people with whom he was personally associated. What they had in common, nonetheless, was an intense concern with the state of their society, with what they saw as its backwardness, its injustice, and its degradation. Calcutta, for the swami, was a cauldron of new ideas, and new ways of moving ideas, and it had a profound influence on the way he would think and work from that time on.

And yet, other commentators have argued, the Bengal Renaissance had its limitations. For all its variety of perspectives, and for all the debate generated between them as the nineteenth century passed, it was in some ways parochial. The voices of the *bhadralok* which made themselves heard were mostly those of upper caste urbanites, and many of the central issues involved reconciling their version of Hinduism with what they had come to understand as enlightened Westernism. Abolishing *sati* and allowing widows to remarry was hardly as much of a problem to the lower castes as it was to the upper castes; arguing the fine points of ancient scriptures in a new culture of critical discourse was not the business of those whose religion was inseparable from local folklore. And thus, to take the view of Arabinda Poddar (1970:245), this renaissance in large part remained restricted within the fences of the banian metropolis; "intellectual ferment hardly moved beyond its outer fringes, where the pull of traditional restraints were still strongly felt and where cultural regenerative aspirations remained largely atrophied."

San Francisco: Against the American Grain

The cultural efflorescence of San Francisco is more recent than those of Vienna and Calcutta. It has been proposed (by Becker and Horowitz, 1971) that San Francisco has long had a "culture of civility," a tolerance of deviance, even a readiness to take difference to be a civic resource. Its history as a seaport, its tradition of radical unions, the fact that it is in large part a city of single people rather than families could all contribute to such a climate: one of some historical depth. Yet only since World War II have its cultural developments really drawn the attention of the world—mostly as critical responses to the culture, politics and economics of mainstream America. With a little hindsight, it is tempting to see some of them also as expressions of the shift of American attention from the Atlantic to the Pacific. In the 1950s, this was the Beat capital (or one of them, with a counterpart across the continent in New York's Greenwich Village); in the late 1960s, a center of flower power, acid rock, and student rebellion; later yet, the site of the greatest elaboration of gay culture.

These are interrelated phenomena, but here I am mostly concerned with the Beat era. The major figures, then, are literary: Kenneth Rexroth, Jack Kerouac, Allen Ginsberg, Gary Snyder, and others. But literary life also connected with music and art, and with the stage performances of Lenny Bruce, the comedian, and with Eastern religion and philosophy, and with Black ethnic culture. If I am biased toward the written word here, it is in large part because this has remained behind as a source (and a source preoccupied with itself) when the performances in other symbolic modes are gone.

Rexroth—poet, translator, cultural critic, and later a somewhat reluctant father figure of the Beat generation—was one of the first to arrive on the scene, in the late 1920s, from Chicago, which had just had its own literary renaissance. The San Francisco he found he described later as "a backwater town." But his own political inclinations resonated with a native streak of libertarian radicalism, descending from the Wobblies, and by the end of World War II, he was in the middle of a circle of people meeting regularly to discuss the coming reconstruction of politics and culture. The city was by then also attracting a number of artists and writers who had been interned in the West during the war years, in camps for conscientious objectors. In the 1950s and early 1960s, Rexroth's home was the locale for gatherings where itinerant writers from elsewhere in the country or the world could meet local writers and radicals. Jack Kerouac showed up there one evening, sat down with a jug of cheap port wine next to him on the floor, and announced that he was a Zen Buddhist; merely to discover, Rexroth was later only too happy to reminisce, that everybody in the room read at least one oriental language, and probably knew a great deal more about Zen than he did. Rexroth took a strong disliking to Kerouac, and hardly ever had a good thing to say about him.

Rexroth's apartment was at the edge of the largely black Fillmore district, but the main arena of the San Francisco Renaissance was the North Beach neighborhood, at one time mostly Italian, then gradually turning into a local bohemia, next to Chinatown. Here were the Hungry i night club, the Vesuvio Bar, the Caffe Trieste, the Co-Existence Bagel Shop, the Cellar Café, and not least, the City Lights Bookstore. City Lights, conveniently next door to the Vesuvio, was founded as the first all-paperback bookstore in America, and with generous late night opening hours and a unique stock of items often hardly available anywhere else (including little magazines of culture and politics produced locally or elsewhere, as well as the output of small presses), it became a place where everybody with an interest in the written word would drop in, browse, and talk. Lenny Bruce, appearing in one or other of the night clubs nearby, knew that this was a good place to look for rap materials.

The main proprietor of the bookstore was himself a leading literary and intellectual figure, Lawrence Ferlinghetti, a navy veteran with a Parisian doctorate in literature who had recently migrated from the East. Ferlinghetti also took City Lights into publishing; and hardly any work on its list achieved more fame (or notoriety) than a long poem named *Howl,* by the until then largely unknown Allen Ginsberg.

It was at the famous poetry reading at the Six Gallery on October 13, 1955, that *Howl* had come instantly into the limelight. This recital had a large part in establishing the concept of poetry readings as public performances on the San Francisco scene. Perhaps the idea had first really caught hold when Dylan Thomas had passed through a few years earlier, engaging local fans in bacchanalian encounters at the Vesuvio before and after his poetry reading. Ferlinghetti, then still a mostly unpaid literary critic, had reviewed Thomas' reading as a new kind of cultural event. Rexroth had initiated the readings at the Six Gallery, known locally as a place where abstract expressionists were being introduced, and on this occasion chaired a gathering of a number of younger writers, some San Francisco natives, some newcomers, of whom Ginsberg was only one. The evening is often credited with having launched the Beats as a literary movement; the air was filled with excitement, and by the time Ginsberg took the stage, he was chanting rather than reading, to what was as much a congregation as an audience. The evening has been described by Kerouac, reputed to have established a somewhat noisy presence cheering his friends, in *The Dharma Bums.*

The authorities found *Howl* obscene. A second shipment from the British printer was seized in the customs but later released; then Ferlinghetti was arrested. The trial found its place in the history of literature. The publisher was acquitted, and the printings of the poem soared.

Writing was the Beats' own main form of expression, but not the only one they cared about. Rexroth was "involved in a nonstop commentary on American culture which always emphasized the unity of the arts" (Cherkovski 1979:77). Ferlinghetti, when he came to San Francisco after years of nomadism, finally found the chance to take up painting, and to enjoy his contacts with San Francisco artists. Not least were many of the Beat writers enchanted with jazz. Their real heroes, it has often been suggested, were Charlie Parker and Lester Young. Rexroth compared the former with Dylan Thomas as well as with Jackson Pollock (the fact that the poetry readings were held in a gallery devoted to abstract expressionism seems to have been no accident), and pioneered a hybrid San Franciscan art form, the poetry recital with jazz accompaniment. Many poets, and many North Beach coffee houses, took up this, perhaps generally with little aesthetic success. On the whole, they did better writing about jazz, and jazz life, as Kerouac did in an early piece published under the pseudonym of Jean-Louis (he was of French-Canadian parentage) but also incorporated into *On the Road*. Rexroth, again, remarked that "there are two things Jack knows nothing about—jazz and Negroes," but this was hardly altogether fair.

The combination, however, should not pass by unnoticed. The fascination with Black culture, and the romantic view of it epitomized in Norman Mailer's essay *The White Negro* (1957), incidentally a City Lights publication, was an integral part of the countercultural alternative of the day. Interracial relationships were a part of the North Beach scenery, disturbing, especially in the combination of black men with white women, to the conservative policemen patroling the neighborhood. The understanding of black life was surely often unrealistic; but at least by way of their involvement with the predominantly black jazzmen's occupational culture, the Beats could form linkages across the ethnic and cultural boundary. Ralph Gleason, a leading jazz critic of the period, had also been quick to identify the new comic Lenny Bruce with the jazz scene, suggesting that his humor was "right out of a roadband sideman's perspective" (quoted by Goldman 1974:210).

There were other such boundaries which the North Beach inhabitants were likewise, to degrees varying between individuals, concerned to transcend. They were in a city on the Pacific, and as Rexroth once put it in an interview (with Meltzer, 1971: 30), "oceans, like steppes, unite as well as separate."San Francisco, he added, also had its internal Oriental life. There were Buddhist temples everywhere.

By some local standards Kerouac's romantic, homemade dabbling with Zen certainly was not terribly impressive. Rexroth translated Chinese and Japanese poetry (although not from the original, but secondhand, from the French), and Ginsberg would involve himself much more deeply with Oriental religions, one after another, than Kerouac did. In any case, both Kerouac and Ginsberg had been drawn to things Oriental before arriving on the

West Coast, although being there surely intensified their interest. Among the painters on the San Francisco scene at the time, there were also those who had spent time in the Orient, who had studied Zen as well as Chinese calligraphy, and who showed evidence of such influences in their art. The writer who was most profoundly concerned with, and knowledgeable about, Oriental thought in an intellectual manner was undoubtedly Gary Snyder, who later took off for many years of study in a Japanese monastery. But Snyder, from a small farm in the American Northwest, and a former graduate student in anthropology and folklore, at the same time brought his interest in American Indian culture to bear on his writing; at the Six Gallery poetry reading where Ginsberg read *Howl,* Snyder read a poem about Coyote, the Indian trickster figure.

Gary Snyder was also a sometime student at the American Academy of Asian Studies, a San Francisco institution which despite its hand-to-mouth existence propagated Oriental religion and philosophy quite influentially. It had a number of Asian faculty members, and enjoyed close relationships with Chinese and Japanese Buddhists in the city, but it mostly catered to the growing interest in Asian culture among more or less educated Euro-Americans. Heading it for some time was Alan Watts, an eccentric and rather self-indulgent Englishman and former ordained Episcopalian minister, who as a speaker and writer with, as he put it himself, an "easy and free-floating attitude to Zen" (and a rather eclectic attitude to religions and popular psychologies generally), served for some time as a main cultural broker between the East and the countercultural West, while slowly drinking himself to death.

But, by then, it was already the 1970s. The Beats had scattered from North Beach long ago (tired, for one thing, of being tourist attractions, but also driven away by police attention and urban renewal), and the survivors had become something else. By the late 1960s, the counterculture was in another part of town, the preferred art forms were rock, posters, and bodily adornment, and while the Beats had had a preference for red wine and marijuana, the hippies were experimenting with LSD. Still, there were also some noticeable connections. If the *Howl* reading had been an epochal event for the Beats, the great Human Be-In of January, 1967, was one for the hippies; and on stage were two of the countercultural elders of the earlier event, Ginsberg and Snyder. Then flower power also declined. The subculture drawing most public attention next was that centered on Castro Street, whose unofficial mayor, Harvey Milk, spoke for the gay community in San Francisco politics. But Milk was killed in City Hall by a frustrated policeman-politician, and then AIDS began to cast its shadow. Meanwhile, one politico-religious movement with a strong appeal to some of the city's disadvantaged also flowered in San Francisco, and gained a measure of influence and acceptance, yet eventually moved far away to a disastrous end in its corner of a South American forest: the People's Temple of the Reverend Jim Jones. The diversity of San Francisco cultural history is continuous, and continues to draw more than local attention, even as it is discontinuous in detail.

Stefan Zweig and Allen Ginsberg both visited Calcutta, and Rabindranath Tagore came to San Francisco. Ferlinghetti has written a lyrical poem named "Short Story on a Painting by Gustav Klimt," and one of Lenny Bruce's close associates studied with Arnold Schönberg. What other connections, of a more general kind, could one make among Vienna, Calcutta, and San Francisco? Beyond their obvious particularities, is there anything more general to be said about the social organization of cultural flow, identifying recurrent characteristics of these urban scenes?

Clearly these three cities are very different in many ways, situated in societies passing through major historical transformations which shape specific cultural content, and in part, no doubt, the intensity of cultural process as well. This I would not dispute. Yet I want to argue in terms of a more general view of urban culture that Vienna, Calcutta, and San Francisco in these periods share some features—in part in common with other large cities, and in part probably to a particular degree among themselves—which contribute significantly to their cultural vitality. There are parallels in their organization of diversity, and coming as close as possible to pinpointing these parallels is my goal here.

Cities Open Toward the World

One phrasing would be that urban cultural process involves a degree of openness in several different ways, and draws perhaps in a couple of ways on some sort of critical mass. Such a formulation might at least give a sense of the kind of argument about to be put forth.

The first kind of openness involves the entanglement of an urban center with wider systems. There is a flow of people and goods as well as meanings in and out of the city; to and from other cities and more distant areas, as well as to and from the surrounding area. Redfield and Singer, in their classic but now rarely read paper on "The Cultural Role of Cities" (1954), made the distinction between cities with an orthogenetic cultural process, which entails the intellectual refinement of the largely homogeneous folk tradition of the surrounding lands, and on the other hand cities with a heterogenetic cultural process, based on the mingling of a plurality of traditions with innovative results. The early development of urbanism in history had a great deal to do with orthogenetic cultural process, but by now there are probably no orthogenetic cities left. In one way or other, all urban centers in our time are heterogenetic, actively combining and merging cultures, working out local reactions to what is initially foreign, and exporting some of the results again.[10]

Vienna, Calcutta, and San Francisco were surely of markedly heterogenetic character in the periods described here. Their internal diversity was not strictly of their own making, and newcomers played a conspicuous part in their cultural life. Let us be reminded here also that Vienna and Calcutta were the Big Apples of larger hinterlands at these times than they are now: Vienna as the capital of the Habsburg empire rather than little Austria, Calcutta as that of an undivided Bengal, but beyond that also of British India as a whole.

Vienna thus attracted many of the best and the brightest from imperial lands soon to break away. A large proportion of the people who would achieve lasting fame were first and second generation Viennese. Sigmund Freud's father was a wool merchant from Moravia. Gustav Mahler was born in a town in Bohemia where his father owned a distillery and a couple of taverns. The architect Adolf Loos was the son of a German stonemason in what is now Brno, Czechoslovakia. A Czech goldsmith was the father of the painter Oskar Kokoschka, while the author Arthur Schnitzler's father was born in Hungary. Theodor Herzl grew up in Budapest. And so forth. To San Francisco came Rexroth from Chicago, Ferlinghetti with a Sorbonne Ph.D., Ginsberg and Kerouac from the East Coast, Oregonian Gary Snyder, and the Englishman Alan Watts.

Calcutta, for its part, is in Bengal, but it has never been wholly a Bengali city. During the years of its history, immigrant groups have created a variety of niches for themselves, from the top to the bottom of city life: Englishmen, Jews, Portuguese, Armenians, Marwaris, Chinese, Sikhs, Biharis, Oriyas, and others. Even with regard to the Bengali, the learned, original, and rather controversial writer Nirad Chaudhuri, who spent much of his early life in the city, has commented in his *Autobiography of an Unknown Indian* that "the oddest thing about Calcutta was that the native human stock did not seem to be capable of taking the best advantage of the soil. With a small number of exceptions the men who made Calcutta the cradle of modern Indian culture were provincials brought up in the city" (1976:372).

The very fact that newcomers are newcomers may indeed contribute to their involvement in cultural innovation; again, where social relationships have to be achieved, as is so often the case in city life, but in particular with regard to those more recently arrived, innovation may serve as a kind of personal currency through which individuals draw attention to themselves.[11] But the openness of the heterogenetic cities should not be seen only, or primarily, in individual terms. At least as importantly, it is an openness to varied traditions, varied systems of meaning and expression. In such terms, Vienna could draw for one thing on the entire ethnic diversity of the Habsburg Empire. It has been suggested that Austrians, in their daily mingling with the other peoples of the empire, developed relativist attitudes—"the almost uncanny ability to see and understand at once all fifty-two sides of a question, and their opposite just as easily" (cited in Johnston 1972:399). But most importantly there was the fact of the relationship between Jews and other Viennese. The ambiguous position of the Jews apparently fostered an ability to look at established truths and priorities from a distance, and to criticize them and play with them. If the point can be made fairly generally about ethnic minorities, as indeed it was in chapter 5, the great influx of eastern Jews to Vienna, and the perhaps unusually intense experience of double vision in their second generation, may have made it especially relevant here.

The openness of cities toward the outside, that is to say,

may widen the horizons of their inhabitants beyond what might be common in more closed communities. In Calcutta, despite its overall ethnic diversity, what mattered most with regard to heterogenetic cultural process was surely the meeting of Indian and Western culture among the *bhadralok*. Rammohun Roy had Bengali lunch and English dinner and drank wine, but took Brahmin cooks to serve him on a journey to England. He also maintained two Calcutta houses—"it was often said that one was in every detail Indian except the owner, while the other was demonstrably European except the owner. The owner was neither here nor there, but had an existence in-between" (Poddar 1970:40).

And in-betweenness was also evident in that house owner's intellectual work. Rammohun was in touch with Unitarians in Europe, and influenced by them, but while they were largely encompassed by one religious tradition which they wanted to reform, the Calcuttan, it has been pointed out, had to think comparatively as he was at the interface of Hinduism with Christianity (and, actually, Islam as well); "as a result his vision sharpened, leaving a narrow sectarian view of the universe behind" (Kopf 1975a:49).

Rammohun Roy was of course a unique case. More generally, it may be said that the Bengal Renaissance was generated partly through the cultural flow, within a form of life framework, of open intellectual interaction with at least segments of the British colonial community in the city; and in large part in response to that state, or at least quasi-state, cultural apparatus through which the colonial power propagated Occidental culture either in undiluted or Orientalist forms. And the *bhadralok* response, fragmented and shifting as it was, organized itself to a degree within a movement framework, either to construct deliberately a better culture or to safeguard, just as deliberately, what was old and threatened.

San Francisco for its part drew selectively on currents of disaffection in America as a whole, as they surfaced after World War II, making the city to some of the newcomers first a sanctuary from tendencies in the wider society, and later a focus of cultural and political rebellion against them. But furthermore, the alternative cultures of San Francisco have drawn both on Oriental civilizations and, to a degree, on American Indian culture for inspiration. Being in the American West and on the Pacific undoubtedly played a part here. And again, there was the part played by American Black ethnic culture.

One might think of this kind of imported cultural heterogeneity as being somehow not part of the essence of urbanism, something that fortuitously just happens to appear again and again in cities. But in fact, cities often owe their existence to their positioning at political and economic crossroads which often turn out to be cultural crossroads as well. And in wider international and regional systems, all kinds of interactions between centers and peripheries are in large part channeled through the hierarchies of urban centers; it is their business to be open. In such ways, Vienna, Calcutta, and San Francisco are hardly atypical, but rather exemplary.

Critical Mass and the Management of Meaning

The importation of diversity, then, is one kind of openness in the cultural order of cities. But diversity also tends to find a promising habitat in the city for other reasons. This may be best understood by way of a rather general argument around the demographic bases of cultural phenomena; around the notion of critical mass.

Urban communities have large, dense populations. This is what most immediately makes us recognize cities when we see them. The concentration of people in space has hardly been a neutral, insignificant circumstance for social and cultural processes, even if it has proven difficult to attribute particular consequences to this factor standing in isolation. Yet in large part, the point must be to see it not just as a concentration of human beings in general, but as a concentration of people with particular, although perhaps varied, characteristics.[12]

Socially organized phenomena often require a population of a certain size. This much can probably be claimed commonsensically, even if it is is difficult to be precise about the number of people that would be required. The notion of critical mass used here, then, is heuristic. In different ways, the concentration of people in cities can help bring about certain kinds of cultural distribution, and can get some kinds of cultural processes going.

The division of labor, as an aspect of the material economy but with the kind of cultural implications discussed earlier in this book, is the most obvious case in point. A city does not usually have a division of labor that is all of its own making, insofar as it also serves the city's surrounding region. But the urban division of labor is further intensified because any specialization that establishes itself there has within relatively easy reach an unusually concentrated population. There is the probability that the city has the critical mass of people (with adequate means) required to support lines of work, and thus forms of knowledge, which could not be supported elsewhere.[13] In the cases we are concerned with here, this is a matter of what material support the city offers for a locally based cultural apparatus, for a set of more or less specialized producers of meaning and cultural form.

Yet critical mass can also be significant in terms of collective intellectual and emotional support for varied structures of meaning. Such support can be directly correlated with material support, insofar as those who provide the latter may also offer the former. In the Viennese instance, it is clear that in a generalized way, the liberal and in significant part Jewish bourgeoisie, prosperous and with some aesthetic and intellectual sensibility, provided much of the wherewithal as well as the appreciation for its cultural productions. In Calcutta, the *bhadralok* generally were receptive to the issues raised and dealt with by the Bengal Renaissance. These were the amateurs, the culturally constituted laymen whom the specialists needed. In both cases, too, material support for the cultural apparatus did not altogether depend on market arrangements, or official forms of redistributive funding for culture, as a fair number of those involved in more specialized cultural production could derive their security from personal or family fortunes.

But material support and appreciative response can also be separated. Subcultures existing on the basis of a relative symmetry of perspectives and a free flow of meaning among participants within a form of life framework do not as such require anything much in the way of material provisioning, but cannot do without some number of people to keep the reciprocities going. And here, on the whole, whatever peculiarity of perspective is involved, the likelihood is again greater in the city than elsewhere (everything else held equal) that it can be collectivized into some form of subculture, and thereby reach fuller expression. There is a greater variety of critical masses, large or small. The condition is simply that people of similar perspectival proclivities can get in touch with one another, and go to work on what they have in common. Every time this condition is met, the city gets another contribution to its proliferation of subcultures.[14]

It is also possible (remember the argument with regard to jazz musicians and others in chapter 5), where subcultures of practitioners form within the cultural apparatus, that there is an audience providing material support, but that the more significant symbolic response to creativity comes from within the more immediately available, personally known subcultural community. This may have been most nearly true in the case of the Beats, who were in the cultural apparatus nationally, or even globally, but whose subculture, one might argue, was based in one neighborhood in San Francisco and in another in New York.

There is also a sort of feedback of the urban propensity for subculture formation into the relationship between the city and its surroundings. For as the city shows itself to be a haven for subcultures, it additionally and selectively attracts those particular migrants who want to involve themselves with them. This, for example, is the way San Francisco grew, as a placc of refuge for 1950s cultural dissidents, and as a center of gay culture in the United States, not to say the world.

The Openness Inside Cities

Yet cultural diversity in itself is hardly enough to turn cities into machineries for more or less continuously innovative cultural production. Another kind of openness seems to help here; the concentration of people in a limited space is important to cultural process not only because it provides critical masses for varied developments, but also because it offers forever new occasions for serendipity: you find things without specifically looking for them, because they are around you all the time. And much of the greatness of Vienna, Calcutta, and San Francisco in the times I am concerned with lies in this, in the fairly easy—not to say insistent—availability of cultural interfaces.

One might argue that some of this kind of involvement

with difference is not serendipitous, not much a matter of chance, insofar as it is again built into the urban order through the division of labor. Because of it, the cultural repertoires of individuals are in a way incomplete, and must therefore be open to one another. Apart from this, however, there is a kind of openness of which cities, and also particular city dwellers, obviously can have more or less.

It is undoubtedly true of some segments of our three cities that they were not much involved in such openness. According to Surajit Sinha, the Bengali anthropologist, "the urban milieu of Calcutta is particularly permissive about the persistence of primordial social identities—languages, dialects, religious groups, castes"; there is a "co-existence of nearly isolated social worlds" (1972:271). The statement pertains to the present, but there is little reason to believe that it would not have been just as true in the century before. (Although I have already argued—apropos the mosaic metaphor, in chapter 2—that ethnographers are somewhat prone to exaggerate such isolation, descriptively and conceptually.) Historians of the Bengal Renaissance, we have also seen, describe its impact outside a relatively limited elite and middle class as modest indeed. Undoubtedly, it could be said about Vienna and San Francisco as well that many inhabitants went about their lives little concerned with the part of their cities in the growth of, respectively, modern and countercultural sensibilities.

Yet there was also something else going on. "The most distinctive feature of Florentine intellectual life was not its variety and complexity—which was matched, to some degree, by Milan, Venice, and Naples—but rather the unusually close rapport between these cultural traditions," writes the historian Brucker of the capital of the Italian renaissance (1969:215), and it is striking that this rapport, this openness, seems to be a regular feature of places of intense cultural productivity. Rather than a flow of meaning divided into a multitude of separate currents, there is an inclusive cultural swirl. This is what more than anything else has intrigued intellectual historians about turn-of-the-century Vienna: the intensity of traffic in meaning and meaningful form within one broad stratum of people, with little or no respect for the kinds of barriers between spheres of thought which we now tend to take for granted. In Paris, London, or Berlin at the same time, Carl Schorske suggests, making a point parallel to Brucker's, "intellectuals in the various branches of high culture, whether academic or aesthetic, journalistic or literary, political or intellectual, scarcely knew each other" (1980:xxvii). In Vienna, on the other hand, they mingled not only with one another, but also with businesspeople and professionals whose cultural concerns were highly developed.

In a similar manner, San Francisco had its openings in the subcultural walls. From Black ethnic culture by way of jazz to Beat literary life, one can see a chain of interlocking subcultures, a flow of cultural influence which entailed selections and transformations, perhaps misunderstandings as well; nonetheless, it was there, as it also was between Oriental culture on the one hand and San Francisco Occidental art and writing on the other.

One may be inclined to think of such management of meaning in network terms. For one thing, individuals may be differently placed with regard to bringing such mingling about. Some people, more or less the quintessential renaissance men, may in themselves combine a range of interests and modes of expression, and support coherence through their own work as well as social cohesion through their contacts. In Vienna, Schönberg, composer but also an accomplished painter and essayist, acknowledging Karl Kraus' influence on him; Kokoschka, painter, playwright, poet, critic. In San Francisco, again, Rexroth was the constant advocate of unity in culture, and the weekly meetings in his apartment could debate literary, philosophical, religious, or political issues; Ferlinghetti wrote as well as painted. Rammohun Roy, Radhakanta Deb, and Bankimchandra were among the generalists of the Bengal Renaissance. But these are all people who are likely to be remembered not least for the enduring value of their own work. Other individuals have perhaps mostly been socially useful, as connecting figures bringing others together in creative circles. Hermann Bahr would be the most obvious Viennese instance.

If some people are more integrative than others, however, the general openness of networks is also significant: an openness which brings together people who are unlike with regard to their dominant concerns or avenues of cultural expression. In *Wittgenstein's Vienna,* Janik and Toulmin (1973:92) illustrate this by pointing out that the composer Anton Bruckner, Gustav Mahler's teacher, gave the physicist Ludwig Boltmann piano lessons; that Mahler consulted Sigmund Freud and used to be a guest in the home of the Wittgenstein family; and that Freud fought a duel with Viktor Adler, later to become a founding father of Austrian socialism. One could add a reminder that von Hofmannsthal attended Mach's lectures and that he borrowed Freud's writings from Hermann Bahr, and that one of Klimt's older painter friends was Mahler's father-in-law. And so on, almost into infinity.[15]

How do such internally diverse networks come about? There is hardly a single answer to the question. It may be, for instance, that in Vienna the shared Jewish background of many of those engaged in varieties of cultural creativity provided one social framework for acquaintance; in Vienna, too, and in Calcutta, the relative prominence of a few educational institutions seems to have meant that individuals of quite different later achievements had been pupils together early in life. In more general terms, it could be argued that the city's openness to the wider society might contribute to the openness within urbanism, insofar as the former brings newcomers to the city who are available to new networks.

Apart from the openness of identifiable personal networks, however, the materials on the three cities also describe other institutions, within different frameworks of cultural flow, which allow a kind of cultural scanning through which serendipity may again operate. Every commentator on turn-of-the-century Vienna dwells lovingly on café life, where relationships could be both formed and maintained, and where new ideas spread rapidly; in the market, no doubt, as far as the provision of material services was concerned, but in the midst of a form of life when it came to the flow of meaning.[16] While the *Jung-Wien* circle was at the Griensteidl as long as it lasted, Karl Kraus, having withdrawn from there, had his own regular table at the Central, where he could be seen with Loos, Kokoschka, and others.

In some ways, the Viennese café was even a material necessity. Housing in the city was notoriously inadequate—crowded, cold, uncomfortable. Thus, the Viennese needed a place of refuge. Yet many cafés, and especially the great ones like the two just mentioned, were much more than that. Some books were written in cafés, and many more hotly discussed. Politicians found more or less willing audiences for their campaigns there, and waiters could direct new guests to tables where particular topics were being discussed. Steady visitors could linger for hours, day after day over a cup of coffee or a glass of wine, and like Trotsky they could earn their local reputation in the café. In the better cafés, one could read Viennese and international newspapers and journals, supplied by the house; only there could be keen competition for these, so that the young Stefan Zweig and his peers were pleased when on the warmest summer days other people left the city and they could have the cafés and their reading materials almost to themselves.

As somewhat more elaborate settings, rather more in the market and part of the cultural apparatus, there were also the cabarets, popular in all the major Central European cities as places where one could eat, drink, and be entertained, with varying degrees of ambition. Karl Kraus was once assaulted in another public place by the irate members of a cabaret ensemble which he had recently reviewed in *Die Fackel.* The one cabaret drawing most attention in Vienna was *Die Fledermaus,* "The Bat," the work of the Secessionist architect Hoffmann, and one to which many Viennese authors contributed, not least Peter Altenberg; Kokoschka put on a technically rather flawed shadow play there.

What did San Francisco and Calcutta have in the way of institutions to keep the cultural flow similarly open? In the former city, the coffee houses and bars—the Co-Existence Bagel Shop, the Hungry i, the Vesuvio—were multipurpose hangouts much like the Viennese cafés.[17] In Calcutta, the factionalism of the *dals,* with their opposing tendencies of fission and fusion, had its part in keeping social life open. Mukherjee suggests that the conflicting loyalties resulting from this helped bring about "an atmosphere where literature and art could flourish," (1975:61), and reminds his readers of T. S. Eliot's view of the importance of diversity and conflict for progress and creativity. Another Calcuttan institution, the *adda,* a kind of salon, would seem to have been even more directly the counterpart of the Viennese café as an arena of sociability. Nirad Chaudhuri has described its place in city life as it was in the early twentieth century, when he was growing up (1976:398 ff.)

The men of Calcutta, according to Chaudhuri, were extremely gregarious, and evinced an "extreme anxiety to avoid boredom at any cost." They were ready to notice any novelty and discuss it with enthusiasm. In the morning, they would wander about in search of casual gossip, while in the evening, the *adda* was a fixed rendezvous. Mostly the gathering place would be the outer parlor of one of the wealthier participants, although an office after office hours, or a tea shop, might also do. Tea would always be available, but hardly anything else, except the company, involving a more or less steady membership who would drop in gradually. If there was a host, in the sense of owner of the house, he was not always present; and when he was, he was not necessarily conspicuous.

Again, at a more formally organized level, the Calcutta of the Bengal Renaissance had a strikingly rich associational life, notably involving a great number of discussion clubs and such entities as the Society for the Acquisition of General Knowledge (a major Young Bengal grouping), the Epistolary Association, the Indian Association for the Cultivation of Science, and the Bengal Social Science Association. Such organizations came and went; they could discuss "all questions connected with local politics, social reform, education, literature, religion, metaphysics, jurisprudence, political economy, scientific outlook, theories of state and of society, colonial administration and the future shape of India" (Poddar 1970:103). Members were kcpt informed about the latest in the world of ideas (and certainly much of this was a matter of keeping an eye on European developments); but the emphasis was indeed often on "general knowledge," not on specialization. Again, for some time, Calcutta had as a recurrent event the Tagores' cultural fair, the Mela, the natural place both to exhibit and perform local work and to inspect it, with many genres coming together in one place.

To help in cultural scanning there are also the media. Apart from the café, journalism played a major part in Viennese culture, most particularly in the form of the *feuilleton;* an essay on any one of a wide variety of topics, often a vignette from concrete life where the writer could place his own subjective experiences and feelings on exhibit. This was the form that Herzl, Bahr, and Altenberg had mastered, and of which Kraus more often than not (but not in Altenberg's case) tended to be sharply critical. The *feuilleton* could have more than a little in common with a sprightly café conversation. It was fast food for thought, quickly produced, often soon forgotten. Yet its characteristic style also had an impact on other writing in the period. Through the *feuilleton* as well as the café, one could fairly effortlessly stay in touch with people, events, and ideas, and perhaps contribute one's own share.

From the *feuilletons* of the *Neue Freie Presse* to the overflowing shelves of the City Lights Bookshop, the media and their outlets also serve serendipity, only widening what is immediately at hand in the street or in the café. One might turn to them more out of curiosity than because one is looking for anything in particular. In 1950s San Francisco, the local radio station KPFA/FM was one of the main institutions of the anti-establishment cultural apparatus. In Calcutta as well, newspapers and journals of all inclinations kept appearing and disappearing. Radhakanta Deb, Rammohun Roy, Bankimchandra Chatterjee were all publicists, and Derozio was trying to start a newspaper just before he died. "One of the great lessons the Swami learnt in Calcutta was no doubt the discovery of two most powerful organs of propaganda: the public lecture and publication," writes Jordens (1978:93) of Dayananda Sarasvati's stay in the city. Dayananda found that the leaders of opinion in Calcutta had their own printing presses, and when the newspapers advertised, his lectures they were a great success.

Someone might object that these are not intrinsically urban phenomena: the nature of these media is precisely to transcend face-to-face relationships and local concentrations of people such as cities. That is true; but it is also a fact that the availability of a rich variety of media, print, or—nowadays—electronic, still has much to do with critical mass. The most convenient place to leaf through a variety of current publications in all of central Europe may still have been in a well-equipped Viennese café, and the newsstand is a very urban institution. For someone like Freud, not much given to socializing outside the medical community, the constant exposure to the local media still placed him squarely in the Viennese cultural context. Yet at the same time, the media brought the world into Vienna.

The café, the *adda,* the amateur society for learning, the book store, the *feuilleton* can thus all serve as the instruments or arenas of quickened and not very predictable cultural flow. In a way, as Simmel suggested, urban life as a whole can be richly serendipitous, involving accidental and unexpected experiences and discoveries. Yet institutions like these bring an even greater concentration of this quality of life. Perhaps such scanning borders on the nonserendipitous, as one may seek out places of this type exactly in order to find out what is going on. Even so, it is on the whole an undirected search, a strategy of situating oneself on the scene of surprises.

The occasions of serendipity, too, may be brought about by a great variety of social and cultural mechanisms. It would appear that the greater internal openness of urban cultural process draws some particular support from those subcultures which have the critical mass, and/or material strength, to maintain their own cultural apparatuses, whether in the market or by way of redistribution. Through these, a traffic in meaning primarily intended for members of the group can also more readily reach others than it would were the subcultural flow inconspicuously, inaccessibly, confined to the personal relationships among members: by way of jazz clubs and Zen temples, Black and Asian cultures in San Francisco went, as it were, public. It would also seem that some cities more than others, for cultural as well as demographic reasons, keep a greater proportion of their inhabitants—and particular inhabitants—in the public view for more of the time. Where the sexes are kept rather strongly segregated, the women are more often at home and the men in the street, and in the cafés. In all our three cities, conspicuously fewer women were participants in the cultural process going on in public places. In Vienna, one basis for the proliferation of cafés seems to have been that as young men had to remain unmarried until economically secure, there were years of their young adult lives when they had nowhere else to go.

Creativity and Perspectives Toward Perspectives

Cultural diversity and vitality thus seem especially likely to go together in a city where, within the critical mass needed for differentiation, there is an interrelatedness among people involved with different cultural forms, as well as other means of cultural scanning. But just what is the nature of the collective, yet differentiated, creative management of culture here?

The processes by which different genres of thought and expression somehow manage to climb on one another's shoulders may yet be poorly understood, and certainly cannot be reconstructed with any greater precision a century later, or even a few decades later, as in our three cases. What is involved, anyhow, is an interplay between perspectives. Different people have their own intellectual problems, and work on them with their own kinds of symbolic materials. But there are also perspectives toward perspectives, and in the cultural swirl of the city the manifestations of other perspectives are not at a distant horizon, or beyond it, but reasonably close at hand. Thus, whatever innovations occur in one field can be seized upon, with approval or critically, to stimulate work in another. The asymmetry of input mode in relationships, to return to one concept from chapter 2, itself becomes culturally generative.

For one thing there may be a sense of affinity, an availability of metaphors. A common feeling of cultural crisis resulting from historical change may add to this sense, even when responses to it may appear to be of all different kinds. In Calcutta, there was the pervasive problem of the relationship between West and East, to be solved in just about every sphere of life and thought. In Vienna, the publicist Kraus, the composer Schönberg, the architect Loos, and the painter Kokoschka could mutually appreciate one another's labor to purify cultural forms. And in the same city, Mach's views of the relationship between reality, the flux of sensory perceptions, and identity could inspire Hofmannsthal as well as the feuilletonists, who in their turn may have left some mark on the style of Arthur Schnitzler's novels, which Freud found coming so remarkably close to his own intellectual struggles with psychoanalysis.

In San Francisco, jazz—the local scene as well as the entire American phenomenon—was central. Although the idea of reading poetry to jazz was a dubious one (a hybrid form as graceful as a steamboat with sails, someone remarked) other influences were more profound. "Abstract expressionist painters," Albert Goldman has argued (1974:190), "were imitating jazz by spattering their canvases with random-looking drips and squirts and by employing these canvases in long impulsively unwound strips that could start and stop anywhere. These same long strips—reflecting the chorus-after-chorus, indefinitely extended jazz solo—turned up inside Jack Kerouac's typewriter, which was specially designed to accommodate a whole roll of paper!"[18] Lenny Bruce, according to Goldman (1974:196), would even explain that there was a kind of unity in the type of abstraction occurring in all the "hip arts," whether jazz, poetry, prose fiction, or painting. The time had come in each of them when their practitioners were so familiar with their old outlines that they could not be bothered to complete them. Instead, one kind or other of abbreviation or short-hand was adopted, carrying the gist of the message without going through the tedium of spelling it out.

As another example of cross-fertilization between expressive forms, there was poet-painter Ferlinghetti's obsession with the idea of turning the arrangement of the words on a page into an effective pictorial presentation—the poem should *look* like its message (Cherkovski 1979:71). And yet while Ferlinghetti was thus experimenting with the written word as picture, there was at the same time the experience of the poetry reading as a cultural form, exercising its own influence on the understanding of poetry itself, and the role of the poet. The readings, Gary Snyder has reminisced, made it clear that poetry is "really an oral art" (1980:163–164). It could evolve at its best communally, in the interaction between the poet and a skilled audience pushing him on to "the difficult, the complex, the outrageous." But this view, Snyder admitted, was also informed by his studies in anthropology, folklore, and linguistics.

The creativity that may come about as perspectives meet with other perspectives does not always grow out of affinity, however. It can also result from their clash. Different cultural forms can inspire one another, but they can also provoke one another through conflict and discord. Again, in Vienna, Calcutta, and San Francisco, new culture often grew in conspicuous opposition to what had gone before it or existed as established culture around it. The picture of Viennese harmony suggested by Stefan Zweig in one of the initial quotations is surely one-sided. *Jung-Wien* and the Secession defined themselves through their departure from what had been at hand; the work of Schönberg and Kokoschka was greeted with immediate, overt hostility; not so few of the major innovators of thought and expression (among them Freud) were deeply ambivalent about Vienna as a place to live in, and many of them moved away, either temporarily or for good. Berlin loomed large as an alternative. And conflicts became sharper over time. If Klimt, Mahler, and Hofmannsthal were rather like reformists within the existing order, people like Loos and Kokoschka were rejectionists. In Calcutta, departures from Hindu conventions in a Westernizing direction were continuously controversial, as in the drawn-out conflict between the Dharma Sabha and the Brahmoists. Street urchins sang ribald songs about Rammohun, who often had to formulate his point of view in the context of public debates. Outraged family elders were ready to assassinate school boys of Derozian inclinations for their misdemeanors; certainly, in both Calcutta and Vienna conflicts frequently focused on the divide between generations. As for San Francisco (whose migrant rebels had perhaps more often left their elders behind somewhere), there may well have been something like a "culture of civility"; Kenneth Rexroth has written in similar terms in his autobiography (1966:366–367). Nonetheless, even there difference has hardly been divorced from conflict. The Beats were harrassed by local police; the 1970s spokesman of the homosexuals was murdered.

Such signs of conflict may all be regrettable in themselves, and yet it would be difficult to deny that the clashes between perspectives have also contributed to the vitality of cultural process in these three cities. Taken-for-grantedness is in large part made impossible, opposition leads to dedoxification, perspectives are sharpened. Cultural co-presence is often most productive of new meaning and form when it is most provocative.

Conclusion: Compartmentalization and Mobility

San Francisco kept producing new cultural forms: counterculture, gay culture. Intellectual and aesthetic life in Vienna stumbled on for some time after the fall of the House of Habsburg, but what was left could hardly survive the return of that past sojourner in the city, Adolf Hitler. In Calcutta, despite all the political or physical problems of the city (or to some degree perhaps because of them), as Satyajit Ray suggested in the second introductory quotation of this chapter, there is still a sense of great vitality. The *adda,* Surajit Sinha notes (1972:273), has continued to be an important institution for the circulation of ideas in Calcutta. And Calcutta is even now a place where a local academic may know "an important dancer, a political leader, a moviemaker" (Sinha 1972:252). A local columnist has calculated that the city has "a reserve army of poets"—some fifteen thousand of them published at one time or other (Mitra 1977:74–77).[19]

To repeat, the cities as we have seen them were in different historical conjunctures, the nature of which can perhaps in each case be stated macroscopically in a few words. The cultures they made at these times have also had different degrees of impact on the world, and perhaps they have been of different enduring weight. Turn-of-the-century Vienna is still in some ways very much alive, but elsewhere, through its ideas, at least as much as in present-day Vienna. For a few years, the Beats drew attention nationally and beyond the United States; but, in the long run, their power to define reality and shape cultural expression has hardly amounted to very much. The influence of the Bengal Renaissance may or may not have reached out effectively into India (opinions differ), but mostly not much further.

What I have tried to identify here, however, are the similarities in the social organization of cultural processes. Like most cities, these three have been open to cultural currents in their wider environment, but looking closer at things, we realize that the historical changes were filtered through the diversity of each city, seen through a multitude of perspectives, mixed with different everyday concerns, and thereby becoming a great deal more culturally complex. The complexity of urban culture partly depends on the importation of varied meanings from the outside, and is partly created and amplified within the city itself, as size and density are exploited for their particular possibilities with regard to the management of culture. Like a great many cities, because of their sizable and concentrated local populations, these three have provided the material bases as well as intellectual and emotional support for quite highly differentiated cultures. Rather more unusually, it would seem, Vienna, Calcutta, and San Francisco have offered environments for a noteworthy openness within the organization of diversity.

As we think about culture, cities can also be good to think with—at least as good as villages. That has been the point of this chapter. As more anthropologists choose to stay in urban settings (for this is where most of them come from, anyway), and try to develop a sense of their internal and external connections (instead of heading for the enclaves, or even constructing them rather arbitrarily in their own minds), as well as of the interplay between the circumstances of cultural production and the productions themselves, our understanding of the making of cultures today will undoubtedly increase in subtlety. When we observe the spatial proximity of the everydays and the avantgardes, then we can also bring their meanings closer to one another.

Yet cities can also have their limitations as frames for cultural study. Taking the historical view of urban cultural process, this becomes especially clear. By way of conclusion, a couple of circumstances must be mentioned in particular.

On the one hand, there is the tendency toward specialization in the management of meaning and meaningful form. In the long term, there may be an overall increase in such specialization; away from intellectuals, toward intelligentsias. Of our three cities, Calcutta and Vienna had the wider coherent fields of cultural efflorescence. In San Francisco, the most recent instance, the universities of the vicinity no doubt played some part in providing the basis of support for a variety of cultural productions, but with the increasing professionalization of Academia, it and Bohemia had obviously drifted apart and viewed one another with some suspicion. As intelligentsias grow, defining their own problems and goals in terms which are increasingly inaccessible for others, and getting their symbolic and material rewards mostly in some way through their peers, there is a compartmentalization of cultural process. Historians and sociologists have documented and analyzed the process whereby American cities, not least, have moved from a civic intellectual life carried by scholars and gentlemen amateurs in interaction, to a situation in which the generalized local framework for cultural production and dissemination has become much less important.[20]

If the tendency is toward such compartmentalization, however, it has also been a fact that cities with more of it have coexisted in time with those with less of it—Florence with Venice and Naples according to Brucker, Vienna with Berlin according to Schorske. Local conditions evidently play a part. Where the patronage and understanding of the laymen of the city still matter—perhaps in the absence of alternatives—or where other frameworks of social organization, whether religion or old school ties, effectively draw together people variously located in the organization of diversity, there perhaps varied cultural currents will again come to mingle, here and there, now and again. And when there are overriding common concerns, when shared conditions of life come to count for more than the particulars of the profession, then people pursuing different lines of cultural work may still find more that is recognizable in each other's efforts, and be stimulated by it.

On the other hand, as a second limiting factor with regard to the ties between contemporary cultural process and urban locality, there is human mobility. That openness to the world which contributes so significantly to the vitality of urban cultures also in a way makes them more fragmented and vulnerable. Anthropologists habitually see people as restricted to places, their thinking mirroring peculiarities of local ecology; "the science of the concrete can thus be written as the poetry of confinement" (Appadurai 1988:38). But urbanites, many of them at least, come and go. This is part of the essence of cities as centers of communication.

Dwarkanath Tagore and Rammohun Roy were not the only Calcuttans on the streets of London. When Mahler, Kokoschka, Zweig, and Freud found Vienna unbearable, they voted with their feet. Greenwich Village, New York, in the 1950s had some of the same local celebrities as North Beach, San Francisco, for these were people whose style of life and thought was on the road.[21] When intelligentsias now turn their backs on their cities, they are often heading for the airport. Nor, obviously, can the study of contemporary cultural complexity allow itself to become imprisoned in even the most interesting of places.

7 The Global Ecumene

Ethnology is in the sadly ludicrous, not to say tragic, position, that at the very moment when it begins to put its workshop in order, to forge its proper tools, to start ready for work on its appointed task, the material of its study melts away with hopeless rapidity. (Bronislaw Malinowski [1922] 1961:xv)

We can easily now conceive of a time when there will be only one culture and one civilization on the entire surface of the earth. I don't believe this will happen, because there are contradictory tendencies always at work—on the one hand towards homogenization and on the other towards new distinctions.
(Claude Lévi-Strauss 1978:20)

Each year in the spring, the countries of Europe meet in a televised song contest, a media event watched by hundreds of millions of people. There is first a national contest in each country to choose its own entry for the international competition. A few years ago, a controversy erupted in Sweden after this national contest. It was quite acceptable that the tune which was first runner-up had been performed by a lady from Finland, and the second runner up by an Afro-American lady who was by now a naturalized Swede. Both were highly thought of and somehow represented that new heterogeneity of Swedish society which had evolved over the last couple of decades. What was controversial was the winning tune, the refrain of which was "Four Buggs and a Coca Cola"; Bugg, like the name of the soft drink, was a brand name (for a chewing gum). Many people thought it improper that the national entry in the European contest should revolve around two brand names. But of the two, Coca Cola was much the more controversial, as it was widely understood as a central symbol of "cultural imperialism." Indeed, a synonym for the latter is "the cocacolonization of the world." Under the circumstances, what drew much less attention was the fact that the winning tune was a calypso, not something one would conventionally think of as typically Swedish, either.

In the end, the text was changed before the European finals, where the Swedish entry finished in the lower end of the field. But that is neither here nor there. For our purposes, what matters is what an incident like this tells us about the kind of cultures we make now.

Long ago, Alfred Kroeber suggested on the one hand that "probably the greater part of every culture has percolated into it," on the other hand that "as soon as a culture has accepted a new item, it tends to lose interest in [its] foreignness of origin" (1948: 257–258). The former seems to be a culture-historical fact. The latter of Kroeber's claims is perhaps at this point more debatable.[1] The interrelatedness of cultures may nowadays force itself upon our awareness more than before, due to its intensity and perhaps its particular current forms. Increasingly, cultural debates around the world are about a loss of integrity in national cultures, about the impact of communication satellites, about the internationalization of youth cultures, about the new cultural diversity created within national boundaries as the natives are joined by migrants and refugees. The origin of new cultural items is becoming a core aspect of the meanings they have to us.[2]

It must now be more difficult than ever, or at least more unreasonable, to see the world (in terms of that metaphor scrutinized in an earlier chapter) as a cultural mosaic, of separate pieces with hard, well-defined edges. Cultural interconnections increasingly reach across the world. More than ever, there is a global ecumene.[3] The entities we routinely call cultures are becoming more like subcultures within this wider entity, with all that this suggests in terms of fuzzy boundaries and more or less arbitrary delimitation of analytical units. To grasp this fact of globalization, in its wide range of manifestations and implications, is the largest task at present confronting a macroanthropology of culture. In this concluding chapter, I want to apply the general point of view developed in the book to at least some aspects of that task.[4]

Centers and Peripheries in Cultural Flow

Until the 1960s or so, acknowledgments of the fact that "we are all in the same world" were mostly pieties, with uncertain political and intellectual implications. Since then, in the social sciences, understandings of globalization have usually involved a view of asymmetry; key conceptual pairs have been center (or core) and periphery, metropolis and satellite.[5]

Asymmetries are present in the global social organization of meaning as well. But what kind of asymmetries are they? How closely aligned are the asymmetries of culture with those of economy, politics, or military might? How do center/periphery relationships in the world affect structures of meaning and cultural expression?

In political and military terms, the world during much of the twentieth century had two superpowers, and whatever freedom of movement other countries exercised, whether great or small, it tended ultimately to be constrained by this arrangement. In economic terms, the century has by and large seen the United States in a dominant position, with a number of lesser powers grouped around it, varyingly in ascent or decline. In cultural terms, would we recognize other powers than these?

As we understand things now, the question has two sides (which may be to simplify matters). There is that cultural production in the periphery which is somehow in response to the political and economic dominance of the center. Here the world system as defined in political and/or economic terms is obviously given cultural recognition of one kind or other. On the other hand, there is the issue of cultural diffusion. What defines the center/periphery relationship here are above all asymmetries, in the terms used before, of input quantity and scale. When the center speaks, the periphery listens, and mostly does not talk back.

In this case, the cultural centers of the world are not by definition identical with political and economic centers. Are they in practice? To begin with, let us just consider this in gross terms, as an issue of the overall cultural influence of nations. It can be argued that the center/periphery relationships of culture are not, at least at any particular point in time, a mere reflection of political and economic power. In the American case, the congruence is undeniable. The general cultural influence of the Soviet Union in the world in the decades of its greatest strength, on the other hand, remained modest compared with its political and military power. Among the lesser powers, Britain and France may at present be stronger as cultural than as economic and political centers; this is perhaps debatable. Japan, on the whole, has at least so far kept a rather lower cultural profile in the world, despite its economic success (and with some exceptions). Most of what it exports does not seem to be identifiably marked by Japaneseness.

If the global pattern of center/periphery relationships in culture thus has some degree of separateness, it is easy to see in some instances what is behind a greater cultural influence. To a degree the present cultural influence of Britain and France still reflects the fact that old-style colonial powers could more or less monopolize the center/periphery cultural flow to its domains. In large parts of the world this even now makes London or Paris not just *a* center but *the* center. In old settler colonies, historical ties are yet closer, as links of kinship and ancestry also connect the periphery to a specific center. In Australia, when critics refer to "the cultural cringe," it is the deference to things English they have in mind. Language is obviously also a factor which may convert political power into cultural influence, and then conserve the latter. As people go on speaking English, French, and Portuguese in postcolonial lands, in postcolonial times, old center/periphery relationships get a prolonged lease on life. If all this means that the center/periphery relationships of culture tend to exhibit some lag relative to present and emergent structures of political and economic power, it might also mean that Japan may well yet come into a position of greater cultural influence in the world.

One might speculate that people also make different assumptions, in a metacultural fashion, about the nature of the relationship between themselves and their culture. By and large, Americans may not expect that the meanings and the cultural forms they invent are only for themselves; possibly because they have seen at home over the years that practically anybody can become an American. The French may see their culture as a gift to the world. There is a *mission civilisatrice.* The Japanese, on the other hand—so it is said—find it a strange notion that anyone can "become Japanese," and they put Japanese culture on exhibit, in the framework of organized international contacts, as a way of displaying irreducible distinctiveness rather than in order to make it spread. (Notably, many of those who engage in introducing aspects of Japanese culture to the world are alien cultural brokers.[6])

Staying with the conception of cultural centers as places

where culture is invented and from which it is diffused, however, one cannot be satisfied with only the very generalized picture of the relative standing of a handful of countries as wholes. Too much is missing, and too much is assumed. Countries do not always exercise their influence at the same level across the gamut of cultural expressions. American influence is at present very diverse, but perhaps most conspicuous in science, technology, and popular culture; French influence on world culture is rather of the high culture variety, and in related fields such as sophisticated food and fashion; there is widespread interest in the organization and internal cultural engineering of Japanese corporations. In such more specialized ways, places like the Vatican or the Shia holy city of Qom also organize parts of the world into center/periphery relationships of culture, for certain purposes.

In this context, one should also keep in mind that particularly in such fields as science and technology, the spread of knowledge between nations can be actively prevented, for reasons of economic, political, and military advantage. Indeed, there are signs that such large-scale restrictive management of knowledge is on the increase.[7] Often, it is primarily a part of competitive relationships between centers, but it constrains the cultural flow between center and periphery as well, maintaining the advantage of the former.

It is another characteristic of the structure of center/periphery relationships that it has many tiers. Some countries have a strong influence in their regions, due to a well-developed cultural apparatus—Mexico in Latin America, for example, and Egypt in the Arab World. A shared language and cultural tradition can be important in this way, at the same time as a sizable domestic market for cultural products can give one country an advantageous position in having something to export to the rest of the region. Such regional centers may base their production on meanings and forms wholly internal to the region, or they may operate as cultural brokers, translating influences from first-tier centers into something more adapted to regional conditions.

World cultural process, it appears, has a much more intricate organization of diversity than is allowed in a picture of a center/periphery structure with just a handful of all-purpose centers. A further issue, obviously, if one tries to arrive at a kind of present-day global cultural flow chart is to what extent the peripheries indeed talk back, which would in large part be a question of the influence of the Third World on the Occident.

Reggae music, swamis, and Latin American novels exemplify the kind of countercurrents from more or less recent cultural history that may first enter one's mind; culture coming fully developed, as it were, from periphery to center, and at the same time culture which the periphery can give away, and keep at the same time. There are indeed instances like these, and while they are not new, they may well be on the increase. A little more will be said about them toward the end of the chapter. Yet desirable as one might find it to be able to speak of world culture in terms of more equal exchange, the conclusion can at present hardly be avoided that asymmetry rules.

But then there are also other kinds of cultural transfers from periphery to center, which in themselves exemplify asymmetry in other manners. One involves particular embodiments of meaning: material objects of art, ritual, or other significance, which are not readily replaceable at the periphery, but which are at one time or other exported, due to the superior economic and political power of the center, and absorbed by its museums or other collections. Here one may indeed see a tangible impoverishment of the cultures of the periphery—often especially in terms of immediate access to the best in one's cultural heritage, as what is removed is what the center defines as the capital-C culture of the periphery. This is now a field of controversy, with the representatives of the periphery demanding the decommoditization and repatriation of artifacts to which they consider their own countries to have a moral right.[8]

There is likewise the kind of periphery-to-center transfer in which people like anthropologists play a part. Much knowledge concerning the periphery is more available in the center than in the periphery itself, and especially to the specialists on the periphery from the center, because of the greater capacity of the center to organize and analyze knowledge in certain ways. The center may extract the raw materials for this knowledge, so to speak, from the periphery, although in that form, knowledge may at the same time remain there. Again, informants and others need not give up the ideas that they give away. The process of refining the materials often occurs only in the knowledge institutions of the center, however, and it is not at all certain that the final product gets back to the periphery. Sometimes, this kind of center/periphery asymmetry is labeled academic imperialism; as we see, it entails a flow in the opposite direction of that usually thought of as cultural imperialism.

Anyway, all this is in gross terms, as a way of beginning to look at cultural management at the most inclusive level. In fact, one does not get very far by talking about the cultural influence of nations, for nations as corporate actors—that is, as states—have only a limited part in the global cultural flow. They may appear in guises such as the USIA, the Fulbright Commission, the British Council, and the Alliance Française, and interact in their own terms in organizations such as UNESCO. Much of the traffic in culture in the world, however, is organized in other terms, transnational rather than literally international. When we talk about American influence or French influence or Mexican influence, we throw together a great many different kinds of asymmetrical relationships, perhaps with some number of symmetrical ones for good measure. Consequently, we are better off looking at the global cultural flow in terms of the four organizational frames of state, market, form of life, movement, and their interrelations.

World Culture, World System

To get some further sense of this, we may consider two prominent but more partial views. One of them suggests that present-day center/periphery relationships in the world will lead to the disappearance of cultural differences: that scenario of global homogenization to which both Malinowski and Lévi-Strauss refer, in different ways, in the quotations above. "One conclusion still seems unanimously shared," claims a prominent media researcher; "the impressive variety of the world's cultural systems is waning due to a process of 'cultural synchronization' that is without historical precedent" (Hamelink 1983:3). Horror tales are told: "The incredibly rich local musical tradition of many Third World countries is rapidly disappearing under the onslaught of dawn-to-dusk North American pop music." "For starving children in the Brazilian city of Recife, to have a Barbie doll seems more important than having food."

This scenario has several things going for it. A quick look

at the world today affords it a degree of intrinsic plausibility; it may seem like a mere continuation of certain present trends. It has, of course, the great advantage of simplicity. And it is dramatic. There is the sense of fatefulness, the prediction of the irreversible loss of large parts of the combined heritage of humanity. As much of the diversity of its behavioral repertoire is wiped out, *Homo sapiens* becomes more like other species—in large part making its own environment, in contrast with them, but at the same time adapting to it in a single, however complex way.

No doubt there is something to this view; yet it so happens that another globalist perspective has quite different implications. In the social sciences, the notion of a world system has become especially linked with the work of Immanuel Wallerstein.[9] The larger part of Wallerstein's work has been in the history of political economy, with culture, as several critics have pointed out, mostly left out.[10] But to the limited extent that he leaves it in, he emphasizes that culture in the contemporary version of a world system is spatially delimited, because the groups in control of states use it to build national identities. The solidarity achieved through these minimizes internal conflict, while it defines the lines of conflict arising from disparities in the international division of labor. Culture can be used by people in the privileged states of the world system core to justify their advantages, or by the relatively advantaged in the peripheral states to define their own oppression by the core.

True, Wallerstein notes, the historical expansion of the world system, entailing the incorporation of new peripheries, involved much cultural diffusion, in fields such as education, religion, language, technology, and law: changes ultimately backed by force. Considerations of efficiency apart, they were expected to create periphery elites culturally separate from the "masses," and loyal to the core powers.[11] But such cultural influences would not influence the large majorities, and in the second or third generation, the elites seized on local tradition to formulate nationalist challenges to foreign domination.

Wallerstein's concern with cultural matters, we can see, has tended to be restricted to an interest in ideology, and he emphasizes the uses of culture in defining those political cleavages which are also territorial. It is interesting to see, however, that his analysis leads him to regard the world system as a source of cultural diversity. Cultural differences within the system are not mere survivals from a past where cultural isolation and autonomy were greater; they can indeed be generated by pressures inherent in the world system itself. A similar point of view is stated by Robert Wuthnow, one of fairly few sociologists of culture concerned with world system studies. Wuthnow notes that the expanding world system creates ideological turmoil in peripheral areas, in the form of revitalization movements in subsistence-level communities, and in the form of ideological revolutions among elites. This, he continues, directly contradicts a common argument by modernization theorists "that the cultural effect of modernization . . . is to act as a so-called universal solvent, producing cultural convergence. Rather, the expansion of core economic and political influence promotes cultural heterogeneity" (Wuthnow 1983:65–66).

The conflict, obviously, is not only with modernization theory, but also with the idea of worldwide homogenization under the aegis of cultural imperialism. Thus, we have here two globalist approaches to culture, if not competing, then at least different in thrust. One of them emphasizes differentiated cultural production in particular places, based on experiences and interests within a world-encompassing structure of social relationships. The other underlines the present powers of global cultural diffusion.

What must be clearly understood here, moreover, is that they are also variously concerned with the different organizational frameworks for cultural flow. Again, Wallerstein emphasizes the state framework in his analysis of the production and dissemination of ideologies of core-periphery distinction and national identity. Current notions of global homogenization, in contrast, are almost entirely preoccupied with the market framework. The prime mover behind this pan-human replication of uniformity is late Western capitalism, equipped with media technology; ignoring, subverting, and devaluing rather than celebrating national boundaries; through commodities, or the mere promise of commodities, luring forever more communities into dependency on the fringes of an expanding worldwide consumer society.

If there are differences between the two approaches, we must also recognize the biases they have in common, and the gaps in their accounts of cultural process. What they share, first of all, is a strong emphasis on the capacity of the world system to shape culture. As critical points of view toward the global political economy, both are preoccupied with the power of the center. What the peripheries do for themselves draws less attention.[12] That is to say, both rather disregard whatever relative autonomy the peripheries may have, and the interplay between the global and the local which may result from this. Both views, in concerning themselves with culture, also obviously focus on its particular political economy, while they may be rather insensitive to other aspects of the growth of the global ecumene.

As far as their relationships to history is concerned, these are somewhat problematic. At first sight, it might appear as if the two views are complementary. Most of Wallerstein's work has dealt with past periods, while the global diffusionist view has attended to the current role of cultural traffic in the world. It might be argued here that the notion of cultural homogenization is really in some ways more in tune with the times, insofar as it highlights the expanded cultural reach of the center. Yet one can hardly just place the two views identified here at different points in history, for while to a certain extent the circumstances favoring homogenization may be of more recent date, it is hardly as if the political and economic differentiation generating cultural diversity has declined as a force more lately. Instead, the situation especially in the latter part of the twentieth century turns especially complicated because of the tension between tendencies. In addition, diffusionist rhetoric sometimes leans toward too ahistorical a conception of the periphery; the murderous threat of cultural imperialism is depicted as involving the high-tech culture of the metropolis, with powerful organizational backing, facing a defenseless, small-scale folk culture. Such encounters do perhaps occur. Yet, in a great many places, decades or centuries of contact and change, of many kinds and intensities, have already shaped that local scene which meet the transnational culture industries of the late twentieth century.

Where have anthropological studies oriented toward a conception of the world system located themselves with reference to these two views? Hitherto, it is Wallerstein's view—or something akin to it—that has been the more influential. These studies have mostly seen the global structures in terms of power and the exploitation of material resources within the international division of labor, and on this basis they have in some instances also dealt with more strictly cultural matters, analyzing the local generation of new structures of meaning and symbolic expression.[13] On the whole, this anthropology has also resembled Wallerstein's work in that it has had a historical bent; it has concentrated on early and middle colonial periods in non-Western societies.

In much of this work, on the other hand, unlike Wallerstein's, there is a more immediate interest in culture within the form of life framework, as we see things here; culture developed and reproduced as adaptive routine, linked to practical circumstances. In addition (and in line with Wuthnow's comments on the effects of world system expansion, as cited above), there has been some research relating to the movement framework, such as on revitalization movements and cargo cults. At times, at least, anthropological studies have furthermore been quite predictably provoked by Wallerstein and other writers on the world system to insist on an analysis where the responses of the periphery are seen as more active, creative, and locally rooted. In *Islands of History,* Marshall Sahlins (1985:viii) thus notes the claim on the part of world system theoreticians that since peripheral societies are open to radical change, externally imposed by Western capitalist expansion, the assumption cannot be entertained that these societies work on some cultural logic of their own; and he retorts that "this is a confusion between an open system and a lack of system."

The combination in this anthropology of an orientation toward history with an emphasis on cultural distinctiveness, as produced mostly within the form of life and movement frameworks, is hardly altogether accidental. Again, in earlier periods, when non-Western societies were increasingly drawn into an interconnected world under European domination, the nature of the interconnections surely were to a great extent quite straightforwardly economic and political; they entailed the extraction of raw materials, and demonstrations of the capacity to use physical force. As yet, the intercontinental influences of a more immediately cultural nature were by comparison often rather weak (missionary work, for instance, apart). There was not so much in the way of a large-scale transfer of meaning systems and symbolic forms. Consequently, non-Western societies were to a fairly great extent left to deal practically and philosophically with their new circumstances through a reworking of their own cultural resources.

But this is not the way things are now, and so we must take changing conditions into account. Certainly, in its insistence that the diversity of cultures must somehow fit into world history, this body of anthropology has usefully thrown doubt on the "the ethnographic present" as a descriptive or prototheoretical device for the construction of an essentially timeless past. And it offers a kind of baseline (all baselines, of course, tend to be relative) for understanding the world as it is now. Eric Wolf's polemically titled *Europe and the People Without History* (1982) is a major example. Yet it is hardly reasonable to turn the study of culture in a global framework altogether into a retreat into history; a study of peoples without a present. And not least in the peripheries of the world system, the present, the real present, has its own characteristics.

Bush and Beento: The World in the Third World

I come back to Nigeria once more. No single Third World country can perfectly exemplify all the variations in center/periphery cultural interrelations and local implications at the periphery. Any one of them, on the other hand, allows us the opportunity to identify some of the variables, and some recurrent tendencies.

When I first became acquainted with Nigeria, several decades ago, I encountered in the local version of English a couple of words which, when put together, now strike me as especially revealing: "bush" and "beento." The latter had become the term for a Nigerian who had been to England, or possibly somewhere else overseas, and returned. During the sojourn abroad, the beento had acquired an advanced education, and so he (for there were rather fewer she beentos) could claim a privileged position in an expanding, at least in part conspicuously meritocratic, national social structure. But hardly less important for the definition of the beento as a social type was the general sophistication which he had acquired abroad, a savoir-faire with regard to the way of life of the metropolis, and an intimate appreciation of its finer points. "Bush," on the other hand, could be used descriptively but would ring in Nigerian ears especially as a denunciation hurled, in richly varying combinations, at adversaries and wrongdoers: an epithet for ignorance and rustic, unsophisticated, uncouth conduct. To be labeled bush in one way or other was to have one's rightful place in modern society put in question.

Beento and bush indeed seem to demarcate, in an embryonic folk model, the space in which contemporary Nigerian national culture has grown. This is not a national culture in the sense of a structure of meaning which is uniform and generally shared within, and distinctive toward the outside. I have in mind rather the entire cultural inventory actually available within the boundaries of the state, the universe of meaning and cultural form within which people live, and which through their lives they give some kind of social organization. At one end of this space, then, with its varied connections and cleavages, there is the openness to the world, more especially to the influence of western Europe and North America. London and New York are by now parts of Nigerian culture, if not as situated experiences, then at least as vibrant images. And metropolitanism is embodied in that figure of a migrant returning home laden with cultural capital. The beento stands, as it were, at the intersection where Wallerstein meets Bourdieu.

In cultural terms, it is at least partly true that what center/periphery relationships order is a charismatic geography, arranged around the bright lights of the metropolis. "Bengal's cultural centre of gravity became located in Calcutta," writes Poddar (1970:243), one of the interpreters of the Bengal Renaissance; but, moreover, "Calcutta's intellectual centre of gravity became located in London. If the promise of Bengal's and also India's regeneration was imported from there, the fatal constraints to its fulfillment were also unloaded from the same ship."

Whatever the consequences may be, places such as London, Paris, New York, and Miami continue to be, or grow into, expatriate capitals of parts of the Third World.[14] It may even seem as if many national cultures now have their centers, their cynosures, outside the territory of the state. In these places, more than elsewhere, their beentos become beentos, not just immigrants in the societies of the center, but also extensions of those societies of the periphery in which they hold continued membership. Such cities are also the centers of a cultural apparatus reaching into Third World national cultures; and not merely because the people of the periphery are allowed in on what the center produces mostly for itself, but also because a considerable part of the production of capital-C and popular culture for the periphery likewise takes place there, or its works are disseminated from there. *Presence Africaine*, the publishing house of Negritude, was a Left Bank phenomenon, and many of the current generation of glossy newsmonthlies for the Third World are edited in London or Paris, by partly Third World staffs.[15] As yet another aspect of the integral role of the metropoles in the national cultures of the periphery, these are the places where exiles go, where shadow politics is conducted, where protest meetings are held, plots hatched, battles over extradition fought. It is where cultural critics can be heard after their voices have been silenced at home.

Within national boundaries, the global center/periphery relationships are linked directly to those of nation and region. To an extent, one may look at all this again in spatial terms (although now a little more close up than we began by doing), as territories are organized by way of hierarchies of urban centers. Capitals—in the Nigerian instance, Lagos—and other large cities become the bridgeheads of transnational cultural influences, through the concentration there of particular institutional and occupational structures, and of groups of people who through their life-styles serve on the national scene as cultural models of metropolitanism. Here are the national jet set, the larger clusters of technocrats and professionals, as well as the representatives from the global center; and here, indeed, one finds in the most complete version what I sketched in chapter 1 as the typical contemporary complex culture.

At the other end of a national cultural spectrum one may find the thousands of rural hamlets to which transnational cultural influences tend to reach in a more fragmented, and perhaps indirect, manner. They are the contemporary approximations of "bush," where the cultural flows within state and market frameworks, and the division of knowledge depending on a division of labor drawn to a great extent from the center, are still weak as compared to that social organization of meaning which belongs mostly within a form of life framework of a pronounced local character.

Not least due to the uneven distribution of influences from the center, cultural diversity tends now to be as great within nations as it is between them.[16] Yet, of course, the terms of urban-rural hierarchy can give only an inexact grasp of the ordering of heterogeneous national cultural inventories. They suggest how a center/periphery structure is laid out over a map which at the same time, it must be understood, may show cultural variations of other derivations. Perhaps these variations also give evidence of globalization working along several lines, at least over time. It is often the case that metropolitan influence does not reach evenly into the various regions of a country. Or if it does so in the end, some parts of the country may have been involved with it earlier than others, and may thereafter continue to have their niches in the national management of culture defined in part by this historical fact. In Nigeria as in other parts of Africa, the head start which various coastal populations had in their involvement with Europe still has a certain impact on the recruitment of intellectual and professional elites, and some other occupational groups.[17] (Good cooks in Nigerian hotels and restaurants, I have been told again and again, come from Calabar, one of the oldest coastal trading towns.)

But these variations which somehow crosscut the current center/periphery structure can also have roots predating the present world system; in Nigeria, they include the diversity of ecological zones, and that of ethnic groups. (Although we now realize that colonialism in some ways affected the constructs of ethnicity as well.) Nigerian ethnography as it has conventionally been written has of course tended to stay fairly close to the "bush" end of the center/periphery cultural space, where these variations are more conspicuous: in local contexts where a Tiv is a Tiv is a Tiv, where one does not have to make distinctions between Tiv peasants and Tiv lawyers, or worry about the nature of the intersect between Tiv culture and the subculture of legal practitioners, or concern oneself with the relationship between the social organizational resilience of Tiv ethnicity and the continuity of Tiv culture. It is such issues that have to be faced, on the other hand, when one seriously confronts the tasks of doing contemporary Nigerian ethnography in a macroanthropological framework.

Frameworks of Cultural Flow: The National and the Transnational

In any case, returning to the center/periphery structure, between the major city and the hamlet there is a network of relationships within which meanings flow continuously, and that network also encompasses that multitude of provincial towns of which in the Nigerian case Kafanchan is one representative. Because of this cultural flow there is now, in the perspectives of most Nigerians, more on this side of the horizon than there was for their ancestors a century ago. During my stays in Kafanchan, I have often found myself somewhat irritated and embarrassed as various townspeople have seen me as a possible resource in implausible schemes for going abroad, or getting into some lucrative import-export business (often import, rather than export, really).

To begin with, I only saw this as a distraction from my purpose of finding out what town life was actually like. With time, I came to realize that these schemes were indeed one part of what it was all about. Such hunches about the good life belonged with the popular tunes about the life-styles of the rich and famous, with that hole-in-the-wall commercial school where adolescents may pick up skills designed to take them from the village to the city, and with the star system of urban folklore, the tales told in beer bars in which politicians, high military officers, and business tycoons become the new tricksters and hero figures. The imagination of these townspeople refused to remain within town limits.

How do people in a place like Kafanchan get their horizons, from where does their view of the world come? Again, while spatial terms and urban-rural contrasts may summarize much of the evidence, culture is primarily a thing of relationships rather than of territory. Thus, we must consider how the relationships are arranged within the various organizational frames—here, primarily state, market, and form of life—to get a sharper sense of how, or to what extent, such a complicated entity as a national culture actually comes to cohere. And as we engage with this task, a more nuanced picture may emerge, not least of what states and markets really do.

By choosing a unit such as Nigeria, of course, we privilege the state framework; but it need not be taken any more as a "given" than the others. Like a great many contemporary Third World states, Nigeria is in large part a product of the global organizational process, especially as shaped by the rise and decline of colonialism. Because of the arbitrariness with which they were set up and their boundaries drawn, some observers would indeed argue that these are precisely states, not nations; local cultural traditions, as developed within the form of life framework, played no part in their definition. Yet often such an argument brackets more recent history, and disregards what states now try to do. As the people of an ex-colony keep on accumulating a common past, and as they are in the sphere of influence of a state cultural apparatus, a national culture even in the sense of something shared and distinctive is brought into existence.

The cultural apparatus of the state, with its asymmetrical ordering of cultural flow, clearly has a major part in setting up the center/periphery relationships within a national culture, through media, schools, universities, museums, civic rituals, or whatever. For ideological purposes, as Wallerstein points out, this apparatus probably emphasizes and promotes internal unity and distinctiveness toward the outside, finding historical legitimacy for this purpose wherever and whenever it can. Away, perhaps, with miniskirts, neckties, and Christian names, all alien items from the metropolis; in with presidential hippopotamus-hide flywhiskers and the management of tradition by "cultural animateurs" employed by the Ministry of Culture.[18] Some peripheral states do more with this than others. Nigeria, with its rather deep internal ethnic and religious cleavages and a rapid turnover of political regimes, has not engaged in such promotional efforts particularly insistently or consistently. The prime African example which might come to mind would rather be the Zairean "authenticity" campaigns of the regime of Mobutu Sese Seko.[19]

Yet the workings of any state cultural apparatus tend to be more multifaceted, and more ambiguous in their outcome. There is some irony in the fact that even as the particular cultural emblems of national distinctiveness are indeed unique, the formula for distinctiveness is in large part transnational: a flag, an anthem.[20] More importantly, the state cannot afford to engage only in a replication of uniformity. Not least through its educational wing, the state cultural apparatus also has a large part in the differentiation, the expansion and reproduction of complexity, deemed necessary for the conduct of the nation's business. In Third World nations, furthermore, this has at the same time been a matter of tying national cultures (in the sense of cultural inventories, as used here) more closely to the global ecumene. As institutional structures for administration, business, and industry, fundamentally inspired by and modeled on those of the center, have been introduced from the top down into the societies of the periphery, they have drawn many of their members into active participation, requiring fairly standardized competences. If some of these are transmitted through institutions of mass education which perhaps above all turn people into modular citizens, there are also those more differentiated educational structures which shape particular categories to particular requirements.[21]

Consequently, the state cultural apparatus tends to have a significant part in constructing the division of labor, and the division of knowledge, within a Third World nation. Following what has been said here before (in chapter 2, to begin with) about the doublesidedness of the division of labor, it helps generate subcultural segmentation at the same time. Many of the subcultures created within this framework—including the cultures of the new meritocracy—tend to have an intrinsic center/periphery orientation at the national level, but it is at the same time in the nature of things that they are continuously open to transnational cultural flow. Some of them may even be considered parts of transnational subcultures, maintained across boundaries through more or less intensive personal interactions or specialized cultural apparatuses. In this way, the state itself seems to ensure that there will be people whose horizons transcend its own territorial limits (see more on this below).

The state, it thus turns out, often actively mediates between the transnational and the national in culture. Turning to the market framework, we are frequently led to assume that it favors the transnational. It is not intrinsically linked to a territory, and the imagery of cultural imperialism shows commoditized culture sweeping in from the center across the periphery.

It is in the market framework that economic power in the world system translates most directly into cultural influence, through a cultural apparatus which, however differentiated and indeed fragmented it may be, creates asymmetry in the cultural flow, and more or less pronounced center/periphery relationships.

Certainly those who operate in the cultural market place often prefer to have national boundaries count for little, and view cultural differences between groups or localities mostly as a nuisance; they want to reach as widely as possible with the same single product. The homogenization of consumers, seen from this perspective, is a cause for celebration rather than regret. "The globalization of markets is at hand," Theodore Levitt, a prominent theorist of marketing, has proclaimed in the *Harvard Business Review,* and he contrasts the multinational with the global corporation. The former "operates in a number of countries, and adjusts its products and practices in each—at high relative costs"; the latter "operates with resolute constancy—at low relative cost—as if the entire world (or major regions of it) were a single entity; it sells the same things in the same way everywhere" (1983:92–93).

The controversy over "Four Buggs and a Coca Cola," the Swedish song contest entry, could be seen in this light. Some listeners would have wanted it to be more nationally distinctive, but no doubt whoever wrote the text and held commercial rights in the tune had one eye on a wider market where Swedishness in itself would not be helpful. Rather self-consciously, it would seem (and in the end, not too successfully), a product was created which could be expected to move with the rhythm of transnationally homogenized culture. Another variety of cultural commodity flow across borders, in contrast, entails little attention of any sort to the characteristics of distant consumers. This is what Karin Barber (1988:25), in an overview of popular culture in Africa, has aptly termed "cultural dumping"—"akin to the dumping of expired drugs and non-functional buses." The cost of taking old Western movies, soap serials, or skin flicks (choosing only examples from the screen) to their final resting place in the Third World is so low that whatever income they generate is almost pure profit: probably an unanticipated addition to whatever they earned in the markets for which they were actually produced. The periphery here is treated to leftovers.

Cultural dumping, however, is hardly what the global homogenization scenario is mostly about. If we try to make the latter as explicit and as credible as we can, as a vision of present and future cultural history, we can perhaps restate it in terms of an ongoing overall reconstruction of peripheral cultures within the global ecumene, primarily characterized by a process of saturation. This might go as follows. As the transnational cultural influences, of whatever sort but certainly in large part market organized, and operating in a continuously open structure, unendingly pound on the sensibilities of the people of the periphery, peripheral culture will step by step assimilate more and more of the imported meanings and forms, becoming gradually indistinguishable from the center. At any one time, what is considered local culture is a little more penetrated by transnational forms than what went before it as local culture—although at any one time also, until the end point is reached, the contrast between local and transnational may still be drawn and still be regarded as significant. The cultural differences which the enthusiasts of national or local distinctiveness celebrate and recommend for safeguarding now may only be a pale reflection of what once existed, and sooner or later they will be gone as well.

What the emphasis on saturation suggests is that the center cumulatively colonizes the minds of the periphery, with a corresponding institutionalization of its forms, getting the periphery so committed to the imports that soon enough there is no real opportunity for choice. The mere fact that these forms originate at the center makes them even more attractive, a peculiar but at times conspicuous aspect of commodity aesthetics in the periphery. This colonization is understood to proceed through relentless cultural bombardment, through the redundancy of its seductive messages. As the market framework of cultural flow interpenetrates with that of forms of life, the latter become reconstructed around their dependence on what was initially alien, using it for their practical adaptations, seeing themselves wholly or at least partially in its mirror.

I will have more to say about the idea of saturation below, but, before that, some brief comments might be in order on the stance of the peripheral state vis-à-vis transnational cultural commodity flows, and generally on the role of material bases in the global political economy of culture.

The state, if it takes an interest in what I have previously termed cultural welfare, may be particularly opposed to cultural dumping. Due to its interests in national cultural coherence and distinctiveness, it may also try to constrain transnational cultural flow more generally. (In passing, early in chapter 4, we have already noted the conflict over the global information order.) Yet the state in the periphery is often a rather weak creature, with little power to impose its will and implement its policy—a "soft state," to borrow the term coined by Gunnar Myrdal (1968)—and this is not least obvious in the area of cultural policy. Thus it has to compromise with, or carry on a rather unsuccessful struggle against, that organized production and dissemination of culture which goes on outside its own framework.

No doubt the performance of the state in managing cultural flow depends in part on material conditions. The soft state is often an impoverished state which can ill afford to maintain a powerful cultural apparatus of its own. Material bases, however, are likely to be no less important in the market framework, for there as well, cultural prestations have to be materially compensated for.

This simple but fundamental fact seems often to get little attention in the global homogenization scenario. There are a range of possibilities. If the involvement with the international division of labor is not to the advantage of the periphery, at any one time or over time, the latter would seem to become a poorer market for the transnational flow of cultural commodities, with the possible exception of that "cultural dumping" which may involve low prices and unattractive goods. Conversely, if some part of the periphery becomes nouveau riche, it may be flooded with the cultural commodities of the center. In recent times, again, the economies of some parts of the global periphery, including Nigeria, have been on a roller coaster ride; small town people who bought imported popular fashions in the marketplace yesterday are perhaps no longer able to do so today. Yet it is hardly clear what are the longer-term implications of such shifts for the transnational cultural market.

One possibility is that when people cannot afford imported cultural commodities, there will be more room for import substitution. But this need not only be an outcome of economic deterioration; it can be the opposite. We must ask, this goes to say, what is the place of locally produced commodities in the cultural market of the periphery. And here the point may need to be made that the market framework, like that of the state, may organize culture in different ways. If one tendency is to homogenize and reach as widely as possible with the same product, there is again the alternative of seeking competitive advantage through distinctiveness, in a particular market segment. The scenario of global homogenization rather too much ignores this alternative, but since it is so often preoccupied with the commodities of popular culture, it is reasonable to make the observation that much of what the entrepreneurs of popular culture in the Third World are doing these days seems to involve carving out such niches.[22] These entrepreneurs do not have the material resources of the culture businesses of the center, but like local entrepreneurs everywhere, they know their territory. Their particular asset is cultural competence, cultural sensibility, growing out of an involvement with local forms of life. Coming out of these themselves, indeed being still in them, they are attuned to the tastes and concerns which can provide markets for particular commodities.

Here it would appear that one can turn the argument about long-term saturation at least some of the way around. The form of life framework, I have said before, also has a redundancy of its own, built up through its ever recurrent daily activities, perhaps as strong as, or stronger than, any redundancy that the market framework can ever achieve. It may involve interpersonal relationships, resulting configurations of self and other, characteristic uses of symbolic modes.[23] One may suspect that there is a core here to which the market framework cannot reach, not even in the longer term, a core of culture which is not itself easily commoditized and to which the commodities of the market are not altogether relevant.

The inherent cultural power of the form of life framework could also be such that it colonizes the market framework, rather than vice versa. This is more in line with what I see, in contrast with the tendency toward saturation, as the maturation tendency; the periphery, seen in this light, takes its time in reshaping that metropolitan culture which reaches there to its own specifications. It is in phase one, so to speak, that the metropolitan forms in the periphery are most marked by their purity; but, on closer scrutiny, they turn out to stand there fairly ineffective, even vulnerable, in their relative isolation—"compartmentalized," as one anthropological vocabulary would have it. In a phase two, and in innumerable phases thereafter, as they are made to interact with whatever else exists in their new setting, there may be a mutual influence, but the metropolitan forms are somehow no longer so easily recognizable: they become hybridized. In these later phases, the terms of the cultural market for one thing are in a reasonable measure set from within the peripheral forms of life, as these have come to be constituted, highly variable of course in the degree to which they are themselves culturally defined in the terms drawn from the center.

In principle, then, it seems entirely possible that the consumer could prefer locally produced cultural goods—if not all the time, at least some of the time. But import substitution in a market framework of cultural flow also requires a sufficient material base.[24] In terms of cultural demographics, there has to be a critical mass of consumers. Nigeria, the most populous country in Africa, and at times quite affluent due to its oil exports, has no doubt been better equipped than many other Third World countries to build up a cultural market of its own. It is also one of those countries which may find some outlets for its cultural commodities in its own wider region, and eventually to some extent reach a wider market yet. That is, it has some potential for becoming a center of sorts in its own right. Smaller national cultural markets may be more dependent on the importation of cultural goods from either regional or global centers, or the market framework for cultural flow may itself become less important.

Popular Culture: The Call of the Center, the Response of the Periphery

As one attempts to get a sense of the management of meaning between center and periphery, in Nigeria as elsewhere in the world, one can hardly ignore popular culture. Hardly any other area of contemporary culture is as strongly associated with the market framework generally, and the transnational flow of cultural commodities particularly. Established assumptions about cultural purity and authenticity come readily to the surface here. Not least among intellectuals and policymakers, the influx of popular culture from the global centers into the peripheries is described rather unremittingly in terms of its destructive and distracting powers. And this is as true in debate in the Third World (or on behalf of the Third World, among interested outsiders) as in a country like Sweden which, if finer distinctions are to be made, would probably be described as part of the semi-periphery (but hardly, on the other hand, of the semi-center) as far as transnational cultural flow is concerned. It is said that local products are threatened with extinction through the importation of "cheap foreign junk." One may detect some hypocrisy here, insofar as it is implied that all local products are of great intellectual or aesthetic merit, never merely cheap local junk.

Produced by the relatively few for a great many consumers, popular culture fits well with a center/periphery structure. Indeed, it may model it. The institutions and the performers of Nigerian popular culture are mostly based in those major urban centers which are at the same time bridgeheads of transnational culture. *Lagos Weekend,* the scandal sheet much enjoyed by the young men-about-town in Kafanchan during my early field periods there, literally placed the capital at the center of their attention. The major sports events occur in the larger cities, and young men have color pictures of British soccer teams on their walls. As popular music groups tour middle-sized and small towns all over the country, they display not only the newest in sounds and in dance but also in fashion and argot. The local commercial artists often draw on the more metropolitan media for ideas. One tailor in Kafanchan had a signboard outside his shop showing his nickname, Ringo Star (sic). In the personal photo albums of young people, pictures of themselves and their friends, in their best outfits and striking sophisticated poses, mix with cutout pictures of athletes, musicians, and movie stars.

Intensely reflexive, popular culture often tells us something about how its producers as well as its consumers see themselves, and in what directions they would like their lives to move.[25] And in Nigeria, popular culture seems fairly permeated with meanings and meaningful forms drawn, or deriving in some other way, from the center. The most relevant contrast to popular culture here, I would suggest, is not, or perhaps only secondarily, high culture, the symbolic forms produced and largely consumed within a cultural elite. It is rather, once more, "bush." Involvement with popular culture in Nigeria appears to be above all a manifestation of metropolis-oriented sophistication and modernity. In a way, it may be more like popular culture as it was in early modern Europe, as described by the historian Peter Burke

(1978)—a field of activity more or less uniting elites and masses in shared pastimes and pleasures. Perhaps this quality of metropolitan-orientedness also accounts for some of what is often referred to as the philistinism of Third World elites. One can reach toward the charisma of the center at least as well through a greater investment in popular culture as through involvement with a more differentiated, less widely understood high culture.

For all this, the center/periphery relationships of popular culture in Nigeria are not of an altogether simple kind. They are asymmetrical, but not free of contradictions, and they do not relegate the periphery to that entirely passive role in cultural construction which the preoccupation with popular culture in the global homogenization scenario seems to suggest.

One aspect of this is that the transnational flow of culture, by giving the periphery access to a wider cultural inventory, provides it with new resources of technology and symbolic expression to refashion and quite probably integrate with what exists of more locally rooted materials.[26] Local cultural entrepreneurs have thus gradually mastered the alien cultural forms, taking them apart to investigate their potentialities in terms of symbolic modes, genres, and organizations of performance. Thus new competences are acquired, and the resulting new forms are more responsive to, and at the same time in part outgrowths of, local everyday life: examples of what I just outlined as the tendency toward maturation, and also of the possibilities of import substitution.

There are good examples of this in music. Popular Nigerian music stars such as Fela Anikulapo-Kuti, Sunny Ade, and Ebenezer Obey have hardly had to fear the foreign competition, and do not enact pale copies of it but perform in styles they have created themselves. Juju music, for example, for some time the dominant popular music form in Western Nigeria, has combined inspirations from more traditional Yoruba music and from highlife, another and rather earlier established popular music form. From modest origins in palm wine bars, it has moved up to large bands performing in night clubs and selling their record albums in large editions. The texts often have their roots in Yoruba praise singing, and likewise show affinities with the religious music of the syncretistic Aladura churches.[27]

In this connection, I should return to the doubts I expressed initially about the sense of time, or more precisely the lacking sense of time, in the scenario of global homogenization. The onslaught of transnational influences, as often described or hinted at, seems rather too sudden. In West Africa, such influences have been filtering into the coastal societies for centuries already, although in earlier periods on a smaller scale and by modest means. There has been time to absorb the foreign influences, to modify the modifications in turn, and to fit shifting cultural forms to developing social structures, to situations and emerging audiences. This is not a scene where the peripheral culture is utterly defenseless, but rather one where locally evolving alternatives to imports are available, and where there are people at hand to perform innovative acts of cultural brokerage.[28]

It is another aspect of the complicated nature of the center/periphery relationships of culture that there is both close attention to the center and what comes out of it and rather ambivalent responses to it. While the celebratory stance toward the center may be dominant, and have logical priority, the typical expressions and personifications of center influence cannot escape unfavorable notice, implicit or explicit. Nigerian popular writing, of which for almost half a century there has been a considerable amount, makes fun both of metropolitan English, too preciously pronounced, and of its corruptions and innovative adaptations in Nigerian everyday discourse. Extreme pidgin forms may be put in the mouth of some characters to define them as country bumpkins, while semiliterate crooks and ruffians make use of big English words. Metropolitan-style honorifics, not least abbreviations of academic credentials, are also much in evidence, mostly for comical effect.

What surely contributes to a certain cultural ambivalence is the fact that the cultural manifestations of center/periphery relationships frequently become inextricably entangled with matters of class. To have wealth and power is to have easier access to the metropolis; and it is through one's relationship to the metropolis that one often gains wealth and power in the periphery. To repeat, like so many Third World countries, Nigeria is a highly meritocratic, credentialist society, where one can carry metropolitan culture on one's sleeve and gain great and very visible advantage from it. The view of the beento, one of the main symbols of the center/periphery relationship in the Nigerian imagination, from below is thus not always sympathetic. Popular writers may describe him as arrogant, distant, and unfriendly. Yet it is another recurrent theme that the returning beento turns into a tragic figure. He has lost touch, his formal skills are not practical, his new universalist morality does not fit into the Nigerian rough-and-tumble.[29] At the same time, in a populist vein, even "bush" can sometimes be used rhetorically to draw attention to a quality of down-to-earth sincerity and lack of affectation.

Then again, there are those television antennae over the roofs of Kafanchan. *Charlie's Angels* are in town, and the Ewings of *Dallas* as well. But they are not alone, and it is not obvious what they accomplish.

One problem with the global homogenization scenario tends to be the quality of the evidence for it. Quite frequently it is anecdotal—"I switched on the television set in my hotel room in Lagos (or Manila, or Tel Aviv, or Geneva), and found that *Dallas* was on." In a more sophisticated version, quantitative evidence is provided that on one Third World television channel or other, some high percentage of the programming is imported.

To be more completely persuasive, arguments about the impact of the transnational cultural flow would have to say something about how people respond to it. The mere fact that Third World television stations buy a lot of imported programs, for example, often has more to do with the fact that they are cheap, instances of cultural dumping, than that audiences are necessarily enthralled with them. We may have little idea about how many television sets are actually on when they are shown, and even less what is the quality of attention to them.

At least as problematic is the sense that people make of the transnational cultural flow.[30] Even when we refer to it as a "flow of meaning," we must keep in mind the uncertainties built into the communicative process. If one cannot be too sure of perfect understanding even in a face-to-face interaction in a local context with much cultural redundancy, the difficulties (or the opportunities for innovative interpretations, if one wants to turn things around) multiply where communication is largely one-way, between people whose perspectives have been shaped in very different contexts, in places very distant from one another. The meaning of the transnational cultural flow is thus in the eye of the beholder: what he sees, we generally know little about.[31]

One intricate issue here is the relationship between different symbolic modes and the global diversity of culture. Do some symbolic forms, in some modes, travel better than others? We know well enough where the barriers of incomprehension are in the linguistic mode. How is the transnational spread of popular culture affected by varying sensibilities with respect to other modes, such as music, or gestures and body movement? One may rather facilely explain the spread of Indian and Hong Kong movies over much of the Third World by referring to the fact that they are cheap (which appeals to distributors) and action-packed (which appeals to somewhat unsophisticated audiences). But the latter point in particular may hide as much as it reveals. What kind, or degree, of precision is there in the audience appreciation of the symbolic forms of another country?[32]

In any case, the beginnings of serious media research by Nigerian scholars show that the most popular series have been those made in the country (cf. Oreh 1985; Vincent 1985). And much of the earthy humor of these series is again generated by local responses to metropolitan influences, as well as by exaggerated displays of metropolitan-derived culture. They regularly show people making fools of themselves as they embrace alien cultural items, and make inept use of them. In one, a prominent business woman is depicted as a member of "the American Dollar Club." In another, when someone tries to change the eating habits of the main character, a local chief, to include European dishes, he stares at the spaghetti and asks what are those worms on his plate.

Current conceptions of cultural imperialism exemplify on the largest imaginable scale the curious fact that according to the economics of culture, to receive may be to lose. In that way, they are a useful antidote to old "white man's burden" notions of the gifts of culture from center to periphery as unadulterated benefaction. Yet it would seem impossible to argue that the transnational cultural influences are generally deleterious. In the areas of scholarship and intellectual life, we hardly take a conflict for granted between the transnational flow of culture and local cultural creativity.[33] Without a certain openness to impulses from the outside world, we would expect science, art, and literature to become impoverished anywhere. Obviously, Nigerian literary life could hardly exist were it not for the importation of literacy and a range of literary forms. But there would not have been a Nigerian Nobel Prize winner in literature in 1986 if Wole Soyinka had not creatively drawn on both a literary expertise drawn mostly from the Occident and an imagination rooted in a Nigerian mythology, and turned them into something unique.

With regard to popular culture, one cannot deny the fact of center/periphery cultural dumping. But if we let ourselves become entirely preoccupied with it, we ignore the possibility that the formal symbol systems of popular culture and the media, and the skills in handling these symbol systems, can be transferred between cultures in more productive ways. As long as there is room for local cultural creativity as well, this may in itself be helped in its continued growth by the availability of a wider range of models.

It may be objected that such notions of cultural enrichment are not to the point, that even if what is imported is seen as equipment, models, and stimuli, these are still destructive insofar as they irreversibly change local culture. Whatever modifications the imports undergo, however much they are integrated with indigenous culture, they will impose alien formats on it. Where literacy comes in, whatever modes of thought may be linked to pure orality are likely to be corrupted.[34] A Nigerian sitcom is still a sitcom. The very shape of popular culture as a social organizational phenomenon, with its great asymmetry in the relationship between performers and audience, might threaten older and more participatory arrangements of cultural expression.

The argument must be taken seriously, but this is one of those instances where often only a thin line can be drawn between a defense of authenticity and an antiquarianism espoused on the behalf of some reluctant other. Even if cultures are not perfectly integrated wholes, they are hardly altogether unintegrated either; and once societies have been changed by large-scale industrial, commercial, administrative, and educational organization, it is difficult to imagine that this would leave no mark on cultural forms more voluntarily chosen, such as those of entertainment. Nigerians could hardly in this postcolonial era switch back completely to their precolonial cultural heritage in the after hours. Pure tradition, and its organizational and technological forms of expression, would not match their everyday experiences and desires. A popular culture, and media technology, are now certainly as much daily necessities for people in large parts of the Third World as they are in the Occident.

The Perspectives of the Footloose

The media, such as television, allow culture to become globalized by neutralizing space. The beento exemplifies another mechanism: people move about.

Many of our notions about human migration are by now actually rather quaint and old-fashioned. In Europe as well as in the United States, research (certain exceptions apart) tends to focus on migrants as immigrants.[35] We assume that people come to a new country to stay, and that just about the only thing that needs to be understood is the relationship between immigrants and their new country. What is origin is past, it seems; links to the old home country are weakened, possibly slowly, but nonetheless surely.

Even used cars and motor roads have their part in invalidating such assumptions, as Mexicans in the United States and Turks in Scandinavia maintain their home links by speeding along the Interstate highway and the *Autobahn*. But this is only a part of something more general. What we see is increasingly the back-and-forth movement of people, on a global scale and in a bewildering variety of forms and frequencies. A great many people of the kind we have thought of as the typical migrants, people in search of work and a better life, return to where they came from after some years, not because they have failed but because that is the way they always planned it. And others come back to visit with some regularity, postponing an answer to the question where they *really* belong, or simply making the question irrelevant.[36]

But then there are also many more kinds of people who are, or have been, on the move: diplomats, businessmen, bureaucrats, academics, tourists, veterans of foreign wars, overseas volunteers, artists, refugees, youths on an intercontinental walkabout. For some of them, changes of scene are parentheses or interludes within a largely sedentary life, while for others, they are recurrent and central to their existence. People can make quick forays from a home base to many other places—for a few hours or days in a week, for a few weeks here and there in a year—or they may shift their bases repeatedly for longer periods. Many of these footloose people are not much like the poor and the wretched whom Emma Lazarus welcomed to America, in those lines inscribed on the Statue of Liberty. They are rather brain drain and jet set, with considerable resources at their disposal. And their movements fit into a yet more varied pattern of long-distance contacts. People can be in touch by way of letter, telephone, and computer, or they can get on a plane and soon be face to face with someone who is far away. Some countries are nations of migrants. Filipinos or Filipinas are health workers in the United States, construction workers in the Middle East, domestics in Hong Kong and Singapore, entertainers throughout much of Southeast Asia, white-collar workers in Papua New Guinea, mail-order brides in western Europe, sailors on the seven seas, professionals in international organizations. There is a growth of new diasporas—of Ethiopians, Ghanaians, Chileans—and new forms for old ones—of Indians and Chinese. And the complexity of identities is at least intimated through hyphenation: Afro-Germans.

What traces do these human passages through geographical space leave on the social organization of meaning in the world?

One must, of course, take into account people's motives for movement. Paul Theroux (1986:133), a writer continuously occupied with themes of journeys, has commented that many people travel for the purpose of "home plus"—Spain is home plus sunshine, India is home plus servants, Africa is home plus elephants and lions. (The perspective, presumably, is from western Europe or North America.) There is no general openness here to a somewhat unpredictable variety of experiences: the benefits of widened horizons are strictly regulated.

Much present-day tourism, for one thing, is of this kind. Organized on a mass basis, it leaves its mark on a host society and its culture. The experience of Europeans or Australians at play becomes something to think about for Africans or Fijians at work.[37] But the "plus," for the tourist, often has little to do with curiosity about alien systems of meaning, and a lot to do with facts of nature, or quasi-nature, such as nice beaches. For the exile, shifted like the tourist directly from one territorial culture to another, but involuntarily, the involvement with a culture away from his homeland is at best home plus safety, or home plus freedom, but often it is just not home at all. Surrounded by the foreign culture, he perhaps tries to keep it at arm's length, and guards what is his own. For most ordinary labor migrants, ideally, going away may be home plus higher income; often the involvement with another culture is not a fringe benefit but a necessary cost. A surrogate home is created with the help of compatriots, in whose circle one feels most comfortable.

One must not exaggerate the cultural implications of migration, then, but neither should they be underestimated. The West African political scene in the late colonial years was transformed by the presence of early beentos and veterans from overseas campaigns during World War II; at about the time of the latter, American scholarly life was enriched by the "illustrious immigrants" from continental Europe; today, Miami is not what it was before 1959. The stranger and the homecomer can both have their distinct voices in place-bound polyphonies.[38]

When people take their "cultural baggage" to another place, their perspectives are yet likely to be altered, temporarily or durably, depending on the way they are inserted into another combination of practical circumstances and currents of meaning. In the form of life framework, there are other constraints, and other opportunities, and what one can observe in other people in one's new surroundings is different from what was there in the place from which one has come. The messages of the cultural apparatus, as organized by the state or the market, are also different, whether that cultural apparatus just ignores the presence of the migrants or somehow acknowledges them—as a market segment to be served with special commodities, or as a particular clientele for a welfare state with some readiness to take cultural differences into account.[39] Special treatment of the latter kinds, naturally, may work as a cultural buffer, conserving more of the perspectives brought from somewhere else. Yet a total encapsulation in a culture one has just somehow brought along is rarely possible, even if approximations, at least in the short term, are common enough.

Looking at things in this manner, however, one is still largely concerned with cultures rooted in territories, and the connections which people create between them by moving about.

Contemporary forms of mobility also entail a growth of another kind of entities: transnational cultures, structures of meaning carried by social networks which are not wholly based in any single territory. The people of the transnational cultures tend to be the frequent travelers, the people based in one place but routinely involved with others in various places elsewhere. Nobody is likely to spend a life—hardly even a day—wholly immersed in a transnational culture. Rather, these people combine involvements with one transnational culture (or possibly more than one) and one or more territorially based cultures. If the latter are likely to encompass the round of everyday life in a community, the transnational cultures usually involve some more narrowly circumscribed field of meaning. Many of them are occupational cultures (often tied to transnational job markets).

The growth and proliferation of such transnational cultures and social networks has been rapid in the present period.[40] (Perhaps the only transnational culture in decline is that of hereditary royalty.) While it makes some sense to see them as a particular type of phenomenon, they must at the same time be seen in their relationships to territorially based cultures. Not least must they be seen in terms of their embeddedness in the center/periphery structure of the world.

If popular culture as transmitted through the transnational market entails great asymmetry, with a mere handful of producers and the greatest possible number of consumers, the transnational occupational cultures are in principle more symmetrical in organization, subcultures maintained in large part within the form of life framework (which thus does not always organize only local cultural flow), perhaps with some cultural apparatus of their own. People from both center and periphery, and from different centers and different peripheries, engage in the ongoing management of meaning within them to a greater extent as both producers and consumers, in a joint construction of meaning and cultural form. Although a relatively even distribution of know-how among them provides the basis for some degree of symmetry in the management of meaning, however, elements in the organization of these cultures still draw them into the center/periphery framework.

Clearly most of these cultures at present have their main sources in Occidental culture. "The whole culture of diplomatic intercourse," Dore writes about one of them, "of bilateral talks, international conferences, nobbling in the lobbies, and partying in the reception rooms—the arts of chairmanship, of cocktail party charm and conference rhetoric, of knowing when to be incisive and when to bore the time away, of judging what will count as a joke and what as an insult—is all part of a world culture as Western in its origins as apple pie" (1984:421–422).[41] It is also often in the center that one finds the greater number of members in the transnational networks in question, as well as the greater resources at their disposal. And insofar as people are initially trained for their positions in the transnational division of labor through some agency of the cultural apparatus, this tends to be either an agency in the center itself or some agency located in the periphery but modeled on that in the center.

Transnational cultures today are thus, usually, in different ways extensions or transformations of the cultures of western Europe and North America. If even the transnational cultures have to have physical centers somewhere, places in which, or from where, their particular meanings are produced and disseminated with particular intensity, or places to which people travel in order to interact in their terms, this is where such centers tend to be located. But away from these centers, too, the institutions of the transnational cultures are often so organized as to make people from western Europe and North America feel as much at home as possible (by using their languages, for one thing).

It is a consequence of this that western Europeans and North Americans can encapsulate themselves culturally not only by staying at home in their territorial cultures. They can also do so—again, to a fairly high degree, although hardly completely—in many of the transnational cultures. For those who are not western Europeans or North Americans, or who do not spend their everyday lives elsewhere in Occidental cultural enclaves, involvement with one of the transnational cultures is more likely a distinctive cultural experience in itself.

It is also true, however, that transnational cultures, if usually of a generalized Occidental derivation, are penetrable to various degrees by the local meanings carried in settings and by participants in particular situations. The conduct of diplomacy, for example, is rather more decontextualized, "according to protocol," than wheeling and dealing in business.[42] And in this as well as in other ways, the transnational cultures, by bringing together people of different territorial cultures in varying locales and constellations, also connect these cultures.

The real significance of the growth of the transnational cultures, one might indeed argue, is often not the new cultural experience that they themselves can offer people—for it is frequently rather restricted in scope and depth—but their mediating possibilities. The transnational cultures provide points of entry into other territorial cultures. Instead of remaining within them, one can use the mobility connected with them to make contact with the meanings of other rounds of life, and gradually incorporate this experience into one's personal perspective. In human history, the direct movement between territorial cultures has often been accidental, a freak occurrence in biographies; if not an expression of sheer personal idiosyncracy, then a result of war, political upheaval or repression, or ecological disaster. Through the transnational networks and cultures, many more people become involved with more cultures—recruited largely on a voluntary basis, but through an institutionalized process.

One may look at this multicultural involvement in terms of the channeling of specific ideas and cultural forms between cultures. On the other hand, it may also be considered with regard to its more general implications for perspectives and for the management of meaning in the interfaces between cultures: what does the multicultural do to the metacultural, to the overall stance toward particular cultures or cultures in general?

One consequence of the increased volume of long-distance movements, and especially of the growth of transnational occupational cultures, is the development in the latter part of the twentieth century of what may be called the culture-shock prevention industry: institutionalized forms for preparing people to cope with other cultures than their own (and the beginnings of yet another profession). "Cross-cultural" training programs are set up to inculcate sensitivity, basic rules of etiquette, and perhaps an appreciation of those other cultures which are of special strategic importance to one's goals: for Westerners in recent times, as culture follows business, especially those of the Arab World and Japan. There is likewise a burgeoning do-it-yourself literature in the field.[43]

What the culture-shock prevention industry actually accomplishes is not so easily evaluated. One may have one's doubts about what quality of understanding can be reached through course work for a couple of days or weeks, or through a frequently unsubtle handbook genre (and as an anthropologist, one perhaps senses an insult to one's credentialed occupational pride). But, at least, they can provide some ideas to work with, and allow some elementary mistakes to be avoided.

For many, however, entering other cultures is first and foremost a personal journey of discovery. There is to begin with those clashes between perspectives, that undermining of the taken for granted, to which the somewhat dramatic term culture shock primarily applies, an undermining for which one may to some extent be prepared. Beyond this, there is the varying readiness to enter more deeply into another structure of meaning. To repeat, not everybody who moves about may want to be immersed in alien culture: the tourist in pursuit of sunshine, the exile relocated more or less against his will. No doubt the willingness to seize such opportunities is also often a very personal character trait. But the individuals involved with the transnational cultures are often in an advantageous position to make the choice. They have the time, during long stays or many of short duration, to explore another local culture, or several of them. Through contacts made by way of the transnational cultures, they can find points of entry. Moreover, always knowing where the exit is, they need not be anxious about preserving some comfortable sense of "at home."

There is an opportunity here, in other words, to become a cosmopolitan. The cosmopolitan is a creature of the organization of diversity in world culture, and consequently deserves some special attention here, as a type.[44] Often the term is used loosely, to describe just about anybody who moves about in the world. But of such people, some would seem more cosmopolitan than others, and others again hardly cosmopolitan at all. A more genuine cosmopolitanism entails a certain metacultural position. There is, first of all, a willingness to engage with the Other, an intellectual and aesthetic stance of openness toward divergent cultural experiences. There can be no cosmopolitans without locals, representatives of more circumscribed territorial cultures. But apart from this appreciative orientation, cosmopolitanism tends also to be a matter of competence, of both a generalized and a more specialized kind. There is the aspect of a personal ability to make one's way into other cultures, through listening, looking, intuiting, and reflecting, and there is cultural competence in the stricter sense of the term, a built-up skill in maneuvering more or less expertly with a particular system of meanings. In its concern with the Other, cosmopolitanism thus becomes a matter of varieties and levels. Cosmopolitans can be dilettantes as well as connoisseurs, and are often both, at different times.[45]

Competence with regard to alien cultures for the cosmopolitan entails a sense of mastery. His understandings have expanded, a little more of the world is under control. Yet there is a curious, apparently paradoxical interplay between mastery and surrender here. It may be one kind of cosmopolitanism where the individual picks from other cultures only those pieces which suit himself. In the long term, this is likely to be the way a cosmopolitan constructs his own unique personal perspective out of an idiosyncratic collection of experiences, although such selectivity can operate in the short term, situationally, as well. In another mode, however, the cosmopolitan does not make invidious distinctions among the particular elements of the alien culture in order to admit some of them into his repertoire and refuse others; he does not negotiate with the other culture but accepts it as a package deal. But even this surrender is a part of the sense of mastery. The cosmopolitan's surrender to the alien culture implies personal autonomy vis-à-vis the culture where he originated. He has his obvious competence with regard to it, but he can choose to disengage from it. He possesses it, it does not possess him. Cosmopolitanism becomes proteanism.

If cosmopolitans are on the move much of the time, they are certainly at home some of the time—quite possibly most of the time. But what, in their case, does this mean?

Perhaps real cosmopolitans, after they have taken out membership in that category, are never quite at home again. Home should be taken-for-grantedness, but if their perspectives have been irreversibly affected by the experience of the alien and the distant, cosmopolitans may not view either the seasons of the year or the minor rituals of everyday life as absolutely natural, obvious, and necessary. There may be a feeling of detachment, perhaps irritation with those committed to the local common sense and unaware of its arbitrariness. Or perhaps the cosmopolitan makes "home" as well one of his several sources of personal meaning, not so different from the others which are further away; or he is pleased with his ability both to surrender to and master this one as well.

Or home is really home, but in a special way: a constant reminder of a precosmopolitan past, a privileged site of nostalgia, where once things seemed fairly simple and straightforward. Or it is again really home, a comfortable place of familiar faces, where one's competence is undisputed and where one does not have to prove it to either oneself or others, but where for much the same reasons there is some risk of boredom.

At home, for most cosmopolitans, most others are locals. This is true in the great majority of territorially based cultures. Conversely, for most of these locals, the cosmopolitan is someone a little unusual, one of us and yet not quite one of us. Someone to be respected for his experiences, possibly, but equally possibly not somebody to be trusted as a matter of course. Trust tends to be a matter of "I know, and I know that you know, and I know that you know that I know." And this formula does not necessarily apply to the relationship between local and cosmopolitan. Where thought control is important, as it has been not least to a number of state apparatuses in history, cosmopolitans are singled out as enemies, and the category is extended to include just about everybody whose horizons are suspected of including ideas from the uncontrollable outside.[46]

Some cosmopolitans are more adept at making the formula of shared knowledge apply again; it becomes their specialty letting others know what they have come across in distant places. What is cosmopolitan can to some extent be channeled into what is local; and precisely because these are on the whole separate spheres the cosmopolitan can become a broker, an entrepreneur who makes a profit. Yet there is a danger that such attempts to make the alien easily accessible only succeeds in trivializing it, and thereby betraying its nature and the character of the real firsthand encounter. Thus, in a way, the more purely cosmopolitan attitude may be to let separate things be separate.

Despite all this, home is not necessarily a place where cosmopolitanism is in exile. It is natural that, in the contemporary world, many local settings are increasingly characterized by cultural diversity. Those of cosmopolitan inclinations may make selective use of their home habitats to maintain their expansive orientation toward the wider world. Other cosmopolitans are perhaps there, whether they in their turn are at home or abroad, and strangers of other than cosmopolitan orientations. Apart from the face-to-face encounters, there are the media—both those intended for local consumption, although they speak of what is distant, and those which are really part of other cultures, like foreign books and films. Again, the power of the media now makes just about everybody a little more cosmopolitan. And one may in the end ask whether it now may even be possible to become a cosmopolitan without going away at all.

Cultural Critics Betwixt and Between

The danger which cosmopolitans may pose to orthodoxy is of course real, but they are not the only danger. As horizons are widened, in whichever way, cultural debate and cultural critique more generally become located within that organization of diversity which transcends community and nation.

Thus, people nowadays often use the distant to criticize what is close at hand. There is the notion that something resembling their utopia, a blueprint for a radical remodeling of local life and thought, actually exists somewhere else. "I have seen the future, and it works," Lincoln Steffens, used to muckraking at home, exclaimed (prematurely, it seems) about the young Soviet Union; since then, in the twentieth century, a variety of countries have appealed to different people for different reasons at different times (Nazi Germany, Mao's China, France for civilization, India for otherworldliness, the Scandinavian countries for welfare, Israel for pioneering spirit, Tanzania for self-reliance, not least the United States for rugged individualism, high tech, and a consumer's Eldorado; Albania, too).[47]

Those organizations for cultural transformation or resistance which we call movements often arise, of course, out of local forms of life, as responses to local circumstances. Yet among them, as well, we see more evidence of globalization: the women's movement, the ecology movement, and the peace movement have not been independently invented in one country after another, even if they draw upon local sources and adapt to local circumstances.[48] They cross national boundaries because much the same problems can be identified in one place after another, and often because the problems themselves are intrinsically transnational. Where there are global movements, too, there can be global, long-distance gurus. Swedish environmentalism resonates in a particular way with Swedish culture in its relationship to nature, but it could still draw early inspiration from Rachel Carson; Swedish feminists have been reading Simone de Beauvoir as well as Germaine Greer.

The flow of ideas and examples here is not all in one direction. The generally egalitarian ethos of many contemporary movements is not easily combined with a natural acceptance of metropolitan dominance. In the Fourth World movement of aboriginal populations—Australian Aborigines, Indians of the Americas, Inuit, Saami, and others—we see the extreme peripheries linking up together for mutual support and for pooling ideas.[49] With regard to the advocacy of this or that country as a model to be emulated, we seem to run into some presumed backwoods utopias at the outskirts of the world, places where people have resolutely chosen their own path (or perhaps some of the people have chosen the path for themselves as well as for others), with such success (in the eyes of some) that other people of the periphery, or even the people of the center, should follow them. These places are seen, then, as laboratories for the world; often small and thus manageable, and devoted to cultural experimentation and invention. Or they are repositories of wisdom lost at home.

Yet much of the time globalized cultural debate follows center/periphery lines in one way or other. At times, the argument is indeed that the periphery will do well to learn from the achievements of the center, and the critical eye is turned toward what is not-center. In much of the world, for long periods at least, Westernization, modernization, and progress have seemed to be practically synonymous terms; whether they are or not was already the issue which the Bengal Renaissance grappled with. At other times, the center itself, or at least its far-reaching influence, is what comes under criticism, as when Swedes get upset about the cocacolonization of a national song contest, or at least sometimes when Nigerians portray the beento in popular literature. But this debate is not just about being for or against the center, and some are also more involved in it than others. "In any community that is attempting to solve the problem of adapting its life to the rhythm of an alien civilization, there is need for a special social class to serve as the human counterpart of the 'transformer' which changes an electric current from one voltage to another," Arnold Toynbee wrote in *The Study of History* (1946:393–394). He identified this class as the intelligentsia, "liaison officers who have learnt the tricks of the intrusive civilization's trade."

What do they do, these liaison officers in the organization of world culture? There are, of course, different ways of liaising. In chapter 5, I distinguished (following Gouldner), as Toynbee most likely did not, between intelligentsia and intellectuals. In the sense used there—and here—the intelligentsia, as specialists in more or less narrowly defined fields, with decontextualized and often credentialed skills, tend to be involved with the kind of transnational cultures whereby the knowledge produced mostly in the center is transmitted rather directly into the cultures of the periphery. The intellectuals, in contrast, are in a more complicated and ambiguous position; liminoid, betwixt and between, in more than one way. Rammohun Roy, the Calcuttan, was an example in his time.[50] It is in the interfaces between center and periphery that much of what there is of intellectual life today, in large parts of the world, is produced. Ideally at least, if they should live up to what one might most highmindedly demand of them, those intellectuals who find themselves inhabiting those interfaces should scrutinize the coherence or incoherence not merely of one local or national culture, but those of different cultures in their interrelations, and eventually perhaps of world culture as such. They should bring one structure of meaning to bear on another, perhaps historically distinct, but no longer necessarily geographically remote. And they should let them reflect on one another, clash against one another. Although their own products may be thought of as high culture, their field of observation is not so confined but includes the entire range of cultural forms. And as far as center/periphery influences are concerned, it is a part of the mandate of intellectuals to comment not only on the flow of meaning as such, but also on the relationship between culture and the political and material conditions shaped by the world system.

George Konrad, the Hungarian author, has portrayed the

transnational culture of intellectuals in terms celebrating a community without boundaries:

> The global flow of information proceeds on many different technical and institutional levels, but on all levels the intellectuals are the ones who know most about one another across the frontiers, who keep in touch with one another, and who feel that they are one another's allies.
>
> We may describe as transnational those intellectuals who are at home in the cultures of other peoples as well as their own. They keep track of what is happening in various places. They have special ties to those countries where they have lived, they have friends all over the world, they hop across the sea to discuss something with their colleagues; they fly to visit one another as easily as their counterparts two hundred years ago rode over to the next town to exchange ideas. (1984:208–209)

This involvement with the wider world is one part of the picture. In his study of the intellectuals of Mexico—who are, of course, not necessarily typical—Camp (1985:52) found that two-thirds had lived abroad for a year or more. And intellectuals may indeed have an elective affinity for cosmopolitanism—in their reflexive, problematizing, generally expansionist management of meaning, the openness and drive toward mastery ideally characteristic of the cosmopolitan would seem to be close at hand.

If intellectuals are cosmopolitans, however, they are also often in one way or other transformers, as Toynbee put it, or mediators, as one might alternatively say, between the transnational and the local, or between local, territorially anchored, cultures. More or less at home in the world and not least in the center, familiar with its tendencies and fashions, the intellectuals of the periphery or semi-periphery bring these back home. Yet they are at the same time frequently open to the flow of meaning from the center and critical of it. Insofar as they have greater access to metropolitan culture than most of their compatriots, they are the latter's informants about the world. As cultural brokers they are in part gatekeepers, deciding on what gets in and what will be kept out, ignored, explicitly rejected. They are also interpreters, who accept the cultural forms of the center not because they are of the center, but because, recontextualized to other conditions, they are (at times) good to think with and express with. Moreover, intellectuals are critics of those currents of culture which they cannot altogether control—not least those of transnational popular culture, and of transnational intelligentsias.

Often, the intellectuals of the periphery are, as a most important part of all this, also guardians of local culture. As cosmopolitans, they may hold a perspective toward it which is rather different from that of most of their neighbors, but nowadays at least, they are likely to argue for its preservation or revitalization rather than its destruction.[51] Consequently, cultural imperialism is what they identify as the great enemy.

In all this, the situation and the activities of intellectuals at the periphery occasionally become rather paradoxical. As critics of alien influences, they may draw on genres of discourse which are themselves imports from the center in their very form. With regard to the minutiae of argument as well, their sources of inspiration may only in part be at home, and in part in the ongoing cultural debates of the center: the adversary culture is also transnational. "Our preoccupation with issues of autonomy and dignity for Africa continually relies on conceptual tools and ideas which draw considerably from European intellectual traditions," writes Ali Mazrui (1976:14), one of the most prolific, and also one of the more controversial, debaters of center/periphery relationships in culture.

Intellectuals, too, operate in a social context, within a network of perspectives. In this regard, their situations may differ considerably. It is in the nature of things that in the centers of world culture, the intellectuals form substantial communities of their own, and are supported by considerable numbers of those "indispensable amateurs" who take an interest in their work mostly as well-informed consumers. Here, intellectual life is largely self-sufficient. The centers may pay some attention to one another, but the tendency in most circles within them has usually been to take little notice of the intellectuals of the periphery, perhaps with the exception of an occasional star: Tagore, Fanon.

At the semi-peripheries of global intellectual life—say, the smaller countries of Europe, the larger countries of Latin America and Asia, or Australia—there is also considerable internal vitality, with producers as well as audiences to keep the cultural debates going. The centers draw a fair amount of attention, but to varying degrees in different local circles. Although the semi-peripheries are to some extent self-sufficient and make some contributions to the transnational flow of intellectual products, they are net importers.

At the real peripheries, intellectuals are often in a much weaker position. In much of the Third World, there is not a sufficient mass of people who are prepared to listen to local intellectuals and provide support for their work, and the local cultural apparatus is too weak to allow them to go about work with some acceptable degree of autonomy and effectiveness. As the cultural market at home is too small, in order to publish, African and Asian writers have often had to submit their work to French or British publishers; to exhibit, their artist colleagues may have to go to London or Paris. Thus the curious situation develops where intellectuals of the periphery speak to their compatriots (or at least have to pretend, both to themselves and to the world, that they do so), but are heard mainly as weak voices at the center, in large part by distant cosmopolitans. With weak public support at home, they can perhaps at best hope for a sinecure within the redistributive economy of the state, but at the same time, as cultural critics, they are vulnerable to state power (from which, at times, they need to be protected through the vigilance of their allies among the transnational intellectuals described by Konrad).

Whether the vantage point toward the center is from the semi-periphery or the real periphery, the most worthwhile stance would appear to be one of an open but critical mind. Not everything that passes for intellectual activity in the present-day linkages between cultures, however, quite measures up to the highest expectations. It is among intellectuals, above all, that "provincialism" is a fighting word in debates about center/periphery relationships. The concept is really ambiguous.[52] There are, in fact, two kinds of provincialism: a provincialism of openness and one of closure. In the extreme form, the provincialism of closure involves a stagnant backwater, largely self-satisfied with a life of ideas which tends toward repetitiousness and involution, a place where mediocrity is safe as competing ideas and more demanding standards of excellence are kept out. The relationship to the center is largely one of refusal.

The provincialism of openness, on the other hand, involves too much deference and mindless mimicry on the part of the periphery toward the center. Here is an audience waiting anxiously to catch the *dernier cri* of the metropolis, perhaps brought back and replayed by an enthusiastic local entrepreneur.[53] It is a provincialism perpetuating the people who are more or less of the periphery as an underclass of cultural process on the world scene, condemned "to live at its outskirts as the hewers of texts and the drawers of book-learning," as Rabindranath Tagore once put it (quoted in Alatas 1977:13). If local talent is to be recognized at home for its achievements, this may occur most certainly, in a roundabout way, only after it has been given its due at the center.

The two forms of provincialism may be unevenly distributed, so that they become dominant, or at least conspicuous, in different places. Perhaps the provincialism of openness occurs more often in the market framework, and the provincialism of closure in that of the state. But they can also occur together; in some places, intellectual life may consist in large part of their mutual recriminations. In the Third World, in the view of many critics (local or otherwise), the view of the charismatic center has often led, at least in one phase or other, to a pronounced provincialism of openness. The intellectuals have been *évolués, ilustrados,* Afro-Saxons. But again, as cultural management is seen as something going on over time, there can be maturation as well as saturation. As long as a local culture remains in existence, with its own assumptions and values, if even only at an implicit, commonsense level, it is possible to draw on it as well, and not only on metropolitan culture, for the critique of metropolitan influences. And the more familiar one becomes with the latter, the better is one able both to criticize them and to recontextualize them, without destroying the context in the process.[54]

Conclusion: A Creolizing World

During the twentieth century—and especially in its latter part—the global ecumene has indeed been an organization of diversity, and one which has also been characterized by diversity in organization. The point of view which I have tried to develop in this chapter can perhaps be summarized as follows:

1. The autonomy and boundedness of cultures must nowadays be understood as a matter of degree;

2. The distribution of culture within the world is affected by a structure of asymmetrical, center/periphery, relationships;

3. These relationships affect cultures, to different degrees, particularly in two analytically distinguishable ways—by shaping the material and power conditions to which cultures adapt, even in their more autonomous cultural processes, and through the more direct influx of initially alien meanings and cultural forms;

4. That influx does not enter into a vacuum, or inscribe itself on a cultural tabula rasa, but enters into various kinds of interaction with already existing meanings and meaningful forms, however these may be socially distributed, in cumulative historical processes;

5. The transnational cultural flow is internally diverse;

6. Market, state, form of life, and movement frameworks for the organization of cultural flow all have their own, somewhat diverse, ways of organizing (which may include promoting, regulating, or preventing) the transnational cultural flow;

7. Not all cultures are local, in the sense of being territorially bounded;

8. And it is hardly self-evident that the end result of the cultural processes connected to transnational center/periphery relationships must be a global homogenization of culture.

Is there, then, any other scenario, any alternative overall conceptualization, which may give us a better grasp of the current interplay between world culture and the national cultures of the periphery?

Whatever anthropologists and their neighbors in other disciplines have been up to in constructing more general points of view toward complexity and change in the Third World, they have hardly ever done justice to the particular qualities of cultural phenomena and cultural processes, as these occur within structures of social relationships. And frameworks which seemed satisfactory at one time have by now been overtaken by events.

During one period—between the 1930s and the 1950s, say—many anthropologists, especially in the United States, were doing acculturation studies.[55] One problem with these was that they often involved a rather weak sense of the political economy of culture, of the overwhelming power of the Western expansion and of the material bases of change. Furthermore, they were inclined to conceptualize situations of culture contact as if they were new or at least recent. It is doubtful if this was more than very rarely justifiable at the time; in any case, another half-century later, such situations have become practically non-existent.

Then, in the 1950s and early 1960s especially (but continuing to some extent still), there was modernization theory. Anthropologists have never been quite as enthusiastic about it as other social scientists, because of its overtones of ethnocentrism and unilinearism. Later on, of course, criticisms have focused, here as well, on the disregard of the center/periphery relationships of the global political economy. For our purposes, it is worth pointing out that modernization theorists have often dwelt on social psychology and patterns of social organization. Of culture, on the other hand, after it has been reduced to Parsonian pattern variables or something similar, there is frequently little left.

A very different framework—again, now several decades old in its most influential formulations—was that dealing with the notion of plural societies, drawing mostly on research experience in colonial plantation societies, with strikingly heterogeneous populations, in Southeast Asia and the Caribbean.[56] Here, the emphasis was on institutionalized cultural separateness, an ethnic or racial division of labor, and the dominance of a single group in the polity. This remains one of the few macroanthropological approaches to the overall organization of cultural complexity but, by now, there are probably in most Third World countries considerably wider areas of the social structure which are relatively open, rather than the restricted niche of any single ascriptively based group. There is also usually a more developed overarching cultural apparatus which breaks down many of the barriers to a society-wide flow of meaning.

And then, more lately—as we have seen—world system theory and what we may think of as radical diffusionism have moved in different directions, in part complementary, but incomplete in their understanding of culture even when put together.

Most likely, I have left out one or two other formulae, frameworks or orientations dealing with similar issues. In any case, at this stage, it seems we can use another guiding imagery which clashes conspicuously with old conceptions of the autonomy and integrity of territorially based cultures, and which thus can serve as a response from cultural studies to the growth of the global ecumene and to notions of the world system elsewhere in the social sciences. The root metaphor I favor, showing up here and there in recent anthropology, is that of creole cultures.[57]

Moving from the social and cultural history of particular colonial societies (where they have tended to apply especially to particular ethnic or racial categories) to the discourse of linguists, creole concepts have become more general in their applications.[58] It is true that linguistic sources of inspiration have not always served cultural analysis well, and whenever one takes an intellectual ride on a metaphor, it is essential that one knows where to get off. But choosing only what suits my purpose from the rather tumultuous diversity of latter-day creolist linguistics (and making perhaps somewhat approximating use of that), I would suggest first of all that creole cultures—like creole languages—are intrinsically of mixed origin, the confluence of two or more widely separate historical currents which interact in what is basically a center/periphery relationship. If our most established understandings of culture indeed seem to delegitimize an interest in such emergent, hybridizing webs of meaning, suggesting that they are artificial, lacking in authenticity—spurious cultures, in Sapir's terms—then such understandings have to be confronted head on.

Moreover, creole cultures have had some time to develop and to move toward a degree of coherence, and to become elaborate and pervasive. Generations of people are being formed from birth by the creole systems of meaning. We are dealing here with something quite other than moments of fresh culture contact, a later time in history.

In creole cultures as I see them, as systems of meaning and expression mapped onto structures of social relations, there is also a continuous spectrum of interacting forms, along which the various contributing historical sources of the culture are differentially visible and active. At one end of the creolizing continuum there is the culture of the center, with its greater prestige, as in language the "Standard"; at the other end are the cultural forms of the farthest periphery, probably in greater parochial variety. Within the form of life framework, groups variously affected by world system constraints and impulses also arrange themselves along the continuum, mixing, observing each other, and commenting on each other; the boundaries between them perhaps more or less blurred depending, for one thing, on the extent to which the forms are also emblematic of group memberships.[59] The asymmetries of cultural flow within market and state frameworks, taking their places within the spectrum, have different points of origin and different reach. Movements arise at different points, at different times. In relation to this, there is a built-in political economy of culture, as social power and material resources are matched with the spectrum of cultural forms.

The cultural processes of creolization are not simply a matter of a constant pressure from the center toward the periphery, but a much more creative interplay. As languages have different dimensions such as grammar, phonology, and lexicon, and as creole languages are formed as unique combinations and creations out of the interaction between languages in these various dimensions, so creole cultures come out of multidimensional cultural encounters and can put things together in new ways. The homegrown uses of symbolic modes can be renewed and expanded through the influx of new cultural technology. In a society where new expertise enters, the concept of the layman has to be constructed, beginning from available sources of common sense. Meanings established in the past change as they are drawn into classificatory schemes brought in from afar. Intellectuals manage local meaning at new levels of metacultural reflection.

Creolization also increasingly allows the periphery to talk back. As it creates a greater affinity between the cultures of center and periphery, and as the latter increasingly uses the same organizational forms and the same technology as the center, not least some of its new cultural commodities become increasingly attractive on a global market. Third World music of a creolized kind becomes world music; and world cities like New York, London, or Paris, in themselves partly extensions of Third World societies, come to exercise some of their influence as cultural switchboards between peripheries (and semi-peripheries), not only as original sources.[60]

This creolist cluster of understandings is a very general one, and it has to be confronted with the particularities of each of those cultures to which there is some chance that it might apply. In this general form, however, it stands opposed to the view of cultures as well-bounded wholes, as well as to assumptions of a replication of uniformity within them. It suggests that the the flow of culture between countries and continents may result in another diversity of culture, based more on interconnections than on autonomy. It also allows the sense of a complex culture as a network of perspectives, or as an ongoing debate. People can come into it from the diaspora, as consultants and advisors, or they can come into it from the multiform local cultures, from the bush. The outcome is not predicted. Creolization thought is open-ended; the tendencies toward maturation and saturation are understood as quite possibly going on side by side, or interweaving. There may come a time of decreolization, the metropolitan Standard eventually becoming dominant, but a creole culture could also stabilize, or the interplay of center and periphery could go on and on, never settling into a fixed form precisely because of the openness of the global whole. What matters is that we are sensitized, through the creolist view, to what general kind of culture this is.

As the world turns, today's periphery may be tomorrow's center. The historian Bernard Bailyn has suggested, in his book *The Peopling of British North America* (1986:112–113), that American culture as it was by the beginning of the eighteenth century "becomes most fully comprehensible when seen as the exotic far Western periphery, a marchland, of the metropolitan European culture system." It is an anachronism, according to Bailyn, to look, as many American historians have done, at colonial America as a frontier, looking forward and outward, anticipating progress, rather than as "a ragged outer margin of a central world, a backward-looking diminishment of metropolitan accomplishment." This may be a controversial point of view. The fact remains, however, that a new culture did grow out of that management of meaning which occurred in this periphery, a culture which went on to turn the tables on the world but which in its internal processes has continued to show the continued fluidity of a creolizing continuum. Anglo culture, the culture of the WASPs, may have provided the metropolis, the Standard, the mainstream, but as it reaches out toward every corner of society, it becomes creolized itself. Ethnic boundaries remain noticeable, yet cultural meanings and forms flow across them. American music with African sources is not necessarily Black music, it may be mountain music or symphony music. You do not have to be Jewish to have *chutzpah;* it may be enough to be a New Yorker.

If some peripheries—in time—become centers, and some old centers pass them as they move in the other direction, what seems unlikely to change, given the way things are, is the organization of the world by way of center/periphery relationships. And as cultural traffic plays its part in this, something like creole cultures may have a larger part in our future than cultures designed, each by itself, to be pieces of a mosaic. Toward the end of the twentieth century, and during the twenty-first, it would seem to be through our grasp of the flux of the global ecumene that we can best make sense of *Homo sapiens.*

Notes

1. The Nature of Culture Today

1. The position paper by Kroeber and Parsons (1958) has provided one of the bases for this view of culture, later influentially propagated not least by Geertz (e.g., 1973). See also the useful reviews by Keesing (1974) and D'Andrade (1984).

2. This is having it both ways on an issue which has sometimes been presented in either/or terms—Clifford Geertz being prominently identified, in the emergent history of culture theory, with one position and Ward Goodenough, somewhat dubiously, with the other (Geertz 1973:10 ff., Goodenough 1981:51 ff.; see also Keesing 1974:84 ff.). As I understand it, if one gives priority to the internal locus of meaning, one risks becoming insensitive to the variety of forms in which culture is embodied, and their particular implications. One may also come to disregard the question of the collectivization of meaning, which can only occur by means of its public manifestations. On the other hand, if one attends only to these overt forms, one may come to neglect not least the problem of perspectivation which will be emphasized here. My position is much like that of Berger and Luckmann (1966); for another statement by an anthropologist on the "double coding" of culture, see Bohannan (1973).

3. The discussion of a concept of perspective in chapter 3 should go some way toward problematizing any understanding of the flow as mere transportation. Generally, understandings of cultural transmission probably have to be to some degree rethought, and made more pluralistic, in the light of work in cognitive psychology. For pointers in this direction, see Bloch (1985:27 ff.) and Sperber (1985).

4. Or, to be less gender-biased, laypersons; I must warn here that whenever in this book I have felt that the use of deliberately gender-neutral terms would still differ so much from ordinary usage that they

might distract readers from the argument, or make the latter clumsier, I have refrained from using them.

5. Some anthropologists, of course, may still take the opinion that, as Appadurai (1986a:357) has put it (critically), "some others are more other than others"; "the anthropology of complex non-Western societies has, until recently, been a second-class citizen in anthropological discourse. This . . . involves a kind of reverse Orientalism, whereby complexity, literacy, historical depth, and structural messiness operate as disqualifications in the struggle of places for a voice in metropolitan theory."

6. In their research on food symbolism, Douglas and Gross (1981) have concerned themselves with measurements of "intricacy" in cultural rule systems; it is noteworthy that the three components of intricacy they suggest (metaphysical, aesthetic, and distributive) are somewhat parallel to the dimensions of complexity discussed here. Yet Douglas and Gross are primarily concerned with intricacy of patterning, rightly pointing out that one can have more intricate patterns using fewer elements and less intricate patterns using more elements. Insofar as my conception of complexity starts out from an understanding that the sheer number of differentiated elements itself makes a culture more or less complex, there is a difference here; however, presumably, the potential for intricate patterning would also be greater with a greater number of available elements, even if that potential may not be realized. If that is so, the analysis of intricacy in the Douglas and Gross sense may seem to be a second step in the analysis of complexity, and one which would seem to be more manageable with a more limited number of elements. When they refer to distribution as a component of intricacy, Douglas and Gross also have in mind a number of things, including the distribution of tasks and privileges among the participants in a meal, but they do not, as I understand them, problematize the distribution of knowledge. Rather, it is assumed that what they deal with are shared rule systems.

7. There are some intriguing guesstimates in this area by D'Andrade (1981:180). Noting that some fifty thousand information "chunks"—units of meaning—are needed to play a sophisticated game of chess, or to speak a language reasonably proficiently, he conjectures that a typical adult probably knows between several hundred thousand and several million chunks. But if knowledge is so distributed in society that everybody does not have all the same chunks, its total information pool may be a hundred to ten thousand times as large as the knowledge of any one individual. It would thus contain something between a few million and ten billion chunks of information.

8. As additional variations of this kind of analysis, one may think of Sider's (1986) argument that culture in class societies grows in the mediation between daily working life and appropriation, and Hobsbawm's (1983) account of the turn-of-the-century mass production of tradition as a phenomenon of state and class.

9. In her critique of the appropriation of early anthropology into the sociology of culture, Archer (1985) points out that what she refers to as "cultural system integration" and "socio-cultural integration" have often been conflated. She does not seem aware, however, of more recent anthropological work of relevance to the issue.

10. No full-scale review of what we will term distributionist thinking in anthropology since Sapir can be undertaken here; Pelto and Pelto (1975) make some attempts in this direction, but from a point of view rather different from mine, and their emphasis is rather on criticizing "uniformist" ethnography. Apart from the comments by Sapir, early writings include Linton's (1936:272 ff.) textbook overview of the organization of culture, where he drew attention to the existence of "universals," "specialties," "alternatives," and "individual peculiarities." Later on, one line of thought has been that of Roberts, beginning with his detailed ethnographic investigation of the variable cultural inventories of three Navaho households (1951). An intriguing comparative sketch of the "information economies" of the Chiricahua Apache, the Cheyenne, the Omaha, and the Mandan (1964) has been followed by detailed studies by Roberts and collaborators of variations in personal meaning systems and small-group cultures; these offer useful examples of perspectivation as discussed in chapter 3 (see, e.g., Roberts, Chiao, and Pandey 1975; Roberts, Morita, and Brown 1986).

Spiro (1951) also adumbrates the interest in cultural distributions from the point of view of psychological anthropology, developed further by Wallace (1961) who proposed that culture could be described as a set of models of standardized exchange sequences, contractual relationships of complementarity which are available to motivated persons for implementation. As long as the resulting actions are predictable, Wallace argued, the people involved need not have any notion whatsoever about what goes on in one another's minds.

Wallace's fairly extreme point of view has drawn some criticism from Schwartz (1978a:435 ff.), who has also contributed importantly to the elaboration of a distributionist view in other publications, drawing to begin with on his work in Manus but proceeding to suggestions with much wider implications (cf. Schwartz 1978a, 1978b, Schwartz and Mead 1961). Goodenough (1971:36 ff.) has carried out a vigorous unpacking of the culture concept, showing that a series of interrelated notions are concealed behind the single term. Building up from a view of the cultural repertoire of the individual, he shows how different sets of standards operate on different occasions, and how the notion of "a culture" can be variously composed from smaller-scale elements (see also Goodenough 1963:257 ff., 1978).

Apart from his comments cited later in the main text, Roger Keesing has also discussed distributive issues in his well-known textbook (1981:71–73), in a monograph on Kwaio religion (1982:198 ff.), in an article on Kwaio women's perspectives (1985), and in a discussion of the notion of "folk models" (1987b). In addition to Fredrik Barth's formulation quoted later in the text, see also another article of his (Barth 1989). Sperber (1985), in a Malinowski lecture, has likewise dwelt on the problem of varyingly narrow and wide distributions of culture, asking for a dialogue between anthropology and psychology in developing an "epidemiology of representations." Why are some representations more contagious than others, spreading efficiently and often swiftly in human populations? The answer, according to Sperber, should lie in a study of the chains of transformations in which mental and public representations follow one another.

Stromberg (1986) has dealt critically with the assumption of shared culture in his study of a Swedish free church congregation, showing the differences in members' understandings of symbolism, and Varenne (1984) has reviewed some of the issues involved in conceptualizing intracultural diversity, in the context of an understanding of American culture. Swartz (1982) offers a comparative study of cultural sharing and distribution, suggesting that members of the same family tend to share more culture, even as they have different positions in the family structure, than do members of different families but of the same family status. For examples of studies in cognitive variability as shown in folk classifications, and discussions of theoretical and methodological problems in this connection, see, for example, Sankoff (1971, 1972), Gardner (1976), Sanjek (1977), and Boster (1985, 1987).

11. The term is used in this manner by Fox (1985), although I draw it more directly from an unpublished paper on the sociology of culture by Bennett Berger. For further comments on culturalism, see Dirlik (1987) and Amin (1989).

12. See, for instance, Moore (1975, 1986, 1987), Turner (1977a), and Vincent (1986).

13. This point of view is now mostly associated in American sociology with symbolic interactionism; in the concern with meaning in process, I see a general affinity between it and Berger's and Luckmann's (1966) sociology of knowledge. It may seem odd to try to combine an interactionist predilection with a concern for macroanthropology, as it is

widely held that interactionism has great difficulty getting above a micro level of analysis. I would like to draw attention, however, to recent sociological debate over micro/macro relationships, where it is increasingly suggested that macrosociology should preferably be grounded in microanalysis, with intensive attention to the manner in which microprocesses are aggregated, and to resultant macrolevel "unintended consequences" (see, e.g., Collins 1981a, 1981b, 1983). This would seem to be much the same general position as that taken, among anthropological interactionists, by Barth (e.g., 1979:79–81). Although, on the whole, the theoretical discussions on this point have not been oriented toward cultural analysis, they would appear generally relevant here as well; not least if one also takes participants' understandings of aggregation and the macrolevel into account. Knorr-Cetina (1981:30 ff.), in her review of attempts to integrate micro- and macrosociologies, indeed suggests that something like this has tended to be a missing link in theoretical work. If one endorses the model of social reality as composed of microsituations, one should "expand this model by taking into account the *macroconstructions endogenous to these situations.*" This is, in her formulation, a "representation hypothesis."

14. Wallace's (1961) viewpoint toward those orderly exchange sequences in which no shared culture is necessary, not even a concern with what goes on in the other's mind, still seems to apply best to very stable interaction routines (of which there are certainly a number in human life). Elsewhere, where interactions are less repetitive and predictable, what one person believes that the other thinks or knows probably again becomes more significant. In Goodenough's conceptualization, there is likewise a bias toward stability: culture is a matter of standards—operating or not operating, but standards nonetheless.

15. The term "management of meaning" probably originates with Cohen and Comaroff (1976), but their use of it was more transactionalist than I generally have in mind here. "Cultural management" has been used in anthropology at least by Fallers (1961) and Roberts (1964). Roberts' mode of using it may be closest to my own.

16. Mazrui (1972:xiv) has proposed this concept.

17. For illuminating approaches to the problem see, for example, Swidler (1986) and Schudson (1989).

18. See Godelier's (1986:3 ff.) useful discussion of the variety of "material realities."

19. Note Appadurai's and Breckenridge's not so nation-oriented but otherwise related conception of public culture as "a *zone* of cultural debate," "an arena where other types, forms and domains of culture are encountering, interrogating and contesting each other in new and unexpected ways" (1988:6).

20. Cf. Wolf (1984:397): "We shall look in vain for a notion of social interaction in Marx, or for a theory of culture. The first we owe to the sociologists, the second to anthropologists."

21. For some brief comments on "the center" in American culture by an anthropologist, see Handler (1988).

22. I have not been back to Kafanchan after the religious riots which broke out there in March, 1987, and which spread from there to other northern Nigerian towns and cities, but I understand that some churches and mosques were destroyed at that time.

23. According to Na'inna (1987:1687), Nigeria at a recent count had at least 23 daily newspapers, 29 weeklies, 9 newspapers in vernacular languages, 54 magazines, 29 radio stations, and 34 television stations.

24. My own understandings here have been helped by the scheme for media analysis proposed by the Israeli psychologist Gavriel Salomon (1979), accounting for media in terms of four classes of attributes: technologies, symbol systems, contents, and situations. If for the purposes of cultural analysis we can treat the technology itself as a given, the other three classes are more or less parallel to the dimensions I have identified.

25. In one of his few references to academic anthropologists (in Stearn, 1967:272–274), McLuhan scorned their limited understandings of the issues he dealt with. They were men of the Gutenberg galaxy, he suggested, importing assumptions from the world of literacy and print into the study of preliterate cultures. This attack was occasioned by Hymes' (1963) review of one of his books.

26. See on the one hand Eisenstein: "Although Marshall McLuhan's work stimulated my historical curiosity, among many of my colleagues it has been counter-productive, discouraging further investigation of print culture or its effects. Concern with the topic at present is likely to be regarded with suspicion, to be labelled 'McLuhanite' and dismissed out of hand" (1979:xvii); and on the other, Booth: "It is unfortunate that McLuhan's love of highjinks and his frequently absurd praise for TV obscured the immensely imaginative way in which he opened up new domains for criticism of the media" (1982:58). But McLuhan's work has not just been either enthusiastically embraced or flatly rejected. In the literature of McLuhanological critique and commentary—see, for example, Stearn (1967), Burke (1968:410–418), Finkelstein (1968), Rosenthal (1968), Miller (1971), Theall (1971), Curtis (1978), Steiner (1979:261–267), and Kroker (1984)—there are also examples of sophisticated cultural analysis. For a portrait of this rather strange man, see Marchand's (1989) biography.

27. In his discussion of "means of communication as means of production," Raymond Williams (1980:55) described these as "amplificatory" and "durative" transformations of communication. Meyrowitz

(1985) has a wide-ranging and imaginative discussion particularly of the spatial implications of electronic media.

28. On the information society in Japan, see Ivy (1988) and Morris-Suzuki (1988).

2. Patterns of Process

1. See Bateson's (1972:130) discussion of redundancy, and—for an anthropological view of variations in social scale in terms of redundancy—Frankenberg's (1966) comparative study of British communities.

2. As shown clearly enough, for instance, in the late 1980s American controversy surrounding Hirsch's *Cultural Literacy* (1987), which claimed to argue for an "anthropological," descriptive sense of cultural sharing, but which nonetheless took an essentially prescriptive stance.

3. Wilson (1983) discusses "cognitive authority" under those conditions where most knowledge is secondhand knowledge. There is not much of an anthropology of expertise, although there is the occasional ethnographic treatment such as that by Errington (1984:102 ff.).

4. The obvious reference here is to Hobsbawm and Ranger (1983).

5. Gusfield (1981) is one of the writers on movements who emphasizes their part in changes in meaning systems.

6. Although the state here may have had its historical roots in a movement, my interpretation here is that this particular movement has been absorbed by the state; and there has mostly been little tolerance for any others operating with any degree of autonomy.

7. See Bensman and Lilienfeld (1973) for an attempt to construct a sociology of knowledge around the experiences of occupations.

8. But the form of life framework, it should be understood, does not include only the working life most directly connected to the division of labor, but also domesticity, sociability, and other kinds of activity involving the same general type of cultural flow.

9. On indexicality in this sense, see the original statement by Bar-Hillel (1954) and Garfinkel (1967). Bernstein's (1971) contrast between restricted and elaborated codes is also relevant here; the former, of course, presuppose more shared meaning than the latter.

3. A Network of Perspectives

1. Habitus is similarly described as a device mediating between personal intake and output, and ordering and being ordered; "structured

structures predisposed to function as structuring structures" (cf. Bourdieu 1977:72, 1984:169–170). Bourdieu moves rather quickly from the individual to the collective level of class, however, and while there is certainly something of value in his view, not least in *Outline of a Theory of Practice* (e.g., 1977:79), of the actor as not particularly knowledgeable about his own actions, it may still be seen as something fairly problematic (cf. Karp 1986:133).

2. There is a visualist bias, obviously, in the term "perspective" which does not entirely suit our purposes here; and, more generally, a bias toward an emphasis on cognition which is not altogether desirable either. But there is hardly another word that so immediately suggests the relationship between social structure and personal meaning. For an illuminating discussion of the implications of the perspective metaphor, see Wilson (1983:3 ff.).

3. My emphasis here, it will be clear, is on the *social* composition of perspectives. The complementary question of the nature of their integration through mental processes is largely disregarded, although the concern with perspectives certainly could be pursued further in this direction. What follows draws on Hannerz (1980:100 ff.), and is also inspired by Barth's (1972) comparative viewpoint toward social organization.

4. Benita Luckmann (1970), writing about "the small life-worlds of modern man," suggests that people now typically relate mostly to the three intersecting microuniverses of family, work, and territorial community; all small, comprehensible, and knowable. Although this is undoubtedly true of many, it is certainly also possible to take an interest in, and even be actively involved with, much more than this. And at least the latter two can have variable implications of scale, sometimes creating quite large and not so transparent worlds. Knorr-Cetina's (1981) discussion of the representation of the macrolevel in microsituations—see chapter 1, note 14—is relevant here.

5. Scheff (1967) is one source for such a reading of Durkheim; taking this formula as a point of departure for developing a more general view toward the social organization of meaning, I also find inspiration in Schutz' (1962:315 ff.) discussion of the reciprocity of perspectives. Goodenough (1971:37) and Keesing (1974:89) similarly define culture in terms of meanings which individuals attribute to one another, and more recently, D'Andrade (1987:113) has noted the three levels of sharing in intersubjectivity. Bohannan (1960) has an illuminating discussion, although in somewhat different terms, of the notion of *conscience collective* in relation to various conceptions of culture in the history of anthropology. The further move to see culture in terms of an organization of similar but varied formulae draws especially on the work by Glaser and Strauss (1964) on "awareness contexts."

The "I know that you know that I know" formula is necessarily the strongest version of the general type, and insofar as one may never know precisely what someone else knows, one should perhaps always, and certainly in many cases, substitute other alternatives for "know" in the social organization of meaning—"assume," "believe," "suspect," etc.

6. The essay on marriage by Berger and Kellner (1964) remains one of the more stimulating analyses of the management of meaning in a dyad.

7. The early history of the concept is a bit obscure. Articles by Green (1946) and Gordon (1947) are sometimes mentioned for significant early uses; but Sapir (1932:236) actually mentions it considerably earlier, as does Linton (1936:275–276).

8. One fairly recent commentator on the idea of subculture suspects that "were it to be introduced today as a new concept in sociology it would be rejected as worthless" (Clarke 1974:428). Another critic, somewhat earlier, finds it strangely underdeveloped: "If chemists had only one word to refer to all colorless liquids and this led them to pay attention to only the two characteristics shared in common, their analysis would be exceedingly primitive." (Yinger 1960:626) Yet critiques by these and other writers (e.g., Fine and Kleinman 1979; Hebdige 1979) contribute to greater sophistication. For a set of early and more recent formulations concerning subcultures and related concepts, see also Arnold (1970).

9. For some representative examples of the work of the "Birmingham School," see Hall and Jefferson (1976), Hall, Hobson, Lowe, and Willis (1980), and Willis (1977).

10. In Goodenough's (1971) distributive model of culture, this is the point made with the concept of an individual's several "operating cultures." On encapsulation and other modes of social existence in complex societies, see Hannerz (1980:255 ff.).

11. On this issue see Bennett Berger (1971:174 ff.).

12. More recent developments of the "social world" concept do not necessarily share this weakness (see, e.g., Strauss 1978, 1982, 1984; Unruh 1979, 1980a, 1980b).

13. Barth's (1984:79–80) discussion of the difference between analyses of ethnicity and of cultural variation makes a similar point very clearly.

14. The work of the "Birmingham School," for example, emphatically locates particular youth cultures in particular class cultures; see Clarke et al. (1982).

15. It should be noted that Barth himself does not in this case appear to think of culture as other than a one-level phenomenon—"one ethnic group, spread over a territory with varying ecologic circumstances, will exhibit regional diversities of overt institutionalized be-

haviour which do not reflect differences in cultural orientation" (1969:12).

16. The term "pluralistic ignorance" is from Allport (1924) by way of Merton (1957:377).

17. Hoggart (1961:77–78) has formulated the point well: "When people feel that they cannot do much about the main elements in their situation, feel it not necessarily with despair or disappointment or resentment but simply as a fact of life, they adopt attitudes toward that situation which allow them to have a livable life under its shadow, a life without a constant or pressing sense of the larger situation." Rodman's (1963) concept of a "value stretch" draws on the same kind of view; see also Hannerz (1969:103; 1971), Bourdieu (1977:77–78), and Molund's (1988) study of a North Indian urban scheduled caste, leading to conclusions in the same vein.

18. One can recognize it, however, in Sahlins' (1985) comments on "meanings at risk," in his discussion of the relationship between structure and history.

19. The point of view stated here is that elaborated by Wulff (1988) in her study of an ethnically mixed group of teenage girls in South London. For conceptions with varying degrees of affinity to the notion of microculture—"small-group culture," "idioculture," "vernacular culture," "indigenous cultural production"—see Roberts (1951), McFeat (1974), Handelman (1987), Fine (1979, 1987:125 ff.), Lantis (1960), and Collins (1979:60 ff.).

20. I am reminded here of Barth's (1975:15) introductory statement concerning a New Guinea mountain people: "The Baktaman are a nation of 183 persons. . . . "

21. The decontextualization may sometimes occur already in the communication between the anthropologist and his informant; see Bourdieu (1977:18) on outsider-oriented discourse as a "system of lacunae."

22. See in this regard Haviland's (1977:171 ff.) discussion of the relationship between gossip and cultural competence, and Whyte's (1974) study of Chinese small-group political ritual, employed as a means of linking the personal to the general through self-criticism, mutual criticism, and the study of central political texts.

23. On such cultures, see the popular work by Deal and Kennedy (1982), an *Administrative Science Quarterly* issue edited by Jelinek et al. (1983), and the volume by Frost et al. (1985)—to mention only a few titles from a rapidly growing literature.

24. An early article by Sykes and Matza (1957) on "techniques of neutralization" among juvenile delinquents is relevant at this point, as is the notion of "accounts" proposed by Scott and Lyman (1968).

25. Frank Parkin's (1972:81) delineation of meaning systems, especially the discussion of the dominant value system, is illuminating here.

26. For classical statements on labeling theory and later discussions, see, for example, Becker (1963), Lemert (1972:62 ff.), Young (1974), Plummer (1979), and Gove (1980). There is some affinity between labeling theory and Bateson's (1972:68 ff.) old notion of schismogenesis.

27. Yinger (1982) offers the most general sociological overview of countercultural phenomena.

28. As Sapir put it, "the economy of interpersonal relations and the friendly ambiguities of language conspire to reinterpret for each individual all behavior which he has under observation in the terms of those meanings which are relevant to his own life. The concept of culture, as it is handled by the cultural anthropologist is necessarily something of a statistical fiction . . . " (1932:237).

29. The distinction made by Goodenough (1971:42) between a culture-subculture relationship analogous to the language-dialect relationship, involving a real affinity, and a relationship between cultures determined mainly by their being within the same societal boundaries, is relevant to this issue.

30. For a discussion of some such variants of performance, see MacAloon (1984).

31. As Eickelman has suggested, "the study of education can be to complex societies what the study of religion has been to societies variously characterized by anthropologists as 'simple,' 'cold,' or 'elementary'" (1978:485). A boldly conceptualized educational anthropology consequently ought to be of central relevance to culture theory; yet this centrality has so far been better realized in sociology than in anthropology, as exemplified by the attention given to the work of Bourdieu and Passeron (1977), Bernstein (1975), and others.

32. See Boli, Ramirez, and Meyer (1986:105).

33. The "production of culture" tendency in American sociology (e.g., Peterson 1976, Becker 1982) demonstrates this successfully. See also Williams (1981).

34. Horton and Wohl, in 1956, described this as "parasocial interaction." The anthropologist John Caughey (1978, 1984) has also discussed such relationships extensively, as "artificial social relations."

35. For a range of views on such issues, see, e.g., Schiller (1974:172 ff.), Williams (1975:135 ff.), Czitrom (1982:193 ff.), Gitlin (1983:325 ff.), Turkle (1984:171 ff.), and Textor (1985).

36. See Goody (1968, 1977, 1986, 1987); and for other anthropological views of literacy, Street (1984) and Finnegan (1988).

37. Olson (1977, 1986, 1988) has other significant discussions of these matters.

38. McArthur (1986) offers an illuminating overview of dictionaries, encyclopedias, and other reference materials—which are, of course, usually organized as enormous lists—in the context of the growth of cultures.

39. Cook-Gumperz (1986) has an illuminating discussion of the views and the practice of popular literacy in Western history. In Sweden, in a similar way, there was for a considerable time a much greater emphasis on reading than on writing, in line with the policy of the national politico-ecclesiastical complex which formed a largely unitary, paternalistic cultural apparatus from the Reformation onwards. In 1686, during the reign of King Charles XI, a church law came into effect requiring that everybody should learn to read, and thus be able to study the Bible. It was the duty of the household to make sure that its members acquired this skill, and they did so by passing it on among themselves. At regular intervals, a clergyman of the state church would come to examine them. The sanctions were effective—those who could not read were not allowed to participate in Holy Communion, nor to marry in church. In this manner, Sweden had achieved nearly universal reading ability by the early nineteenth century, before it had anything much in the way of a national school system. But the emphasis on reading was such that this skill had jumped far ahead of that of writing by 1700, and it then took nearly two centuries for the latter to catch up (cf. Johansson 1981).

40. On film literacy, see, for example, Worth (1981:108 ff.) and Cole and Keyssar (1985); on computer literacy, Kemeny (1983).

41. For examples of attention to it, however, see the discussions by Wilensky (1964) and Gottdiener (1985). Anthropologists actually evolved the beginnings of an understanding of the interplay between subcultures and the cultural apparatus some decades ago, in their studies of civilizations (see, e.g., Marriott 1955, 1959; Redfield 1956; Singer 1972:250 ff.). In the latter, a cultural apparatus was certainly present, staffed by priests and literati who took the raw materials of folk consciousness, refined them into a great tradition, and then broadcast it to both inspire and constrain a resultant, dependent little tradition—or traditions, as the latter were often localized and thus diverse even within the range of reach of one great tradition. Yet the little traditions were not mere passive recipients of cultural flow from the civilizational centers. They also had their own internal life, and took from the offerings of the great tradition and interpreted it in large part as would fit their circumstances and collectivized local perspectives. There were thus, in the anthropological terms of the times, simultaneous processes of universalization and parochialization.

42. Gellner (1987:13 ff.; see also 1983:24 ff.) emphatically distinguishes between two kinds of division of labor, and two kinds of complex societies, along such lines.

43. For another critical review, see Bennett (1982).

44. See also Steiner (1979:50–51). Needless to say, while reception of the electronic media can more readily be collectivized, it does not have to be so. Salomon (1979:187 ff.), in a study comparing the "television literacy" of Israeli and American children, found that the former more often viewed television in the company of their parents, and related their greater viewing skills partly to this fact.

45. Research on "patterns of cultural choice" within the sociology of culture represents one approach to the study of relationships between subcultures and cultural apparatus (see Peterson 1983). The most extreme instance of a dependence of the former on the latter might be that where an entire subculture seems to develop around a copyrighted, commoditized game of "fantasy role playing" (cf. Fine 1983, Dayan 1986).

46. Marx's original statement is in *The Eighteenth Brumaire* (1957:109); the issue has drawn considerable discussion in research on British class structure and class consciousness (cf. Bulmer 1975). See also chapter 5, note 2, and the relevant passage in the main text.

47. Fine and Kleinman (1979:8) point out that where most of the individuals carrying a subculture are not in effective interaction, various forms of "interlocks" can serve to integrate the subcultural community. A subcultural apparatus is clearly one of them.

48. See Gans' (1974:25) discussion of the difference between creator-orientation and user-orientation.

49. On the former possibility, see Cohen (1972) and Cohen and Young (1973).

4. Unfree Flow

1. For a brief summary, see Schiller (1989:327 ff.).

2. Sharrock's (1974) comments on "owning knowledge" are of a general interest here.

3. The discussion of reciprocity, redistribution, and market exchange here draws on Polanyi (1957a:47–55; 1957b:250 ff.). See also Sahlins (1965) on generalized reciprocity and Boulding's (1970:141 ff.) related treatment of the "grant system" and the "exchange system" in the essay "Knowledge as a Commodity."

4. Goldfarb's (1982) comparative study of the United States and Poland illuminates various issues involved in the production and dis-

semination of culture through the cultural apparatus under market and redistributive arrangements; see also Di Maggio's (1977) analysis of the impact of market structures on cultural production. For a study in a mixed cultural economy, see Ericson's (1988) study of the art world in Stockholm.

5. This, of course, is only an instance of the issues of social system/cultural system interrelatedness discussed in chapter 1.

6. See, for example, Giddens (1979:188): "To analyse the ideological aspects of symbolic orders . . . is to examine *how structures of signification are mobilised to legitimate the sectional interests of hegemonic groups*" (emphasis in original).

7. A statement by Wolf suggests the first of these possibilities: "The development of an overall hegemonic pattern or 'design for living' is not so much the victory of a collective cognitive logic or aesthetic impulse as the development of redundancy—the continuous repetition, in diverse instrumental domains, of the same basic propositions regarding the nature of constructed reality" (1982:388). Geertz emphasizes the other in his discussion of ideology as a cultural system: "Its style is ornate, vivid, deliberately suggestive: by objectifying moral sentiment through the same devices as science shuns, it seeks to motivate action" (1973:231).

8. The name of one of the greatest recent performers in the politics of symbolism indeed turns out to be an anagram of *Negara.*

9. See Abercrombie, Hill, and Turner (1980:155), who conclude that in late capitalist society, it is true that the agencies of ideological transmission are well developed, but that their potential is not realized; in part because of the incoherence of the dominant ideology itself, in part because of a continuing autonomy on the part of working-class culture.

10. Disinformation is obviously another, related variant of engineered ignorance, making people believe that they know when they do not.

11. For relevant ethnographically based discussions see, for example, Murphy (1980) and Lindstrom (1984).

12. See Appignanesi and Maitland (1989), Akhtar (1989), and Ruthven (1990) for a variety of views, and the editorial comments in *Public Culture* (Appadurai and Breckenridge 1989), a later issue of the same journal (including Spivak 1989), and Asad (1990) and Fischer and Abedi (1990) for anthropological and other analytical comments.

13. See, for example, Sampson (1984) on the cultural apparatus, censorship, and rumor in Romania under the Ceausescu regime.

14. In the case of ethnicity, obviously, a tendency to mutual exclusivity between groups may leave all about similarly advantaged and disadvantaged. Where there is inequality among ethnic groups with re-

gard to assets, however, there can be winners and losers in ethnic organization, some being rather more excluded than included.

15. Bourdieu's (1984) work on taste judgments as cultural capital is conspicuously important in this area, even though one may hold that its ethnography is very French, and perhaps characteristically pre-1970s, pre-genre blurring, prepostmodernist, as well.

16. See also Keil's (1966:43) remarks along similar lines. Note moreover, in a similar vein, Harold Bloom's argument that creativity in poetry is rooted in an anxiety of influence—"where generosity is involved, the poets influenced are minor or weaker; the more generosity, and the more mutual it is, the poorer the poets involved." Consequently, "the history of fruitful poetic influence . . . is a history of anxiety and self-saving caricature, of distortion, of perverse, willful revisionism . . . " (1973:30).

17. For an extended discussion of this complex of "commodity aesthetics" in contemporary capitalism, see Haug (1986).

18. Apart from what is said in the text, see, for example, Scoditti (1982) on a Melanesian master carver's "copyright" over symbols.

19. For discussions of credentialism, see Collins (1979, 1981c) —the latter is one of the few studies taking the issue at least partly out of the contemporary context—and Freidson (1984). On the whole, credentialism in contemporary society has close links to professionalism, but it is hardly confined to the professions. The established art academies in Europe, for example, have also been credentialist (cf. Peterson and White 1979).

20. Cf. Hayek: "We need to remember only how much we have to learn in any occupation after we have completed our theoretical training, how big a part of our working life we spend learning particular jobs, and how valuable an asset in all walks of life is knowledge of people, of local conditions, and special circumstances. . . . It is a curious fact that this sort of knowledge should today be generally regarded with a kind of contempt, and that anyone who by such knowledge gains an advantage over somebody better equipped with theoretical or technical knowledge is thought to have acted almost disreputably" (1945:522).

21. In his novel *The Songlines,* Bruce Chatwin (1988:47) has an intriguing passage where a white Australian hanger-on of the Aboriginal Land Rights movement expounds on the idea of "deprogramming" sacred knowledge; as it had fallen into the hands of white people through fraud or force, it was now to be returned as cultural property to the original owners. Archives were to be examined for unpublished materials on the Aborigines, and the relevant pages returned to the rightful "owners"; copyright would be transferred from the authors of books to the people they described; photographs returned to the photographed, or their de-

scendants; recorded tapes to the recorded; and so on. It is interesting that Chatwin's tale finds some resonance in the property notions of Australian Aborigines touched upon above.

22. On this question, see Baudrillard (1981:102).

23. For views of the historical development of copyright, see Parsons (1974) and Loewenstein (1985); the current situation is discussed by Ploman (1985) and Ploman and Hamilton (1980).

24. Bledstein goes as far as to suggest that catastrophe has regularly been made to appear as the alternative to expert power: "Professionals tended to confide the worst, often evoking images of disaster and even a horrible death. The physician might hint at the possibility of an undetected cancer, leaving the patient to his own thoughts. The lawyer might threaten the client with high bail, a long trial, and visions of being locked up and sexually abused in jail. The professor might intimidate the student with failure in his studies, which might permanently obstruct the pursuit of a promising career. The policeman might menace the average citizen with pictures of meaningless, catastrophic, and racial violence in the streets, especially at the hands of a mugger or psychopath" (1976: 99). Note also Susan Sontag's (1979a) comments on the malignant uses of illness as metaphor.

25. For examples of some of the variations here, see the discussion concerning "the informed client" in medical care by Nelson and McGough (1983), and Cain's (1983) study of British general-practice lawyers, suggesting that what the latter primarily do, as "organic intellectuals of the bourgeoisie," is indeed to translate the particularities of their clients' cases into a transsituational legal discourse, in order to reach outcomes directly retranslatable into clients' own wishes.

5. Growth, Flux, Coherence

1. This usage may be contested. While I claim that common sense is largely implicit and unreflective, it is true that rhetorical appeals to "common sense" occur precisely at points where there is explicit, more or less focused controversy over something. Yet I would argue that the point of these appeals is precisely to shift a fact or assumption into the realm of the taken-for-granted. It would appear that my understanding is similar to that of Gramsci (1971:323 ff.); see on this also Giddens (1976:114–115).

2. One approximate example of this in the literature is that of the English farm worker who has limited contact with others in a similar situation and who therefore tends to act deferentially within a situation-

al definition based on his patron's perspective, rather than on the basis of an awareness of class interests anchored in his own position. See especially Newby (1977); also Chapter 3, note 46, and the passage in the main text to which it refers.

3. See, for example, Goldman (1971:169 ff.); also Rosaldo (1987, 1988) on Mexican-American culture as a border culture.

4. The argument has been stated in the most pointed terms, and perhaps rather too much as a just-so story, by Cuddihy (1974); modern thought, he argues, has grown in large part of the encounter, in Europe during the last two centuries, between *Yiddishkeit* and civility. Marx, Freud, Lévi-Strauss and other Jewish intellectuals have been forever aware of the contrast between their own people and the *goyim;* critical perhaps of a failure of emancipation among the former, but mostly intent on revealing what is under the surface of civility of the others. Seemingly engaged in a continuous celebration of tactlessness on every arena, Marx tried to lay bare the crudity of capitalism, concealed by the discreet charm of the bourgeoisie. Freud, in a Vienna where Jewish intellectuals were preeminent but where anti-Semitism was gathering force (see chapter 6), dealt a blow to sexual decorum, at the very heart of the order of civility. Lévi-Strauss investigates the hidden logic of culture and opposes *savoir-vivre* to *savoir-faire* in a study of "the origin of table manners." And why this concern with binary oppositions? Cuddihy concludes by quoting, not Lévi-Strauss, but Alexander Portnoy's complaint to his parents: "The very first distinction I learned from you, I am sure, was not night and day, or hot and cold, but *goyische* and Jewish!"

5. On the awareness and the cultural productivity of exiles, see for example an essay by Said (1984). Steiner (1975:10) notes the significance of exile to contemporary literature; writers like Nabokov, Borges, and Beckett have stood "in a relation of dialectical hesitance not only toward one native tongue . . . but toward several languages." See also Mannheim's (1936:6 ff.) comments on the consequences of social mobility, and the essays by Schutz (1964) on "The Stranger" and "The Homecomer."

6. It may be inserted here that when the division of knowledge is built on expansionist expertise, as discussed below, the general-purpose wisdom of accumulated experience is correspondingly devalued; the consequence tends to be that, in contemporary cultures, old age becomes less rewarding.

7. It is true that Gouldner (1976:62–64), in introducing this concept, makes the point that there is a single culture of critical discourse shared by contemporary intellectuals and intelligentsia. As I use the notion, however, I will assume that while such an overall similarity

may exist in the ordering of the management of meaning, there is segmentation on the basis of meaning content, so that the use of the plural form can also be justified.

8. See Gouldner (1976:57–64) for the most extended discussion of Bernstein's (1971, 1975) relevance to his analysis.

9. Although Gouldner made his comments on intellectuals and intelligentsia as a part of his analysis of "the new class" in Western societies, we leave the debate over that phenomenon aside here. His distinction between these two concepts may be compared to Richard Hofstadter's contrast between the qualities of "intelligence" and "intellect" in *Anti-Intellectualism in American Life:* "intelligence is an excellence of mind that is employed within a fairly narrow, immediate, and predictable range; it is a manipulative, adjustive, unfailingly practical quality. . . . Intelligence works within the framework of limited but clearly stated goals, and may be quick to shear away questions of thought that do not seem to help in reaching them. . . . Intellect, on the other hand, is the critical, creative, and contemplative side of mind. Whereas intelligence seeks to grasp, manipulate, reorder, adjust, intellect examines, ponders, wonders, theorizes, criticizes, imagines" (1963:24–25).

In nineteenth-century Russia, the people to whom the term 'intelligentsia' first applied may have been rather more like Gouldnerian intellectuals; under Stalinism there was little room for them, so that the new Soviet intelligentsia was indeed more of an intelligentsia (to the extent that the term was not just used to describe all white-collar workers). On these complicated matters, see, for example, Malia (1960).

Although Gouldner's simple contrast suits our purposes here well enough, it is certainly possible to develop further distinctions among the variety of people showing some concentrated involvement with ideas. For a more elaborate typology, see for instance Carroll (1978).

10. Cf. Kadushin on value concepts (such as "freedom of speech," "rights of man," or "justice"): "Because these symbols are defined essentially in their application rather than in any abstract formulation, any member of society who knows the terms can manipulate them with fair ease. Precisely because value concepts can be so easily applied to a variety of situations, most societies have a relatively small set of persons, called intellectuals, who are creatively expert in finding the relationship of one value concept to another and in tracing the use and application of these concepts in a society's tradition" (1974:6).

11. There are really several ways in which contemporary liminoidity contrasts with the liminality of ritual: the former, Turner (1977b; cf. 1982:32 ff.) points out, involves most people in leisure rather than work, it is voluntary rather than mandatory, it occurs at the margins

and interstices of social life rather than at its center, and its products tend to be individualized rather than fundamentally collective.

12. Note Turner's observations on Muchona's deep involvement in ethnographer-informant discussions of symbolism: "At such times he had the bright hard eye of some raptor, hawk, or kite, as he poised over a definitive explanation. Watching him, I sometimes used to fancy that he would have been truly at home scoring debating points on a don's dais, gowned or perhaps in a habit. He delighted in making explicit what he had known subliminally about his own religion" (1960:342). This perspective seemed to have been shaped by his experience as a stranger in the local community: "Beneath his jester's mask, and under his apparent timidity, he may have cherished hatred against those more securely placed in the ordered groupings of society. Such hatred may itself have given him a certain clairvoyance into tense relationships in the kinship and political systems" (1960:350).

With regard to the uses of contrasting experiences, Gouldner (1985:204 ff.) has taken Marx's theoretical achievements as the point of departure for an extended comment on the nature of intellectual creativity. The fundamental source of the latter, he argues, "entails an ability to *cross the boundaries* of an intellectual tradition and thus to escape control by a single perspective." More precisely, one has to have access to several perspectives (or "languages"); to move between them in a way which deviates from any conventional division of labor between them; and yet to order them in a firm hierarchy. See also the appendix on creativity by Karen Lucas in the same volume.

Mary Douglas, in "Pascal's Great Wager," (1985) has another version of the marginality argument, suggesting that radical skepticism grows where relative privilege is combined with powerlessness.

13. For further comments on the role of competition and conflict in intellectual life, see for example Bourdieu's essay "Intellectual Field and Creative Project" (1969), and the formulation by Collins: "Intellectual life is a multisided conversation (to be sure, mainly carried out on paper). Though this implies at least a certain degree of consensus, it also very much consists of arguments. For the aim of intellectual life, above all, is to be heard, to publicize one's views, and to receive recognition for them. The structure of intellectual life inevitably builds in an element of conflict. . . . The strategic problem of any intellectual is to be maximally original while yet maximally relevant to what the community is prepared to hear. For this reason, the intellectual world is inevitably a matter of alliances and coalitions, of ideas that build on and extend the relevance of other ideas, of researches that buttress or overthrow existing models that have cumulated in previous research" (1986:1337).

Note also Geertz' (1973:29) comment on interpretive anthropology: " . . . a science whose progress is marked less by a perfection of consensus than by a refinement of debate. What gets better is the precision with which we vex each other."

14. Hollinger (1975:135) argues in a similar vein that American intellectuals by the middle of the twentieth century built a new cosmopolitanism on the variety of ethnic heritages that were at the same time drawn upon and transcended.

15. The debate referred to here, of course, has been concerned largely with the relationship of intellectuals to the class structure, although it is restated here in more general terms.

16. On the relationship between media and qualities of intellectual life, see also Simonds (1982).

17. The classic work on mnemonic uses of the environment is Frances Yates' *The Art of Memory* (1966). For an interpretation of Trobriand myth along similar lines, see Harwood (1976).

18. On the mnemonic aspects of oral poetry, see especially the work of Lord (1960) and Havelock (1963).

19. Of course, media lend themselves unequally to the storage of meaning. Some are only or mostly involved in instant transmission, like the telephone. And where recording occurs, it is still true that certain documents are more lasting than others. Harold Innis (1950, 1951), the Canadian economic historian who was a highly original thinker on communication and culture—and an important influence on McLuhan (cf. Carey 1967)—noted that early technologies of literacy may have had different implications in this respect. Writing on stone, clay, or parchment was very durable, but difficult to move around. It tended to direct attention toward history and tradition, toward religious rather than worldly authority. Writing on paper or papyrus was mobile but perishable, a technology for far-flung empires.

20. This is, in fact, as true of biography as of longer-term history; because of the ease with which photographs can be taken, for example, we can have fairly complete pictorial records of stages in a person's life, including changes in appearance, contexts, and personal relationships, instead of the single portrait painting of pre-photography elite individuals. Photographs promote nostalgia, Susan Sontag suggests; they also "testify to time's relentless melt" (1979b:15). I have pointed to this relationship between technology and identity elsewhere (Hannerz 1983).

21. This figure pertains to the nonacademic intellectuals, while the academics read somewhat fewer of these journals. On the other hand, they most likely read a number of other journals in their respective academic fields.

22. The suggestion that intelligentsia styles of work may occur

in the arts is certainly no denial of the fact that the notion of paradigm may apply in rather different ways between the sciences and the arts, and within each of them in different instances; see Clignet (1979).

23. For an ethnographic study of consciousness raising through personal narratives in women's rap groups, see Kalcik (1975).

24. Foucault's (1981:126 ff.) concept of the "specific intellectual" appears to relate most closely to this type of movement intellectual; well-educated, with a direct, localized connection to a specific body of knowledge and its institutions, speaking on the basis of this positioned experience. See also Poster (1984), who compares Foucault's "specific intellectual" with the Sartrean "universal intellectual"; there is a variation on the Gramsci/Mannheim theme here.

25. Gouldner (1979:59) remarks on this that the language of critical discourse treats the relationship between its speakers and those spoken about as a relationship between judges and judged; "it implies that the established social hierarchy is only a semblance and that the deeper, more important distinction is between those who speak and understand truly and those who do not."

26. For an ethnographic example, see Fisher's (1985:87 ff.) description of Barbadian villagers' notion of "studiation"; too much education endangers sanity. Borgström's (1974:75 ff.) study of ideas about deviance in rural northern Sweden suggests that the same view is common there as well.

27. American antispecialist populism has strong historical roots. Shils has noted that "when populism goes on the warpath, among those they wish to strike are the 'overeducated', those who are 'too clever,' 'the highbrows,' the 'longhairs,' the 'eggheads,' whose education has led them away from the simple wisdom and virtue of the people" (1956:100). And according to Hofstadter, "In the original American populistic dream, the omnicompetence of the common man was fundamental and indispensable. . . . What used to be a jocular and usually benign ridicule of intellect and formal training has turned into a malign resentment of the intellectual in his capacity as expert" (1963:34).

28. See also the less familiar studies by, for example, Cameron (1954) and Merriam and Mack (1960).

29. Gregory Bateson (1972:134–135) cites Samuel Butler and Zen Buddhism on the same point: "the better an organism 'knows' something, the less conscious it becomes of its knowledge."

30. Goldfarb (1982:35–37), in his study of cultural freedom in Eastern Europe and the United States, describes an experimental Hungarian theater group which moved, in the 1970s, from the political constraints of Budapest to the tolerant climate of off-off-Broadway, New York. If the Theater Squat would thrive in the market anywhere, it ought

to be there. Despite an international reputation, however, the group found its performances poorly attended, and some had to be canceled for lack of an audience.

31. See Clark (1983:113–115, 173) on the importance of guild structures in contemporary academic life; for further comments on the dominant orientation toward peers in this context, see also Jencks and Riesman (1968:201 ff.) and Culler (1988:28 ff.).

32. Crane (1976) has reviewed types of reward structures in science, art, and religion.

33. A study of art publics in Israel, by Liah Greenfield (1984), illustrates such coherence by elective affinity more concretely. The Israeli art world, Greenfield suggests, has a dual structure which emerged in the late 1960s. One subsystem involves conceptual and other abstract artists, public institutions such as museums, and most art critics. The other subsystem encompasses the creators of figurative art, and the commercial art market. But the two also have largely separate publics, of differing characteristics. The friends of figurative art are found in business and the professions. Their trained perspective is to attach value to competence, as evinced in a product. In figurative art they can make their own judgment on this basis, without the aid of intermediate authorities.

Conceptualist art, on the other hand, has its supporters principally among people with a training in the humanities or social sciences, and with work relating to this. They are more likely to be interested in the plurality of perspectives and in originality and creativity as such; they, therefore, also find pleasure in knowing more about the artist and the process of artistic creation, rather than only in the product. As they grant, and actually relish, the fact that not everything about the art they enjoy is obvious, they take a strong interest in the commentary of such intermediate specialists as art critics. It hardly seems accidental, either, that institutions such as museums play the greater part in this subsystem of the art world. They tend to make the cultural producers themselves, and people closely aligned with them in their understanding of the meaning systems in question, more autonomous in the control of reward structures. Still, for the friends of conceptual art, elective affinities do not go all the way. For help with the extra effort of more complete sense-making and appreciation, they need the assistance of art critics.

34. In *another* role in his repertoire, of course, an amateur may be a real member.

35. On the problems of such criticism, see, for example, Barzun's (1982:3–29) essay "Music into Words."

36. Interdisciplinary work does tend to be a secondary pursuit, and is not always highly thought of. Most radically, interdisciplinary relationships may be created in order to produce intellectuals, people who make a habit or even a virtue of crossing boundaries. More pragmatically, it may have the purpose of solving some limited, sharply defined problem. It earns a bad name where it is a preoccupation of dilettantes ("if you cannot master one discipline, try two") or dominated by the shady practices of cognitive entrepreneurship ("pick up the basics of a discipline where it is dirt cheap, and get rich quick by trading it to those who never heard it before"). It may draw most successfully on original coherence work when individuals construct their own unique boundary-crossing networks of relationships to colleagues, conferences, books, and journals in pursuit of their own research objectives—what Donald Campbell (1969) has described as "the fish scale model of omniscience" (with each scholar having an area of activity and competence partially overlapping with those of several others, and wholly identical with nobody's). Yet, such an informal social organization of knowledge can come into conflict with the institutional order of disciplines, and with established understandings of professional identity. Nationally, locally, and over time, however, there is much variation in the receptivity to interdisciplinary work; some academias appear profligate in their readiness to set up and support new quasi-disciplines and programs, and then to undermine them and disband them later on. Elsewhere, the emphasis on established disciplines is rigid: career paths, socialization patterns, and administrative decisions all contribute to keeping boundaries neat, and areas of incoherence safe.

37. Apart from the viewpoints on the matter cited in the text, see also Bateson (1972:495), on the definition of a high civilization: "There shall be diversity in the civilization, not only to accommodate the genetic and experiential diversity of persons, but also to provide the flexibility and 'preadaptation' necessary for unpredictable change."

38. A developed version of such reasoning has also been offered by Salzman (1981), suggesting that societies maintain flexibility through multiformity and fluidity; they keep alternatives "on reserve," in various ways. Salzman identifies five. Alternatives can be in durable storage in texts, sacred or otherwise authoritative; they can be periodically enacted in ritual, even when they do not occur in everyday life; they can be maintained by deviant minorities; they may be asserted as realities in ideology, even if the ideology is hardly an accurate description of the way things actually are; or the members of a society may engage in a range of ongoing adaptations, among which they could redistribute themselves if conditions were to change.

6. The Urban Swirl

1. This, as I understand it, is also approximately what Bourdieu says about the role of urbanism in the "emergence of a field of discussion" in a remarkable 11-line, 132-word sentence, in a note in *Outline of a Theory of Practice* (1977:233).

2. Rather than cluttering the text with citations, I will use this note to give an overall account of where I have dipped, rather less than systematically, into the very large literature on the three cities—a literature that only goes on growing.

For Vienna, the books by Johnston (1972), Janik and Toulmin (1973), Schorske (1980), and Spiel (1987) have been central sources for the overall view. Janik's (1981) review of the Schorske book, and LaCapra's (1983:84 ff.) review of the Janik and Toulmin volume, have provided a sense of where areas of disagreement exist, even if I have not paid much attention to them here. Schorske's (1978) article on generational tensions in Viennese culture has also been useful. Rozenblit (1983), Beller (1989), and the volume edited by Oxaal, Pollak, and Botz (1987) offer various views of the Jewish community, Zweig's (1943) autobiography provides a firsthand account of intellectual life, and various publications centering on Freud (Schick 1969; Gay 1978:29 ff.; Walkup 1986), Kraus (Heller 1973; Stern 1975; Timms 1986; Zohn 1986), Hofmannsthal (Broch 1984), Kokoschka (Whitford 1986), Hitler (Jones 1983), and Viennese art (Schorske 1986) have been additional pieces of the picture; see also Steiner's (1985) comments occasioned by Broch's book on Hofmannsthal.

As far as Calcutta is concerned, I have been aided by the several works by Kopf (1969, 1975a and 1975b, 1979) and Kling (1975, 1976), as well as by the overviews of the Bengali Renaissance by Mukhopadhyay (1979), Poddar (1970), Sarkar (1970), and Sastri (1972). Pradip Sinha (1978) on Calcutta urban history has been useful, as has S. N. Mukherjee (1970, 1975) on urban politics and factionalism. Of writings on particular individuals and their activities and experiences in Calcutta, I have drawn on Hay (1965) and Nag (1972) on Rammohun Roy, Clark (1961), Meenakshi Mukherjee (1985:38 ff.), Partha Chatterjee (1986:54 ff.) on Bankimchandra Chatterjee, Kripalani (1962) on Rabindranath Tagore, and Jordens (1978) on Dayananda Sarasvati. Chapters in Bose (1967) and Surajit Sinha (1972) have provided general insights into the past and present of Calcutta. Broomfield's (1968) and Ray's (1984) studies of Bengali politics deal in large part with a later period than that of central interest here but have still been of some interest; I should also mention studies of various particular Calcuttan topics by Baumer (1975), Bhattacharya (1974), Crane (1983), and Gray (1975).

A general sense of the Beat period in San Francisco can be gained from Ferlinghetti and Peters (1980), Honan (1987), and Meltzer (1971). The biographies of Kenneth Rexroth (Gibson 1972), Jack Kerouac (Charters 1973; McNally 1979), Lawrence Ferlinghetti (Cherkovski 1979), Lenny Bruce (Goldman 1974) and Alan Watts (Furlong 1986) have been enlightening, as have been some of the writings of Rexroth (1957, 1966, 1970); Kerouac (1955, 1958); and Snyder (1980), themselves. Fields (1981) and Jackson (1988) deal usefully with the Oriental connection, and Herron (1985) provides a street-by-street understanding of literary San Francisco.

While I do not actually deal with the hippie period and the development of gay culture in San Francisco, I would add that I have found Perry's (1984) history of the former, and FitzGerald's (1986) discussion of the gay community in *Cities on a Hill*, generally useful for background understandings.

3. It is perhaps too easy to forget that quite other kinds of cultural forms than those of Freud, Zweig, Schönberg, and Kraus were also produced, reinvented, transformed, elaborated, and otherwise worked over in Vienna during the same period. The idea of Germanic superiority was cultivated in several varieties, from the theatrical politics of Georg von Schönerer by way of the mysticism and antisemitic eroticism of the former monk Adolf Josef Lanz "von Liebenfels" (publisher of the journal *Ostara*), and the mythologizing of Aryan supremacy of the magician Guido von List, to the quasi-biological racism of Houston Stewart Chamberlain, who lived in Vienna for twenty years.

4. This is the way the story is usually told, but Spiel (1987:59) has Trotsky's name in the anecdote as Bronstein, his original name. It does not seem altogether clear under what name he was known, and to whom, in this period.

5. Musil's *The Man Without Qualities*, a novel published in several volumes but still incomplete at the time of the author's death, gives a vivid picture of the mood of the late Habsburg era.

6. Gay (1978:34) emphasizes that Freud was not a part of the Viennese intellectual scene in the sense of having much personal contact with its other major participants, but this would hardly mean that he could remain unaware of its concerns and achievements.

7. For those whose view of Orientalism has been shaped mostly by Said's (1978) critique, the idea of a progressive, syncretizing Orientalism may be puzzling; but see Kopf's (1980) comments on Said, as well as Inden's (1986) discussion of Orientalist constructions of India.

8. There was also a more conservative branch of the Tagores; see Kling (1976:18).

9. See his comment, as quoted by Gray: "Whose words are one in his mind, ten in speech, a hundred in writing, and a thousand in a

quarrel, he is a babu. Whose strength is one thing in his hand, ten times greater in his mouth, a hundred times greater on the written page, and out of sight at the time for work, he is a babu. Whose intelligence in his childhood is in books, in youth in a bottle, in adulthood in his wife's *ancal,* he is a babu. Whose god of good fortune is the British, whose guru is the teacher of the Brahmo religion, whose Veda is the native newspaper, and whose place of pilgrimage is the National Theatre, he is a babu. Who is a Christian to the missionaries, a Brahmo to Kesabcandra, a Hindu to his father, and an atheist to brahman beggars, he is a babu. Who takes water at home, liquor in his friend's house, a tongue lashing in the prostitute's quarters, and a collaring at his Master Sahib's house, he is a babu. Who despises the use of oil at bath time, his own finger at meal time, and his mother's tongue at conversation time, he is a babu. Whose concern is only with clothing, whose diligence is pursuing a good job, whose only respect is for his wife or mistress, and whose anger is only for good books, without doubt, he is a babu" (1975:122).

10. Redfield and Singer (1954:62–63) raise the question whether, after decolonization, some non-Western cities could reverse from a heterogenetic to an orthogenetic role; however, they find it improbable. McGee (1971:121 ff.), taking up their conceptualization in a discussion of Kuala Lumpur, also emphasizes the difficulties inherent in such a transformation.

11. See again "Making Distinctions," in chapter 4.

12. There are parallels between my argument here and that of Claude Fischer (1975).

13. Simmel (1964:420), describing cities as "seats of the highest economic division of labor," refers to the Parisian occupation of the *quatorzième:* "persons who identify themselves by signs on their residences and who are ready at the dinner hour in correct attire, so that they can be quickly called upon if a dinner party should consist of thirteen persons."

14. Robert Park, in his classic paper "The City: Suggestions for the Investigation of Human Behavior in the Urban Environment," first published in 1916, already made this point: "Association with others of their own ilk provides also not merely a stimulus, but a moral support for the traits they have in common which they would not find in a less select society" (1952:51). While this particular sentence occurs in the context of a discussion of deviant behavior, his argument was more general.

15. Timms (1986:8), in his Kraus biography, has a diagram of intersecting intellectual circles in Vienna, but the technique of representation hardly allows him to show the real intricacy of networks. One of

the most celebrated instances of Viennese network density, of course, is the serial polyandry of Alma Mahler.

16. Coser (1965) discusses other such settings of intellectual life: the French rococo salon and the eighteenth-century coffeehouse in London.

17. Nathe's (1978) study of a hippie-era San Francisco coffee house shows particularly clearly the great possibilities for cultural scanning in an institution combining a great range of activities.

18. Rexroth (1970:1 ff.) and Kerouac's biographer McNally (1979: 149) draw similar parallels between—in the former case—Dylan Thomas, Charlie Parker, and Jackson Pollock, and—in the latter case—Kerouac, Parker, and Pollock.

19. A latter-day visitor to Calcutta, Geoffrey Moorhouse, also notes that around College Street there is one of the largest secondhand book markets in the world, and that every weekend on the Maidan (the large park around Fort William), "poets recite their verses to each other, composers sing the ballad they have just finished, artists discuss their most recent brushwork and lots of people simply roll up to listen" (1974:190).

20. See, for example, the work of Bender (1979, 1984)—whose proposal for studying public culture I referred to in chapter 1—and comments on the compartmentalization of recent times by Bell (1976:102 ff.) and Jacoby (1987).

21. On the mobility of twentieth-century Bohemia and its California bases, see Miller: "Via 29 Palms, Venice, Claremont, Santa Barbara, Big Sur, the Monterey Peninsula, Santa Cruz, Palo Alto, Frisco-Berkeley, Marin, Mendocino, Eugene, Portland, Seattle, the network runs from Mexico to Vancouver and Alaska: via other stations it runs from Frisco to Chicago, Cambridge and New York, London, Paris, Tangier—in all an underground railroad connecting a series of stations and terminals . . . through which, hitching, driving, riding in boxcars, the same population flowed and flows" (1977:228). Sukenick (1987) draws a picture of the Greenwich Village scene paralleling that of North Beach during the Beat period.

7. The Global Ecumene

1. Yet hardly wholly untrue. Linton's (1936:326–327) formulation of the "one hundred percent American" life remains the classic reminder of the diverse origins of familiar things; Befu (1983:243) has adapted Linton's statement to describe what is "one hundred percent

Japanese"; Raymond Williams (1985:177) has perhaps independently come up with a strikingly similar account of what being British amounts to.

2. See Bar-Haim's (1987) discussion of this in the context of Eastern European youth culture.

3. Kopytoff (1987:10) defines the ecumene as a "region of persistent cultural interaction and exchange." Kroeber, recalling that the Greeks in antiquity used this term for "the inhabited world," comments that it "has a modern utility as a convenient designation of the total area reached by traceable diffusion influences from the main higher centers of Eurasia at which most new culture had up to then been produced" (1948:423). Again, a world culture ordered by center/periphery relationships. See also Kroeber's (1945) Huxley Memorial Lecture.

4. For another approach to the problem, see Appadurai (1990).

5. The core/periphery conceptual pair (at times with semi-periphery thrown in to form a trio) is favored by Wallerstein; the metropolis/satellite contrast may remain most strongly associated with Frank (e.g., 1967); Shils (e.g., 1975), although writing from a very different perspective, may have done more than anybody else to put the center/periphery pair into circulation. For a slightly earlier attempt to formulate sociology at a global level, see Moore (1966).

6. A comment by the Indian scholar Amar Nath Pandeya at a meeting of Asian academics is to the point: "We in India receive information on Japanese society and science via America, and Americans' image of Japan is given to us as if it were what Japan really is. Japan exports cars and machines, but not culture or science; Japanese scholars and academic circles are not responsive to international needs. What we want to know is not the American people's view of Japan, but the Japanese people's view of Japan . . . " (Abdel-Malek and Pandeya 1981:12).

7. See, for example, contributions to the volume edited by Gibbons and Wittrock (1985).

8. See discussions of such issues in McBryde (1985).

9. The sources I draw on here are particularly Wallerstein (1974:347 ff.) and (1984:159 ff.). Wallerstein (1990) is an additional attempt to deal with questions of culture in world system studies.

10. See, for example, Collins (1981c:45 ff.); Chirot and Hall (1982); Ragin and Chirot (1984:303–304); and Robertson and Lechner (1985). Wallerstein has more recently gone some distance toward responding to such criticisms; see the last item cited in note 9. This does not, however, appear to mark any more dramatic departure from views stated earlier.

11. Wallerstein's interpretation indeed brings to mind here Lord Macaulay's "Minutes on Education," as relating to the nineteenth-

century Raj: "We must do our best to form a class who may be interpreters between us and the millions whom we govern; a class of persons, Indian in blood and colour, but English in taste, in opinion, in morals, and in intellect" (quoted by Poddar, 1970:36).

12. Cf. Ortner: "History is often treated as some thing that arrives, like a ship, from outside the society in question. Thus we do not get the history *of* that society, but the impact of (our) history *on* that society" (1984:143).

13. June Nash (1981) has reviewed relatively early work with such an orientation.

14. Cf. Naipaul: "Cities like London were to change. They were to cease being more or less national cities; they were to become cities of the world, modern-day Romes, establishing the pattern of what great cities should be, in the eyes of islanders like myself and people even more remote in language and culture. They were to be cities visited for learning and elegant goods and manners and freedom by all the barbarian peoples of the globe, people of forest and desert, Arabs, Africans, Malays" (1987:141–142).

Several books published almost simultaneously view the relationship of Miami to Latin America from different angles (Allman 1987; Didion 1987; Rieff 1987).

15. Similarly, the corporate headquarters and part of the editorial offices of the largest Latin American magazine publisher, with more than fifty periodicals, are in Miami (Volsky 1989).

16. It is one aspect of this that, according to Theodore Levitt (1983:94), the theorist of market globalization to whom further reference will be made in the text further on, "a market segment in one country is seldom alone. . . . Even small local segments have their global equivalents elsewhere."

17. Curtin (1984:247 ff.) offers a more general overview of early "fringe westernization."

18. On "cultural animateurs," see Shaw (1972).

19. On authenticity in Zaire, see Callaghy (1980); and for a portrayal of its reexported form in Togo, Packer (1988:101 ff.).

20. On such aspects of the transnational in the national, see Löfgren (1989).

21. On the importance of mass education in the construction of citizenry, see Boli, Ramirez, and Meyer (1986).

22. Peter Manuel (1988:94), in his ethnomusicological survey, concludes that "it may seem that every prominent West African musician has coined some label for his particular fusion of traditional and modern sounds."

23. I am reminded here of Wolf's (1966) comment that what is

referred to as "national character" is often lodged in such contexts and relationships.

24. And since cultural technologies are variously costly, import substitution may also become feasible at different levels in each case.

25. Fabian (1978) was one of the earlier anthropologists to comment on the significance, and—at least at the time of his writing—the comparative paucity, of studies of Third World popular culture. For a review of the growing body of work on African popular culture, see the study by Barber (1987) quoted in the text; Siegel's *Solo in the New Order* (1986) is another ethnography allowing a good view of a Third World popular culture.

26. As Sahlins (1985:viii) has it (in the quite different context of eighteenth-century Hawaii), "European wealth is harnessed to the reproduction and even the creative transformation of their own cultural order."

27. For insights into the West African popular music world, see Moore (1982), Chernoff (1985), Collins (1985), and Waterman (1988).

28. Laing (1986) also refers to West African instances in his enlightening critical overview of center/periphery relationships in popular music, and the applicability of the "cultural imperialism" thesis.

29. For examples, see Aluko (1964) and the more sophisticated Achebe (1961).

30. In a critical review of notions of "cultural dependency" in relation to the media, Boyd-Barrett (1982:193) has pointed to a theoretical and methodological lag in much Third World media research. While the latter, not least that cited in support of the global homogenization scenario, often continues to engage in naively positivistic forms of content analysis, the tendency in the Occident has increasingly been to emphasize the context in communications are received, and the individual's capacity for selection as well as selective retention. As the periphery picks up what the center is discarding, perhaps we have here another instance of cultural dumping?

31. A classic instance from anthropology is the Tiv reinterpretation of Hamlet, as recounted by Laura Bohannan (1966). A news item concerning *Dallas,* the television serial, in the *International Herald Tribune* tells a similar story (Friedman 1986). A team of communication researchers at Hebrew University in Jerusalem conducted a study of how Israelis of different national origins decoded American television programs generally, and *Dallas* specifically. The most striking finding was that the groups came up with quite divergent interpretations of the program. Recent Russian immigrants were suspicious of the show and paid attention to the credits to find out who was the power behind it. One of them said, "They want us to think the rich are unhappy so we average

people will feel more content." They also looked in a rather deterministic way at the activities of the characters—JR did what he did because he had to, as a businessman. The Moroccan Jews as well as the Israeli Arabs saw the show as some sort of a depiction of reality, but a reality they were uncomfortable with. The Arabs did not want to watch *Dallas* in mixed company, and when it had shown Sue Ellen leaving her husband JR to go and live with her lover, this group of viewers apparently unconsciously censored the occurrence and reported that she had returned to her father. The kibbutz Israeli were most like Americans in their response, according to this study. They related to it playfully, as a source of fantasy.

32. Worth (1981:72) touches on such problems in his discussion of film anthropology, as he asks how cinematic understandings are distributed. Do "film language" communities have anything to do with language communities; do they relate to the distribution of cognitive styles? Sperber's (1985) "epidemiological" concern with the differential cognitive contagiousness of representations may also be related to transnational cultural flows in different symbolic modes.

33. Although in terms of what will be said below, the disadvantages of a "provincialism of openness" should not be forgotten.

34. See, for example, Rodgers' (1984) analysis of the impact of literacy on Batak thinking about kinship.

35. Gmelch (1980) reviews many of the exceptions.

36. See, for example, Sutton on Caribbean migrants in New York: "Both Hispanics and Afro-Caribbeans reconstitute their lives in New York City by means of a 'cross roads' process created by the mutual interaction of happenings in New York and the Caribbean. In general contrast with the situation of European immigrants, New York's Caribbean population is exposed to a more continuous and intense bi-directional flow of peoples, ideas, practices, and ideologies between the Caribbean region and New York City. These bi-directional exchanges and interactions have generated what can be called a transnational socio-cultural system, a distinctly unitary though not unified transmission belt that reworks and further creolizes Caribbean culture and identities, both in New York and the Caribbean" (1987:19–20).

37. The anthropology of tourism is becoming quite voluminous; for a rather early review, see Graburn (1983). Wagner (1977) offers a view of the play/work encounter between Scandinavians and Gambians.

38. See, again (as in note 4, chapter 5), Schutz' (1964) classic essays on these two types. Eva Hoffman's *Lost in Translation* (1989), a portrayal of her passage from Krakow to the New World, is a noteworthy literary account of the shifts in a migrant's perspective.

39. For an example of the latter, see Björklund's (1981) case

study of the experience of the Suryoye, a Christian group from the Middle East, with the Swedish state.

40. I discuss these developments in network terms in Hannerz (1991a). For an interpretation of their historical background, see Field (1971). Ziman (1977) comments on the circulation of people and ideas within the transnational scientific community.

41. See Moore (1985) for a discussion of the situation of Third World diplomats within this framework. Another example of asymmetry in transnational cultures can be found in the "invisible colleges" of academics referred to in chapter 3, on which Altbach has these comments: "In most fields, scholarship is international and key leaders come from many countries. But . . . there are considerable imbalances in the system. Today's invisible colleges, in most fields of knowledge, are dominated by the metropolitan universities in the Western industrialized nations, particularly by North America and Britain. The key journals are published in these locations. The main evaluators, journal editors, publishing advisors, and other influential scholars are located in the major universities of the West. And . . . the network functions mostly in English. Scholars in peripheral institutions have little access to the mainstream and find it difficult to keep fully informed and up to date. They are simply not included in the informal networks and are frequently unaware of the latest developments and trends" (1987:177). On transnational occupational cultures, see also Golding (1977) and Sauvant (1976). A colleague and I have commented on transnational and center/periphery aspects of the global organization of anthropology (Gerholm and Hannerz 1982:5–13).

42. For an insider's revelations of business considerations in Middle Eastern contexts, see Aburish (1985).

43. Harris and Moran tell the reader of their textbook *Managing Cultural Differences* (1987:xii) that "it is structured around *the global manager,* an innovative concept on the cutting edge of international management that can prepare the reader to cope with a rapidly changing business environment" and that it is "in tune with the megatrend toward globalization, whether in the economy or marketplace, in communication or transportation, in management or the professions, in human services or militarization." The purpose is "not only to help you better cope with cultural differences, but to facilitate cultural synergy." The compiler of the volume *Do's and Taboos Around the World,* issued by the Parker Pen Company, describes his goals in the foreword: "Ideally, this book will help each world traveler grow little invisible antennae that will sense incoming messages about cultural differences and nuances. An appreciation and understanding of these differences will prevent embarrassment, unhappiness, and failure. In fact, learning through travel about these cultural differences can be both challenging and fun" (Axtell

1985). And travelers in Southeast Asia will come across a series of guides to countries in the region, collectively entitled "Culture Shock" (e.g., Roces and Roces 1985).

44. The cosmopolitan/local distinction has been a part of the sociological vocabulary for close to half a century now, since Robert Merton (1957:387 ff.) developed it out of a study, during World War II, of "patterns of influence" in a small town on the eastern seaboard of the United States. At that time (and certainly in that place), the distinction could hardly be set in anything but a national context. The cosmopolitans of the town were those who thought and who lived their lives within the structure of the nation rather than purely within the structure of the locality. Since then, the scale of culture and social structure has grown, so that what was cosmopolitan in the early 1940s may be counted as a moderate form of localism by now. For a portrayal of the contemporary cosmopolitan, see Backer (1987).

45. The dilettante, remember, is "one who delights"; someone whose curiosity takes him a bit beyond ordinary knowledge, although in a gentlemanly way he refrains from becoming a specialist (see chapter 5).

46. In China, cosmopolitans were "the filthy ninth" on the list of enemies of the Cultural Revolution; for a discussion of the theme in modern Chinese history see Levenson (1971). Note also White's (1988) discussion of the prevalent Japanese treatment of ex-expatriates as culturally polluted.

47. For major studies of twentieth-century political pilgrimages on the left, see Caute (1973) and Hollander (1981); the latter also has a brief update on travelers to Cuba and Nicaragua (Hollander 1986). Mazrui (1969:255 ff.) has commented on "Tanzaphilia," that wave, now apparently past, of admiration and goodwill for the Tanzanian efforts in nation building.

48. On the whole, it should be said, these movements have attracted more followers in the center and semi-periphery than in the periphery of the world system.

49. It is true that these contacts, at least initially, may have benefited from some brokerage by well-wishers at the center.

50. The situation of intellectuals at the periphery is the topic of an ever-growing number of analyses; see, for example, Alatas (1977), Goonatilake (1982), Jha (1977), Laroui (1976), and Shils (1972:335 ff.). But one would want more detailed studies along the lines of Camp's (1985) work, or that on American intellectuals by Kadushin (1974), not to speak of studies focusing more particularly on how intellectuals engage in the management of meaning.

51. See also, for example, Osiel (1984) on Brazilian intellectuals.

52. On provincialism, see also Shils (1972:355 ff.).

53. A Japanese colleague claims that this take-home work is

referred to in Japan as verticalization: one takes something written from the left to the right and rewrites it in Japanese script, from top to bottom.

54. See, for example, some of the portraits of major twentieth-century Islamic intellectuals in the volume edited by Esposito (1983).

55. The memorandum by Redfield, Linton, and Herskovits (1936) and the discussion by Barnett et al. (1954) were among the central formulations of the acculturation framework.

56. The plural society concept originally came out of the economist Furnivall's (1948) work in Southeast Asia, but was brought into anthropology particularly by M. G. Smith in a number of writings mostly collected in his 1965 volume. A large number of critiques and reformulations complicate the view of the pluralist framework and are not really taken into account here; however, see, for example, Morris (1967), Despres (1968), and Kuper and Smith (1969).

57. Drummond (1980; see also 1978) may offer the hitherto most detailed discussion of the value of creole concepts to cultural studies, in his interpretation of ethnicity and culture in Guyana. Fabian (1978:317) uses the pidgin/creole contrast more in passing, suggesting that colonialism in Africa ("frequently disjointed, hastily thrown together for the purpose of establishing political footholds") produced pidgin cultures, whereas more viable creole syntheses came into existence in later periods. Graburn (1984:402 ff.) sees new creole art forms, anchored in the reformulated consciousness of Third and Fourth World peoples, expanding beyond the restricted codes of tourist art, and Jackson (1989) argues that pidgin and creole concepts allow a better understanding of the culturally volatile situation of South American forest Indians as they are being included in a wider cultural order. For earlier versions of my argument here, see Hannerz (1987, 1988).

58. For discussions of regionally restricted conceptions of creolism, in the New World context, see, for example, Adams (1959) and Brathwaite (1971:xiii ff.). Creolist linguistics has grown from a minor specialty involving perhaps a dozen practitioners in the 1950s to a volatile field involving a thousand scholars or so now (according to DeCamp, 1977:7). For an overview of the issues and the state of knowledge, see, for example, Muehlhäusler (1986).

59. On the varying relationships between racial and ethnic categories and creolization, see, for example, Raymond Smith (n.d.) and Patterson (1975), as well as Drummond's work referred to in note 56.

60. I develop this perspective toward world cities in Hannerz (1991b). For lively discussions of some aspects of what one might term the countercreolization of the center, see Hebdige (1987) on Caribbean music, its changes and migrations, and Feld (1988), in his brief notes on "world beat."

References

Abdel-Malek, Anouar and Amar Nath Pandeya, eds. 1981. *Intellectual Creativity in Endogenous Culture.* Tokyo: The United Nations University.

Abercrombie, Nicholas, Stephen Hill, and Bryan S. Turner. 1980. *The Dominant Ideology Thesis.* London: George Allen & Unwin.

Aberle, David F. 1960. The Influence of Linguistics on Early Culture and Personality Theory. In Gertrude E. Dole and Robert L. Carneiro, eds., *Essays in the Science of Culture.* New York: Crowell.

Aburish, Said K. 1985. *Pay-Off.* London: Deutsch.

Achebe, Chinua. 1961. *No Longer at Ease.* London: Heinemann.

Adams, Richard N. 1959. On the Relation Between Plantation and "Creole Cultures." In *Plantation Systems of the New World.* Washington, D.C.: Pan American Union.

Akhtar, Shabbir. 1989. *Be Careful with Muhammad!* London: Bellew.

Alatas, Syed Hussein. 1977. *Intellectuals in Developing Societies.* London: Cass.

Allman, T. D. 1987. *Miami.* New York: Atlantic Monthly Press.

Allport, Floyd W. 1924. *Social Psychology.* Boston: Houghton Mifflin.

Altbach, Philip G. 1987. *The Knowledge Context.* Albany: State University of New York Press.

Aluko, T. M. 1964. *One Man, One Matchet.* London: Heinemann.

Amin, Samir. 1989. *Eurocentrism.* New York: Monthly Review Press.

Anderson, Benedict. 1983. *Imagined Communities.* London: Verso/New Left Books.

Appadurai, Arjun. 1986a. Theory in Anthropology: Center and Periphery. *Comparative Studies in Society and History* 28:356–361.

—— 1986b. Is Homo Hierarchicus? *American Ethnologist* 13:745–761.

—— 1988. Putting Hierarchy in Its Place. *Cultural Anthropology* 3:36–49.

—— 1990. Disjuncture and Difference in the Global Cultural Economy. *Public Culture* 2(2):1–24.

Appadurai, Arjun and Carol A. Breckenridge. 1988. Why Public Culture? *Public Culture* 1(1):5–9.

—— 1989. Editors' Comments: On Fictionalizing the Real. *Public Culture* 1(2):i–v.

Appignanesi, Lisa and Sara Maitland, eds. 1989. *The Rushdie File.* London: Fourth Estate.

Archer, Margaret S. 1985. The Myth of Cultural Integration. *British Journal of Sociology* 36:333–353.

Arnold, David O., ed. 1970. *The Sociology of Subcultures.* Berkeley: Glendessary Press.

Asad, Talal. 1990. Ethnography, Literature, and Politics: Some Readings and Uses of Salman Rushdie's *The Satanic Verses. Cultural Anthropology* 5:239–269.

Axtell, Roger E. 1985. *Do's and Taboos Around the World.* New York: Wiley.

Backer, Dorothy. 1987. Rootless. *American Scholar* 56:269–274.

Bailyn, Bernard. 1986. *The Peopling of British North America.* New York: Knopf.

Barber, Karin. 1987. Popular Arts in Africa. *African Studies Review* 30 (3):1–78.

Bar-Haim, Gabriel. 1987. The Meaning of Western Commercial Artifacts for Eastern European Youth. *Journal of Contemporary Ethnography* 16:205–226.

Bar-Hillel, Yehoshua. 1954. Indexical Expressions. *Mind* 63:359–379.

Barnett, H. G., Leonard Broom, Bernard J. Siegel, Evon Z. Vogt, and James B. Watson. 1954. Acculturation: An Exploratory Formulation. *American Anthropologist* 56:973–1002.

Barth, Fredrik. 1969. Introduction. *In Ethnic Groups and Boundaries.* Oslo: Universitetsforlaget.

—— 1972. Analytical Dimensions in the Comparison of Social Organizations. *American Anthropologist* 74:207–220.

—— 1975. *Ritual and Knowledge Among the Baktaman of New Guinea.* New Haven: Yale University Press.

—— 1979. *Process and Form in Social Life.* London: Routledge and Kegan Paul.

—— 1984. Problems in Conceptualizing Cultural Pluralism, with Illustrations from Sohar, Oman. In David Maybury-Lewis, ed., *The Prospects for Plural Societies.* Washington, D.C.: American Ethnological Society.

—— 1987. *Cosmologies in the Making.* Cambridge: Cambridge University Press.

—— 1989. The Analysis of Culture in Complex Societies. *Ethnos* 54: 120–142.

Barzun, Jacques. 1982. *Critical Questions.* Chicago: University of Chicago Press.

Bateson, Gregory. 1972. *Steps to an Ecology of Mind.* New York: Ballantine.

Baudrillard, Jean. 1981. *For a Critique of the Political Economy of the Sign.* St. Louis: Telos Press.

Baumer, Rachel Van M. 1975. The Reinterpretation of Dharma in Nineteenth-Century Bengal: Righteous Conduct for Man in the Modern World. In Rachel Van M. Baumer, ed., *Aspects of Bengali History and Society.* Honolulu: University Press of Hawaii.

Becker, Howard S. 1963. *Outsiders.* New York: Free Press.

—— 1982. *Art Worlds.* Berkeley: University of California Press.

Becker, Howard S. and Irving Louis Horowitz. 1971. The Culture of Civility. In Howard S. Becker, ed., *Culture and Civility in San Francisco.* Chicago: Transaction/Aldine.

Befu, Harumi. 1983. Internationalization of Japan and Nihon Bunkaron. In Hiroshi Mannari and Harumi Befu, eds., *The Challenge of Japan's Internationalization.* Tokyo: Kodansha International.

Bell, Daniel. 1976. *The Cultural Contradictions of Capitalism.* London: Heinemann.

Beller, Steven. 1989. *Vienna and the Jews, 1867–1938.* Cambridge: Cambridge University Press.

Bender, Thomas. 1979. The Cultures of Intellectual Life: The City and the Professions. In John Higham and Paul K. Conkin, eds., *New Directions in American Intellectual History.* Baltimore: Johns Hopkins University Press.

—— 1984. The Erosion of Public Culture: Cities, Discourses, and Professional Disciplines. In Thomas L. Haskell, ed., *The Authority of Experts.* Bloomington: Indiana University Press.

—— 1986. Wholes and Parts: The Need for Synthesis in American History. *Journal of American History* 73:120–136.

Benjamin, Walter. 1969. *Illuminations.* New York: Schocken.

Bennett, Tony. 1982. Theories of the Media, Theories of Society. In Michael Gurevitch, Tony Bennett, James Curran and Janet Woollacott, eds., *Culture, Society and the Media.* London: Methuen.

Bensman, Joseph and Robert Lilienfeld. 1973. *Craft and Consciousness.* New York: Wiley.

Berger, Bennett M. 1971. *Looking for America.* Englewood Cliffs, N.J.: Prentice-Hall.

Berger, Peter L. and Hansfried Kellner. 1964. Marriage and the Construction of Reality. *Diogenes* 46: 1–24.

Berger, Peter L., and Thomas Luckmann. 1966. *The Social Construction of Reality.* Garden City, N.Y.: Doubleday.

Berlin, Isaiah. 1978. *Russian Thinkers.* New York: Viking.

Bernstein, Basil. 1971. *Class, Codes, and Control.* vol 1. London: Routledge and Kegan Paul.

—— 1975. *Class, Codes, and Control.* vol. 3. London: Routledge and Kegan Paul.

Bhattacharya, Sabyasachi. 1974. Positivism in 19th Century Bengal: Diffusion of European Intellectual Influence in India. In *Indian Society.* New Delhi: People's Publishing House.

Björklund, Ulf. 1981. *North to Another Country.* Stockholm Studies in Social Anthropology, No. 9. Stockholm: Department of Social Anthropology, University of Stockholm.

Bledstein, Burton J. 1976. *The Culture of Professionalism.* New York: Norton.

Bloch, Maurice. 1977. The Past and the Present in the Present. *Man* 12:278–292.

—— 1985. From Cognition to Ideology. In Richard Fardon, ed., *Power and Knowledge.* Edinburgh: Scottish Academic Press.

Bloom, Harold. 1973. *The Anxiety of Influence.* New York: Oxford University Press.

Bohannan, Laura. 1966. Shakespeare in the Bush. *Natural History* 75 (7):28–33.

Bohannan, Paul. 1960. Conscience Collective and Culture. In Kurt H. Wolff, ed., *Emile Durkheim, 1858-1917.* Columbus: Ohio State University Press.

—— 1973. Rethinking Culture: A Project for Current Anthropologists. *Current Anthropology* 14:357–372.

Boli, John, Francisco O. Ramirez, and John W. Meyer. 1986. Explaining the Origins and Expansion of Mass Education. In Philip G. Altbach and Gail P. Kelly, eds., *New Approaches to Comparative Education.* Chicago: University of Chicago Press.

Booth, Wayne C. 1982. The Company We Keep: Self-Making in Imaginative Art, Old and New. *Daedalus* 111(4):33–59.

Borgström, Bengt-Erik. 1974. Outsiders Within: The Management of Mental Deviance in a North Swedish Community. *Ethnos* 39: 63–82.

Bose, Nirmal Kumar. 1967. *Culture and Society in India.* Bombay: Asia Publishing House.

Boster, James S. 1985. "Requiem for the Omniscient Informant": There's Life in the Old Girl Yet. In Janet W.D. Dougherty, ed., *Directions in Cognitive Anthropology.* Urbana and Chicago: University of Illinois Press.

Boster, James S., ed. 1987. Intracultural Variation. *American Behavioral Scientist* 31(2).

Boulding, Kenneth E. 1966. The Economics of Knowledge and the Knowledge of Economics. *American Economic Review* 56(2):1–13.

—— 1970. *Beyond Economics.* Ann Arbor: University of Michigan Press.

Bourdieu, Pierre. 1969. Intellectual Field and Creative Project. *Social Science Information* 8(2):89–119.

—— 1977. *Outline of a Theory of Practice.* Cambridge: Cambridge University Press.

—— 1984. *Distinction.* Cambridge, Mass.: Harvard University Press.

Bourdieu, Pierre and Jean-Claude Passeron. 1977. *Reproduction in Education, Society and Culture.* Beverly Hills: Sage.

Boyd-Barrett, J. O. 1982. Cultural Dependency and the Mass Media. In Michael Gurevitch, Tony Bennett, James Curran, and Janet Woollacott, eds., *Culture, Society and the Media.* London: Methuen.

Bradbury, Ray. 1953. *Fahrenheit 451.* New York: Random House.

Brathwaite, Edward. 1971. *The Development of Creole Society in Jamaica, 1770–1820.* London: Oxford University Press.

Broch, Hermann. 1984. *Hugo von Hofmannsthal and His Time.* Chicago: University of Chicago Press.

Broomfield, J. H. 1968. *Elite Conflict in a Plural Society.* Berkeley and Los Angeles: University of California Press.

Brucker, Gene A. 1969. *Renaissance Florence.* New York: Wiley.

Bulmer, Martin, ed., 1975. *Working-Class Images of Society.* London: Routledge and Kegan Paul.

Burke, Kenneth. 1968. *Language as Symbolic Action.* Berkeley and Los Angeles: University of California Press.

Burke, Peter. 1978. *Popular Culture in Early Modern Europe.* New York: Harper & Row.

Cain, Maureen. 1983. The General Practice Lawyer and the Client: Towards a Radical Conception. In Robert Dingwall and Philip Lewis, eds., *The Sociology of the Professions.* London: Macmillan.

Callaghy, Thomas M. 1980. State-Subject Communication in Zaire: Domination and the Concept of Domain Consensus. *Journal of Modern African Studies* 18:469–492.

Cameron, William Bruce. 1954. Sociological Notes on the Jam Session. *Social Forces* 33:177–182.

Camp, Roderic A. 1985. *Intellectuals and the State in Twentieth-Century Mexico.* Austin: University of Texas Press.

Campbell, Donald T. 1969. Ethnocentrism of Disciplines and the Fish-Scale Model of Omniscience. In Muzafer Sherif and Carolyn W. Sherif, eds., *Interdisciplinary Relationships in the Social Sciences.* Chicago: Aldine.

Carey, James W. 1967. Harold Adams Innis and Marshall McLuhan. *Antioch Review* 27:5–31.
Carroll, John. 1978. In Spite of Intellectuals. *Theory and Society* 6:133–150.
Caughey, John L. 1978. Artificial Social Relations in Modern America. *American Quarterly* 30:70–89.
—— 1984. *Imaginary Social Worlds.* Lincoln: University of Nebraska Press.
Caute, David. 1973. *The Fellow-Travellers.* New York: Macmillan.
Charters, Ann. 1973. *Kerouac.* San Francisco: Straight Arrow Books.
Chatterjee, Partha. 1986. *Nationalist Thought and the Colonial World.* London: Zed.
Chatwin, Bruce. 1988. *The Songlines.* London: Picador/Pan.
Cherkovski, Neeli. 1979. *Ferlinghetti.* Garden City, NY: Doubleday.
Chernoff, John M. 1985. Africa Come Back: The Popular Music of West Africa. In Geoffrey Haydon and Dennis Marks, eds., *Repercussions: A Celebration of African-American Music.* London: Century.
Chirot, Daniel and Thomas D. Hall. 1982. World-System Theory. *Annual Review of Sociology* 8:81–106.
Clark, Burton. 1983. *The Higher Education System.* Berkeley and Los Angeles: University of California Press.
Clark, T. W. 1961. The Role of Bankimcandra in the Development of Nationalism. In C. H. Phillips, ed., *Historians of India, Pakistan, and Ceylon.* London: Oxford University Press.
Clarke, John, Stuart Hall, Tony Jefferson, and Brian Roberts. 1982. Subcultures, Cultures and Class: A Theoretcal Overview. In Stuart Hall and Tony Jefferson, eds., *Resistance Through Rituals.* London: Hutchinson.
Clarke, Michael. 1974. On the Concept of 'Sub-culture.' *British Journal of Sociology* 25:428–441.
Clifford, James. 1983. On Ethnographic Authority. *Representations* 2: 118–146.
Clignet, Remi. 1979. The Variability of Paradigms in the Production of Culture: A Comparison of the Arts and the Sciences. *American Sociological Review* 44:392–409.
Cohen, Albert M. 1955. *Delinquent Boys.* Glencoe, IL: Free Press.
Cohen, Anthony P. and John L Comaroff. 1976. The Management of Meaning: On the Phenomenology of Political Transactions. In Bruce Kapferer, ed., *Transaction and Meaning.* Philadelphia: Institute for the Study of Human Issues.
Cohn, Bernard S. 1987. *An Anthropologist Among the Historians and Other Essays.* Delhi: Oxford University Press.

Cohen, Stanley. 1972. *Folk Devils and Moral Panics.* London: MacGibbon and Kee.

Cohen, Stanley and Jock Young, eds. 1973. *The Manufacture of News.* London: Constable.

Cole, Michael and Helen Keyssar. 1985. The Concept of Literacy in Print and Film. In David R. Olson, Nancy Torrance, and Angela Hildyard, eds., *Literacy, Language, and Learning.* Cambridge: Cambridge University Press.

Collins, John. 1985. *African Pop Roots.* London: Foulsham.

Collins, Randall. 1979. *The Credential Society.* New York: Academic Press.

—— 1981a. On the Microfoundations of Macrosociology. *American Journal of Sociology* 86:984–1014.

—— 1981b. Micro-Translation as a Theory-Building Strategy. In K. Knorr-Cetina and A. V. Cicourel, eds., *Advances in Social Theory and Methodology.* Boston: Routledge and Kegan Paul.

—— 1981c. *Sociology Since Midcentury.* New York: Academic Press.

—— 1983. Micromethods as a Basis for Macrosociology. *Urban Life* 12:184–202.

—— 1986. Is 1980s Sociology in the Doldrums? *American Journal of Sociology* 91:1336–1355.

Cook-Gumperz, Jenny. 1986. Literacy and Schooling: An Unchanging Equation? In Jenny Cook-Gumperz, ed., *The Social Construction of Literacy.* Cambridge: Cambridge University Press.

Coser, Lewis A. 1965. *Men of Ideas.* New York: Free Press.

Crane, Diana. 1972. *Invisible Colleges.* Chicago: University of Chicago Press.

—— 1976. Reward Systems in Art, Science, and Religion. *American Behavioral Scientist* 19:719–734.

Crane, Robert I. 1983. The Press and Local Associations as Manifestations of Change in Late Nineteenth Century Calcutta. In G. R. Gupta, ed., *Urban India.* New Delhi: Vikas.

Cuddihy, John M. 1974. *The Ordeal of Civility.* New York: Basic Books.

Culler, Jonathan. 1988. *Framing the Sign.* Norman: University of Oklahoma Press.

Curtin, Philip D. 1984. *Cross-Cultural Trade in World History.* Cambridge: Cambridge University Press.

Curtis, James M. 1978. *Culture as Polyphony.* Columbia: University of Missouri Press.

Czitrom, Daniel J. 1982. *Media and the American Mind.* Chapel Hill: University of North Carolina Press.

Dahrendorf, Ralf. 1970. The Intellectual and Society: The Social Function of the "Fool" in the Twentieth Century. In Philip

Rieff, ed., *On Intellectuals.* Garden City, N.Y.: Anchor/Doubleday.

D'Andrade, Roy G. 1981. The Cultural Part of Cognition. *Cognitive Science* 5:179–195.

—— 1984. Cultural Meaning Systems. In Richard A. Shweder and Robert A. LeVine, eds., *Culture Theory.* Cambridge: Cambridge University Press.

—— 1987. A Folk Model of the Mind. In Dorothy Holland and Naomi Quinn, eds., *Cultural Models in Language and Thought.* Cambridge: Cambridge University Press.

Darnton, Robert. 1975. Writing News and Telling Stories. *Daedalus* 104(2):175–194.

Dayan, Daniel. 1986. Review Essay: Copyrighted Subcultures. *American Journal of Sociology* 91:1219–1228.

Deal, Terrence E., and Allan A. Kennedy. 1982. *Corporate Cultures.* Reading, Mass: Addison-Wesley.

Debray, Régis. 1981. *Teachers, Writers, Celebrities.* London: Verso/NLB.

DeCamp, David. 1977. The Development of Pidgin and Creole Studies. In Albert Valdman, ed., *Pidgin and Creole Linguistics.* Bloomington: Indiana University Press.

Despres, Leo A. 1968. Anthropological Theory, Cultural Pluralism, and the Study of Complex Societies. *Current Anthropology* 9:3–26.

Didion, Joan. 1987. *Miami.* New York: Simon & Schuster.

Di Maggio, Paul. 1977. Market Structure, the Creative Process, and Popular Culture: Toward an Organizational Reinterpretation of Mass-Culture Theory. *Journal of Popular Culture* 11:436–452.

Dirlik, Arif. 1987. Culturalism as Hegemonic Ideology and Liberating Practice. *Cultural Critique* 6:13–50.

Dore, Ronald. 1976. *The Diploma Disease.* Berkeley and Los Angeles: University of California Press.

—— 1984. Unity and Diversity in World Culture. In Hedley Bull and Adam Watson, eds., *The Expansion of International Society.* Oxford: Oxford University Press.

Douglas, Mary. 1978. *Cultural Bias.* London: Royal Anthropological Institute.

—— 1985. Pascal's Great Wager. *L'Homme* 25(1):13–30.

Douglas, Mary and Jonathan Gross. 1981. Food and Culture: Measuring the Intricacy of Rule Systems. *Social Science Information* 20:1–35.

Drummond, Lee. 1978. The Transatlantic Nanny: Notes on a Comparative Semiotics of the Family in English-Speaking Societies. *American Ethnologist* 5:30–43.

—— 1980. The Cultural Continuum: A Theory of Intersystems. *Man* 5:352–374.

Eickelman, Dale F. 1978. The Art of Memory: Islamic Education and Its Social Reproduction. *Comparative Studies in Society and History* 20:485–516.

Eisenstein, Elizabeth L. 1979. *The Printing Press as an Agent of Change.* Cambridge: Cambridge University Press.

Ellison, Ralph. 1964. *Shadow and Act.* New York: Random House.

Ericson, Deborah. 1988. *In the Stockholm Art World.* Stockholm Studies in Social Anthropology, no. 17. Stockholm: Department of Social Anthropology, University of Stockholm.

Erikson, Kai T. 1976. *Everything in Its Path.* New York: Simon & Schuster.

Errington, Frederick K. 1984. *Manners and Meaning in West Sumatra.* New Haven: Yale University Press.

Esposito, John L., ed. 1983. *Voices of Resurgent Islam.* New York: Oxford University Press.

Fabian, Johannes. 1978. Popular Culture in Africa: Findings and Conjectures. *Africa* 48:315–334.

Fallers, Lloyd A. 1961. Ideology and Culture in Uganda Nationalism. *American Anthropologist* 63:677–686.

Feierman, Steven. 1986. Popular Control over the Institutions of Health: A Historical Study. In Murray Last and G. L. Chivanduka, eds., *The Professionalisation of African Medicine.* Manchester: Manchester University Press.

Feld, Steven. 1988. Notes on World Beat. *Public Culture* 1(1):31–37.

Ferlinghetti, Lawrence and Nancy J. Peters. 1980. *Literary San Francisco.* New York: Harper & Row.

Field, James A., Jr. 1971. Transnationalism and the New Tribe. *International Organization* 25:353–362.

Fields, Rick. 1981. *How the Swans Came to the Lake.* Boulder: Shambala.

Fine, Gary Alan. 1979. Small Groups and Culture Creation: The Idioculture of Little League Baseball Teams. *American Sociological Review* 44:733–745.

—— 1983. *Shared Fantasy.* Chicago: University of Chicago Press.

—— 1987. *With the Boys.* Chicago: University of Chicago Press.

Fine, Gary Alan and Sherryl Kleinman. 1979. Rethinking Subculture: An Interactionist Analysis. *American Journal of Sociology* 85: 1–20.

Finkelstein, Sidney W. 1968. *Sense and Nonsense of McLuhan.* New York: International Publishers.

Finnegan, Ruth. 1988. *Literacy and Orality.* Oxford: Blackwell.

Fischer, Claude S. 1975. Toward a Subcultural Theory of Urbanism. *American Journal of Sociology* 80:1319–1341.

Fischer, John L. 1975. The Individual as a Crucial Locus of Culture. In

Thomas R. Williams, ed., *Socialization and Communication in Primary Groups.* The Hague: Mouton.

Fischer, Michael M. J., and Mehdi Abedi. 1990. Bombay Talkies, the Word and the World: Salman Rushdie's *Satanic Verses. Cultural Anthropology* 5:107–159.

Fisher, Lawrence E. 1985. *Colonial Madness.* New Brunswick, N.J.: Rutgers University Press.

FitzGerald, Frances. 1986. *Cities on a Hill.* New York: Simon & Schuster.

Foucault, Michel. 1981. *Power/Knowledge.* New York: Pantheon.

Fox, Richard G. 1985. *Lions of the Punjab.* Berkeley: University of California Press.

Frank, Andre Gunder. 1967. *Capitalism and Underdevelopment in Latin America.* New York: Monthly Review Press.

Frankenberg, Ronald. 1966. *Communities in Britain.* Harmondsworth: Penguin.

Freidson, Eliot. 1984. Are Professions Necessary? In Thomas L. Haskell, ed., *The Authority of Experts.* Bloomington: Indiana University Press.

Friedman, Thomas L. 1986. Israeli Cultural Groups View 'Dallas' but See a Different Show. *International Herald Tribune,* April 3.

Frost, Peter J., Larry F. Moore, Meryl Reis Louis, Craig C. Lundberg, and Joanne Martin, eds. 1985. *Organizational Culture.* Beverly Hills, CA: Sage.

Furlong, Monica. 1986. *Zen Effects: The Life of Alan Watts.* Boston: Houghton Mifflin.

Furnivall, J. S. 1948. *Colonial Policy and Practice.* London: Cambridge University Press.

Gans, Herbert J. 1974. *Popular Culture and High Culture.* New York: Basic Books.

Gardner, Peter M. 1976. Birds, Words and a Requiem for the Omniscient Informant. *American Ethnologist* 3:446–468.

Garfinkel, Harold. 1967. *Studies in Ethnomethodology.* Englewood Cliffs, N.J.: Prentice-Hall.

Gay, Peter. 1978. *Freud, Jews and Other Germans.* New York: Oxford University Press.

Geertz, Clifford. 1957. Ritual and Social Change: A Javanese Example. *American Anthropologist* 59:32–54.

—— 1973. *The Interpretation of Cultures.* New York: Basic Books.

—— 1975. Common Sense as a Cultural System. *Antioch Review* 33:5–26.

Gellner, Ernest. 1983. *Nations and Nationalism.* Oxford: Blackwell.

—— 1987. *Culture, Identity, and Politics.* Cambridge: Cambridge University Press.

Gerholm, Tomas and Ulf Hannerz. 1982. Introduction: the Shaping of National Anthropologies. *Ethnos* 47:5–35.
Gibbons, Michael and Björn Wittrock, eds. 1985. *Science as a Commodity.* Harlow, Essex: Longman.
Gibson, Morgan. 1972. *Kenneth Rexroth.* New York: Twayne.
Giddens, Anthony. 1976. *New Rules of Sociological Method.* London: Hutchinson.
—— 1979. *Central Problems in Social Theory.* London: Macmillan.
Gitlin, Todd. 1983. *Inside Prime Time.* New York: Pantheon.
Glaser, Barney G. and Anselm L. Strauss. 1964. Awareness Contexts and Social Interaction. *American Sociological Review* 29:669–679.
Gmelch, George. 1980. Return Migration. *Annual Review of Anthropology* 9:135–159. Palo Alto, Cal: Annual Reviews.
Godelier, Maurice. 1986. *The Mental and the Material.* London: Verso.
Goldfarb, Jeffrey C. 1982. *On Cultural Freedom.* Chicago: University of Chicago Press.
Golding, Peter. 1977. Media Professionalism in the Third World: The Transfer of an Ideology. In James Curran, Michael Gurevitch, and Janet Woollacott, eds., *Mass Communication and Society.* London: Arnold.
Goldman, Albert. 1971. *Freakshow.* New York: Atheneum.
—— 1974. *Ladies and Gentlemen, Lenny Bruce!* New York: Random House.
Goodenough, Ward H. 1963. *Cooperation in Change.* New York: Russell Sage Foundation.
—— 1971. *Culture, Language, and Society.* Reading, Mass: Addison-Wesley.
—— 1978. Multiculturalism as the Normal Human Experience. In Elizabeth M. Eddy and William L. Partridge, eds., *Applied Anthropology in America.* New York: Columbia University Press.
—— 1981. *Culture, Language, and Society.* 2d ed. Menlo Park, Cal.: Benjamin/Cummings.
Goody, Jack. 1977. *The Domestication of the Savage Mind.* Cambridge: Cambridge University Press.
—— 1986. *The Logic of Writing and the Organization of Society.* Cambridge: Cambridge University Press.
—— 1987. *The Interface Between the Written and the Oral.* Cambridge: Cambridge University Press.
Goody, Jack, ed. 1968. *Literacy in Traditional Societies.* Cambridge: Cambridge University Press.
Goonatilake, Susantha. 1982. *Crippled Minds.* New Delhi: Vikas.
Gordon, Milton M. 1947. The Concept of Sub-Culture and Its Application. *Social Forces* 26:40–42.

Gottdiener, Mark. 1985. Hegemony and Mass Culture: A Semiotic Approach. *American Journal of Sociology* 90:979–1001.

Gouldner, Alvin W. 1976. *The Dialectic of Ideology and Technology.* London: Macmillan.

—— 1979. *The Future of Intellectuals and the Rise of the New Class.* London: Macmillan.

—— 1985. *Against Fragmentation.* New York: Oxford University Press.

Gove, Walter R., ed. 1980. *The Labelling of Deviance.* Beverly Hills: Sage.

Graburn, Nelson H. H. 1983. The Anthropology of Tourism. *Annals of Tourism Research* 10:9–33.

—— 1984. The Evolution of Tourist Arts. *Annals of Tourism Research* 11:393–419.

Gramsci, Antonio. 1971. *Selections from the Prison Notebooks.* London: Lawrence and Wishart.

Gray, John N. 1975. Bengal and Britain: Culture Contact and the Reinterpretation of Hinduism in the Nineteenth Century. In Rachel Van M. Baumer, ed., *Aspects of Bengali History and Society.* Honolulu: University of Hawaii Press.

Green, Arnold W. 1946. Sociological Analysis of Horney and Fromm. *American Journal of Sociology* 51:533–540.

Greenfield, Liah. 1984. The Role of the Public in the Success of Artistic Styles. *Archives Européennes de Sociologie* 25:83–98.

Griaule, Marcel. 1965. *Conversations with Ogotemmeli.* London: Oxford University Press.

Griswold, Wendy. 1981. American Character and the American Novel: An Expansion of Reflection Theory in the Sociology of Literature. *American Journal of Sociology* 86:740–765.

Gusfield, Joseph R. 1981. Social Movements and Social Change: Perspectives of Linearity and Fluidity. In *Research in Social Movements, Conflict and Change,* vol. 4. Greenwich, Conn: JAI Press.

Hall, Stuart and Tony Jefferson, eds. 1976. *Resistance through Rituals.* London: Hutchinson.

Hall, Stuart, Dorothy Hobson, Andrew Lowe, and Paul Willis, eds. 1980. *Culture, Media, Language.* London: Hutchinson.

Hamelink, Cees T. 1983. *Cultural Autonomy in Global Communications.* New York: Longman.

Handelman, Don. 1987. Micro-Structure and Micro-Process: The Development of Infrastructure in Two Israeli Work Settings. *Social Analysis* 22:73–103.

Handler, Richard. 1988. The Center in American Culture: Analysis and Critique. *Anthropological Quarterly* 61:1–2.

Hannerz, Ulf. 1969. *Soulside.* New York: Columbia University Press.

—— 1971. The Study of Afro-American Cultural Dynamics. *Southwestern Journal of Anthropology* 27:181–200.

—— 1980. *Exploring the City.* New York: Columbia University Press.

—— 1983. Tools of Identity and Imagination. In Anita Jacobson-Widding, ed., *Identity: Personal and Socio-Cultural.* Uppsala: Almqvist & Wiksell International.

—— 1986. Theory in Anthropology: Small is Beautiful? Anthropological Theory and Complex Cultures. *Comparative Studies in Society and History* 28:362–367.

—— 1987. The World in Creolisation. *Africa* 57:546–559.

—— 1988. American Culture: Creolized, Creolizing. In Erik Åsard, ed., *American Culture: Creolized, Creolizing and Other Lectures from the NAAS Biennial Conference in Uppsala, May 28–31, 1987.* Uppsala: Swedish Institute for North American Studies.

—— 1989a. Notes on the Global Ecumene. *Public Culture* 1(2):66–75.

—— 1989b. Culture Between Center and Periphery: Toward a Macroanthropology. *Ethnos* 54:200–216.

—— 1990. Cosmopolitans and Locals in World Culture. *Theory, Culture and Society* 7(2-3):237–251.

—— 1991a. The Global Ecumene as a Network of Networks. In Adam Kuper, ed., *Conceptualising Societies.* London: Routledge.

—— 1991b. The Cultural Role of World Cities. In Anthony Cohen and Katsuyoshi Fukui, eds., *The Age of the City.* Edinburgh: Edinburgh University Press.

Harris, Neil. 1985. Who Owns Our Myths? Heroism and Copyright in an Age of Mass Culture. *Social Research* 52:241–267.

Harris, Philip R. and Robert T. Moran. 1987. *Managing Cultural Differences.* 2d ed. Houston: Gulf Publishing Company.

Harwood, Frances. 1976. Myth, Memory, and the Oral Tradition: Cicero in the Trobriands. *American Anthropologist* 78:783–796.

Haug, Wolfgang F. 1986. *Critique of Commodity Aesthetics.* Cambridge, U.K.: Polity Press.

Havelock, Eric A. 1963. *Preface to Plato.* Cambridge, Mass: Harvard University Press.

Haviland, John B. 1977. *Gossip, Reputation, and Knowledge in Zinacantan.* Chicago: University of Chicago Press.

Hay, Stephen N. 1965. Western and Indigenous Elements in Modern Indian Thought: The Case of Rammohun Roy. In M. B. Janssen, ed., *Changing Attitudes Towards Modernization.* Princeton: Princeton University Press.

Hayek, F. A. 1945. The Use of Knowledge in Society. *American Economic Review* 35:519–530.

Heath, Shirley B. 1983. *Ways with Words.* Cambridge: Cambridge University Press.
Hebdige, Dick. 1979. *Subculture.* London: Methuen.
—— 1987. *Cut'n'Mix.* London: Methuen.
Heller, Erich. 1973. Dark Laughter. *New York Review of Books* (May 3) 21–25.
Herron, Don. 1985. *The Literary World of San Francisco and Its Environs.* San Francisco: City Lights.
Hirsch, E. D., Jr. 1987. *Cultural Literacy.* Boston: Houghton Mifflin.
Hobsbawm, Eric. 1983. Mass-Producing Traditions: Europe, 1870–1914. In Eric Hobsbawm and Terence Ranger, eds., *The Invention of Tradition.* Cambridge: Cambridge University Press.
Hobsbawm, Eric and Terence Ranger, eds. 1983. *The Invention of Tradition.* Cambridge: Cambridge University Press.
Hoffman, Eva. 1989. *Lost in Translation.* New York: Dutton.
Hofstadter, Richard. 1963. *Anti-Intellectualism in American Life.* New York: Vintage/Random House.
Hoggart, Richard. 1961. *The Uses of Literacy.* Boston: Beacon.
Hollander, Paul. 1981. *Political Pilgrims.* New York: Oxford University Press.
—— 1986. Political Tourism in Cuba and Nicaragua. *Society* 23(4): 28–37.
Hollinger, David A. 1975. Ethnic Diversity, Cosmopolitanism and the Emergence of the American Liberal Intelligentsia. *American Quarterly* 27:133–151.
Holzner, Burkart and John H. Marx. 1979. *Knowledge Application.* Boston: Allyn and Bacon.
Honan, Park, ed. 1987. *The Beats.* London: Dent.
Horton, Donald and R. Richard Wohl. 1956. Mass Communication and Para-social Interaction. *Psychiatry* 19:215–229.
Horton, Robin. 1982. Tradition and Modernity Revisited. In Martin Hollis and Steven Lukes, eds., *Rationality and Relativism.* Oxford: Blackwell.
Hughes, Everett C. 1961. *Students' Culture and Perspectives.* Lawrence: University of Kansas School of Law.
Hymes, Dell. 1963. Review of Marshall McLuhan, *The Gutenberg Galaxy. American Anthropologist,* 65:478.
Illich, Ivan. 1977. Disabling Professions. In *Disabling Professions.* London: Marion Boyars.
Inden, Ronald. 1986. Orientalist Constructions of India. *Modern Asian Studies* 20:401–446.
Innis, Harold A. 1950. *Empire and Communications.* London: Oxford University Press.

—— 1951. *The Bias of Communication.* Toronto: University of Toronto Press.

Ivy, Marilyn. 1988. Critical Texts, Mass Artifacts: The Consumption of Knowledge in Postmodern Japan. *South Atlantic Quarterly* 87: 419–444.

Jackson, Carl. 1988. The Counterculture Looks East: Beat Writers and Asian Religion. *American Studies* 29:51–70.

Jackson, Jean. 1989. Is There a Way to Talk about Culture Without Making Enemies? *Dialectical Anthropology* 14:127–143.

Jacoby, Russell. 1987. *The Last Intellectuals.* New York: Basic Books.

Janik, Allan. 1981. Schorske's Vienna. *Archives Européennes de Sociologie* 22:354–364.

Janik, Allan and Stephen Toulmin. 1973. *Wittgenstein's Vienna.* New York: Simon & Schuster.

Jelinek, Mariann, Linda Smircich, and Paul Hirsch, eds., 1983. Organizational Culture. *Administrative Science Quarterly* 28(3).

Jencks, Christopher and David Riesman. 1968. *The Academic Revolution.* Garden City, N.Y.: Doubleday.

Jha, Akhileshwar. 1977. *Intellectuals at the Crossroads.* New Delhi: Vikas.

Johansson, Egil. 1981. The History of Literacy in Sweden. In Harvey J. Graff, ed., *Literacy and Social Development in the West.* Cambridge: Cambridge University Press.

Johnson, Richard. 1986. The Story So Far: And Further Transformations? In David Punter, ed., *Introduction to Contemporary Cultural Studies.* London: Longman.

Johnston, William M. 1972. *The Austrian Mind.* Berkeley: University of California Press.

Jones, J. Sydney. 1983. *Hitler in Vienna 1907–1913.* New York: Stein and Day.

Jones, Leroi. 1963. *Blues People.* New York: Morrow.

Jordens, J. T. F. 1978. *Dayananda Sarasvati.* Delhi: Oxford University Press.

Kadushin, Charles. 1974. *The American Intellectual Elite.* Boston: Little, Brown.

Kalcik, Susan. 1975. " . . . like Ann's Gynecologist or the Time I Was Almost Raped": Personal Narratives in Women's Rap Groups. In Claire R. Farrer, ed., *Women and Folklore.* Austin: University of Texas Press.

Karp, Ivan. 1986. Agency and Social Theory: A Review of Anthony Giddens. *American Ethnologist* 13:131–137.

Keesing, Roger M. 1974. Theories of Culture. *Annual Review of Anthropology* 3:73–97. Palo Alto, Cal: Annual Reviews.

—— 1981. *Cultural Anthropology.* 2d ed. New York: Holt, Rinehart & Winston.
—— 1982. *Kwaio Religion.* New York: Columbia University Press.
—— 1985. Kwaio Women Speak: The Micropolitics of Autobiography in a Solomon Island Society. *American Anthropologist* 87: 27–39.
—— 1987a. Anthropology as Interpretive Quest. *Current Anthropology* 28:161–176.
—— 1987b. Models, "Folk" and "Cultural": Paradigms Regained. In Dorothy Holland and Naomi Quinn, eds., *Cultural Models in Language and Thought.* Cambridge: Cambridge University Press.
Keil, Charles. 1966. *Urban Blues.* Chicago: University of Chicago Press.
Kemeny, John G. 1983. The Case for Computer Literacy. *Daedalus* 112(2):211–230.
Kerouac, Jack. 1955. *On the Road.* New York: Viking.
—— 1958. *The Dharma Bums.* New York: Viking.
Klapp, Orrin E. 1969. *Collective Search for Identity.* New York: Holt, Rinehart & Winston.
Kleinman, Arthur. 1980. *Patients and Healers in the Context of Culture.* Berkeley: University of California Press.
Kling, Blair B. 1975. Economic Foundations of the Bengal Renaissance. In Rachel Van M. Baumer, ed., *Aspects of Bengali History and Society.* Honolulu: University Press of Hawaii.
—— 1976. *Partner in Empire.* Berkeley: University of California Press.
Knorr-Cetina, Karin D. 1981. Introduction: The Micro-Sociological Challenge of Macro-Sociology: Towards a Reconstruction of Social Theory and Methodology. In K. Knorr-Cetina and A.V. Cicourel, eds., *Advances in Social Theory and Methodology: Toward an Integration of Micro- and Macro-Sociologies.* Boston: Routledge and Kegan Paul.
Kolakowski, Leszek. 1989. On Total Control and Its Contradictions: The Power of Information. *Encounter* 73(2):65–71.
Konrad, Georg. 1984. *Antipolitics.* San Diego and New York: Harcourt Brace Jovanovich.
Konrad, Georg and Ivan Szelényi. 1979. *The Intellectuals on the Road to Class Power.* New York: Harcourt Brace Jovanovich.
Kopf, David. 1969. *British Orientalism and the Bengal Renaissance.* Berkeley: University of California Press.
—— 1975a. The Universal Man and the Yellow Dog: The Orientalist Legacy and the Problem of Brahmo Identity in the Bengal Renaissance. In Rachel Van M.Baumer, ed., *Aspects of Bengali History and Society.* Honolulu: University Press of Hawaii.
—— 1975b. A Bibliographic Essay on Bengal Studies in the United States.

In Rachel Van M. Baumer, ed., *Aspects of Bengali History and Society.* Honolulu: University of Hawaii Press.

—— 1979. *The Brahmo Samaj and the Shaping of the Modern Indian Mind.* Princeton: Princeton University Press.

—— 1980. Hermeneutics Versus History. *Journal of Asian Studies* 39: 495–506.

Kopytoff, Igor. 1987. The Internal African Frontier: The Making of African Political Culture. In Igor Kopytoff, ed., *The African Frontier.* Bloomington: Indiana University Press.

Kripalani, Krishna. 1962. *Tagore.* New York: Grove Press.

Kroeber, A. L. 1945. The Ancient *Oikoumene* as an Historic Culture Aggregate. *Journal of the Royal Anthropological Institute* 75:9–20.

—— 1948. *Anthropology.* New York: Harcourt, Brace.

—— 1953. Introduction. In A. L. Kroeber, ed., *Anthropology Today.* Chicago: University of Chicago Press.

Kroeber, A. L. and Talcott Parsons. 1958. The Concepts of Culture and of Social System. *American Sociological Review* 23:582–583.

Kroker, Arthur. 1984. Processed World: Technology and Culture in the Thought of Marshall McLuhan. *Philosophy of the Social Sciences* 14:433–459.

Kuper, Leo and M. G. Smith. 1969. *Pluralism in Africa.* Berkeley and Los Angeles: University of California Press.

LaCapra, Dominick. 1983. *Rethinking Intellectual History.* Ithaca: Cornell University Press.

Laing, Dave. 1986. The Music Industry and the 'Cultural Imperialism' Thesis. *Media, Culture and Society* 8:331–341.

Lakoff, George and Mark Johnson. 1980. *Metaphors We Live By.* Chicago: University of Chicago Press.

Lantis, Margaret. 1960. Vernacular Culture. *American Anthropologist* 62:202–216.

Laroui, Abdallah. 1976. *The Crisis of the Arab Intellectual.* Berkeley: University of California Press.

Lasch, Christopher. 1977. *Haven in a Heartless World.* New York: Basic Books.

Last, Murray, and G. L. Chivanduka, eds., 1986. *The Professionalisation of African Medicine.* Manchester: Manchester University Press.

Lemert, Edwin M. 1972. *Human Deviance, Social Problems, and Social Control.* 2d ed. Englewood Cliffs, N.J.: Prentice-Hall.

Levenson, Joseph R. 1971. *Revolution and Cosmopolitanism.* Berkeley: University of California Press.

Lévi-Strauss, Claude. 1978. *Myth and Meaning.* London: Routledge & Kegan Paul.

Levitt, Theodore. 1983. The Globalization of Markets. *Harvard Business Review* 61(3): 92–102.

Lindstrom, Lamont. 1984. Doctor, Lawyer, Wise Man, Priest: Big-men and Knowledge in Melanesia. *Man* 19:291–309.

Linton, Ralph. 1936. *The Study of Man.* New York: Appleton-Century-Crofts.

Lippincott, Bruce. 1958. Aspects of the Jam Session. In Ralph Gleason, ed., *Jam Session.* New York: Putnam.

Loewenstein, Joseph. 1985. The Script in the Marketplace. *Representations* 12:101–114.

Löfgren, Orvar. 1989. The Nationalization of Culture. *Ethnologia Europaea* 19:5–24.

Lord, Albert B. 1960. *The Singer of Tales.* Cambridge: Harvard University Press.

Luckmann, Benita. 1970. The Small Life-Worlds of Modern Man. *Social Research* 37:580–596.

MacAloon, John J. 1984. Olympic Games and the Theory of Spectacle in Modern Societies. In John J. MacAloon, ed., *Rite, Drama, Festival, Spectacle.* Philadelphia: Institute for the Study of Human Issues.

Machlup, Fritz. 1980. *Knowledge and Knowledge Production.* Princeton: Princeton University Press.

Mailer, Norman. 1957. *The White Negro.* San Francisco: City Lights.

Malia, Martin. 1960. What Is the Intelligentsia? *Daedalus* 89:441–458.

Malinowski, Bronislaw. 1961. *Argonauts of the Western Pacific.* New York: Dutton. (First published 1922.)

Mannheim, Karl. 1936. *Ideology and Utopia.* New York: Harcourt, Brace & World.

Manuel, Peter. 1988. *Popular Musics of the Non-Western World.* New York: Oxford University Press.

Marchand, Philip. 1989. *Marshall McLuhan.* New York: Ticknor & Fields.

Marcus, George E. 1986. Contemporary Problems of Ethnography in the Modern World System. In James Clifford and George E. Marcus, eds., *Writing Culture.* Berkeley: University of California Press.

Marcus, George E. and Michael M. J. Fischer. 1986. *Anthropology as Cultural Critique.* Chicago: University of Chicago Press.

Marriott, McKim. 1955. Little Communities in an Indigenous Civilization. In McKim Marriott, ed., *Village India.* Chicago: University of Chicago Press.

—— 1959. Changing Channels of Cultural Transmission in Indian Civilization. In Verne F. Ray, ed., *Intermediate Societies, Social Mobility and Communication.* Proceedings of the American Ethnological Society. Seattle: University of Washington Press.

Marx, Karl. 1957. *The Eighteenth Brumaire of Louis Bonaparte.* New York: International Publishers.

Mazrui, Ali A. 1969. *Violence and Thought.* London: Longman.

—— 1972. *Cultural Engineering and Nation-Building in East Africa.* Evanston: Northwestern University Press.

—— 1976. *A World Federation of Cultures.* New York: Free Press.

McArthur, Tom. 1986. *Worlds of Reference.* Cambridge: Cambridge University Press.

McBryde, Isabel, ed. 1985. *Who Owns the Past?* Melbourne: Oxford University Press.

McFeat, Tom. 1974. *Small-Group Cultures.* New York: Pergamon.

McGee, T. G. 1971. *The Urbanization Process in the Third World.* London: Bell.

McLuhan, Marshall. 1962. *The Gutenberg Galaxy.* Toronto: University of Toronto Press.

—— 1964. *Understanding Media.* New York: McGraw-Hill.

McNally, Dennis. 1979. *Desolate Angel.* New York: Random House.

Medawar, Peter. 1984. *Pluto's Republic.* Oxford: Oxford University Press.

Mehta, Ved. 1970. *Portrait of India.* New York: Farrar, Straus & Giroux.

Meltzer, David, ed. 1971. *The San Francisco Poets.* New York: Ballantine.

Merriam, Alan P. and Raymond W. Mack. 1960. The Jazz Community. *Social Forces* 38:211–222.

Merton, Robert K. 1957. *Social Theory and Social Structure.* Glencoe, Ill.: Free Press.

Meyrowitz, Joshua. 1985. *No Sense of Place.* New York: Oxford University Press.

Michaels, Eric. 1985. Constraints on Knowledge in an Economy of Oral Information. *Current Anthropology* 26:505–510.

Miller, Jonathan. 1971. *McLuhan.* London: Fontana.

Miller, Richard. 1977. *Bohemia.* Chicago: Nelson-Hall.

Mills, C. Wright. 1963. *Power, Politics, and People.* New York: Ballantine.

Mitra, Ashok. 1977. *Calcutta Diary.* London: Cass.

Molund, Stefan. 1988. *First We are People.* Stockholm Studies in Social Anthropology, no. 20. Stockholm: Department of Social Anthropology, University of Stockholm.

Moore, Carlos. 1982. *Fela, Fela.* London: Allison & Busby.

Moore, Robert J. 1985. *Third-World Diplomats in Dialogue with the First World.* London: Macmillan.

Moore, Sally F. 1976. Epilogue: Uncertainties in Situations, Indeterminacies in Culture. In Sally F. Moore and Barbara G. Myerhoff,

eds., *Symbol and Politics in Communal Ideology.* Ithaca: Cornell University Press.
—— 1986. *Social Facts and Fabrications.* Cambridge: Cambridge University Press.
—— 1987. Explaining the Present: Theoretical Dilemmas in Processual Ethnography. *American Ethnologist* 14:727–736.
Moore, Wilbert E. 1966. Global Sociology: The World as a Singular System. *American Journal of Sociology* 71:475–482.
Moorhouse, Geoffrey. 1974. *Calcutta.* Harmondsworth: Penguin.
Morris, H. S. 1967. Some Aspects of the Concept Plural Society. *Man* 2:169–184.
Morris-Suzuki, Tessa. 1988. *Beyond Computopia.* London: Kegan Paul International.
Muehlhäusler, Peter. 1986. *Pidgin & Creole Linguistics.* Oxford: Blackwell.
Mukherjee, Meenakshi. 1985. *Realism and Reality.* Delhi: Oxford University Press.
Mukherjee, S. N. 1970. Class, Caste and Politics in Calcutta, 1815–38. In Edmund Leach and S. N. Mukherjee, eds., *Elites in South Asia.* Cambridge: Cambridge University Press.
—— 1975. Daladali in Calcutta in the Nineteenth Century. *Modern Asian Studies* 9:59–80.
Mukhopadhyay, Amal Kumar. 1979. *The Bengali Intellectual Tradition.* Calcutta: K. P. Bagchi.
Mulkay, M. J., and B. S. Turner. 1971. Over-Production of Personnel and Innovation in Three Social Settings. *Sociology* 5:47–61.
Murphy, William P. 1980. Secret Knowledge as Property and Power in Kpelle Society: Elders Versus Youth. *Africa* 50:193–207.
Musil, Robert. 1953–1960. *The Man Without Qualities.* London: Secker and Warburg.
Myrdal, Gunnar. 1968. *Asian Drama.* New York: Pantheon.
Nag, Jamuna. 1972. *Raja Rammohun Roy.* New Delhi: Sterling.
Na'inna, Salisu. 1987. Tribulations in the Media. *West Africa* (August 31) pp. 1687–1688.
Naipaul, V. S. 1987. *The Enigma of Arrival.* New York: Knopf.
Nash, June. 1981. Ethnographic Aspects of the World Capitalist System. *Annual Review of Anthropology* 10:393–423. Palo Alto, Cal: Annual Reviews.
Nathe, Patricia A. 1978. Prickly Pear Coffee House: The Hangout. *Urban Life* 5:75–104.
Nelson, Margaret K. and Helen L. McGough. 1983. The Informed Client: A Case Study in the Illusion of Autonomy. *Symbolic Interaction* 6:35–50.

Newby, Howard. 1977. *The Deferential Worker.* Harmondsworth: Allen Lane.

Olson, David R. 1977. From Utterance to Text: The Bias of Language in Speech and Writing. *Harvard Educational Review* 47:257–281.

—— 1986. Interpreting Texts and Interpreting Nature: The Effects of Literacy on Hermeneutics and Epistemology. *Visible Language* 20:302–317.

—— 1988. Mind and Media: The Epistemic Functions of Literacy. *Journal of Communication* 38(3):27–36.

Ong, Walter J. 1968. Knowledge in Time. In Walter J. Ong, ed., *Knowledge and the Future of Man.* New York: Holt, Rinehart & Winston.

Oreh, O. O. 1985. *Masquerade* and other Plays on Nigerian Television. In Frank Okwu Ugboajah, ed., *Mass Communication, Culture and Society in West Africa.* München: Hans Zell/K.G. Saur.

Ortner, Sherry. 1984. Theory in Anthropology Since the Sixties. *Comparative Studies in Society and History* 26:126–166.

Osiel, Mark J. 1984. Going to the People: Popular Culture and the Intellectuals in Brazil. *Archives Européennes de Sociologie* 25:245–275.

Oxaal, Ivar, Michael Pollak, and Gerhard Botz. eds. 1987. *Jews, Antisemitism and Culture in Vienna.* London: Routledge & Kegan Paul.

Packer, George. 1988. *The Village of Waiting.* New York: Vintage.

Park, Robert E. 1952. *Human Communities.* Glencoe, Ill.: Free Press.

Parkin, Frank. 1972. *Class Inequality and Political Order.* London: Paladin.

Parsons, Ian. 1974. Copyright and Society. In Asa Briggs, ed., *Essays in the History of Publishing.* London: Longman.

Patterson, Orlando. 1975. Context and Choice in Ethnic Allegiance: A Theoretical Framework and Caribbean Case Study. In Nathan Glazer and Daniel P. Moynihan, eds., *Ethnicity.* Cambridge, Mass: Harvard University Press.

Pelto, Pertti J. and Gretel H. Pelto. 1975. Intra-Cultural Diversity: Some Theoretical Issues. *American Ethnologist* 2:1–18.

Perry, Charles. 1984. *The Haight-Ashbury.* New York: Rolling Stone/Random House.

Peterson, Richard A. ed. 1976. The Production of Culture. *American Behavioral Scientist* 19(6).

—— ed. 1983. Patterns of Cultural Choice. *American Behavioral Scientist* 26(4).

Peterson, Richard A. and Howard White. 1979. The Simplex Located in Art Worlds. *Urban Life* 7:411–439.

Ploman, Edward W. 1985. Copyright: Where Do We Go from Here? In Philip G. Altbach, Amadio A. Arboleda, and S. Gopinathan, eds., *Publishing in the Third World.* Portsmouth, N.H.: Heinemann.

Ploman, Edward W. and L. Clark Hamilton. 1980. *Copyright.* London: Routledge & Kegan Paul.

Plummer, Ken. 1979. Misunderstanding Labelling Perspectives. In David Downes and Paul Rock, eds., *Deviant Interpretations.* Oxford: Martin Robertson.

Poddar, Arabinda. 1970. *Renaissance in Bengal.* Simla: Indian Institute of Advanced Study.

Polanyi, Karl. 1957a. *The Great Transformation.* Boston: Beacon Press.

—— 1957b. The Economy as Instituted Process. In Karl Polanyi, Conrad M. Arensberg, and Harry W. Pearson, eds., *Trade and Market in the Early Empires.* Glencoe, Ill.: Free Press.

Poster, Mark. 1984. Sartre's Concept of the Intellectual: A Foucauldian Critique. In Norman F. Cantor and Nathalia King, eds., *Notebooks in Cultural Analysis,* 1. Durham: Duke University Press.

Pratt, Mary Louise. 1987. Linguistic Utopias. In Nigel Fabb, Derek Attridge, Alan Durant, and Colin MacCabe, eds., *The Linguistics of Writing.* Manchester: Manchester University Press.

Putnam, Hilary. 1975. *Mind, Language and Reality.* Cambridge: Cambridge University Press.

Ragin, Charles and Daniel Chirot. 1984. The World System of Immanuel Wallerstein: Sociology and Politics as History. In Theda Skocpol, ed., *Vision and Method in Historical Sociology.* Cambridge: Cambridge University Press.

Ray, Rajat Kanta. 1984. *Social Conflict and Political Unrest in Bengal 1875–1927.* Delhi: Oxford University Press.

Redfield, Robert. 1947. The Folk Society. *American Journal of Sociology* 52:293–308.

—— 1956. *Peasant Society and Culture.* Chicago: University of Chicago Press.

—— 1962. *Human Nature and the Study of Society.* Chicago: University of Chicago Press.

Redfield, Robert, Ralph Linton, and Melville J. Herskovits. 1936. A Memorandum for the Study of Acculturation. *American Anthropologist* 38:149–152.

Redfield, Robert and Milton Singer. 1954. The Cultural Role of Cities. *Economic Development and Cultural Change* 3:53–73.

Rexroth, Kenneth. 1957. San Francisco Letter. *Evergreen Review* 1(2):5–14.

—— 1966. *An Autobiographical Novel.* Garden City, N.Y.: Doubleday.

—— 1970. *The Alternative Society.* New York: Herder and Herder.

Rieff, David. 1987. *Going to Miami.* Boston: Little, Brown.

Roberts, John M. 1951. *Three Navaho Households.* Papers of the Peabody Museum of American Archaeology and Ethnology, Harvard University, 40(3).

—— 1964. The Self-Management of Cultures. In Ward H. Goodenough, ed., *Explorations in Cultural Anthropology.* New York: McGraw-Hill.

Roberts, John M., Chien Chiao, and Triloki N. Pandey. 1975. Meaningful God Sets from a Chinese Personal Pantheon and a Hindu Personal Pantheon. *Ethnology* 14:121–148.

Roberts, John M., Saburo Morita, and L. Keith Brown. 1986. Personal Categories for Japanese Sacred Places and Gods: Views Elicited from a Conjugal Pair. *American Anthropologist* 88:807–824.

Robertson, Roland and Frank Lechner. 1985. Modernization, Globalization and the Problem of Culture in World-Systems Theory. *Theory, Culture and Society* 2(3):103–117.

Roces, Alfredo and Grace Roces. 1985. *Culture Shock! Philippines.* Singapore: Times Books International.

Rodgers, Susan. 1984. Orality, Literacy, and Batak Concepts of Marriage Alliance. *Journal of Anthropological Research* 40:433–450.

Rodman, Hyman. 1963. The Lower-Class Value Stretch. *Social Forces* 42:205–215.

Rosaldo, Renato. 1987. Politics, Patriarchs, and Laughter. *Cultural Critique* 6:65–86.

—— 1988. Ideology, Place, and People Without Culture. *Cultural Anthropology* 3:77–87.

Rosenthal, Raymond. ed. 1968. *McLuhan: Pro and Con.* New York: Funk & Wagnalls.

Rozenblit, Marsha L. 1983. *The Jews of Vienna 1867–1914.* Albany: State University of New York Press.

Ruthven, Malise. 1990. *A Satanic Affair.* London: Chatto & Windus.

Sahlins, Marshall D. 1965. On the Sociology of Primitive Exchange. In Michael Banton, ed., *The Relevance of Models for Social Anthropology.* London: Tavistock.

—— 1976. *Culture and Practical Reason.* Chicago: University of Chicago Press.

—— 1985. *Islands of History.* Chicago: University of Chicago Press.

Said, Edward W. 1978. *Orientalism.* New York: Pantheon.

—— 1984. The Mind of Winter: Reflections on Life in Exile. *Harpers Magazine* (September) 49–55.

Salomon, Gavriel. 1979. *Interaction of Media, Cognition, and Learning.* San Francisco: Jossey-Bass.

Salzman, Philip Carl. 1981. Culture as Enhabilmentis. In Ladislav Holy and Milan Stuchlik, eds., *The Structure of Folk Models.* London: Academic Press.

Sampson, Steven. 1984. Rumours in Socialist Romania. *Survey* 28 (4):142–164.

Sanjek, Roger. 1977. Cognitive Maps of the Ethnic Domain in Urban Ghana: Reflections on Variability and Change. *American Ethnologist* 4:603–622.

Sankoff, Gillian. 1971. Quantitative Analysis of Sharing and Variability in a Cognitive Model. *Ethnology* 10:389–408.

—— 1972. Cognitive Variability and New Guinea Social Organization: The Buang Dgwa. *American Anthropologist* 74:555–566.

Sansom, Basil. 1980. *The Camp at Wallaby Cross.* Canberra: Australian Institute of Aboriginal Studies.

Sapir, Edward. 1932. Cultural Anthropology and Psychiatry. *Journal of Abnormal and Social Psychology* 27:229–242.

—— 1938. Why Cultural Anthropology Needs the Psychiatrist. *Psychiatry* 1:7–12.

—— 1985. *Selected Writings in Language, Culture, and Personality.* Berkeley: University of California Press.

Sarkar, Susobhan. 1970. *Bengal Renaissance and Other Essays.* New Delhi: People's Publishing House.

Sastri, Sivanath. 1972. *A History of the Renaissance in Bengal.* Calcutta: Editions Indian.

Sauvant, Karl P. 1976. The Potential of Multinational Enterprises as Vehicles for the Transmission of Business Culture. In Karl P. Sauvant and Farid G. Lavipour, eds., *Controlling Multinational Enterprises.* Boulder: Westview.

Scheff, 1967. Toward a Sociological Model of Consensus. *American Sociological Review* 32:32–46.

Schick, Alfred. 1969. The Vienna of Sigmund Freud. *Psychoanalytical Review* 55:529–551.

Schiller, Herbert I. 1974. *The Mind Managers.* Boston: Beacon Press.

—— 1989. The Privatization and Transnationalization of Culture. In Ian Angus and Sut Jhally, eds., *Cultural Politics in Contemporary America.* New York: Routledge.

Schorske, Carl E. 1978. Generational Tension and Cultural Change: Reflections on the Case of Vienna. *Daedalus* 107(4):111–122.

—— 1980. *Fin-de-Siècle Vienna.* New York: Knopf.

—— 1986. MOMA's Vienna. *New York Review of Books* (September 25):19–24.

Schudson, Michael. 1989. How Culture Works: Perspectives from Media Studies on the Efficacy of Symbols. *Theory and Society* 18:153–180.

Schutz, Alfred. 1964. *Collected Papers, II: Studies in Social Theory.* The Hague: Martinus Nijhoff.

—— 1967. *Collected Papers, I: The Problem of Social Reality.* The Hague: Martinus Nijhoff.

Schwartz, Theodore. 1978a. Where is the Culture? Personality and the Distributive Locus of Culture. In George D. Spindler, ed., *The Making of Psychological Anthropology.* Berkeley and Los Angeles: University of California Press.

—— 1978b. The Size and Shape of a Culture. In Fredrik Barth, ed., *Scale and Social Organization.* Oslo: Universitetsforlaget.

Schwartz, Theodore and Margaret Mead. 1961. Micro- and Macrocultural Models for Cultural Evolution. *Anthropological Linguistics* 3:1–7.

Scoditti, Giancarlo M. G. 1982. Aesthetics: The Significance of Apprenticeship on Kitawa. *Man* 17:74–91.

Scott, Marvin B. and Stanford M. Lyman. 1968. Accounts. *American Sociological Review* 33:46–62.

Sharrock, W. W. 1974. On Owning Knowledge. In Roy Turner, ed., *Ethnomethodology.* Harmondsworth: Penguin.

Shaw, Roy. 1972. The Cultural "Animateur" in Contemporary Society. *Cahiers d'Histoire Mondiale* 14:460–472.

Shils, Edward. 1956. *The Torment of Secrecy.* New York: Free Press.

—— 1972. *The Intellectuals and the Powers.* Chicago: University of Chicago Press.

—— 1975. *Center and Periphery.* Chicago: University of Chicago Press.

Sider, Gerald. 1986. *Culture and Class in Anthropology and History.* Cambridge: Cambridge University Press.

Siegel, James T. 1986. *Solo in the New Order.* Princeton: Princeton University Press.

Simmel, Georg. 1964. *The Sociology of Georg Simmel.* New York: Free Press.

Simonds, A. P. 1982. On Being Informed. *Theory and Society* 11:587–616.

Singer, Milton. 1972. *When a Great Tradition Modernizes.* London: Pall Mall.

Sinha, Pradip. 1978. *Calcutta in Urban History.* Calcutta: Firma KLM Private.

Sinha, Surajit, ed. 1972. *Cultural Profile of Calcutta.* Calcutta: Indian Anthropological Society.

Smith, M. G. 1965. *The Plural Society in the British West Indies.* Berkeley and Los Angeles: University of California Press.

Smith, Raymond. n.d. People and Change. *New World* (Jamaica), Guyana Independence Issue.

Snow, C. P. 1964. *The Two Cultures: and a Second Look.* Cambridge: Cambridge University Press.

Snyder, Gary. 1980. *The Real Work.* New York: New Directions.

Sontag, Susan. 1967. *Against Interpretation.* New York: Delta.

—— 1979a. *Illness as Metaphor.* New York: Vintage Books/Random House.

—— 1979b. *On Photography.* Harmondsworth: Penguin.

Sperber, Dan. 1985. Anthropology and Psychology: Towards an Epidemiology of Representations. *Man* 20:73–89.

Spiel, Hilde. 1987. *Vienna's Golden Autumn 1866–1938.* London: Weidenfeld and Nicolson.

Spiro, Melford. 1951. Culture and Personality: The Natural History of a False Dichotomy. *Psychiatry* 14:19–46.

Spivak, Gayatri Chakravorty. 1989. Reading *The Satanic Verses. Public Culture* 2(1):79–99.

Stearn, Gerald E., ed. 1967. *McLuhan: Hot and Cool.* New York: Dial Press.

Steiner, George. 1975. *Extraterritorial.* Harmondsworth: Penguin.

—— 1979. *Language and Silence.* Harmondsworth: Penguin.

—— 1980. *On Difficulty.* Oxford: Oxford University Press.

—— 1985. Dream City. *New Yorker* (January 28):92–97.

Stern, J. P. 1975. Karl Kraus and the Idea of Literature. *Encounter* 45 (2):37–48.

Strauss, Anselm L. 1978. A Social World Perspective. In Norman K. Denzin, ed. *Studies in Symbolic Interaction,* 1. Greenwich, Conn: JAI Press.

—— 1982. Social Worlds and Their Segmentation Processes. In Norman K. Denzin, ed., *Studies in Symbolic Interaction,* 4. Greenwich, Conn: JAI Press.

—— 1984. Social Worlds and Legitimation Processes. In Norman K. Denzin, ed., *Studies in Symbolic Interaction,* 5. Greenwich, Conn: JAI Press.

Street, Brian V. 1984. *Literacy in Theory and Practice.* Cambridge: Cambridge University Press.

Stromberg, Peter G. 1986. *Symbols of Community.* Tucson: University of Arizona Press.

Sukenick, Ronald. 1987. *Down and In.* New York: Morrow.

Sutton, Constance R. 1987. The Caribbeanization of New York City and the Emergence of a Transnational Socio-cultural System. In

Constance R. Sutton and Elsa M. Chaney, eds., *Caribbean Life in New York City.* New York: Center for Migration Studies of New York.

Swartz, Marc J. 1982. Cultural Sharing and Cultural Theory: Some Findings of a Five-Society Study. *American Anthropologist* 84:314–338.

Swidler, Ann. 1986. Culture in Action: Symbols and Strategies. *American Sociological Review* 51:273–286.

Sykes, Gresham M. and David Matza. 1957. Techniques of Neutralization: A Theory of Delinquency. *American Sociological Review* 22:664–670.

Textor, Robert B. 1985. Anticipatory Anthropology and the Telemicroelectronic Revolution: A Preliminary Report from Silicon Valley. *Anthropology and Education Quarterly* 16:3–30.

Theall, Donald F. *The Medium Is the Rear View Mirror.* Montreal: McGill-Queen's University Press.

Theroux, Paul. 1986. *Sunrise with Seamonsters.* Harmondsworth: Penguin.

Timms, Edward. 1986. *Karl Kraus, Apocalyptic Satirist.* New Haven: Yale University Press.

Toynbee, Arnold J. 1947. *A Study of History.* New York: Oxford University Press. (Abridged edition.)

Trilling, Lionel. 1965. *Beyond Culture.* New York: Viking.

Turkle, Sherry. 1978. *Psychoanalytic Politics.* New York: Basic Books.

—— 1984. *The Second Self.* New York: Simon and Schuster.

Turner, Victor. 1960. Muchona the Hornet, Interpreter of Religion. In Joseph B. Casagrande, ed., *In the Company of Man.* New York: Harper.

—— 1974. *Dramas, Fields, and Metaphors.* Ithaca: Cornell University Press.

—— 1977a. Process, System, and Symbol: A New Anthropological Synthesis. *Daedalus* 106(3):61–80.

—— 1977b. Variations on a Theme of Liminality. In Sally Falk Moore and Barbara G. Myerhoff, eds., *Secular Ritual.* Assen: van Gorcum.

—— 1982. *From Ritual to Theatre.* New York: Performing Arts Journal Publications.

Unruh, David R. 1979. Characteristics and Types of Participation in Social Worlds. *Symbolic Interaction* 2:115–129.

—— 1980a. The Nature of Social Worlds. *Pacific Sociological Review* 23:271–296.

—— 1980b. The Social Organization of Older People: A Social World Perspective. In Norman K. Denzin, ed., *Studies in Symbolic Interaction,* 3. Greenwich, Conn: JAI Press.

Varenne, Hervé. 1984. Collective Representation in American Anthropological Conversations: Individual and Culture. *Current Anthropology* 25:281–191.

Vincent, Joan. 1986. System and Process, 1974–1985. *Annual Review of Anthropology* 15:99–119.

Vincent, Theo. 1985. Television Drama in Nigeria: A Critical Assessment. In Frank Okwu Ugboajah, ed., *Mass Communication, Culture and Society in West Africa.* München: Hans Zell/K. G. Saur.

Volsky, George. 1989. Magazine Publisher Is Sold. *New York Times,* May 3.

Wagner, Ulla. 1977. Out of Time and Place—Mass Tourism and Charter Trips. *Ethnos* 42:38–52.

Walkup, James. 1986. Order and Disorder in Freud's Vienna. *Social Research,* 53:579–590.

Wallace, Anthony F. C. 1961. *Culture and Personality.* New York: Random House.

Wallerstein, Immanuel. 1974. *The Modern World-System.* New York: Academic Press.

—— 1984. *The Politics of the World-Economy.* Cambridge: Cambridge University Press.

—— 1990. Culture as the Ideological Battleground of the Modern World-System. *Theory, Culture and Society* 7(2–3):31–55.

Ward, Barbara E. 1965. Varieties of the Conscious Model: The Fishermen of South China. In Michael Banton, ed., *The Relevance of Models for Social Anthropology.* London: Tavistock.

—— 1966. Sociological Self-Awareness: Some Uses of the Conscious Model. *Man* 1:201–215.

—— 1977. Readers and Audiences: An Exploration of the Spread of Traditional Chinese Culture. In Ravindra K. Jain, ed., *Text and Context.* Philadelphia: Institute for the Study of Human Issues.

Waterman, Christopher A. 1988. Asíkò, Sákárà and Palmwine: Popular Music and Social Identity in Inter-War Lagos, Nigeria. *Urban Anthropology* 17:229–258.

White, Merry. 1988. *The Japanese Overseas.* New York: Free Press.

Whitford, Frank. 1986. *Oskar Kokoschka.* London: Weidenfeld and Nicolson.

Whyte, Martin K. 1974. *Small Groups and Political Rituals in China.* Berkeley: University of California Press.

Wilensky, Harold L. 1964. Mass Society and Mass Culture: Interdependence or Independence? *American Sociological Review,* 29:173–197.

Williams, Raymond. 1959. *Culture and Society.* Garden City, N.Y.: Anchor/Doubleday.

—— 1975. *Television: Technology and Cultural Form.* New York: Schocken.

—— 1980. *Problems in Materialism and Culture.* London: Verso/NLB.

—— 1981. *Culture.* London: Fontana.

—— 1985. *Towards 2000.* Harmondsworth: Penguin.

Willis, Paul E. 1977. *Learning to Labour.* Farnborough: Saxon House.

Wilson, Patrick. 1983. *Second-Hand Knowledge.* Westport, Conn: Greenwood Press.

Wolf, Eric R. 1966. Kinship, Friendship, and Patron-Client Relations in Complex Societies. In Michael Banton, ed., *The Social Anthropology of Complex Societies.* London: Tavistock.

—— 1982. *Europe and the People Without History.* Berkeley and Los Angeles: University of California Press.

—— 1984. Culture: Panacea or Problem? *American Antiquity* 49:393–400.

Worth, Sol. 1981. *Studying Visual Communication.* Philadelphia: University of Pennsylvania Press.

Wulff, Helena. 1988. *Twenty Girls.* Stockholm Studies in Social Anthropology, no. 21. Stockholm: Department of Social Anthropology, University of Stockholm.

Wuthnow, Robert. 1983. Cultural Crises. In Albert Bergesen, ed., *Crises in the World-System.* Beverly Hills: Sage.

Yates, Frances A. 1966. *The Art of Memory.* Chicago: University of Chicago Press.

Yinger, J. Milton. 1960. Contraculture and Subculture. *American Sociological Review* 25:625–635.

—— 1982. *Countercultures.* New York: Free Press.

Young, Jock. 1974. New Directions in Subcultural Theory. In John Rex, ed., *Approaches to Sociology.* London: Routledge & Kegan Paul.

Ziman, John M. 1977. Ideas Move Around Inside People. *Minerva* 15:83–93.

Zohn, Harry. 1986. The Stature of Karl Kraus. *Midstream* 32(3):42–48.

Zola, Irving K. 1977. Healthism and Disabling Medicalization. In *Disabling Professions.* London: Marion Boyars.

Zweig, Stefan. 1943. *The World of Yesterday.* London: Cassell.

Index